THE SUBJECT OF HOLOCAUST

JEWISH LITERATURE AND CULTURE

Alvin H. Rosenfeld, *editor*

THE SUBJECT OF HOLOCAUST FICTION

Emily Miller Budick

Indiana University Press

Bloomington & Indianapolis

This book is a publication of

Indiana University Press
Office of Scholarly Publishing
Herman B Wells Library 350
1320 East 10th Street
Bloomington, Indiana 47405 USA

iupress.indiana.edu

Manufactured in the United States of America

Library of Congress Cataloging-in-Publication Data

Budick, E. Miller, author.
    The subject of Holocaust fiction / Emily Miller Budick.
    pages cm. — (Jewish literature and culture)
    Includes bibliographical references and index.
    ISBN 978-0-253-01630-0 (pb : alk. paper) — ISBN 978-0-
253-01626-3 (cl : alk. paper) — ISBN 978-0-253-01632-4 (eb)
    1. Holocaust, Jewish (1939–1945), in literature. I. Title.
    PN56.H55B83 2015+
    809.3'9358405318—dc23
                                                    2014041962

1 2 3 4 5   20 19 18 17 16 15

For

Hananel, Micha, Amos, and Noga Almakies
Tzeelah, Avital, and Carmel Sharon

You are the joys of your grandparents' lives. May you each grow into the person you wish to become; may you continue to include your grandparents in your lives; and may you always be mindful not only of the sadness and tragedies of the Jewish past but also of its triumphs.

This book is also dedicated to the memory of our son

Yochanan Budick

who, had he lived, would certainly have been, like his siblings, nieces, and nephews, a vibrant contributor to the life of the people he so loved.

Contents

Acknowledgments   *ix*

Introduction   *1*

Prologue: Ghostwriting the Holocaust:
The Ghost Writer, The Diary, The Kindly Ones, and Me   *19*

SECTION I. Psychoanalytic Listening and Fictions of the Holocaust

1   Voyeurism, Complicated Mourning, and the Fetish:
Cynthia Ozick's *The Shawl*   *41*

2   Forced Confessions:
Subject Position, Framing, and the "Art" of Spiegelman's *Maus*   *70*

3   Aryeh Lev Stollman's *The Far Euphrates:*
Re-Picturing the Pre-Memory Moment   *100*

SECTION II. Golems, Ghosts, Idols, and Messiahs:
Complicated Mourning and the Intertextual
Construction of a Jewish Symptom

4   Bruno Schulz, the Messiah, and Ghost/writing the Past   *127*

5   A Jewish History of Blocked Mourning and Love   *146*

6   See Under: Mourning   *163*

SECTION III. Mourning Becomes the Nations: Styron, Schlink, Sebald

7   Blacks, Jews, and Southerners in William Styron's *Sophie's Choice*   *185*

8   (Re)Reading the Holocaust from a German Point of View:
Bernhard Schlink's *The Reader*   *195*

9 Mourning and Melancholia in W. G. Sebald's *Austerlitz*   209

Epilogue: Holocaust, Apartheid, and the Slaughter of Animals:
J. M. Coetzee's *Elizabeth Costello* and Cora Diamond's
"Difficulty of Reality"   228

Bibliography   239
Index   247

Acknowledgments

THIS BOOK HAS been a long time in the writing. Many of the debts I have amassed are now so woven into the fabric of my being, let alone into the book itself, that I can no longer pick them apart. Therefore, to all my friends and family, colleagues and students, with whom I've entered into conversation on this subject, I am thankful for the enlightenment and illumination I have received. You know who you are.

Some debts are easier to retrieve, such as the journals and collections that have not only given me permission to reprint from the materials that went into writing this book but also helped to shape that material in the first place. Therefore, I want to thank the journal *Common Knowledge,* which first printed an early version of the *Ghost Writer* arguments as "The Haunted House of Fiction: Ghostwriting the Holocaust," *Common Knowledge* 5 (1996): 120–35, and *Prooftexts,* which published "Forced Confessions: History, Psychoanalysis, and the 'Art' of Holocaust Fiction; The Case of Art Spiegelman's *Maus,*" *Prooftexts* 21 (2002): 379–98. My gratitude also goes to Marc Lee Raphael, whose two conferences resulted in "Psychoanalysis, Epistemology, and Holocaust Fiction: The Case of Cynthia Ozick's *The Shawl,*" in *The Representation of the Holocaust in Literature and Film,* ed. Marc Lee Raphael (Williamsburg, VA: College of William and Mary, 2003), 1:1–28, and "The Holocaust, Trauma, and the Jewish Fiction of *Tzimtzum:* Aryeh Lev Stollman's *Far Euphrates,*" in *The Representation of the Holocaust in Literature and Film,* ed. Marc Lee Raphael (Williamsburg, VA: College of William and Mary, 2007), 2:24–39. Many of the materials that constitute section 2 of the book first appeared in an essay titled "Survivor Guilt and Incomplete Mourning: The Symptoms of a Jewish Literary Canon," in *Arguing the Modern Jewish Canon: Essays on Literature and Culture in Honor of Ruth. R. Wisse,* ed. Justin Cammy, Dara Horn, Alyssa Quint, and Rachel Rubinstein (Cambridge, MA: Harvard University Press, 2008), 517–31.

From February 2012 to November 2012 I was a fellow at the Center for Advanced Holocaust Studies, United States Holocaust Memorial Museum, in Washington, D.C. I am grateful to the museum staff and to Phyllis Greenberg Heideman and Richard D. Heideman, who provided the fellowship that paid for my stay there.

I am especially thankful to Rami Aronzon, with whom I coauthored the book that was my introduction into the field of the unconscious mind: *Psychotherapy and the Everyday Life.* Even though this was a practical book rather than a scholarly book, it provided me with the background in Freud's theories of mind, without which I would never have found a way to read and respond to the Holocaust fictions that I have engaged with here. Rami was a mentor, guide, and, finally, good friend. Without the education I received from him, this book could never have been written.

My interest in Jewish literature is intimately bound up with my children and my grandchildren, who have inherited the history my authors have written about. They are also a part of the project of the future, which certainly will be worthy of the Jewish achievements of the past. Hopefully this future will also secure a safer world for all of us, Jews and non-Jews alike.

My husband, Sandy, needs no words from me to know how much a part of my life's enterprise he is in all of its dimensions. If not for him, I would not have wound up in Israel; would not have understood how intimately my being is wound up in my Jewishness; would not have come to question my commitments and then reestablish them on my own, somewhat different grounds.

Finally, I want to thank my readers Anita Norich and Elizabeth Baer for extremely helpful comments, and, of course the editors at Indiana University Press: Raina Polivka, music, film, and humanities editor; Jenna Whittaker, assistant sponsoring editor; my project editor, Michelle Sybert; and my fabulous copyeditor, Jill R. Hughes, who located and uprooted many embarrassing errors. The text is much cleaner for Jill's skillful scalpel. Series editor Professor Alvin Rosenfeld, who also read and commented on the manuscript, has been a dear colleague and friend throughout.

THE SUBJECT OF HOLOCAUST FICTION

Introduction

I T H A S B E E N many years since Holocaust fiction has had to establish its legitimacy against the charge that a fictional text is either inadequate, inappropriate, or even endangering to the task of representing the Nazi genocide of the Second World War. Yet some of the issues raised in relation to what exactly an artistic representation may be understood to be representing, and at what cost, remain pertinent to our fullest appreciation of the best Holocaust literature. If this body of texts is to become an inseparable part of the literary canon and not just a set of special writings to which we grant a privileged status because of the gravity of the events they record (not to mention their relative historical proximity), then establishing the credentials of these texts on more purely aesthetic and literary grounds becomes imperative. This is not to say that preserving the texts' relationship to the events that produced them in the first place is not an equally important goal. The preservation of historical knowledge is an essential objective for any culture. In the case of the Holocaust, as with other fraught historical catastrophes, casting doubt on whether events occurred and dismissing the gravity of their consequences for real human beings and communities are anathema both to the writers of the texts and to the participants in the events that the texts fictionalize. This is equally true, one hopes, for readers. Nonetheless, the preservation of historicity may not be the primary province of literary fictions. Indeed, it may be in the very nature of fiction to trouble the waters of historical validity and veracity. Literary texts, whatever their subjects and ethical goals, function in specifically literary ways. And that might well mean that their narrative procedures clash with their historical aspirations.

In the following pages I argue that Holocaust fiction, no less than great fiction generally, proceeds through the flawed, often faulty subjectivities of its characters. This prominence of the subjectivity of characters (even in dire circumstances, the historical accuracy of which is not up for dispute) produces in readers a heightened sense of their own subjectivity in relation to what they are reading, as well as to their perceptions of reality generally. Until now, most critics of Holocaust fiction, whatever their particular theoretical frameworks or selection of texts, have tended to read the fictions as fictionalized histories—that is, as transparencies through which we are able to glimpse the virtually inconceivable and unrepresentable horrors of the Holocaust experience, including the concentration camp. My objective is to restore to these fictions the primary work of fiction itself, which is to complicate the relationship between the fictional representation and the world that the text purports to be representing. The Holocaust fictions that concern me, and that I consider not only legitimate engagements with the events of the Second World War but also great works of literature, are in no way forms of Holocaust denial. They are also not attempts at relativizing events. In this study I do not read memoirs, autobiographies, or even fictionalized autobiographies. I read fictions. Historical accounts establish one sort of contract with the reader, fictional texts another. A memoir is one kind of text; a fiction is another. My claim is that fiction does a certain sort of narrative work. That work cannot be dismissed or even relegated to a secondary position even if the literary work has multiple other objectives, such as a wish for historical commemoration, an expression of personal grief or guilt, or a desire to mourn the victims of catastrophe. Therefore, the word "subject" in the title of this book does not refer to the topic, theme, or even intention of Holocaust fiction. Rather it refers to the subject-hood of the characters/victims in a text and the subjectivity of the text itself. It refers as well to the reader whose subject position, is, through the texts' strategies, made of concern to the reader. By "subject position" I mean simply, albeit also complexly, all of those factors that make each and every one of us who we are. This means, in relation to the fictions we read, those features of our lives and psyches that lead us, for example, to read Holocaust texts in the first place and then to respond to them in certain ways. To read people's stories of suffering and degradation without attempting as much as is humanly possible to interrogate our reasons for reading and reacting to these stories is to risk, on the one hand, the worst kind of simplification of the texts and, on the other, the abuse or misuse of other people's experiences. Holocaust fiction is an arena in which Holocaust narratives can come under the self-scrutiny of writers and readers both. It can become a model for the reader of the ways we human beings can engage the horrific experiences of other people with full respect for the differences between their real and often unbearable suffering and our sympathies, their subject positions and our own.

Holocaust Criticism in Historical Perspective

The by now ample field of scholarship on Holocaust fiction and poetry, by such insightful critics as Lawrence Langer, Alvin Rosenfeld, Sidra Ezrahi, James Young, Geoffrey Hartman, Susan Gubar, Marianne Hirsch, Sara Horowitz, Michael Rothberg, and others, has already established certain of the ways this body of texts not only builds on existing literary conventions but also, through the creative genius of the writers, transforms the canon of which it is a part. This relationship between tradition and the individual talent (to apply here T. S. Eliot's famous definition) is paralleled by the equally important relationship between tradition and the individual talent of the critics who have analyzed and theorized these texts, producing in the process new ways of conceptualizing and interpreting literature itself. And yet there are problems, especially in relation to literary texts that are not fictionalized historical, autobiographical, or biographical accounts, but full-fledged fabrications, often by writers who neither experienced nor witnessed the events of the Second World War. In this book I build on other critics' important forays into the field of Holocaust literature. My hope is to contribute to the further transformation of the tradition of Holocaust literary studies. But I also wish to complicate our reading of Holocaust fictions by suggesting how fiction is also at odds with the tasks of historical commemoration. Fiction, I maintain, cannot but prompt us to question our knowledge of events. In a way that documentary and historical accounts do not and perhaps cannot, fiction also highlights the centrality of subjectivity or subject position in the processes by which we know—or think we know—the quotidian realm of external facts and events. Such a focus on subjectivity can well carry over into our relation to more purely historical narratives as well. Holocaust fiction, like other historical fiction, produces what we might think of as a form of historical skepticism. In so doing it endangers our acceptance of the straightforward veracity of historical knowledge. Yet such writing can also deepen the challenges of confronting human experiences of devastation. It can open the subject of the Holocaust to a broader comprehension of both victims and victimizers and of what their stories require of us, both ethically and intellectually. Fiction in general, and historical fiction in particular, is a form of moral thinking in which there is no "moral" as such, but, rather, the production of the terms and conditions by which ethical judgments can and must be reached. For this reason, the dangers posed by Holocaust fiction are well worth the yield in deepening and producing nuances in our ethical thinking, even about so catastrophic an event as the Holocaust.

Bernard Harrison (2006), in a recent essay on "Aharon Appelfeld and the Problem of Holocaust Fiction," has aptly and succinctly summarized the cases both for and against Holocaust fiction. Harrison uses a major philosopher in Holocaust studies, Berel Lang, to set up the case against writing Holocaust fiction, to which Harrison, as a philosopher, then responds. According to Lang, as Harrison summarizes his arguments:

1. Imaginative fiction lives by the representation and analysis of individual consciousness in all its diversity. It is . . . essential to our understanding of the Holocaust . . . to see that by its nature, it denied the diversity of consciousness.
2. Fiction opens a space of narrative contingency, between the writer, his fiction, and what that fiction is notionally "about." Within that space a vast ar-

ray of possibilities open up, between which the writer is free to choose, precisely because that choice is not determined by his subject matter. Whatever choice he makes, he risks falsifying that subject matter in at least two ways. On the one hand, his choices will exhibit a bias determined by his personality and outlook. . . . That in turn will work to further personalize a peculiarly and essentially impersonal body of history events.

3. Any fiction . . . tends to impose a structure, of plot and denouement on the events it describes, and will thus invite the reader to see those events as instantiating some general pattern inherent in human life. (80–81)

In countering what he acknowledges as Lang's well-made points, Harrison argues that "literature, good literature . . . teaches the reader what words mean, and how things look through the prism of those meanings. . . . [It] forces language honestly to explore its own roots; to offer the reader, in terms of *knowledge-of* rather than *knowledge-about,* an account of human reality" (88–91). While not quite taking into account Lang's third objection to Holocaust narrative (which I deal with in chapter 1), Harrison counters Lang by noting how fiction encourages us to acknowledge the subjectivity of knowledge, how what we imagine to be historical "truth" is always informed by the humanly embodied formulation of that truth. In other words, there is no "truth" outside the human subject that either experiences events or records or reads them.

In arguing this way Harrison succeeds a line of critics of Holocaust literature who have demonstrated how Holocaust fiction and poetry, as well as more historical writing such as memoirs and diaries, have not only augmented our more factual knowledge of the Jewish genocide of the Second World War but also, more importantly, defined the uniqueness of its specific horrors. In the views of major critics, Holocaust writing has no less than transformed what we understand writing to be. As Alvin Rosenfeld, quoting Elie Wiesel, already put the case in one of the earliest studies of Holocaust literature, "At Auschwitz, not only man died but also the idea of man" (1980, 5). Or as Sidra DeKoven Ezrahi phrased it in a study that, like Rosenfeld's *A Double Dying,* also came out in 1980, "The implementation of the Final Solution—not an eruption of chaotic forces of violence but a systematized, mechanized, and socially organized program—was a mockery of the very idea of culture that had survived into the twentieth century" (2–3). Thus, the corpus of Holocaust texts, as Rosenfeld cogently argued, cannot be defined simply by a shared subject matter. Rather, as a body of writings it must convey the force of the death of the idea of man and culture at Auschwitz. It must compel the writer and the reader to fundamentally change their modes of comprehension such that what emerges in and through the text is the deformation of language, literature, and culture. As Ezrahi put it, "The distorted image of the human form which the artist might present as but a mirror of nature transformed can hardly be contained within the traditional perimeters of mimetic art, because although

Holocaust literature is a reflection of recent history it cannot draw upon the time-less archetypes of human experience and human behavior which can render un-lived events familiar through the medium of the imagination" (2–3). "The challenge to the literary imagination," wrote another, even earlier critic of Holocaust fiction, Lawrence Langer, "is to find a way of making" "accessible to the mind and emotions of the reader" the "fundamental truth" that not only "our conception of reality, but its very nature" were transformed as a result of Dachau and Auschwitz (1975, xii).

Each of these books proceeds through readings of individual texts, and the power of each study inheres in its ability to illuminate those texts. Nonetheless, a more generalizable literary portrait of *l'univers concentrationnaire* emerges through the combined effect of these critical studies. This portrait brings into powerful relief not only the horrible suffering of the victims but also their dehumanization, the reduction of their world to a set of arbitrary and absurd rules in which survival had less to do with having your wits about you than with pure, unpredictable luck.

There are a range of defenses of Holocaust fictions that are pertinent to, though not at the center of, my current enterprise. As I have argued in several essays and in my book on Aharon Appelfeld (Budick 2004), one supreme value of fiction over more historical accounts is that it personalizes victims. As Appelfeld once put it in *Beyond Despair,* fiction renders the faceless millions as discrete human beings, both reversing the Nazis' intention of making the Jew disappear and simultaneously restoring to each person the uniqueness and specificity that often becomes attenuated even after the war (1994, 21–22, 38, 80). "I remain a private survivor," claims the narrator of Imre Kertész's *Kaddish for a Child Unborn,* meaning that he remains a uniquely individual person and that much of his survivor experience must of necessity remain private and personal (1997, 12). Fiction also makes of the victims' stories not merely the record of technologically and historically horrific events but expressions of human personality in all of its many dimensions. For this reason Holocaust protagonists in novels such as Saul Bellow's *Mr. Sammler's Planet* (1970), Cynthia Ozick's *The Shawl* (1990), Art Spiegelman's *Maus* (2011a; first published in two volumes in 1986 and 1991), and many of Aharon Appelfeld's books are often—in contradiction to what we might expect of fictions like these—not very likeable characters. Ozick's Rosa in *The Shawl,* for example, is a self-hating (hence auto-anti-Semitic) snob, who, like the father in Appelfeld's *Age of Wonders* (1981), has contempt for Eastern European and religious Jewry. Art Spiegelman's father in *Maus* is similarly unlikeable in many ways, even before his wartime experiences. In so presenting these characters, the texts provide their survivors with psycho-biographies that individualize their personalities. They suggest not only that these individuals existed in all their human discreteness before the war but also that the war did not wholly

determine who they were and who they would become. Such a view of the "survivor" also complicates our view of their suffering or deaths. Indeed, it ups the
ante. Through these texts we come to realize that what is most abhorrent about
the Holocaust is not that good, innocent people died, but that people, period,
died, and for no reason other than their being Jewish or part Jewish or gypsy or
homosexual or handicapped. The appropriate punishment for being a snob like
Rosa or Vladek Spiegelman is not a labor camp, a concentration camp, rape, or
the death of a child.

In the same vein, but in a reversal of the texts' presentation of the victim and
more a consequence of the texts' dynamics than anything that the texts represent
directly, is how Holocaust fiction complicates our view of the victimizer. It is certainly not the case that Holocaust fictions (at least not the texts that concern me)
soften the line between victim and victimizer. Victimizers are guilty of crimes
for which they deserve both the legal punishment and moral repudiation they receive. Nonetheless, victimizers are also human beings, and human beings cannot
be reduced to the status of a victimizer any more than a victim can be reduced
to the status of a survivor—as if calling someone a victimizer explains what that
means. One does not have to go so far as to argue, as does Hannah Arendt, for
the banality of evil. Evil is hardly banal. But neither is evil, as Stanley Cavell put
it in *The Claim of Reason,* the behavior of monsters: "To understand Nazism," he
writes, "whatever that will mean, will be to understand it as a human possibility;
monstrous, unforgiveable, but not therefore the conduct of monsters. Monsters
are not unforgivable, and not forgivable. We do not bear the right internal relation to them for forgiveness to apply" (1999, 377–78). One might have to apply to
victims a version of the argument made in relation to survivors, which differentiates between guilt and shame. There may be a difference, let us say, between guilt
and what one might call shamefulness. Not all victimizers are guilty in the same
ways and of the same things. They did not all do what they did, or did not do,
for the same reasons. To understand the Holocaust is to understand this fact. It
is also to at least try to understand why people behaved as they did. The guilt of
those who actively slaughtered Jews shades into shameful behavior, which defined the actions not only of the German, Polish, and Hungarian civilian population but even of the Allied nations like Great Britain and the United States, who
did little to rescue Jews during the war. This might not cheer us. It shouldn't. But
it is sobering to keep in mind something else that Stanley Cavell writes in relation to the Holocaust: that a question we must all ask ourselves always is "Where
is one now, and how is one living with, hence counting upon, injustice?" (2010,
349). Mass slaughter of innocent human beings hardly ended with the end of the
Second World War, either in relation to the Jews (who in the view of many remain
endangered, at least in Israel) or to other ethnic or national groups. It exists in
our world as it did in the 1930s and 1940s. It may well be the case for Jews that the

specificity of their history—centuries of persecution and pogroms that culminate in a Holocaust—suggests a special need for caution and attentiveness to threat. Anti-Semitism is no figment of the Jewish imagination. It may also, however, be the case, for Jews and non-Jews alike, that self-skepticism and self-scrutiny around the questions "How would I have behaved?" and "How do I behave now?" are absolutely essential to everything we understand moral inquiry to be.

If the Holocaust narrative becomes simply about the Jewish (or gypsy, homosexual, or handicapped) victim, who is good, and the German (or Nazi, Polish, or anti-Semitic) victimizer, who is bad, then the story of the Holocaust becomes simple and straightforward. There are good people, and there are bad people. It is as simple as that. The story yields no complexity of knowledge about any other human situation in which any of us (Jews, Germans, and others) might find ourselves. Nor does it help us to understand how the Holocaust itself transpired. It certainly does not produce in us a need for self-interrogation. Such self-interrogation is a paramount consequence of most literary fictions. It is a feature of great Holocaust fiction as well. It is possible to argue, and I have done so elsewhere, that Nazism might be defined as just that attempt to reduce the world into the good guys and the bad guys—Aryans and Jews—such that a similar simplification on the parts of texts would be a philo-Semitic reversal of the dynamics that produced the Holocaust in the first place. This subject will recur in relation to some antifascist postmodernist positions in which the Jew once again becomes a trope for other concerns, even if in a philo-Semitic mode. The subject also occupies me in relation to Bernhard Schlink's *The Reader* (2008). Readers have objected to Schlink's novel because it seems to let the Nazis off too easily by representing them through an illiterate woman who is herself a victim. Yet, *The Reader* opens up to view important areas for the reader's self-interrogation. It enables the reader to question his or her own relation not only to the Holocaust but also to other human events that we may not (to pick up Schlink's major metaphor) be able to "read" with full comprehension.

In the 1990s and thereafter the scholars who follow the first generation of critics tend to continue in the directions pioneered by them. In particular, critics focus on the kinds of antimimetic, even surrealist forms of representation that seemed to be required in order to convey the horrors of the Holocaust. Michael Rothberg quite brilliantly captures the mimetic force of the antimimetic, nonrealist tradition of Holocaust writing (both in fiction and nonfiction) in *Traumatic Realism: The Demands of Holocaust Representation,* where he examines how "the intersection of the everyday and the extreme in the experience and writing of Holocaust survivors" discovers in what Rothberg calls traumatic realism "an aesthetic and cognitive solution to the conflicting demands inherent in representing and understanding genocide" (2000, 9). In a similar vein, Sara Horowitz, in *Voicing the Void: Muteness and Memory in Holocaust Fiction,* explores "the trope of muteness," which, she notes, is "predominant in Holocaust narratives of all sorts" but "functions in fiction deliberately and explicitly to raise and explore connections and disjunctures among fictional constructs, textual omissions, and historical events." Voicing the void produces what Horowitz calls a "poetics of atrocity" (1997, 1–2, 25). Such a poetics is defined by the way it acknowledges and frames the limits of speech, thus managing to "say" the unsayable. Despite the apparent contradictions between Horowitz's book and David Patterson's *The Shriek of Silence: A Phenomenology of the Holocaust Novel,* Patterson's book also looks at how textual meaning is constructed via an idea of muteness. "The Holocaust novel," writes Patterson, "is not primarily an attempt to recount the details of a particular occurrence, to depict a reality that transcends the imagination, or to describe a horror inaccessible to a limited language. It is, rather, an event and an endeavor to fetch the word from the silence of exile and restore it to its meaning" (1992, 5). Lea Fridman (2000) argues in a similar vein. The "event" to which Patterson refers is the literary event for the reader, the way the reader comes to experience the "silence" and in this way may lead the word back from its exile. The idea of literature as an "event," as something that happens to the reader through the text, is important to my own focus on how Holocaust fiction "frames" the subject position of the reader. But Horowitz's point that insofar as the silence in the text often replicates the unspeakableness at the heart of the victim's experience also cautions us against imagining that our eventful relation to the text is anything like the events that befell the victims.

Whether Holocaust scholars have focused on the continuity between Holocaust literature and other bodies of Jewish texts (as do Alan Mintz in *Hurban: Responses to Catastrophe in Hebrew Literature* [1984] and David Roskies in *Against the Apocalypse: Responses to Catastrophe in Modern Jewish Culture* [1999]), on gender issues or the second generation (like Alan Berger in *Children of Job: American Second-Generation Witnesses to the Holocaust* [1997]), or on national responses (S. Lillian Kremer, *Witness through the Imagination: Jewish American Holocaust Literature* [1989]), literary criticism has tended, until recently, to posit a fairly unambiguous relationship to the events of the Holocaust on the parts of writers both of primary texts (whether fictions, autobiographical fictions, memoirs, or diaries) and of secondary texts, including their own. Holocaust writing and the critique of that writing have been understood to be in the service of preserving historical knowledge of the Holocaust, however difficult a task that is. Texts remember the Holocaust and commemorate its victims by producing in the reader something like an experience of the horror and pain, dislocation and loss, suffered by the victims. It is only more recently that critics such as Michael Rothberg (in *Traumatic Realism* [2000]), Gary Weissman (in *Fantasies of Witnessing: Postwar Efforts to Experience the Holocaust* [2004]), Walter Benn Michaels (in an essay titled "'You who never was there': Slavery and the New Historicism, Deconstruction and the Holocaust" [1996]), Lawrence Langer (in *Preempting the Holo-*

caust [2000] and *Using and Abusing the Holocaust* [2006]), and Alvin Rosenfeld (in *The End of the Holocaust* [2011]) have begun to question some of the motives for and consequences of Holocaust writing. In a review of several twenty-first-century studies of the Holocaust, many of them dealing with the exploitation or "misuse" of the Holocaust subject, Eric Sundquist notes in Norma Rosen's *Touching Evil,* a very early Holocaust novel about two non-Jewish women, the "prescient dramatization of the ways in which 'identification' and 'witnessing,' with their attendant problems of corrosion, voyeurism, projection, replication, and the like, were bound to become key themes in Holocaust studies" (2006, 65). Not only that, Sundquist continues, but a novel such as this "confronts us with the disturbing probability that the atrocities of Judeocide are seductive, a kind of pornography through which we lose our innocence, whatever the motive or epiphany" (65). Sundquist also cites Emily Prager's 1992 *Eve's Tattoo* in this context (65). To what degree, these texts and their critics are asking, can any of us remain un-implicated in our interest in the Holocaust? To what extent do we, perhaps unwittingly, violate the privacy or integrity of victims, exploiting their suffering for purposes of our own (even noble purposes), or using the Holocaust as a screen onto which to project our own fantasies and fears, desires and beliefs? These are vital questions. They are questions that are inevitable when we deal with fictional writings. They are the questions that govern my readings in this book.

Skepticism, History, Fiction

As historical fiction, Holocaust fiction is governed by and produces many of the same complexities and philosophical depths that pertain to the genre of historical fiction as such. First and foremost, historical fiction, as I have argued in my two books on the American romance tradition—*Fiction and Historical Consciousness* (1989) and *Engendering Romance* (1994)—has to be understood as foregrounding the subjectivities of interpretive process that pertain to the writing both of history and of fiction. Historical fiction, we might say, produces a theory of historical consciousness. It constructs a theory of how we come to know and understand events that occurred in the past. The ways historical fiction contributes to our understanding of epistemology—that is, how it illuminates how we *know* things about the world—were the emphasis of my first foray into the field of Holocaust writing, my book *Aharon Appelfeld: Acknowledging the Holocaust* (2004), as well as several essays on Holocaust fiction that I have published over the last several years (Budick 1996, 2003, 2007). As Stanley Cavell (1976) has so importantly put the matter in the context of philosophical skepticism, philosophers are on to something when they claim that we can never know, as factual knowledge, beyond the shadow of a doubt, certain things about the world, such as what another person is feeling or suffering or whether the evidences of our senses are conveying objectively accurate readings about external reality. However, that does not mean—and Cavell insists on this—that we do not still "know" certain things about the world and other people. What Cavell (1987) calls "disowning knowledge" is not a genuine expression of skepticism. It is, rather, a refusal to acknowledge that we do indeed "know" certain things, even if such knowledge is not founded on purely evidentiary materials. We know, for example, what another person's words are asking of us. We also know that another human being *is* a human being, even if we try to deny that knowledge.

Events that occurred in the past and that can never be made present to us in any tangible way constitute a particular class of events to which our human senses cannot provide absolute verification. History, therefore, produces a particular form of the philosophical skeptical dilemma. This by no means suggests that historical "knowledge" is to be dissolved in an absolute and radical relativism or denial (as in Holocaust denial). Historical *fiction*, of which Holocaust fiction is one variety, uses such historical skepticism in order to directly confront the tension between what Cavell differentiates as knowing as opposed to acknowledging. If a text is a great work of historical fiction, it never totally resolves the question of its relationship to the historical events to which it gestures. Rather, it opens up the question of knowledge as seriously worthy of our attention. For critics like James Young, Geoffrey Hartman, and others, the epistemological insights produced by Holocaust literature are a major feature of how this body of texts works and why it is important to both literary and historical writings. The brilliance of a text like Art Spiegelman's *Maus,* for example, has precisely to do with the way it gives us (rather literally) a picture of how we come to know and transcribe historical events, which, as Young points out, can never be understood in isolation of the subjective mind that is interpreting those events. "The truths of the Holocaust," writes Young, "inhere in the ways we understand, interpret, and write its history. . . . This is not to deny the historical facts of the Holocaust outside of their narrative framing, but only to emphasize the difficulty of interpreting, expressing, and acting on these facts outside of the ways we frame them" (1998, 1–3). Young also argues this point in his book *At Memory's Edge* (2000, 12–41); Dominick LaCapra makes a similar point in *Representing the Holocaust* (1994, 139–79). I suggest that this "constitutive relationship between the present and different moments of the past," as Michael Rothberg (2000, 209) puts it, pertains to the reader as much as to the author or characters of a literary text.

In my readings of what I consider to be some of the very best Holocaust fictions ever written, I go beyond the more purely epistemological questions that historical Holocaust fictions raise, with which I, like others, have already dealt. I probe more deeply issues of subject position, as Dominick LaCapra and Elizabeth Bellamy (among others) have defined them. That is, I show how Holocaust fiction, deliberately and almost in defiance of what we might deem proper to a fiction of this sort, constructs a subjectivity that calls into question the motivations and actions not only of the characters in the text and of its author, but, ultimately and more importantly, for reasons both ethical and epistemological, also of the reader. In other words, I read Holocaust fictions through a psychoanalytic lens in order to pull into focus processes of fantasy formation, projection, repression, and other of the defense mechanisms that remain largely unconscious to us (as they generally do) when we read texts. These are the psychological mechanisms by which we unconsciously (which is to say inadvertently) transform texts from external events in an external world to highly personal and subjective expressions of self.

What permits the kind of analysis I have done in this book is (at least in part) the lapse of time between the events of the Holocaust and the present moment. In the many decades since the Holocaust and the publication of the first major works of Holocaust literature—Primo Levi's memoirs and philosophical writings and Elie Wiesel's autobiographical fictions—our relation to the events of the Second World War has been radically altered. Some of this change has come about because of the traditions of writing themselves, both fictional and critical. Recent authors have felt freer to write fictions that are not histories in fictional dress. But the change is also a consequence of the temporal distance itself. To be sure, distance produces certain pressures on historical and fictional writing, which have to go forward without benefit of witness testimony and perhaps without a readership inclined to want to explore a subject that has already received extensive literary and historical treatment. Subsequent events also sometimes cast a shadow backward that makes it difficult to express emotions and responses simply and purely. Time and distance, however, also provide new possibilities for analyzing and theorizing both the historical events and the fictional representations of them. They permit the application of the most literary of readings, which is to say they allow us to engage in asking questions of these fictions that raise ethical, psychological, and moral issues not only about the victimizers but about the victims, and finally, and most importantly for my purposes, about us, the inheritors of this history.

Let me be very clear about this: I do not indulge in anything as obscene as Holocaust denial or the kind of revisionist thinking that either reverses the positions of the victims and the victimizers or evens the score. Rather, I employ the same skepticist lens to Holocaust fictions that I apply whenever I read a work of fiction, in order to accord the text its full due as a literary work. By definition a work of fiction is under no obligation whatsoever to stick to the historical facts or, for that matter, external reality. Therefore, by the very fact of its being a fiction—a kind of sanctioned or contractual fabrication or lie—fiction necessarily raises questions concerning the external veracity of its representations. Historical fictions (except for allohistories) very often add certain constraints to this contract. Holocaust fiction certainly does not abandon its commitment to some measure of correlation between the events within the fictive world and the historical record. Nonetheless, whatever Holocaust fiction or any other sort of historical fiction might be imagined to achieve, the one thing it *cannot* be entrusted to do is to preserve the *historical* record of the events it records as pure and unadulterated reliable history.

Even nonfictional historical writings, as many historians have observed, risk distortions, since, as James Young has so aptly demonstrated, the only thing that writing (even autobiographical and historical writing) can evidence is the act of writing itself:

> Inasmuch as the diarists and memoirists see themselves as traces of experiences, and their words as extensions of themselves, the link between words and events seems quite literally *self*-evident: that which has touched the writer's hand would now touch the reader. . . .
> But for the reader with only words on a page, the authority for this link is absent. . . . What was evidence for the writer at the moment he wrote is now, after it leaves his hand, only a detached and free-floating sign, at the mercy of all who read and misread it. (1988, 24; italics in original)

A similar argument pertains to photographs. Yet whatever problems inhere in historical accounts of the nonfictional variety—whether these accounts are witness testimonies, memoirs, diaries, or histories—the existence in the world outside the text of external evidences and documents, to which the text can be understood as directing our attention, produces the possibility of a level of verification and validation that fictional texts can never provide, at least not if they are to remain *literary* works in the fullest possible sense of the term. However much we might acknowledge or even prioritize the subjectivities that produce interpretation of historical events within the discipline known as history, that discipline is predicated upon the possibility of some sort of proof or at least general rational consensus concerning the text's assertions. As a discipline, history conceives of itself as having something accurate to say about actual events in the real world. Historical writing would violate its contract with its reader if it were to begin to make things up.

Of course, subjectivity may be inevitable in the writing of historical accounts, but to some degree at least, subjectivity is a feature of the perceiving mind that the historian must seek to contain. This is *not* to say that historians have to overcome all affective responses altogether (LaCapra has argued this case brilliantly in *History and Memory after Auschwitz* [1998]). However, they must curb them. This is not so for the writer of fictional texts. For the creative writer, subjectivity is the virtue most in demand. Affect with its framing subjectivities is a major component both in the composition of the fictional text and in its subsequent reception by a reader.

By employing psychoanalytic (and, on occasion, neuropsychoanalytic) concepts, I do not mean to locate, either in authors or in characters, the outlines of certain Freudian plots. This was the fashion in Freudian criticism of the early and mid-twentieth century, when Freud first came into literary-critical fashion. Rather (and following the work of critics such as Peter Brooks in books like *Psychoanalysis and Storytelling* [1994]), I take seriously the significance for literary texts of the structure of unconscious processes. Whatever we might think of one Freudian plot or another, Freud did contribute to the history of Western thought a theory of the dynamic unconscious that even the most ardent Freud bashers tend to take for granted in their own writings and theories. The unconscious components of our thinking include a neurologically defined unconscious, which consists of those neurological events that regulate both our thinking and our acting. However, the unconscious processes of the mind also include a psychodynamic unconscious, which has to do with the repression or sublimation of feelings, thoughts, wishes, desires, anxieties, and so on. In all likelihood these were once known to us, although they might not have been. Now, however, they no longer constitute the conscious, rational, intellectual terrain of our thinking and acting. Yet to some degree they influence our every thought and behavior (Budick 2008). In some of the texts I am concerned with (Aryeh Lev Stollman's *Far Euphrates* [1997], for example), the neurobiological unconscious features in my interpretation. My primary interest, however, lies more with the dynamic unconscious. This is true in relation to the text itself as text and, just as importantly, to the reader. By examining those unconscious processes, and by drawing from them certain ethical implications, I believe we are able to experience the text more fully, especially in relation to our own unconscious processes of mind in our reading of the text. It took new historicist critics some years to begin to interrogate their own biases in relation to the biases of the authors and texts they were intent upon exposing in their readings. Such biases do not consist exclusively of blatant prejudices of which we might become intellectually self-aware. Rather, they also and even more primarily involve those precipitates of our deepest fears, frustrations, angers, and wishes that unconsciously and yet persistently influence who we are and how we think: for example, how our parents' or communities' experiences of the Holocaust (either as victims or as witnesses from afar) become part of an internal landscape of anxiety about the outside world; how their expressions *and* repressions affect how we see both ourselves and others in that world; or, for that matter, how our resentment of our parents and their generation for whatever they have instilled within us might play out in our own psychological ways of being in the world. This is in large part the subject of Philip Roth's *The Ghost Writer* (1995), which is a brilliant exercise in discovering how we convert other people and their experiences into expressions of our deepest desires and anxieties.

Scholars of the Holocaust also need to subject themselves to this lens of psychoanalytic self-scrutiny, although I must add here that while I train a psychoanalytic eye on my own subject position, I in no way wish to incriminate or implicate any of us in the field of Holocaust studies, whether literary authors, critics, or historians. I have tremendous respect for the scholarship that has been done in this field and for many of the novels, short stories, and poems that have been written. My objective is to take advantage of our distance from the events of the Second World War in order to open up questions of an epistemological, psychological, and, finally, ethical nature that would have been unseemly to raise half a century ago and that would still be inappropriate in relation to the auto-biographical narratives of individuals who suffered the events of the Holocaust. I choose to use psychoanalytic categories, not to catch anyone up short, but, rather, and again following the work of Cavell, to make good on the idea that "fantasy shadows anything we can understand reality to be" (1996, 97). Therefore, a fictional text or a critical one will inevitably present ideas through fantasies, wishes, anxieties, fears, desires, and the like.

In this study I am not reading for the unconscious of the author. Nor am I reading for the unconscious of the characters, at least not as a final goal, although I often proceed through such an investigation of the characters' unacknowledged and often concealed motivations in both their behaviors and in the ways they tell the stories of their horrific experiences. My major purpose is to probe the unconscious of the fictional text itself as the various literary devices that go into constructing the text produce something very like a consciousness or mind. I want to fathom what sorts of fantasies, wishes, and fears the text entertains in relation to the events it narrates so as to be able to examine what in us as readers and Holocaust scholars represents both legitimate and illegitimate investments in the subject. I am less interested in what Gary Weissman (2004) has identified (quite insightfully) as fantasies of witnessing, which have more to do with a sense of our own "guilt" for not having experienced the awful events about which we are writing than with probing other sorts of fears, anxieties, and even aspirations that are prompted in us by Holocaust fictions. I examine how the literary text itself implicates the reader in what could be thought of us as a voyeuristic overinvestment in the subject of the Holocaust, as when a text like Cynthia Ozick's *The Shawl* forces us into the position of being curious (however embarrassed we are by our interest) as to whether or not the protagonist Rosa's infant daughter was or was not a product of rape or, in the case of Stollman's *Far Euphrates,* when the text seems to be asking us to picture a castrated man. What does it mean for any of us to pry into the dirty laundry of the past (to pick up another image from *The Shawl*)? By what right do any of us, even the children of survivors like Artie in Spiegelman's *Maus,* compel others to recount to us the indignities and humiliations they suffered in the camps and ghettos? Artie Spiegelman forces his father to tell a story his father has no need or desire to tell. How much is Artie's coerciveness a reflection of our own? And what does A/art know about this problem of what I call forced confessions?

We have all become very familiar with certain pictures and stories of Holocaust atrocities, such as the photo shown to the protagonist of Stollman's novel. These images may still be difficult to bear, but they might also be less stressful than other, more ordinary, mundane, and even compromising matters, not to mention morally questionable ones that might pertain just as powerfully, perhaps even more so, to individual people's experiences. We might also feel that listening to stories in a certain way threatens to compromise our fullest sympathies for the narrators of those stories. For example, what if we doubt that Rosa in *The Shawl* is telling us the whole truth about what happened to her infant daughter? What if her fantasy of resurrecting the dead child in the present only repeats a fantasy of resurrection that already began in the camps? What powers of sympathy and understanding would that story demand of us, which perhaps we feel inadequate to provide? And why, then, might we prefer to read the story in some other, potentially less off-putting, way?

This book is divided into six parts. In the prologue I interrogate my own subject position on the subject of the Holocaust. I do that by reading two very different kinds of fiction side by side. One is a novel that is not, in my view, essentially a Holocaust novel, although many have taken it to be one, precisely because it plays the game of seeming to be one. Jonathan Littell's *The Kindly Ones* (2009) gives us the story of the Holocaust from the perspective of the perpetrator, who is also, in this novel, a sexual deviant and a psychopath. Indeed, it is difficult not to wonder whether the memoir that the protagonist is writing is not more about his sexual deviancy than about the Holocaust, making the Holocaust the cover story for a much more mundane and ordinarily perverted life. *The Kindly Ones,* I believe, holds up a dark, distorted, and yet frighteningly revealing mirror to the field of Holocaust studies itself, which has everything to do with our sometimes prurient interest in other people's suffering and with how we do and do not see ourselves reflected in narratives of the Holocaust. It also exposes to view how we use the Holocaust to justify our talking about other things that we would not be permitted to discuss, or would not permit ourselves to discuss, were it not under the cover of the Holocaust.

In order to discuss Littell's novel I revisit the controversy that was waged some years ago concerning whether *The Diary of Anne Frank* (1929–1945) constituted an appropriate vehicle of Holocaust representation. This involves my looking at Philip Roth's (in)famous novel *The Ghost Writer* as well, not to mention some subsequent entries into this field of Anne Frank fantasies: Nathan Englander's *What We Talk About When We Talk About Anne Frank* and Shalom Auslander's *Hope: A Tragedy,* both published in 2012. In this regard I also bring to bear my own personal experience of the *Diary of Anne Frank* and its place in the development of my own Holocaust consciousness, well before I moved into the academic study of literary texts. I am concerned in this section with what it means that human beings have an all-important fantasy life (as defined by philosophers and psychoanalysts such as Stanley Cavell, Jonathan Lear, Eric Santner, and Slavoj Žižek) and how this might have to be factored self-consciously into our reading of Holocaust narratives.

I move from here to section 1, "Psychoanalytic Listening and Fictions of the Holocaust," which consists of extended readings of what are for me three of the finest Holocaust fictions ever written: Cynthia Ozick's *The Shawl,* Art Spiegelman's *Maus,* and Aryeh Lev Stollman's *Far Euphrates.* In each case I bring into focus the subject position of the text (not necessarily, I hasten to emphasize again, that of the author) and thereby the potential and possibly flawed subject position of the reader of the text, which the text is deliberately or inadvertently exposing. Rape, infanticide, and bodily mutilation all hover at the borders of our anxieties, fears, and curiosities, quite irrespective of our interest in the Holocaust. In "Golems, Ghosts, Idols, and Messiahs: Complicated Mourning and the Intertextual Construction of a Jewish Symptom," section 2, I engage a set of fictions that are clearly in dialogue with one another and that in their intertextuality express an idea of Jewish guilt concerning the enormity of historical Jewish suffering and persecution. My texts here include Cynthia Ozick's *The Messiah of Stockholm* (1987); Philip Roth's *The Prague Orgy,* the epilogue to *Zuckerman Bound* (1985), and "Looking at Kafka" (1975); David Grossman's *See Under: Love* (1989); Aharon Appelfeld's *Age of Wonders* (1981); Anne Michaels's *Fugitive Pieces* (1998); Nicole Krauss's *History of Love* (2010) and *Great House* (2006); Dara Horn's *The World to Come* (2006); Jonathan Safran Foer's *Tree of Codes* (2010); and Michael Chabon's *The Final Solution* (2004) and *The Amazing Adventures of Kavalier and Clay* (2000). Almost all of these works are obsessed with the real-life murdered Jewish writer Bruno Schultz. Almost all of them deal with lost or imagined Jewish manuscripts and the subsequent inheritance of Jewish textual traditions. While these texts expose the obsessions of their characters, they themselves also exhibit some of their characters' symptoms. These texts are exercises in the failure to mourn, which ultimately point the way to a form of mourning that is recognizably Jewish and that enables the reader as well as the writer of the text to put the past to rest with dignity and without forgetfulness.

My third section, titled "Mourning Becomes the Nations," deals with Holocaust texts by non-Jewish authors. My objective here is to read the Holocaust-inflected subject position of the "other" in relation to Jewish history. My objects of investigation include William Styron's *Sophie's Choice* (1979), Bernhard Schlink's *The Reader* (2008), and W. G. Sebald's *Austerlitz* (2001). As Christine Berberich has argued in a review essay of recent Holocaust studies, "positionality"—"author background, origin, and writing incentive"—matters (2006, 568). In this section I investigate how positionality matters, specifically in relation to non-Jewish authors, and what kinds of transformations such Holocaust narratives produce in our understanding of the Holocaust as a topic of non-Holocaust-related discourses. Non-Jewish sites of Holocaust reflection in various ways return me to Jonathan Littell's book and with how the Holocaust can become fused with and thereby become a cover for other subjects and interests. Therefore, in my epilogue I examine one final text—J. M. Coetzee's *The Lives of Animals* (2003a)—in order to address the question of who does or does not have the right to deal with the Holocaust and what governs an appropriate application to this subject. Coetzee's lectures and their subsequent appearance in his novel *Elizabeth Costello* (2003b) raise the problem of using and abusing the Holocaust not only within the text itself but also, of course, through the text, which after its publication became a topic of conversation among several extremely prominent literary critics and philosophers in a separately published volume. This conversation is as fascinating as the text itself. It not only exemplifies the problem of subject position but also provides philosophical and scholarly bases for us to define more precisely what it means for human beings to confront and respond to the difficult narratives of suffering and pain that comprise the Holocaust experience, not to mention other experiences of suffering and pain as well.

Prologue: Ghostwriting the Holocaust

The Ghost Writer, The Diary,
The Kindly Ones, *and Me*

In this prologue I examine two literary texts that highlight the problem of subject position. I also consider my own response to these two texts and to *The Diary of Anne Frank,* which features as a major source of conflict in one of these texts and in Holocaust literary scholarship generally. Too often we implicate the subject position of authors and critics without taking into account how our own subject positions influence our judgment and our responses. I do not want to err in that direction.

One of the only texts in contemporary Jewish American fiction to garner as much critical backlash from critics as Philip Roth's *Ghost Writer* (1995) is the very text that other critics and the general Jewish public felt Roth had violated in *The Ghost Writer*—that is, *The Diary of Anne Frank.* For such prominent writers and intellectuals as Cynthia Ozick (1997), Alvin Rosenfeld (1991, 2011), and Lawrence Langer (1998, 2006), the *Diary* was problematic not because of anything that Anne Frank wrote in her diary, but because of how the book was taken up in contemporary culture, often as the only work of Holocaust literature that some readers ever read. From the time of its publication in the various languages in which it has appeared, the *Diary* has seemed to some to pull away from the kind of rigorous, historical analysis of the Holocaust that is required in order to understand the horrors of what happened to the Jews of Europe. As the diary of a thirteen-year-old girl in hiding, which ends before her incarceration and death in a concentration camp, the *Diary* necessarily stops short of portraying either the harrowing experience of the camps or the extermination of the Jews. Furthermore, as the narrative of an adolescent falling in love for the first time, fighting with her parents, and fantasizing about who she will become after the war, the book offers itself up (especially for younger readers, of whom there are many) as an object of easy identification, as Susan Bernstein (2003), among others, has argued. These features of the *Diary* are exacerbated in the stage and film versions of the book, which end on the note of affirmation also struck by the book that all people are basically good. That might be a thought many of us wish to believe and abide by, but it does not quite capture the emotional and moral tenor of the Holocaust. As Lawrence Langer puts it in *Using and Abusing the Holocaust,* the *Diary* provided "support for the welcome notion that in the midst of chaos, even the chaos of mass murder, the human imagination, to say nothing of other features of the self, can remain untainted by the enormity of the crime" (2006, 19). Thus, as Alvin Rosenfeld notes in *The End of the Holocaust,* no lesser a figure than former U.S. president Ronald Reagan, when he finally visited Bergen-Belsen, recycled Anne's oft-quoted words: "I still believe that people are really good at heart. . . . If I look up into the heavens, I think it will all come right, that this cruelty, too, will end, and that peace and tranquility will return again" (2011, 118; Rosenfeld devotes two chapters to the *Diary*). It is as if Bergen-Belsen can somehow be made to contribute to this thirteen-year-old's vision of hope for the future.

Since Roth's *Ghost Writer* so brilliantly captures both the adolescent quality of Anne and the fantasizing tendencies of her public (as much among adult readers as among more youthful ones), it is difficult to quite fathom the anger against Roth produced by his book, which, when all is said and done, is a fairly recognizable bildungsroman, in which the major protagonist, Nathan Zuckerman, records both his visit to an older Jewish writer, who is his model of artistic success, and his conflict with family and community over his recently published short story. That story, like much of Roth's writing, is a satirical critique of Jewish Americans. *The Ghost Writer,* then, is essentially a portrait of the artist as a young Jewish man who, like James Joyce, is torn between his loyalties to his family and community, on the one hand, and, on the other, his wish to be an unfettered author in the high style of Henry James. Of course, much of the negative response to Roth's novel came from that same general reading public that Roth is taking to task in his book through the depiction of Zuckerman's parents and his parents' advocates, Judge Wapter and his wife. If within the novel Roth's enduring alter ego Nathan Zuckerman has violated the sensibility of the Jewish community through his depiction of a sordid family feud (hence his father's and the judge's responses), the novel itself alienates Jewish readers in the real world through Roth's resurrection of Anne Frank as a character within the novel, albeit clearly marked as his character's neurotic fantasy. Nonetheless, other, more scholarly readers (Jack Beatty [1979], for example) have objected to Roth's book as well.

I do not want to dismiss out of hand the book's problematic relationship to the *Diary* or, for that matter, to the Holocaust. When the protagonist-author-narrator of *The Ghost Writer* rails at his mother that "we are not the wretched of Belsen," the Holocaust happened "in Europe—not in Newark" (1995, 106), we are meant to hear the voice of an immature young man who is in considerable resistance to the details of Jewish history, not to mention his parents. Even the fact that *The Ghost Writer* is a multiply framed text, in which the author Roth produces an older Nathan Zuckerman narrating the events of his younger self, does not quite get Roth off the hook, since the book does fabricate a compelling story about an Anne Frank who survives the Holocaust. Roth's *Ghost Writer,* like many of his other texts, is highly irreverent (Rubin-Dorsky 1989). Its interrogation of American Jewry is fierce, and its tendencies toward what the book itself identifies as sacrilege are potent. Yet these are also the singular strengths of the novel, which produce its extraordinary brilliance. For a reader like myself, coming to Roth long after the Holocaust, *The Ghost Writer* is in no way a problematic text, even though Anne Frank is an icon of my own youth, as she is for many readers of Roth's novel. Nonetheless, since I have never suffered anxieties concerning *Jewish* persecution, for me the text is brilliant satire and completely unthreatening. Of course, as I noted in my study *Blacks and Jews in Literary Conversation* (1998), I had quite a different response to Roth's *Counterlife* (1986), in which at least part of the object of ridicule is Israeli politics. In relation to the subject matter of that text, I felt quite vulnerable. Therefore, I found the text both offensive and endangering until upon subsequent readings I could see what the text might actually be getting at that made my response both unsophisticated and unprofessional (Budick 1998, 202). Clarifying subject position in relation to any text (and not only Holocaust fiction) may be necessary to going the distance in reading the author's text, and not only our own. In relation to *The Ghost Writer,* however, I never suffered a moment's doubt about its legitimacy as a literary text.

Although humorous in the extreme, *The Ghost Writer* is a serious book, written by a serious writer. Roth's invention of an Anne Frank who is as much a mirror of his young narrator-writer as she is of the larger community who idolizes her suggests how conscious Roth's text is of how the events of the Holocaust might well become screens onto which readers of many different persuasions can project their own private fantasies and fears (Spargo 2001; Budick 1996). Thus, Nathan's story of Anne is cordoned off from the text as a short story titled "Femme Fatale," which Nathan is quick to interpret quite self-knowingly in the next and final section of the novel. "The loving father who must be relinquished for the sake of his child's art," Zuckerman acknowledges, "was not hers; he was mine" (Roth 1995, 168). And he continues in a passage that, by using the word "fiction" in two different senses, shifts from Zuckerman's voice within the novel to Roth's outside and through it:

> To be wed somehow to you, I thought, my unassailable advocate, my invulnerable ally, my shield against their charges of defection and betrayal and reckless, heinous informing! Oh, marry me, Anne Frank, exonerate me before my outraged elders of this idiotic indictment! Heedless of Jewish feelings? Indifferent to Jewish survival? Brutish about their well-being? Who dares to accuse of such unthinking crimes the husband of Anne Frank!
>
> But, alas, I could not lift her out of her sacred book and make her a character in this life. . . . The rest was so much fiction, the unchallengeable answer to their questionnaire that I proposed to offer the Wapters. And far from being unchallengeable, far from acquitting me of their charges and restoring to me my cherished blamelessness, a fiction that of course would seem to them a desecration even more vile than the one they had read. (170–71)

When Zuckerman says that "the rest was so much fiction," he means, simply, that his story of Amy as Anne is just a made-up story, a fiction in the sense of a fantasy produced by an overly melodramatic young man. However, when the passage ends by saying that this "fiction" would come to seem a "desecration even more vile than the one they had read," the term shifts registers. Insofar as there *is* no published "fiction" by Nathan Zuckerman in which Nathan marries Anne—that is, there is only this text, which is written by Roth about a character named Nathan—the fiction being referred to in the second instance is Roth's. Roth knows that his novel is going to be perceived as a desecration that is only going to worsen his relations with the Jewish community. And yet he publishes this sacrilege anyway. And he is right about its public reception.

It is a credit to Roth's incredible genius that the Anne Frank whom Zuckerman produces more closely corresponds to the Anne Frank in the unexpurgated editions of the *Diary* than in the original text read by the Wapters and others. I think this is a source of gratification to many of us for whom Anne served a certain psychological function in our lives. In the unrevised version that finally came out only in 1986 in Dutch, prepared by the Netherlands State Institute for War Documentation (the English translation to follow in 1989 and the revised edition in 2003), Anne is far more feisty, gutsy, and devoted to her art than in the originally published *Diary*—just the way Roth/Zuckerman imagines her (Budick 1996).

Despite this, however—and Roth knows it—Nathan's Anne is just as much a projection onto the historical Anne Frank as is the community's Anne. Roth's novel is fully conscious of the ways reading trades in subjectivities. As he later puts it in *The Prague Orgy*, which completes the Zuckerman trilogy, *Zuckerman Bound*, that *The Ghost Writer* initiates, "There's nothing that can't be done to a book, no cause in which even the most innocent of all books cannot be enlisted, not only by *them*, but by you and me. . . . Mightier than the *sword*? This place [Czechoslovakia] is proof that a book isn't as mighty as the mind of its most benighted reader" (1985, 759). This comment covers the community's construction of Anne as well as Nathan's. Judge Wapter acts in Roth's novel as the judge and jury of Jewish values in America and therefore of who represents the Jewish people: "We were all poor people in a new land," the judge writes to Zuckerman, "struggling for our basic needs, our social and civil rights, and our spiritual dignity" (1995, 100). For him Anne is the symbolic representation of that reality.

That the person to dictate to Zuckerman is a judge or that the story that lands Zuckerman in trouble with his family and the community has to do with a trial is not incidental to what Roth is attempting to achieve in his book. What Roth's *Ghost Writer* puts on display is how the "truth" can no more be preserved by history or by the legal system than it can by the flights of fancy we call literature. Nathan's short story "Higher Education" is about Jews being judged and sentenced (much like Zuckerman in relation to Wapter), and there is no sense in that story that justice is being served. The judge in the story is not Jewish. And he decides an inheritance issue in favor of Nathan's rather scandalous Uncle Sydney (whom the young Nathan admires) over the aspiring doctors-to-be twin sons of his aunt Essie. What is significant about both Uncle Sydney and Aunt Essie that Nathan's critics do not seem to notice (any more than they notice it in relation to Roth's short story "The Defender of the Faith," in which, while one of his Jewish soldiers is manipulative, the other, more central protagonist is a loyal American) is that both are very active defenders of the faith—in a positive sense: Uncle Sydney is reputed to have thrown overboard a poker player who called him a dirty Jew (this might not have been a detail in the story, but it is a detail of Roth's text), while Aunt Essie manages to break the hand of a sex offender in a movie theater with a hammer she keeps in her purse. The story's final image, as recorded in Zuckerman's paraphrase, says it all: "My story . . . concluded with Essie taking aim" (Roth 1995, 83). The story, we might say, takes aim as well, not against the Jewish family (as Nathan's critics read it), but against the unwillingness of some Jews (but not Aunt Essie) to strike back.

There is for Roth an education that might be higher than the higher education provided in graduate schools and medical colleges. Nathan presents strong Jews, who are not victims and who are capable of defending themselves. Indeed, that is Nathan's take on Anne Frank: Nathan's Anne survives. She also refuses to be seen as a victim, either as a child in England or later as a young woman in America. For Nathan and Roth, "Higher Education" would seem to have to do not with the professional or monetary aspirations of Jews, but with learning certain historical lessons, including what it means to take power into one's own hands—whether through physical violence (Sydney and Essie) or through the more cultural venue afforded by literature (Anne Frank and Nathan Zuckerman). A hammer taking aim, after all, is a bit like a pen in midair.

That Zuckerman's short story is about a trial serves another purpose as well. In preferring *The Diary of Anne Frank* to Nathan Zuckerman's short story, the community is not only opting for more favorable as opposed to more critical presentations of Jewish life; they are also signaling their preference for historical accounts over fictional ones. Indeed, the objections to Roth's resurrection of Anne in his novel have to do primarily with its assault against the historical record. Yet what Roth seems aware of in the novel, perhaps as a consequence of his many trips to Europe as a part of the Writers from the Other Europe project, is the controversy raging there over the *Diary*'s authenticity. A hotly contested issue, beginning in the late '50s and peaking in the '70s, was whether or not the *Diary* was actually written by Anne Frank or was ghostwritten by her father or by novelist Meyer Levin. The charge that the *Diary* was ghostwritten took two different forms. The milder version had Otto Frank and Levin (in collaboration with translators and typists) revising the *Diary.* The other, more radical and violent charge claimed that Otto Frank and Levin had themselves authored the *Diary,* wholly fabricating its events (Budick 1996).

Even before Roth's fictionalization of the *Diary,* in other words, there were those who claimed it was a fiction and dismissed it accordingly. Thus, for example, in *Anne Frank's Diary: A HOAX,* which was published in 1979, shortly after *The Ghost Writer,* a man named Ditlieb Felderer attempted to expose, quite against what he claims to be his great reluctance to do so, "the colossal hoax surrounding the Anne Frank diary." In Felderer's view of things, Anne Frank is the "pinnacle of the Holocaust theory" and the publication of her diary was "a racket . . . prompted by the callous spirit of people" trying to slander the Germans and the Dutch. To this end, Felderer questions everything from the feasibility that a young girl wrote this diary, to whether the descriptions of the diary by those who found it correspond to the length of the published document, to the possibility that the Holocaust never even occurred. "It is alleged," writes Felderer,

> that Anne Frank died at the Bergen-Belsen concentration camp due to typhus in March 1945. . . . If the purpose was to exterminate all Jews as is alleged we find it most strange why this girl was first sent to Westerbork, and then . . . to Auschwitz-Birkenau [and that] in December 1944 Anne arrived in Bergen-Belsen with her sister Margot—a long distance from Auschwitz, not to die of "gassing" but of typhus. All this sort of shipping back and forth seems most incongruous to us if we are to believe that "extermination" story. How anyone in a time of full scale war, where transportation and food supplies are severely hampered, can proceed in this manner to "exterminate" people is beyond our comprehension. The whole matter reaches the ultimate in silliness when we are further told that the father, instead of being gassed to death, as was the original purpose, ends up being **hospitalized** at Auschwitz, surviving the ordeal. . . . The logic of this would mean that the Germans wanted people to be **healthy** before they were sent to the gas chambers. (1979, iii–iv, 1–2; boldface in original)

There is very little intellectual rigor, plenty of distortion, and no small measure of plain anti-Semitism in this little pamphlet. (At one point Felderer writes, "Whether the nicknames [in the published version] are found in the original we do not know but if they do, they indicate the girl was a spoiled brat whose parents had neglected to inculcate common courtesy. No decently brought up child would have used these nick-names" [12].) Nonetheless, I quote from this text not to accord it legitimacy, but to make several points about the relationship between fiction and historical evidence, which Roth seems to have comprehended when he wrote his novel. First of all, the very existence of Felderer's text confirms a major insight of *The Ghost Writer.* Even documents and evidentiary materials, which we imagine to be beyond dispute, can, and more importantly, will be challenged. There is no protection against Holocaust denial. People who perversely want to deny what happened will deny it. Second, the challenge against the historicity of the Holocaust will itself take the form of evidence and proof. Felderer's book is amply annotated and footnoted throughout, providing a scholarly apparatus that would appear to make his argument incontestable. Finally, the issue of proof, in the case of the *Diary* and similar texts, is messy for at least one reason that has nothing whatsoever to do with how historical facts can be intentionally distorted. The events of the Holocaust are inherently incoherent and incomprehensible. Felderer is hardly wrong that it does not make sense that there were hospitals in concentration camps or that in defiance of their own best military interests the Nazis invested inordinate resources in transporting Jews hither and yon.

But there is even more to the Anne Frank controversy than this. Occurring at the same time as the denials of the *Diary*'s authenticity was another event that even further complicated the issue of historical proof: Meyer Levin's legal proceedings against Otto Frank for the American rights to the play version of the *Diary*. This widely publicized struggle between the author who had fought so hard for the *Diary*'s publication in the United States and the man who had compiled the original typescript of the book played right into the hands of the *Diary*'s deniers. For what seemed to be happening in the courts was a legal battle between two authors for the copyright of a text that each one claimed to be his, and, therefore, by definition, not that of Anne Frank. As if that were not sufficient to appear to justify suspicions about the *Diary*'s authenticity, Otto Frank had indeed revised his daughter's text, a process of revision that was deepened and further complicated by the various individuals involved in the *Diary*'s transcription and subsequent translation. Many of these revisions were minor and of the sort that any text might undergo in the process of its publication, especially given the condition of the manuscript upon its retrieval and given the further distortions inevitable in the process of its translation. None of the revisions warranted the claim that the *Diary* was a forgery and a fake—in a word, a fiction. But some of Otto Frank's revisions were extensive.

The Jewish community, Roth knows, is seriously mistaken when it imagines that the factual record will secure its interests and guarantee the preservation of the memory of the murdered six million. History is not necessarily a defender of truth and a protector of fact—hence the novel's virtual obsession with the language of judges, juries, and the law. How, this book asks, does one prove, as in a court of law, the "truth" about the past, especially in relation to something as inherently unbelievable as the Holocaust? In proceeding this way Roth also invokes the context in which the Holocaust entered into American consciousness: through the Nuremberg trials immediately following the war (1945–1946) and the trial of Adolf Eichmann in 1961. These trials did not prevent Holocaust denial. The question of legal justice versus ethical judgment and the degree to which the courts can provide verification of the events of the Second World War is a primary subject in Bernhard Schlink's *The Reader*, which is also, like *The Ghost*

Writer, a bildungsroman—albeit of a German lawyer-to-be rather than a young Jewish artist. Against Holocaust denial even the *Diary* provides no defense. "Did six million really die?" Roth has his anti-Semitic Diasporist anti-Roth ask in *Operation Shylock*. "Come off it. The Jews pulled a fast one on us again, keeping alive their new religion. Holocaustomania. Read the revisionists. What it really comes down to is *there were no gas chambers*" (1993, 253; italics in original).

There were, of course, gas chambers, and yet Roth's anti-Roth is not completely wrong that American Jews may have constructed a new religion out of the Holocaust. In the third of the Zuckerman novels, *The Anatomy Lesson* (in Roth 1985; originally published 1983), Roth includes the following poignant detail concerning the protagonist's dying mother:

> A year after his [father's] death she developed a brain tumor. . . . Four months later, when they admitted her again, she was able to recognize her neurologist when he came by the room, but when he asked if she could write her name for him on a piece of paper, she took the pen from his hand and instead of "Selma" wrote the word "Holocaust" perfectly spelled. This was in Miami Beach in 1970, inscribed by a woman whose writings otherwise consisted of recipes on index cards, several thousand thank-you notes, and a voluminous file of knitting instructions. Zuckerman was pretty sure that before that morning she'd never even spoken the word aloud. Her responsibility wasn't brooding on horrors but sitting at night getting the knitting done and planning the next day's chores. But she had a tumor in her head the size of a lemon, and it seemed to have forced out everything except the one word. That it couldn't dislodge. It must have been there all the time without their even knowing. (1985, 447)

Roth's figure of the Holocaust lodged in the brain of the American-born Jewish mother in a 1983 American Jewish novel that seems in no way a work of Holocaust fiction can be taken as a measure of the place of the Holocaust in the Jewish American imagination. As Norma Rosen put it in the foreword to the 1989 republication of her 1969 novel, *Touching Evil*, "As safe Americans we were not there. Since then, in imagination, we are seldom anywhere else" (3). For most Jewish Americans and many non-Jewish Americans as well, this Holocaust consciousness is largely unspoken, and as compared with the daily concerns of ordinary life it is of almost radical "disconcern." As Roth puts it, "it" is there all the time, without anyone knowing it is there. The sliding referent for the word "it" in Roth's last sentence suggests that "it" is perhaps also nothing less than a cancerous growth that just might dislodge everything else in its mortally destructive insistence, a "murdered eye," as Cynthia Ozick puts it in *The Messiah of Stockholm*, through which the post-Holocaust generations, especially Jews, are condemned to see the world (1987, 3).

Thus, it is hardly out of keeping with a certain view of American Jewry for Shalom Auslander in *Hope: A Tragedy* (2012) to have his protagonist Solomon Kugel's mother invent Holocaust experiences for herself and for the rest of the members of her family:

For some time now, Mother had been putting together a family scrapbook for Jonah [her grandson]. . . . To her dismay . . . the photographs told a very different story from the one she remembered, or wanted to tell, or wanted Jonah to be told. . . . So she began to include, here and there, a new photograph of prisoners at Buchenwald, some press clipping about pogroms in the Soviet Union, a collage of Kristallnacht, corpse piles at Dachau, mass graves at Auschwitz, until these terrifying images of history's tragic victims equaled, and soon outnumbered, the photographs of any actual Kugels. (105–106)

Mother, the book tells us, is "suffering from post-traumatic effects from a genocide that happened, but not to her" (160). Auslander calls his version of Holocaustomania "not-traumatic-enough-stress disorder" (173).

Auslander is clearly following Roth's lead when he resurrects Anne Frank, albeit, as is appropriate for a writer younger than Roth, Auslander's Anne is an old woman rather than a potential love interest (lest we miss the link to Roth, Roth is explicitly named several times in the novel). Auslander's Anne, we might say, is a double resurrection. She is the ghost not only of Anne Frank herself but of Roth's Anne as well. And she represents the continuing Jewish American obsession with Anne Frank and the Holocaust (Roth himself resurrects Anne once again in *Exit Ghost* in 2007). "By the time Mother had given [*The Diary of Anne Frank*] to him to read," we are told in Auslander's novel, "she'd already made him read Elie Wiesel's *Night*, and *Dawn*, and *Day*, and Primo Levi's *If This Is a Man*; and sit through all three hours of Stanley Kramer's *Judgment at Nuremberg*, all seven and a half hours of NBC's *Holocaust*, and all nine hours of Claude Lanzmann's *Shoah*" (2012, 105). Despite his resentment of his mother, Kugel finds himself incapable of freeing himself of her Holocaust obsession and getting rid of the madwoman in the attic (to invoke the title of Sandra Gilbert's and Susan Gubar's groundbreaking feminist study). The simple fact, Kugel decides, is that "a Jew can't throw Anne Frank out of his house" (154). Nor, for that matter, we discover, can a German: "How could a German throw Anne Frank out of his attic?" the former (German) owner of the house remarks. "Can you imagine the headlines? *Nazis Strike Again? Local Man Makes It Six Million and One?*" (152). "We've all got our crosses to bear," says the German to the Jew, a tad insensitive to the content of his metaphor (155). Nonetheless, in Auslander's book Germans and Jews *both* experience themselves as victims of the Holocaust, which neither one of them can get past.

Like Roth's Anne, Auslander's is the irreverent, sacrilegious, rebellious writer that Auslander, like Roth, would be. She is, in Kugel's mother's verdict, after she has read Anne's most recent manuscript, nothing less than a "fucking WHORE," a "bitch": "Anne Frank would never write those things," Mrs. Kugel declares. "Anne Frank would never *think* those things" (278; italics in original). Auslander's Anne, in other words, is definitely not the "poor murdered child" (278) that the *Diary*'s history has made of her. Rather she is a Jewish writer, like Kafka (112), like Roth, and like Auslander. "Do you really think that anyone would have read that fucking book if she had survived?" Kugel's wife asks him, coming to the same conclusion as Anne in *The Ghost Writer*. "People read Anne Frank because Anne Frank died," she concludes (162), and she repeats this sentiment later in the novel (183). Auslander's Anne, like Roth's, knows this is the sad truth. "They wanted her to be their blind girl," Auslander's Anne says of Helen Keller. "Their deaf angel. Me, I'm the sufferer. I'm the dead girl. I'm Miss Holocaust, 1945. The prize is a crown of thorns and eternal victimhood. Jesus was a Jew . . . but I'm the Jewish Jesus" (266). Anne would prefer it be otherwise. "I want to be Anne Frank without the Holocaust," she explains, "but I use the Holocaust to subsist. . . . To that I plead guilty" (244). So might Roth and Auslander or, for that matter, Holocaust critics (myself included). Such Holocaustomania comes at a high cost. In an attempt to destroy Anne's new manuscript, Kugel's mother manages to burn down the house as well, killing her son in the process. "I've been charged with saving her," Kugel's mother says to him. "Even if it means letting her die?" To which Kugel's mother answers yes (262). Ironically Mrs. Kugel prophesies the end to the novel, in which what she saves is only the unsullied image of the Jewish martyr who is a projection onto Anne and not Anne herself.

For Sol Kugel Jewish identity is inseparably a part of his "guilt" about the Holocaust, which is expressed in terms of his guilt about owning his new (haunted) house (99). It is also part and parcel of his anxieties for his survival (92, 170). As Roth put it in *The Prague Orgy,* "the national anthem of the Jewish homeland" ought to be "such things can happen . . . such things happen to me, to him, to her, to you, to us." And Roth goes on as only Roth can: "When you see the Jewish faces mastering anxiety and feigning innocence and registering astonishment at their own fortitude—you ought to stand and put your hand to your heart" (1985, 762). Who will save the Jews of America if another Holocaust ensues? This is Nathan Englander's protagonists' question as well in his short story "What We Talk About When We Talk About Anne Frank?" (which is also the title of the 2012 volume of stories in which this one appears). The only common denominator linking the two radically different Jewish couples in Englander's story—the one secular, the other ultra-Orthodox—is the question of who will hide them in what attic should there be another Holocaust. This is the Jewish question from the Jewish point of view, and it does not go away with time.

* * *

What the Roth, Auslander, and Englander books all expose is not only the manipulative, fantasizing, exploitative dimension of the public's imagination of Anne and the Holocaust but also a parallel obsession with Anne and the Holocaust on the parts of even those writers who are critical of the public fascination with Anne—namely, Roth, Auslander, and Englander themselves. Indeed, as I have begun to suggest, Anne Frank was one of my own early obsessions. It was my own experience of reading the *Diary* so many years ago that first exposed me to the brutal and terrifying facts of the Holocaust, which thereafter became the basis not only for certain of my own fantasies and fears but for the narrative frame into which I could express those fantasies and fears and others as well. For many of us growing up in the suburbs of the United States in assimilated Jewish homes, the Nazis did not represent a genuine threat. Being Jewish was also not a source of anxiety. Being young and female, however, was. Therefore, the Nazis metamorphosed into a more existential threat, more like dragons and monsters in fairy tales than real human beings. We invented games of hiding. We shared our hideaways with one another, and we imagined our forms of resistance. Our images of violence and violation were very often taken from more explicit Holocaust accounts. And just as Anne's blossoming into sexual maturity became a source of identification for us, so did what we imagined had happened, if not to her, then to others like her, when her sexual maturity was achieved. Indeed, given how much our adolescent sense of the Holocaust had to do with fears of sexual violation, it is nothing less than amazing how long it took professional Holocaust studies to recognize publicly the incidents of rape, sexual coercion, and sexual violence in the ghettos and camps. Almost all of our imaginings, of course, had to be kept back from our parents, who, like Anne's parents, would have been impotent to help us in any event and who could hardly be entrusted with our rather scandalous and embarrassing scenarios of victimization. I was already a college graduate when I went with my husband to live in Israel, but in my imagination of things I went (at least in part) because of Margot Frank, Anne's more Zionistic sister, who was murdered and therefore could not fulfill her dream. To some degree I was living my life not only for the murdered Anne but for her murdered sister, Margot, too. That American Jewish tendency to produce Jewish identity on the basis of the Holocaust exists in Israel as well. "Playing with the Holocaust," as James Young terms it, "not lightheartedly . . . but in the obsessive earnestness of children trying to work through a family's trauma," suggests how we learn "to imagine history, not as it really happened, but as it mattered" in our lives. Young records his own youthful experience of "playing with the Holocaust," what I would call, simply, playing Holocaust (2000b, 42).

To what degree such Holocaust fantasies continue to shadow the more intellectual, academic project of a book like my own is difficult to say, even for me. But it is clear that insofar as the Holocaust was a major force of both American and Jewish—not to mention Israeli—identity for me, the subject is hardly without more personal and even more juvenile resonances. I put this up front because, as I have already said, what I have defined as my subject in this book is the subjectivity that frames any writer's or reader's view of any subject, including the Holocaust, and that includes my own. The Holocaust matters not only because of its moral and historical gravity, which is tremendous, but also because it triggers in many of us (especially if we are Jewish) fantasies of both victimhood and defiance. We want our victims, and we want our heroes. Those fantasies affect the way we relate to the experiences of others.

* * *

For this reason a book like Jonathan Littell's *The Kindly Ones* (2009) may occasion our repulsion (it certainly disgusted me), because, like Roth's *The Ghost Writer* so many years earlier (or perhaps like the Auslander and Englander books today), it seems to violate the sanctity of the subject. It might even (if only imaginatively) seem to replicate the murder of the Jewish subject. But if *The Ghost Writer* and *Hope: A Tragedy* are mildly salacious, *The Kindly Ones* is downright pornographic. Not only does the novel's hero, Maximilian Aue—who is an S.S. officer recording, after the end of the war and in exacting detail, his involvement in the murder of the Jews—spend a good amount of time (like the more youthful and innocent Zuckerman) masturbating, but he is also a sexual pervert and a matricide. I must confess that there were sections of the novel that were too off-putting for me to read. These were not, strangely enough, the sections dealing with the Holocaust, which were straightforward and factual, and also fairly familiar. Rather, the hero's perversions—such as masturbating all over his mother's house—were just too nauseating for me to tolerate. I do not for a moment think that my inability to read the text does not have something to do with my own limitations as a reader. But it also tells me something about how Littell's novel might be understood in the context of Holocaust fiction. It suggests to me how well Littell understands how inured we have become to the recitation of Holocaust horrors, which, surely, have to be less tolerable to read about than someone's jerking off.

In her essay on *The Kindly Ones,* titled "When the Perpetrator Becomes a Reliance Witness," Susan Rubin Suleiman summarizes both the considerable praise for the book and the just as considerable attack against it, with which I can sympathize, despite my finally feeling that this is an extraordinary novel. The condemnations of the book concern themselves with (among other things) the text's lack of verisimilitude, its sensationalism, and its fascination with violence. Basically, the book has seemed an obscene affront to the subject of the Holocaust. In the views of the novel's critics, the Holocaust cannot be dealt with through the same kinds of literary representations that are permitted other events or situations. Furthermore, as Suleiman notes, "The extended representation of [the] character's subjectivity . . . necessarily requires a degree of empathy." That is difficult for most of us to accord a Nazi like Aue. "Even if the character is loathsome, he . . . must at least be recognized as human, hence sharing some characteristics with the rest of us" (2009, 9). As Suleiman recognizes, this points an accusing finger not only, perhaps, away from the perpetrator, which is problematic enough, but also toward us.

Of course, this is one of the virtues of Littell's text: it does not leave the reader out of the equation. Certainly we cannot dismiss how the book delivers an electrifying, terrifying picture of the systematic murder and extermination of the Jews, down to counting the calories necessary to keep Jews alive long enough for them to work for a few months before they either die on their own or are gassed. For this the book has to be praised. But it is this latter role of testimony that for Suleiman also produces part of our objection to the novel: that the perpetrator gains the status of a witness, although here again, as she points out, the book also does service to the cause of Holocaust fiction by making it lucidly clear that a Holocaust novel, like any other piece of writing, is a constructed narrative. It is not a transparent, impartial presentation of facts, but the expression of a subjective perception, often behind another subjective perception—that is, the author behind the narrator.

I would suggest that *The Kindly Ones* is even more subversive than Suleiman allows. Aue is not a "reliable witness," even though he is a storehouse of information. Indeed, *The Kindly Ones* is not really a Holocaust novel at all, or, at least, not directly so. Rather, it is a book about a kind of fascination with the Holocaust that is, or at least can be, its own sort of perversion. In fact, the book is basically a psychopath's exhibitionist display of his sexual deviancy, which includes his incestuous affair with his sister, his masturbatory escapades, and, finally, his act of matricide, when he also kills his stepfather as well, as if for good measure. It is this story, I suggest, that the narrator (not Littell) wants to broadcast to the world; and the only way he knows he can get away with telling this story is by cloaking his text as a Holocaust account. There is no business, as has been said, like *shoah* business, and both Littell and his character know this. Indeed, given how delusional the narrator is—to the point that he cannot even remember murdering his own mother—it is not impossible to posit that Aue never was a Nazi. It may well be the case that he invents this identity for himself because it glorifies to himself who he is, alongside giving him a forum for declaring to the world his bizarre picture of reality. This would make Aue an inverted and perverted mirror of the mother in Shalom Auslander's *Hope*. Just as the mother sees herself as the Nazis' victim, so Aue fantasizes himself as the Nazi victimizer. To have written *The Kindly Ones,* Aue didn't need to have been a Nazi. Rather, he only needed to do a certain amount of research, which is confirmed by the fact that, indeed, the literal author Jonathan Littell did do this research and wrote this book. The inclusion of the "Glossary" at the end of the novel evidences the degree to which this fiction is also a work of research. The glossary signs the author's name to the text, not Aue's.

It is no accident that from the very beginning of the novel, the book signals its affinity to the tradition of Edgar Allan Poe's psychotic fantasies, a literary tradition that would be well known to the American author who grew up in France, where Poe is even more popular than in his native United States. "Some time ago," Aue tells us very early on in the narrative,

> my wife brought home a black cat. She probably thought it would make me happy. . . . Whenever I tried to pet it, to show my goodwill, it would slip away to sit on the windowsill and stare at me with its yellow eyes; if I tried to pick it up and hold it, it would scratch me. At night, on the other hand, it would come and curl up in a ball on my chest, a stifling weight, and in my sleep I would dream I was being smothered beneath a heap of stones. With my memories, it's been more or less the same. (Littell 2009, 5–6)

Poe's fictions are everywhere about madmen, as is the case with "The Black Cat" and others of the tales of conscience and revenge ("The Tell-Tale Heart," "The Imp of the Perverse," and "William Wilson"). These stories are also, like Aue's narrative, confessions that finally (albeit inadvertently or at least unconsciously) culminate in the protagonist's arrest and execution. For this reason Poe's are tales of suicide as much as of murder. So might Littell's be such a tale of self-destruction. Although Aue claims that he is not confessing, that in fact he feels no remorse, it is clear throughout the narrative that he suffers from guilt (he has a range of stomach ailments) and that his 999-page narrative is a confession, which could well culminate in his arrest and death.

Another indicator that Aue's confession is of a piece with those of Poe's narrators is the incestuous relationship between Aue and his twin sister, whose name, Una, recalls Poe's angelic colloquies (both the incestuous relationship and the location of the masturbatory scene in the family home look in the direction of "The Fall of the House of Usher"). Throughout his fiction, Poe's narrators murder the women in their lives, not always mothers, but almost always mother substitutes. That the narrator of Littell's book is not aware of murdering his mother and stepfather and that he has this sense "of always observing myself; it was as if a film camera were fixed just above me" (107) also makes him like one of Poe's narrators: delusional and self-alienated. "I am a man like other men, I am a man like you," the narrator protests as the pitch of his hysteria rises. "I tell you I am just like you!" (24). Like Poe's narrators, Littell's Aue doth protest too much. Aue is not like us at all, and not just because he was a Nazi, *if* indeed he was.

This reading of Aue does not deny that Littell's novel gives us a tremendous amount of information about the Holocaust. As already noted, the book superbly captures the "automaton-like" scientism that went into calculating calories or how many human bodies might be incinerated in a day (879). A fascinating aspect of Littell's novel that cannot be dismissed is, in a kind of reversal of the stereotype of the Jew as feminized male, the representation of the feminization of the Nazi soldier. Not only does Aue dream of himself as a woman, but he also attributes Hitler's hatred of homosexuality to the influence of the Jews: "the Christian prohibition," he argues, "is a Jewish superstition" (195). "When Germany is purified of its Jews, it will have to be purified of their pernicious ideas too" (199). That Aue is himself circumcised ("Oh it's nothing," he says, "a teenage infection" [199]) makes of Aue either a nominal Jew or a self-hating Jew, thus suggesting how Nazism constituted an attempt to condemn and disown aspects of the self that one both wished to deny and to preserve. This, too, would link Littell's novel with the Poe tradition of the doppelgänger, especially as embodied in Poe's tales of ratiocination (the Dupin stories) and in works like "William Wilson" and the other tales of conscience and revenge, in which what one is attempting to kill off is one's mirror self-reflection. As I already noted, homicide is often suicide in Poe's fiction, and that is not a bad interpretation of Nazi genocidal policy: by killing the Jews, the Nazis would kill their disavowed mirror image of themselves.

If Littell's novel has seemed to some to let the German people off too easily by imagining the Nazi as psychopath (paralleling the argument against Bernhard Schlink's *The Reader* that Schlink excuses Nazi behavior by portraying Nazis as illiterate and uneducated), I suggest that to read the novel this way is to miss how carefully constructed the book is to not excuse the Nazis. Indeed, the text goes further: it suggests how the exploitation of the Holocaust for any purpose whatsoever is abhorrent. Insofar as any work of fiction (or, for that matter, memoir or history) benefits its author, texts have to find ways to signal their awareness of their own culpability without falling into a silence that simply evades the Holocaust altogether.

Like *The Ghost Writer*, Littell's *The Kindly Ones* discomforts. In this way both books lead us to question our own motivations and our own responses, including the pleasure we might find in other people's humiliations or perversions. I found Littell's *The Kindly Ones* as unpleasant a read as I once found *The Diary of Anne Frank* a sympathetic friend and Roth's book a brilliant satire. But neither identification with nor repulsion by a text is an appropriate response to a Holocaust narrative, of whatever kind. If the Holocaust is to be more than a screen for our fantasy projections—whatever kinds of projections those might be—then we need to be able to create distance between ourselves and the texts we read. We must be able to interrogate ourselves alongside the perpetrators. And we must be able to grant the unbridgeable distance between our experiences and those of the individuals who suffered the Holocaust firsthand.

Both Roth and Littell seem to me great writers because of the degree to which they are conscious of the difference between fiction and fact and the degree to which narrative inevitably brings to its stories unconscious factors and features. I begin *The Subject of Holocaust Fiction* with Roth's *The Ghost Writer* and Littell's

The Kindly Ones for several reasons. First, neither is, by conventional definition, a Holocaust novel: Roth's (which precedes the subsequent flow of Holocaust novels) because the Holocaust is secondary to the book's attempt to depict the portrait of the young Jewish artist, both in relation to his precursor writers (James, Joyce) and to his community; Littell's (coming very late in the game) because, as I have suggested, its purpose seems to be the subversion of the genre or at least an exposure of some of its more problematic aspects. Second, both books deal with the problem of subject position, which is a defining feature of great literary texts. By emphasizing how Holocaust fictions, like other fictions, call into question the objectivity of our perceptions, I hope to help secure Holocaust fiction for the canon of great literature. The best Holocaust fiction, I suggest, requires no special pleading, even if, as historical fiction, not to mention fiction about a barely comprehensible, major catastrophic event, it requires a special kind of reading, one that takes the historical record and real human lives into account.

* * *

Since this prologue is an attempt to bring into play my own subject position, this is the place to explain my choice of texts. Since I am interested in fiction, I have *not* discussed memoirs or autobiographies, even fictionalized ones, such as the novels of Elie Wiesel. Whatever rhetorical devices go into telling historical narratives (Primo Levi's books, for example), people's stories, when they are told in the first person, are generally not shared with us so that we can critique or psychoanalyze them, unless, of course, we are health professionals who are being told these stories for the purposes of psychological intervention. It is presumptuous and unethical for anyone else (including a literary critic) to question people's stories of suffering and pain. Therefore, I have chosen to deal only with fictions, and I have primarily stayed with novels that are fairly well known and have been accorded the respect of other critics as far as their seriousness as works of art.

I have also preferred nonrealist novels to works of realism. Realist fiction can legitimately be read more like fictionalized documentaries or histories than imaginative explorations of their subject. In other words, they may be read more as attempts to record events than to interpret them. Many Holocaust novels have indeed been read this way. Therefore, I have not dealt with early entries into the field of Holocaust fiction (such as books by Leon Uris and Herman Wouk). These books certainly served to introduce the Holocaust into the public imagination, but they do not seem to me the kinds of works of literature that raise interpretive issues, at least not of the sort that interest me in this book. Moving in the opposite direction, I have also avoided texts like Jerzy Kosinski's *The Painted Bird*. *The Painted Bird* is surely not a work of realist fiction. Nonetheless, it seems to me so highly sensationalistic as to flood the subject of the Holocaust with a kind of excess that, in my view and in the same way as Littell's Aue, does damage to the subject. Littell is in control of this sensationalism; Koskinski, I feel, is not. I also have not revisited texts that I have dealt with extensively in the past. Therefore, while I could have included an extended reading of Saul Bellow's *Mr. Sammler's Planet,* which certainly suggests how Sammler's contemporary politics reflect his Holocaust experience, I did not, since I discuss that book at length in *Blacks and Jews in Literary Conversation.* Similarly concerning the extraordinary fiction of Aharon Appelfeld, my book-length study *Aharon Appelfeld's Fiction: Acknowledging the Holocaust* was the inception for the present project. Therefore, I have dealt with only one of Appelfeld's novels, since it fit so perfectly into the general argument of section 2 of this book, and I did not want to leave Appelfeld (one of the most important and prolific writers on the Holocaust) unrepresented. I have not gone back and discussed his other fictions.

In sum, I chose to discuss Holocaust novels that, in my judgment, constitute great works of art, those that make us conscious of the degree to which we are readers of texts and therefore being called upon to think about the relationship between imagination and reality and the moral force of that relationship. For me being a reader means taking experience secondhand, mediated by words and by other people's imaginations. Human subjects suffered the Holocaust; human subjects write stories about their experiences; human subjects read those stories. The recognition or acknowledgment of the human is every bit the life force of great Holocaust fiction and its greatest ethical contribution.

Section I
Psychoanalytic Listening and Fictions of the Holocaust

As is probably clear by now, I am going to read Holocaust fictions psychoanalytically, as expressing and exposing unconscious positions on the parts of texts and readers alike. In this section, therefore, I "listen" to three superb Holocaust fictions with what Theodor Reik, using a phrase from Nietzsche's *Beyond Good and Evil,* designates "the third ear." "The psychoanalyst," writes Reik, "has to learn how one mind speaks to another beyond words and in silence. He must learn to listen 'with the third ear.' It is not true that you have to shout to make yourself understood. When you wish to be heard, you whisper" (1949, 144). My intention in the three readings in this section is to listen to what these texts "whisper" outside the margins and between the lines. I read them through a psychoanalytical third ear in order to understand them not only more fully but, finally, more compassionately and, hopefully, with a significant degree of self-consciousness as well. "A little more or a little less sincerity," writes Reik, "a small plus or minus of moral courage, is what decides whether we understand ourselves and others" (59–60). In other words, sometimes we need a bit more bravery and a little less bravado in order to read texts. What prompts Reik's observation is his realization that in interpreting one of his own dreams he had omitted a significant aspect of the context: anti-Semitism. What this leads to for Reik is a discussion of Jews (like himself) who are ashamed of being Jewish. "Not analysis, but the analyst," writes Reik, "makes us understand the meanings of those puzzling processes of the unconscious," and for Reik part and parcel of this process is interrogating one's own interior consciousness, including one's responses to other people's words (67, 146–47). I apply this paradigm of reading with a multiply attuned third ear (or eye) to the relationship between the reader and the text. It is often through the reader's interrogation of his own subject position in relation to the text that the reader can unravel the text's deepest and most significant meanings.

I have described the features of psychoanalytic listening that I apply to the reading of literary fictions in my book coauthored with Rami Aronzon in 2008. They can be summarized as follows:

1. Listening psychoanalytically means listening for the surplus in a narrative, for the "what else" of the story, which is to say for both its unconscious *as well as* its conscious contents and structures. A work of art contains highly crafted conscious contents and structures. Those do not, however, preclude features of the unconscious.

2. Listening psychoanalytically means listening neutrally, nonjudgmentally, and nondefensively. This means neither approving nor disapproving nor even supporting the teller of the story. Shoshana Feldman and Dori Laub (1992) have argued that our job as readers (or listeners) of people's narratives is to witness them. That means we must support the storyteller in the details of the story, whether we find them credible or not. It may be the case that when we listen to Holocaust testimonies or read them as memoirs or diaries, it is incumbent upon us not to assume a psychoanalytic stance in relation to the material presented. After all, most of us are not professional psychotherapists. Furthermore, most oral testimony given by Holocaust survivors is not being told to us for the purposes of our psychoanalytic insights. This is precisely the situation of the father, Vladek, in relation to his son in Art Spiegelman's *Maus*. But a fictional text is *not* oral testimony, and fictional characters are certainly not endangered by our forays into a psychoanalytic response to the material presented. What we can say about the text *Maus* is quite different from what we can say about the survivor Vladek's story or, for that matter, about his son's narrative of his reception of that story. Listening nondefensively also means not permitting ourselves to react to what we might find offensive in the text, as, for example (especially if we are Jewish readers), the auto-anti-Semitism of a protagonist such as Rosa in Ozick's *The Shawl*.

3. Psychoanalytical listening assumes there is always more story to be told. This means there is also always more listening to be done. Analysis is never over, and in the process of its being heard and heard again and returned to the client for her own self-listening, the story is itself always in the process of dynamic change. This means that, in relation to our reading of literary texts, our analysis of the text, fed back into our reading of that text, will also produce a new text in its wake. We can never factor out either the endless meaningfulness of the text or its self-transformation as it becomes subject to our conscious and unconscious processes. The reader is responsible for her interpretation of and relationship to the text, and she must assume that responsibility.

4. Psychoanalytic listening proceeds on the assumption that a story told to another is also, even primarily, a story told to the self—a story, to recur to

Reik's language, told in whispers. To listen psychoanalytically, then, is often less to hear than to overhear a story. For this reason the purpose of psychoanalytic listening is not to interpret for the patient, but to give the story back to the narrator in such a way that the storyteller can interpret for himself.

5. This idea of returning the story to the teller, when the teller is a written narrative, means not preempting the text's rights to its own insights. We need to credit the text with a degree of self-knowledge that we are merely helping to assist into greater clarity.

6. Finally, listening psychoanalytically means also listening to our own responses, to our own unconscious processes and materials, which very often are the triggers for our interpretations of other people's stories. I do not want to fall back on the definition of literary texts as providing some sort of "as-if" life training for the reader, although this is probably as good a definition as any of what fiction is and how it works.

Whatever other benefits listening to Holocaust fictions with a third ear might provide, however, one way that it functions, which my readings are intended to highlight, is how the text's psychoanalytic processes become an avenue into witnessing the reader's own unconscious wishes, fears, fantasies, and desires. Listening psychoanalytically to Holocaust fictions might help us to identify what in *us* resists hearing certain things in Holocaust narratives and what that says about who we are and what needs to change in us so that we can more fully and deeply comprehend other people's tales of suffering. Part of what Holocaust fiction can serve to help us develop is our fullest capacity for the sympathetic—nonjudgmental, undefended, and non-self-referential—listening to other people's stories. Those might be aspects of reading that we might want to bring to any literary text. They are essential in relation to Holocaust fiction, where our relationship to fictive stories ultimately helps configure our relationship to history as well.

1 Voyeurism, Complicated Mourning, and the Fetish

Cynthia Ozick's The Shawl

By THE TIME we meet Rosa Lublin in the second part of Cynthia Ozick's novella *The Shawl* (1990), she is "a madwoman and a scavenger." She has given up her store in New York ("she smashed it up herself") and moved to Miami (113). A Holocaust survivor and a refugee in America, Rosa destroys her store because, as she puts it, "whoever came, they were like deaf people. Whatever you explained to them, they didn't understand" (27). This is the assumption she also makes about the man to whom she is now explaining these things. "Whatever I would say," she says to Simon Persky, "you would be deaf" (27). The "you" reaches disturbingly out of the text and speaks to us, the readers, as well. How we might not remain deaf to Rosa's story is part of the challenge the story issues to its readers. Yet to hear Rosa's story in all of its complexity and detail, we must listen in a special sort of way. In order to hear the story, not only as Rosa gives it to us in factual detail but also in its psychological undercurrents, we must listen in a way that even those of us who *do* listen to Holocaust narratives quite regularly, or at least believe ourselves to be listening, may need to learn. This may mean we might also have to unlearn certain aspects of our regular listening or, to bring this back to the realm of literary, reading practices. It might also mean hearing a story that Rosa herself does not fully intend to tell us.

The Dysfunctional Narrator

Ozick's *Shawl* proceeds in two parts. The first part, the short story titled "The Shawl," is a lyrical, almost poetic account of a forced march, which delivers the major protagonist, Rosa Lublin; her baby daughter, Magda; and her niece, Stella, to a labor camp, where Magda ultimately dies. The second part "Rosa" is a longer, more realistic narrative. It concerns the very bitter and dysfunctional Rosa after the war and after she has relocated to Florida and become a recluse. Rosa's only meaningful relationship is with her dead child, whom she treats as if she were alive, until she meets Simon Persky and begins to enter into a relationship with him. The novella in its entirety has something important to tell us not only about the degradation suffered by survivors like Rosa both during and after the war but also about the world's reluctance to hear such survivor stories—or to hear them fully. For, ironically, and more importantly, however much the book has something to say about the world's unwillingness to hear the story of the Holocaust, it also has something to offer about the opposite phenomenon: our often too avid interest in the events of the Holocaust and the ways we hear those events according to preconceived notions about what happened and to whom.

What is clear from the beginning of *The Shawl* is that unlike the protagonists in other Holocaust narratives (for example, Vladek in *Maus* or Hannalore in *The Far Euphrates*), Rosa does want someone to hear her story of devastation and loss, or at least to hear the part of the story she wants to tell. But no one will listen. Or, more precisely, no one will listen in a way Rosa considers as listening. There is someone in the story, aside from Simon Persky later on, who is willing, even eager, to hear Rosa's story. That someone is Dr. Tree, a Holocaust scholar of sorts, who is actively soliciting Rosa's participation in his scientific study of survivors. As someone who is so interested in hearing stories of the Holocaust that he seeks them out, Dr. Tree is discomfortingly like us, the readers of Ozick's text, since anyone who picks up Ozick's book to read it is, by definition, not representative of that part of the population who refuses to hear Rosa's story. Dr. Tree, we are told, has "lately begun to amass survivor data." It is for this reason that he would like to conduct "an in-depth interview" with Rosa. "Though I am not myself a physician," Tree explains, "I am presently working on a study . . . designed to research the theory . . . known generally as Repressed Animation. Without at this stage going into detail, it may be of some preliminary use to you to know that investigations so far reveal an astonishing generalized minimalization during any extended period of stress resulting from incarceration, exposure, and malnutrition" (1990, 36). The consequence of this minimalization, according to Dr. Tree, is a state of "non-attachment," of "consummated indifference": "they gave up craving and began to function in terms of non-functioning" (36–38). Dr. Tree gives us a definition that recalls the *Mussulman,* the camp inmate on the verge of death, who has given up the will to live and whose zombie-like qualities are picked up in many a Holocaust novel and critical essay.

Since by most conventional standards (including her own) Rosa is "mad," Tree's diagnosis cannot be dismissed out of hand. This is not in the least to diminish the force of Rosa's objection to participating in Tree's study: "Disease, disease! . . . An excitement over other people's suffering. They let their mouths water up. Stories about children running blood in America from sores, what muck" (36). There is something moderately distasteful in the public interest in the Holocaust, especially in relation to the shame, humiliation, and, finally, psychological distress of the "survivors." "Whatever stains in the crotch are nobody's business," Rosa quite rightly admonishes not only the characters in the text but us, too, for we would miss the thrust of Rosa's ire were we to exclude ourselves from her accusation (34).

There are survivors, like Rosa, who need to be heard in very personal, affective, and nonhistorical ways, precisely as we might hear someone in a psychoanalytic situation. In other words, some people, like Rosa, need to be heard from within the sheer madness of their storytelling by listeners (like Persky or like us) who are willing to entertain madness as a legitimate mode of narrative expression, even if, or especially because, it does nothing less than drag us into its madness. To be sure, this madness (the storyteller's and finally our own) threatens to dissolve the story's relationship to historical fact and documentation. It threatens to virtually disqualify the narrative as testimony altogether. And this is the bind: a Holocaust narrative that causes us to question its historical bases is anathema, no less to the teller than to us. Yet for us to hear Holocaust narratives as if they were strictly historical accounts flattens and distorts them in equally problematic ways. Some survivors do suffer from what Tree is calling "Repressed Animation," "generalized minimalization," "non-attachment," and "consummate indifference." These may be crude, reductive, and perhaps even non-illuminating ways of defining what ails Rosa. Yet some survivors (Rosa among them) do suffer from neurotic and psychotic symptoms. We need to be able to hear their stories not in spite of their pathologies, but through them and through our own (hopefully less severe) psychopathologies as well.

Rosa's rather unsympathetic niece, Stella, who "took psychology courses at the New School at night," has other, more familiar-sounding, perhaps less off-putting names than Tree's for Rosa's condition: "fetish" and "trauma" (31). But "psychoanalysis" (29) is clearly under scrutiny, if not outright attack, in Ozick's text along with Holocaust studies in general. Nonetheless, just as we would be overreacting were we to chuck the enterprise of Holocaust studies because it can become too subjective and even prurient, so too psychoanalysis may have something to contribute to our understanding of Holocaust narratives. Even more important, perhaps, psychoanalysis might provide a vocabulary and a technology for our effectively listening to and responding to survivor stories like Rosa's. As everyone, including Rosa, is agreed, Rosa is "crazy." How else can we explain her attachment to her dead daughter's shawl (which is basically a fetish [31]), or her narrowing down the range of her relationships to letters and phone calls with that daughter and her niece, Stella (whom she despises; is this not something we might label generalized minimalization or nonattachment?), or how she animates the dead child's spirit, making her come alive again? The psychoanalytic name for this, to add to an already overlong list, is "complicated mourning."

"Complicated mourning," as described by Vamik D. Volkan in *Linking Objects and Linking Phenomena* (1981), involves the internalization (introjection) of the lost loved object. Incapable of mourning so as to get through the mourning process and back to life again, the mourner attempts through various means to keep the dead person alive. Therefore, the deceased person remains a living entity within the mourner. Such a diagnosis of Rosa's situation will no more surprise or disturb readers of the novella who are interested in such psychoanalytic terms of description than the previously mentioned terms like "trauma," "fetish," or the "transitional object" (as discussed by Andrew Gordon [1994]), which in terms of complicated mourning might be called a "linking object." Indeed "linking objects," "fetishism," and "complicated mourning" collectively name parts of a single psychological condition. Yet the question remains of what value these psychoanalytic terms might be for us in reading—which is to say in listening to—Rosa's (and Ozick's) story. These psychoanalytic categories are not only vital to our interpreting Rosa's story; they are also pertinent to how we understand our own relation to the text.

We have come a long way in psychoanalytic literary criticism from the old Freudianism, in which texts were read as allegories of pathological conditions pertaining to either the characters or the author. Psychoanalytic categories are no longer assumed to be the objective facts of which literary texts are merely the fictional illustrations. Yet psychoanalysis does offer certain assistance in interpreting the literary text. Of course, Rosa is a fictional character, and whatever she says or thinks or does is being constructed by Ozick, whose mind is not Rosa's. We might just want to dismiss the complexities of Rosa's ambiguities and ambivalences for the depths of clarity of Ozick's literary purposes. Even if writers may be assumed to create fiction out of the unconscious as well as conscious components of their own minds, those conscious components are there in abundance. Writers cognitively, intellectually determine much about the final product we call the story, and without a doubt *The Shawl* is a highly crafted work of fiction. It deploys several literary strategies for making ethical and even ideological points about the Holocaust and about Jewish identity before, after, and during the events, although we also need to see that ideology bears with it its own deeply unconscious motivations.

Ozick is not Rosa. Yet if a writer is a great writer—and I think Ozick is such a writer—then, as Freud claimed long ago in "Creative Writers and Day-Dreaming" (1978a; originally published 1908), she articulates archaic fantasies, which inhabit all of us. The "essential *ars poetica*," of the creative writer, says Freud, "lies in the technique of overcoming the feeling of repulsion in us which is undoubtedly connected with the barriers that rise between each single ego and the others. . . . The writer softens the character of his egoistic day-dreams by altering and disguising it, and he bribes us by the purely formal—that is, aesthetic—yield of pleasure which he offers us in the presentation of his phantasies" (153; italics in original). Located in Rosa—whose name is a translation into English of Ozick's Hebrew name, Shoshanah—there clearly is a part of Ozick's own psyche functioning *as if* Ozick had had the horrific experiences of this woman, whom she so devotedly produces for us on the page: her own world of paper and pen, in its small stillness, so like Rosa's, as Rosa writes letter after letter to her dead daughter. Ozick's gift as a writer is her ability to put herself into this other consciousness in the condition of *as if*. It is her talent to let this consciousness speak to us of its pain and torment and even of its less savory fantasies, unfettered by the processes of intellect that generally defend us against such unguarded expressions of self. There is a depth to Rosa's madness that demands to be read, precisely because Ozick's great talent has constructed it for us to explore.

It is in terms of plumbing the depths of Rosa's story that the psychoanalytic model has something special to offer. We may be able to understand *The Shawl* without access to terms like "fetish," "transitional [linking] object," "trauma," or "complicated mourning," but these words are at least no worse than others we might use to try to describe Rosa's situation. Insofar as understanding Rosa or people like her has something to do with being able to comprehend what they are suffering, the terms have value. But the psychoanalytic model has something more to offer. This is its insistence that listening is an ongoing process that is never exhausted. Even more crucially, such listening never exhausts the narrative that it is hearing. Or, more precisely, it never exhausts the narrative it is overhearing, because, as I have already noted, psychoanalytic thinking also attends to the way a story told to another person might nonetheless be primarily a story told to the self. Of this story we are merely eavesdroppers. We as much listen *in* on these stories as we listen *to* them. This also means that these stories are *not* asking us to respond to and act upon them, at least not in any direct way. That Rosa's ideal listener is her dead daughter, Magda, who is not (unless we believe in ghosts) a separate entity but a part of Rosa herself, provides clear evidence that Rosa's addressee is herself, not us.

That there is always more story to be heard will turn out to be a very important psychoanalytic insistence in reading Ozick's novella, since most critics have concluded too quickly how the two parts of the narrative fit together. Readers of *The Shawl* have tended to assume that part 1 of the narrative, dealing with the forced march to the labor camp, contains the factual bases of Rosa's experience, which account for Rosa's behavior in part 2 of the novella. These bases seem to be as follows: after a forced march, Rosa, Stella, and Magda (who has been hidden by Rosa in her shawl and has thus gone undetected) arrive together at the camp; Stella at some point steals the shawl; and the child, searching for her shawl, wanders into the camp arena, where the camp guard throws her against the electric fence surrounding the camp and the child dies. As Rosa herself summarizes the story in part 2 of *The Shawl*: "The lost babe. Murdered. Thrown against the fence, barbed, thorned, electrified, grid and griddle" (31). Yet to hear fully what Rosa is saying in Miami we must hear what the short story, which is also focalized through Rosa, is not telling us or, more precisely, also telling us but in occluded and fantastic ways. Most of us, I think, have stopped short of hearing that other story. As a result we have also not encountered the troubling issue of authenticity in Ozick's fiction: of whether Rosa's narrative is factually accurate (and, if so, accurate of what exactly?) and if and how it matters whether a particular survivor narrative is "truthful" in the factual, epistemological, historical sense. Stopping short of hearing the full narrative also prohibits our understanding of Rosa's psychological prehistory and how this, as much as any of the horrific events that befall her during the Holocaust itself, has determined who she is. Additionally, it blocks our self-interrogation as readers of Rosa's and, finally, of Ozick's story.

The Narrative of Shame

"Consider also the special word they used," Rosa rails at us in the second story, "Rosa": "*survivor.* . . . As long as they didn't have to say *human being*" (Ozick 1990, 36). In order for us to acknowledge that the "survivor" is a "human being" in every sense of the word, we have to hear in their stories the life that preceded the devastation, even or especially where this life is not an ideal one. And to do this we must, even at the risk of disliking or finding fault with the survivor, grant the same psychological complexity to the human beings who suffered the catastrophe as to those who did not. Rosa's repeated conjuring of the dead child, Magda, like her attachment to Magda's shawl, does contain a story that Rosa wishes and needs to tell, albeit not to Dr. Tree or Stella, who just might give names to her condition and, even more painfully, judge her for what her story reveals about her. We the readers might not want to hear this story. Yet to refuse to hear Rosa's story in its entirety is to refuse to hear her at all. And that makes us no different from the customers in her shop.

Since Rosa's ideal audience is her dead daughter, Magda, let us pursue Rosa's narrative as a story told to Magda. The word "deaf," which Rosa hurls at Persky and uses to describe her customers in New York City, first occurs in the text, almost bizarrely, in the short story that precedes "Rosa," where it concerns her baby daughter. Rosa is afraid that the infant Magda might be "defective, without a voice; perhaps she was deaf" (7). Rosa would first and foremost have Magda hear her story, which is, of course, in part why she must keep the dead child alive: in order to have her listen to what her mother needs to tell her. "You're always prodding me for these old memories," Rosa writes to Magda. "If not for you, I would have buried them all" (42). Therefore, Rosa's truest story is best glimpsed, or, more precisely, overheard, in the letters she writes to Magda, which is the part of her that is prodding her to remember the past. This story is also contained in what Rosa calls her "private words" (70). These are the words that she neither writes nor speaks, many of which are captured in the free-associative thoughts that hover around her acts of letter writing. These letters and thoughts, we are made to understand, are expressed in literary Polish, Rosa's mother tongue. Therefore, they come closer than anything Rosa might say in broken English (to her customers, to Persky, to Stella, or to us) to expressing the truth of Rosa's experience.

To you, Rosa tells her daughter, I tell no lies. Even if we sense that Rosa does misrepresent the truth to some extent even to Magda (i.e., to herself), what she says to Magda comes as close to "the" truth as we or Rosa will ever come. That there is no absolute, unambiguous truth ever and that all of us are always to some degree or other distorting the truth, even to ourselves, are facets of the wisdom this novella has to teach us about listening to other people's stories. To hear the truth of Rosa's story, to hear what it is that she wishes us to hear on the unconscious rather than conscious level, we need to hear how her words make sense as a narrative that, whatever lies Rosa might be telling in the ways she consciously, rationally, constructs her story, itself tells no lies. Associative links, like the genre of fiction, produce a contract with the story's audience (which, in the case of associative links, is also the storyteller) that exists outside the definition or concept of lying. Associative thinking simply tells a different kind of story, organized around a different kind of truth.

Ozick's text provides us with only two of Rosa's letters to Magda, although we receive some fragments of a third letter as well. The letters contain many "definite facts" (66), as Rosa calls them, that constitute much of the narrative she had tried unsuccessfully to tell to the customers in her shop. That these "facts" were told in the shop in bits and pieces of broken English suggests how fragmented, partial, and inadequately they told the story that Rosa was trying so desperately to tell. To be sure, through these same "definite facts" Ozick and Rosa provide their readers/listeners with important information about the Holocaust, in particular as it relates to the somewhat less well rehearsed experience of the ghetto. These include the utter ordinariness of the life surrounding the ghetto, the number of witnesses who had to know what was going on but who chose to do and say nothing, the ingenuity of the Nazis in imprisoning the Jews, the abominable conditions within the ghetto itself ("the most repulsive slum, deep in slops and vermin and a toilet not fit for the lowest criminal" [67]), and so forth. Both Ozick and Rosa would have us know these things. Yet these definite facts are far less important, at least to Rosa's narrative, than the inner story she needs to tell her daughter and herself. Insofar as a part of Ozick's purpose is to tell us this inner story as well, the definite facts are also less important to Ozick's story.

Therefore, we need to interrogate carefully the images through which Rosa tells her "factual" story. One of these images is "the tramcar in the Ghetto" (66), which, it turns out, opens onto the scene of Rosa's suffering in more ways than one. The tramcar is not exclusively or even primarily a literal artifact or historical detail of the past, even though it is that as well. Rather, the tramcar (like Ozick's shawl, albeit not, perhaps, Rosa's) is already a metonymy both of the events it intends to convey and, even more important, of memories and feelings surrounding those events. Rosa's repetition (to Magda) of what she had said about the tramcar to the customers in her shop before she smashed it up (as she would have liked to have smashed up the tramcar) and what she wanted them to understand by it (which is in part this fact of her violent desire) gets to the heart of at least one aspect of what makes Rosa's narrative of the ghetto almost impossible for any of her customers to hear. Rosa would also like to smash her listeners to smithereens, not least because of what the narrative also expresses, which is also difficult for us readers/listeners to hear: Rosa's sense of aristocratic entitlement and superiority over us common folk and plebeians and her total embarrassment at falling from her former place of privilege. It is this arrogance and its unexpressed underbelly of shame that Rosa repeatedly expresses to Persky when she tells him rather nastily, "My Warsaw isn't your Warsaw," "Your Warsaw isn't my Warsaw" (19, 22).

Here is the story Rosa tries to tell her customers about her experience in the ghetto, which they refuse to hear:

> When I told about the tramcar, no one ever understood it ran on tracks! Everyone always thought of buses. Well, they couldn't tear up the tracks, they couldn't get rid of the overhead electric wires, could they? The point is they couldn't reroute the whole tram system; so, you know, they didn't. The tramcar came right through the middle of the Ghetto. What they did was build a sort of overhanging pedestrian bridge for the Jews, so they couldn't get near the tramcar to escape on it into the other part of Warsaw. The other side of the wall.
>
> The most astounding thing was that the most ordinary streetcar, bumping along on the most ordinary trolley tracks, and carrying the most ordinary citizens going from one section of Warsaw to another, ran straight into the place of our misery. Every day, and several times a day, we had these witnesses. Every day they saw us—women with shopping sacks; and once I noted a head of lettuce sticking up out of the top of a sack—green lettuce! I thought my salivary glands would split with aching for that leafy greenness. . . . And in this place now I am like the woman who held the lettuce in the tramcar. I said all this in my store, talking to the deaf. How I became like the woman with the lettuce. (67–69)

What primarily organizes Rosa's choice of story, in particular the choice of metonymic figure around which she organizes that story, is her sense of deprivation, the way in which, as she puts it elsewhere, her life—not just any life, but this life of privilege—has been stolen from her. Rosa's is a shame narrative, and this is a difficult aspect of Rosa's narrative for us to hear: how she is ashamed to be reduced to someone like us. Rosa's life was to have been one of superiority over those Polish peasants who roam freely and well fed throughout Rosa's Warsaw while Rosa is left to salivate with animal hunger over a head of lettuce. Indeed, her sense of diminishment by them is conveyed by the way her position above has been made into a mockery by the pedestrian bridge that connects the parts of the ghetto. She towers above the peasants only in some meaningless, architectural way. Rosa is equally mortified to have been "billeted" along with another group of "peasants," with whom she also does not belong: those "teeming Mockowiczes and Rabinowiczes and Perskys and Finkelsteins, with all their bad-smelling grandfathers and their hordes of feeble children," "these old Jew peasants worn out from their rituals and superstitions, phylacteries on their foreheads sticking up so stupidly, like unicorn horns" (66–67).

What makes Rosa's arrogance and snobbism especially difficult for Jewish readers is that these Jews for whom she has such contempt are very likely more like *our* relatives than is Rosa herself. They are our grandparents and great-grandparents. And this is also likely the same population that makes up the customers in her shop. They are the New York Perskys. "In this place now," Rosa says to them, without any sense of the offense she is offering in her bid to make them listen to her, "I am like the woman who held the lettuce in the tramcar. I said all this in my store, talking to the deaf. How I became like the woman with the lettuce." "My Warsaw is not your Warsaw."

Rosa feels sullied by the ghetto, and she carries those feelings of humiliation and shame with her into her present life, first in New York and then in Miami. But Rosa's shame has to do with more than the humiliation of living in the ghetto:

> Two long whole rolls of glinting dentures smiled at her; he was proud to be a flirt.
> "You read Yiddish?" the old man said.
> "No."
> "You can speak a few words maybe?"
> "No." My Warsaw isn't your Warsaw. But she remembered her grandmother's cradle-croonings: . . . *Unter Reyzls vigele shteyt a klorvays tsigele.* How Rosa's mother despised those sounds! When the drying cycle ended, Rosa noticed that the old man handled the clothes like an expert. She was ashamed for him to touch her underpants. *Under Rosa's cradle there's a clearwhite little goat.* (19; italics in original)

Not without reason does Ozick stage this first meeting with Persky in a Laundromat. Nor is it insignificant that what Rosa is made to notice is how Persky handles her "underpants," or that later, after Rosa gets home, she is certain that a pair of her underpants is missing (she later finds them): "Then it came to her that Persky had her underpants in his pocket. Oh, degrading. The shame. Pain in the loins."

... What could a man, half a widower, do with a pair of female bloomers? ... A sex maniac ... his parts starved. Whatever stains in the crotch are nobody's business" (34). Persky, because of his name, his Yiddish, and his lower-class status, does more than revive memories of the filthy, degrading, shameful conditions of the ghetto. He reminds her of the "pain in the loins," which has a far more specific reference.

That the words of her grandmother's song refer to a "clear-white little goat" under her cradle may contain in Rosa's hearing of it a sexual innuendo. The words correspond to the vulnerability she was exposed to in the ghetto simply by virtue of the lack of sanitary conditions and the forced cohabitation in small spaces with other Jews. Rosa's vulnerability and the "pain in the loins," however, also lead from matters of filth and lack of privacy to other sorts of humiliation far more harrowing, which may also have inherently to do with the conditions of ghetto life. Joan Ringelheim (1985, 1998), Myrna Goldenberg (1998), and Felicja Karay (1998) have countered the long entertained contention that Jewish women were not raped during the Holocaust. They were not only subject to violent rape by Germans both in the ghettos and in the camps, these critics point out, but they were vulnerable as well to both rape and sexual coercion within the ghettos by their fellow Jews. Since Jewish men were often placed higher in the hierarchy of the ghetto, with greater access to food and other resources, making oneself sexually available could sometimes secure for oneself or one's family the protection necessary to survive. This is the theme of one of Ida Fink's most memorable short stories, "Aryan Papers."

"Stella's accusations," insists Rosa in one of the letters she writes to her dead daughter, "are all Stella's own excretion. Your father was not a German. I was forced by a German, it's true, and more than once, but I was too sick to conceive. ... No lies come out of me to you. You are pure" (Ozick 1990, 43). "Excretion" is just the right term for Rosa to use to describe Stella's accusation that Magda is the consequence of a "pain in the loins." Rosa's insistence on "cleanliness" in relation to her letter writing and her claim that Magda is "pure" attempt to reverse her sense of shame in relation to Magda's birth. The same logic pertains to her lines toward the end of the novella, when Magda "behave[s] as if she was ashamed," and Rosa is prompted to say to her not only, "don't be ashamed" but also, tellingly, "I am not ashamed of your presence." It is Rosa, of course, and not Magda, who feels shame, and Rosa on some level knows this. That is why she imputes shame to Magda. The idea of being ashamed, in other words, originates in Rosa's consciousness, not Magda's, which does not exist except as Rosa's fantasy. Even if Magda's father is her gentile Polish lover, as Rosa claims, and not a German, an illegitimate child produced of a union between a Christian and a Jew in the 1930s or '40s cannot but occasion embarrassment on Rosa's part, however much she denies that. Even a Jewish father would not have protected Magda from being an illegitimate child.

Because the text never clarifies who fathered Magda, the reader is tempted to want to solve this mystery. Yet as Rosa so succinctly puts it, the "pain in the loins is nobody's business," certainly not ours. What, then, does constitute our proper business as readers? And how are we supposed to act on that business responsibly? In *At Memory's Edge: After-Images of the Holocaust in Contemporary Art and Architecture,* James E. Young (2000b) cites an event that at the time also made a profound impression on me along similar lines:

> When confronted by leaders of the ultra-Orthodox community in Jerusalem, the curators of Israel's national Holocaust memorial museum, Yad Vashem, refused to remove wall-sized photographs taken by the Nazis of naked Jewish women on their way to the gas chambers at Treblinka. . . . The museum replied that because this degradation, too, was part of the reality of the Holocaust, it had to be shown as part of the historical record. . . . In the eyes of the religious community, however, the humiliation and violation of these women's modesty was as much a part of the crime as their eventual murder. That their modesty would be violated yet again by the viewers now might even suggest not so much a repetition of the crime as an extension of it. . . . Despite the curators' stated aim of maintaining the exhibit's historical integrity, the museum may have refused to acknowledge another historical reality: the possibility of their visitors' pornographic gaze. (56–57)

This is surely a heightened, even overdetermined case of what Michael Rothberg, in *Traumatic Realism,* calls "Holocaust pornography," the idea that "there might be something *pornographic* about making images and ultimately commodities out of the Holocaust" (2000, 187–88; italics in original). How much more pornographic is the very graphic exposure of devastated, humiliated bodies and lives, which invites the uninvited gaze of others, even if in the service of historical knowledge and memory?

Despite the fact that Rosa's narrative is explicitly and repeatedly that of a self-hating Jew and is continuously offensive to readers as well as to other characters within the story (and after the Holocaust, self-hating Jews might not seem in any way morally superior to Jew-hating Nazis), nonetheless, we, like Persky, must be willing to hear Rosa's story, dispassionately and disinterestedly, without making too many inquiries into precisely what happened to her. We must also be willing to forebear any reference to ourselves—indeed, any reference whatsoever to moral or ethical considerations—if we are to hear her story as what it is: an expression of pain, whether in the loins or elsewhere, as legitimate as any other expression of pain, despite its lack of generosity and moral underpinnings. As we shall see once again in Art Spiegelman's *Maus* when he records an instance of his father's racism, suffering does not provide human beings with an education in ethics. Thus, Ozick is careful to include in *The Shawl* evidence of both Rosa's anti-gay sentiments and her lack of respect for culturally or racially different others, such as the hotel receptionist.

The Narrative of Guilt

Ozick's presentation of Rosa's story, including Rosa's own narrative of that story, may have as one primary purpose a wish to inform us of something about the ghetto. It might also be a plea to the reader to tolerate the arrogance, snobbism, and general bad behavior of certain survivors whose pain is no less real for their objectionable personalities (as I have already observed, both Art Spiegelman's father, Vladek, and Saul Bellow's Mr. Sammler, not to mention a variety of Aharon Appelfeld's characters, are people of this sort). But neither of these purposes primarily defines Rosa's reasons for telling her story in the ways that she tells it. Nor do these purposes get at what her story is really about. For concealed within the story of the tramcar and the ghetto is another story that is far more central to Rosa's consciousness and psychological being than are either the objective or even the emotional facts concerning the ghetto. If we are to truly hear Rosa's story, we are going to have to hear the story hidden behind not only the facts recorded in her letters and the violent anger being expressed through those facts and the terrible self-recrimination but also the guilt that they contain. For more than shame, Rosa also feels guilt in relation to the death of Magda.

As Ruth Leys points out in her book *From Guilt to Shame*, the term "shame" enters into the discussion of survivor experiences in order to counter the inevitable "taint of collusion" that the previously dominant term—"survivor's guilt"—had produced. The "general privilege [accorded] to shame over guilt," she writes, "can be situated in the context of a broad shift . . . in the medical and psychiatric sciences, literary criticism, and even philosophy away from the 'moral' concept of guilt in favor of the ethically different or 'freer' concept of shame" (2009, 7). Shame interprets trauma in a particular way Leys explains in her earlier book *Trauma*: the *mimetic* theory of trauma, which produces an internal affinity to the idea of survivor's guilt, "holds that trauma . . . can be understood as involving a kind of hypnotic imitation of or regressive identification with the original traumatogenic person, scene, or event, with the result that the subject is fated to act it out or in other ways imitate it" (2000, 8). The "*antimimetic* theory" repudiates this "mimetic notion . . . in favor of the opposite idea that the subject remains aloof from the traumatic experience . . . a spectator of the scene, which he can therefore see and represent to himself" (9). For this reason there is an affinity between the antimimetic theory and shame. "Guilt," Leys explains, "concerns your actions." Shame concerns "who you are" (11).

Rosa, I suggest, does experience shame both in relation to her experience of being incarcerated in the ghetto and in relation to her being sexually abused. In relation to her daughter, however, she feels guilt. Her conjuring of the dead child acts out and imitates the original traumatic moment and the subsequent moments in the camp that are also already moments of traumatic repetition.

Although most readers have shied away from reading "The Shawl" as anything but a highly lyrical, poetic representation of the murder of Magda, as a work of fiction the story is already an interpretive conundrum. Do we take the story as another set of "definite facts" (like the description of the ghetto) against which to understand Rosa's later life as represented in "Rosa"? Or do we take the story as already a fantasy projection of Rosa's mind? "The Shawl" is as much focalized through Rosa as is the later story. That is, whatever we understand the objective realities to be in "The Shawl," they are already being rendered through Rosa's consciousness. "Stella, cold, cold, the coldness of hell," "The Shawl" begins (Ozick 1990, 3). These thoughts, with their focus on Stella, the description of her as "cold," and the lack of logic in defining that coldness as being of hell, clearly belong to Rosa's mind, not some external, omniscient authorial consciousness. Significant, too, is that image after image from "The Shawl" will recur in "Rosa," thus making "Rosa" an extension of the consciousness first expressed in "The Shawl." This pattern of repetition opens up at least two antithetical interpretive options. The first, which I think most readers have followed, is that we read "Rosa" as a picture of a mind caught in an endless repetition compulsion, endlessly repeating events that occurred in the camp, as recorded in "The Shawl." The second is that we understand the first section as already a fantasy of Rosa's imagination, already playing out the delusions that will come to seem delusional to us only in the second part of the novella. Not only does "The Shawl" contain the images that recur in "Rosa," but those images already circulate and repeat themselves madly, almost obsessively, within the short story itself.

If "The Shawl" is indeed of a piece with "Rosa" and is therefore itself already the reflection of a fantasy, what might that fantasy be? In other words, what might we imagine to have produced the psychotic events recorded in "The Shawl" if that is what those events are? And why might it be difficult for us readers to ask questions concerning the authenticity of the "definite facts" presented in the short story?

Let us take "The Shawl" for a moment as most readers have taken it, as a more or less authentic rendering of the events that occurred to Rosa, Stella, and Magda on the forced march to a concentration camp and then in the camp itself, where Magda meets her violent death in a manner that those of us who have read enough Holocaust narratives have come to recognize as not so uncommon. In *Maus* Vladek Spiegelman also refers to children being smashed to death against walls, a site of brutality recorded as well by Aharon Appelfeld in his memoir, *The Story of a Life* (1999). Ozick herself recalls reading such a detail and surmises that it might have lodged in her imagination and given birth to the story. To be sure, there are aspects of the narrative in "The Shawl" that defy belief, such as Magda's survival during the march and for some period of time in the camp. But most of us who have read Holocaust memoirs, histories, and fictions are used to the exceptions that prove the rule. We accept the kinds of fabrications that go with trying to produce a significant story of the horrors of the concentration camps. Our objections to the Roberto Benigni film *Life Is Beautiful* (1997), if we have any, do not generally have to do with the improbability of the child being incarcerated along with his father. That is a literary conceit with which we are familiar and with which most of us can live.

So to take the short story as it has generally be understood and interpret the "Rosa" sequence in relation to it, Rosa's letters to Magda, including the tramcar narrative and the associative thoughts that accompany her letter writing, must at least be understood to incorporate, in highly distorted and occluded ways— almost as in a kind of dream work—the story of Magda's death in the camp. With every fiber of her being in every way and at every moment, Rosa relives the scene of Magda's murder, which she would also deny, by resurrecting the dead daughter. Thus, even without regard to the story of Magda, Florida for Rosa is already a scene of endless repetition and replay of the camp: "the streets were a furnace, the sun an executioner. Every day without fail it blazed and blazed," "she felt she was in hell" (Ozick 1990, 14). Or later: "Everything, everything is on fire! Florida is burning" (39). Rosa builds on these physical facts of her environment to imprison herself in a room as sordid and oppressive as the place she occupied in the camp barracks, although she does draw the line at wearing any clothing with stripes. As is characteristic of someone suffering from a repetition compulsion, she will not budge from this spot, which encapsulates the scene of Magda's death, although we might already point out that the work camp in which Magda dies has no crematorium, and the images of fire in "The Shawl" have to do with electricity and not with the smoke and ashes of the death camps. There is an imprecision here to which we might do well to attend.

The thread of repetition runs even more precisely through the tramcar story that Rosa tells her customers, which she then records in her letters to Magda. Thus, the tramcar, running on "overhead electric wires" through a concentration-camp-like ghetto surrounded by a "wall," evokes the site of Magda's future death: the camp where the electric wires run atop the walls of the enclosure. Even the object of Rosa's desire in the ghetto sequence, the head of lettuce, becomes in this story of "repressed animation" a potential if highly crazed and wild vehicle for symbolizing the dead daughter, whose head looms like a lantern over the final sequence of the novella and that moments earlier had been configured by Rosa as a "little doll's head," the shawl thrown over "the knob of the [telephone] receiver" (66). Animation is abundant in this story, whether repressed or not. Rosa sees Magda everywhere. She would revive her everywhere. But reviving her everywhere, she also kills her over and over again. Indeed, she electrocutes her over and over again in what the text calls the "blazing flying current" of Rosa's mind, which represents both the act of writing and the electricity of her inner consciousness (69). This word "electricity" also transports the novella into biblical contexts that both illuminate and further problematize the text, as we shall see.

In his discussion of complicated mourning Volkan (1981) describes the ambivalent feelings about the lost love object that produce this kind of mourning. Given the enormity of the horror Rosa has experienced—and our profound empathy with the pain it entails—it might seem indecorous at best, brutally hostile at worst, to contemplate the possible complexities of Rosa's feelings for her daughter. Our views of motherhood are not all that different from Rosa's. Rosa would "prove herself pure: a Madonna"; she would be the quintessential mother: "I'm a mother," she says to Persky, "the same as your wife, no different" (Ozick 1990, 59). We might add that she is no different from us, who may well be mother-readers, and, if not mother-readers, then, like Persky, the husbands, sons, or daughters of such mothers. How, then, could we possibly suspect of Rosa the bereaved mother that she might, for example, have suffered feelings of ambivalence about Magda's birth, some of which she may even have projected and displaced onto Stella as Stella's hostility to Magda rather than her own? Wouldn't such a suspicion be tantamount to turning our backs on Rosa's suffering, becoming, like her customers or Stella, deaf to her story of catastrophic loss?

And yet might it not be possible that if we could get past the clichés of pure and sacred motherhood that we share with Rosa—indeed, if Rosa herself could get past that fantasy about her relationship to her child—we might discover equally profound bases for sympathizing with Rosa? For Rosa such listening might even enable her to sympathize with, and finally forgive, herself so that she might finally lay the child to rest, mourn her death, and get on with her life. Such a possibility has practical, theoretical, and, finally, ethical implications for how we hear Holocaust narratives, whether factual or fictive.

The images and phrases of the opening short story, the story that gives us the scene of Magda's murder at the hands of the camp guard, which later recur in Rosa's telling of her story of the ghetto and in her conjuring of the dead child, are too numerous to cite completely. They include such images and moments as "the sunheat [that] murmured of another life, of butterflies in summer," the "dandelions and deep-colored violets . . . innocent tiger lilies, tall, lifting their orange bonnets . . . moth[s]"; and "She looked like a butterfly, touching a silver vine" (8–9). These images recur throughout the section of the novella titled "Rosa." A few examples include images of Magda as a "butterfly" (64, 69) or a lioness (43), specifically a yellow lioness (39), a "yellow blossom" (44) "all in flower" (64), her hair as "yellow as buttercups" (65). But it is in the story's final sequence that the images cluster in powerful density, reproducing the scene of Magda's death, which Rosa would deny, but which in writing she not only exposes but also (literally, perhaps, as we shall see) replicates:

[Rosa] was tired from writing so much, even though this time she was not using her regular pen, she was writing inside a blazing flying current, a terrible
beak of light bleeding out a kind of cuneiform on the underside of her brain.
The drudgery of reminiscence brought fatigue, she felt glazed, lethargic. And
Magda! Already she was turning away. Away. The blue of her dress was only a
speck in Rosa's eye. Magda did not even stay to claim her letter: there it flick-
ered, unfinished like an ember, all because of the ringing from the floor near
the bed. Voices, sounds, echoes, noise—Magda collapsed at any stir, fearful
as a phantom. She behaved at these moments as if she was ashamed, and hid
herself. Magda, my beloved, don't be ashamed! Butterfly, I am not ashamed
of your presence: only come to me, come to me again, if no longer now, then
later, always come. These were Rosa's private words; but she was stoic, tamed;
she did not say them aloud to Magda. Pure Magda, head as bright as a lantern.

The shawled telephone, little grimy silent god, so long comatose—now,
like Magda, animated at will, ardent with its cry (69–70).

When Rosa says to Magda in the first of her two long letters to her daughter, "I'm
saving you" (42), she means literally that she is saving the opening of the box
containing the child's shawl until later, when she can better relish it. Yet, as with
so much else of what Rosa says, both to Magda and to us, she exposes precisely
what opening the box with the shawl is actually meant to accomplish: she would
save her daughter. She would keep her alive. However, as Magda's disappearance
from the final scene and the ardent cry of the telephone indicate, Rosa cannot
do this, and on some level she knows it. Hence, Rosa's conflicted state of mind,
her unrest in the presence of the facts as she presents them, that her daughter is
indeed alive and a successful professor of philosophy in New York City, or is she
a doctor? Rosa presents both versions.

When Rosa reassures her daughter, "I pretend you died" "to soothe [Stella's]
dementia" (42), we might well hear the opposite claim: I pretend that you lived, in
order to soothe my own guilt. "Stella was alive," Rosa thinks to herself, "why not
Magda?" (35). Furthermore, the claim that Magda is still alive might well describe
not only the present moment of Rosa's reality but an earlier moment as well. A
curious feature of "The Shawl" is that when we are given the no-win situation in
which Rosa finds herself as she sees the child totter toward the fence—whether
to run after the child or go back for the shawl, for which the child is presumably
searching—the choice she has to make is precisely *not* about the impending death
of the child at all but, rather, about whether she wants to risk rendering the child
silent by giving her the shawl. In the final moments of the story the question of
Magda's survival is again *not* at the center of the passage, since by now Magda
is already dead. These are the two scenes of dilemma, the second of which concludes the short story:

Fetch, get, bring! But she did not know which to go after first, Magda or the
shawl. If she jumped out into the arena to snatch Magda up, the howling would

not stop, because Magda would still not have the shawl, but if she ran back into the barracks to find the shawl, and if she found it, and if she came after Magda holding it and shaking it, then she would get Magda back, Magda would put the shawl in her mouth and turn dumb again. (8)

She only stood, because if she ran they would shoot, and if she tried to pick up the sticks of Magda's body they would shoot, and if she let the wolf's screech ascending now through the ladder of her skeleton break out, they would shoot; so she took Magda's shawl and filled her own mouth with it . . . until she was swallowing up the wolf's screech and tasting the cinnamon and almond depth of Magda's saliva; and Rosa drank Magda's shawl until it dried. (10)

What story, in addition to the ostensible one Rosa seems to be telling, might these two passages also be telling us?

From the beginning of "The Shawl," images of death crowd around the baby Magda. Of course, these could only be intended by the author to foreshadow Magda's imminent death; or they might represent Rosa's own premonition that the baby's death is imminent (how could it not be?) Yet those images might also contain glimmers of the reality of Magda's situation, which her mother would consciously deny: that "Magda, curled up between sore breasts . . . [and] wound up in the shawl" (3), is already dead. The windings of the shawl already associate it with the winding sheets and shrouds of burial, not to mention the prayer shawl in which religious Jews are buried. And if Magda wasn't dead at the beginning of the march, then she might well be dead by the time Stella and Rosa reach the camp. "Rosa knew Magda was going to die very soon; she should have been dead already, but she had been buried away deep inside the magic shawl, mistaken there for the shivering mound of Rosa's breasts; Rosa clung to the shawl as if it covered only herself. Magda was mute. She never cried" (5–6). "Buried" away in the shawl, Magda never cries, not only, perhaps, because she "should have been dead already," but because she *is* dead already. It is not only "as if" the shawl covers nothing more than the shivering mound of Rosa's empty breasts. That may be all that it covers, unless, of course, it also covers the body of the dead baby.

Unless we ourselves believe in magic, the "magic shawl" that "could nourish an infant for three days and three nights" does not exist, except in Rosa's imagination, as informed in this instance by the story of Christ's resurrection—not an insignificant or incidental intertextual reference, which will recur in the novella. The reality of Rosa's and Magda's situation is harsher and bleaker. "There was not enough milk; sometimes Magda sucked air; then she screamed. . . . One mite of a tooth sticking up . . . an elfin tombstone of white marble. . . . Magda relinquished Rosa's teats. . . . Magda took the corner of the shawl and milked it instead" (3–4). At the very least, this version of the story helps locate the depth of Rosa's guilt in having survived. Not only was she unable to intervene to save her daughter from a violent murder at the hands of others, but she was also unable to perform the most elementary of maternal functions, such as nursing her baby. Seeing the fantasy behind Rosa's fantasy—the fantasy in the short story that becomes the basis for the complicated mourning exhibited in "Rosa"—helps us to add depth to our understanding of Rosa. But it adds another element as well, one that is harder for both us and Rosa to cope with: Rosa's rage at the child, who confronts her with her inadequacy as a mother and who almost literally sucks her dry. Unable to save the child, the child might also have contributed to hastening the mother's death, as she's imagined doing when Rosa deliberates whether or not to run after the child's dead body. From some point of view, Magda should never have been born.

"Stella was ravenous," we are told through Rosa's consciousness, "a growing child herself." "Rosa was ravenous, but also not; she learned from Magda how to drink the taste of a finger in one's mouth. They were in a place without pity, all pity was annihilated in Rosa, she looked at Stella's bones without pity. She was sure that Stella was waiting for Magda to die so that she could put her teeth into the little thighs," her "spindles" of legs, so like Stella's own "knees [which were] tumors on sticks, her elbows chicken bones" (3). "'Aryan,' Stella said . . . and Rosa thought how Stella gazed at Magda like a young cannibal. And the time that Stella said 'Aryan,' it sounded to Rosa as if Stella had really said 'Let us devour her'" (5). Might we not understand the "growing child" Stella, who is being looked at by Rosa "without pity," to be the object of Rosa's own ravenous hunger, which she then projects onto Stella as Stella's wish to devour Magda? As the text tells us directly, it is only "as if" Stella has said "let us devour her." These thoughts belong to Rosa, not to Stella. Indeed, a few pages later, toward the beginning of "Rosa," before we have had time to forget the cannibal imagery of "The Shawl," we are told explicitly that Rosa has "cannibal dreams about Stella" (15). These dreams might well recall to Rosa that projection of her own cannibal wishes onto Stella in the camp. That the word Rosa hears as "devour" is the word "Aryan" links the shamefulness of Rosa's cannibal wishes not only with the guilt attached to the death of baby Magda but also to the shame Rosa feels about her birth, and, finally, to the guilt she feels for that shame. That she claims the baby as the source of her ability to resist such tawdry thoughts only deepens our sense of how Rosa's idealizations of the baby might well be a cover for her knowledge of her less than ideal self.

From the start what courses through Rosa, we are told, is not the milk that might sustain the life of her baby, but an "electric current." This internal electricity has an external correlative as well. "Sometimes the electricity inside the fence would seem to hum," we are told. "Stella said it was only an imagining, but Rosa heard real sounds in the wire: grainy sad voices. The farther she was from the fence, the more clearly the voices crowded at her. The lamenting voices strummed so convincingly, so passionately, it was impossible to suspect them of being phantoms" (9). Even though this passage occurs at the moment of Magda's death, it refers back to Rosa's experience of the camp from the start. And that produces a chronological confusion that exposes what might actually have happened to Magda. As the "mute" and "dumb" child is fantasized by Rosa to toddle off to her electrocution on the very same electric fence that from the start has spoken the words Rosa needs to hear from Magda, Magda finally seems to speak those words, only to have them gobbled up by the fence, which has spoken them from the start: "Maaa— . . . Maaaa . . . aaa," says the child (8); and "the electric voices [of the fence] began to chatter wildly. 'Maamaa, maaa-maaa,' they all hummed together" (9).

The electric voices that swallow up Magda's voice seem to be activated only now, in the final moments of the story. Yet they were there from the beginning, inhabiting Rosa's imagination and producing the hum of internal knowledge that Rosa would deny—both that Magda is dead and that she lives only in the electrical activity of her mother's brain. "Rosa knew that Magda was going to die very soon," "Rosa saw that today Magda was going to die," she "saw that Magda was going to die," the text repeats, producing a distinct hum of its own (5, 7, 8). And yet in the midst of this hum of knowledge, a "fearful joy ran in Rosa's two palms, her fingers were on fire, she was astonished, febrile: Magda, in the sunlight, swaying on her pencil legs, was howling" (7). Logic falls away in these passages: Magda is going to die and yet Rosa experiences a fearful joy, specifically in her fingers, which soon take on the quality of a child swaying on "pencil legs" and howling. Rosa writes Magda into life; she writes her words in the electric current of her brain, here as later, when she writes letters to the dead child in order to keep her alive.

The lapse of logic that is the magical moment of the mother's recovery of the child as a feature of her own imaginative life is replicated in the lapse of temporal sequence in the passage about the hum of the fence that I have already begun to quote. I repeat the beginning so as to bring into view the unmarked shift in the passage from past to present that blurs the distinction between the two:

> Sometimes the electricity inside the fence would seem to hum; even Stella said it was only an imagining, but Rosa heard real sounds in the wire: grainy sad voices. The farther she was from the fence, the more clearly the voices crowded at her. The lamenting voices strummed so convincingly, so passionately, it was impossible to suspect them of being phantoms. [unmarked shift] The voices told her to hold up the shawl, high; the voices told her to shake it, to whip with it, to unfurl it like a flag. Rosa lifted, shook, whipped, unfurled. (9)

Miraculously, magically, with a wave of the magic shawl, abracadabra, Rosa conjures the living child, who is about to be delivered high on the shoulders of the camp guard to a death that will transfigure the child into a permanent hum of language within Rosa's brain, saying the word Rosa most needs to hear: Mama. When Rosa takes pen to paper, she will resurrect this moment, not of Magda's death, but of her coming to life again, as the child becomes one with the current that is not only the electric fence but also the "blazing flying current, a terrible beak of light bleeding out a kind of cuneiform on the underside of [Rosa's] brain." Not only is Rosa, in her fantasy, not responsible for Magda's death (the guard is), but she also is the savior who brings her to life everlasting *in this world* (after three days and three nights).

Fetish, Teleology, and Redemptive History

We are now in a position to understand what Rosa means when she defines the power of "living language" as the "power to make history, to tell, to explain. To retrieve, to reprieve! / To lie" (44), and she repeats: "To retrieve, to reprieve" (45). Rosa's story, whether as reflected in "The Shawl" or in "Rosa," is no lie. But neither is it documentary history. It is, in all the varieties of its telling, retrieval of an associative sort, in the service of both self-acquittal and respite from the unendurable pain of the child's death. Whether as the fantasy of the child's murder at the hands of the camp guard or as what was already the fantasy of her resurrection after her death on the forced march, the power that fuels Rosa's fantasy is *living* electric language. This living electric current of words can as easily kill the child as save her, because Rosa's words also contain and expose—in occluded ways—the equally vital, living truth that the grieving mother would but cannot deny: that the child at her empty breast, is dead, hidden under Rosa's shawl.

Self-consciousness, Theodor Reik reminds us in *Listening with a Third Ear* (1949), always contains an element of self-critique, self-knowledge, which is why we sometimes avoid it. To hear the definite facts and external horrors of the Holocaust is not necessarily to hear the more internal and even more terrifying horrors of the sort that Rosa has endured. How could any mother live with her sense of having failed her baby? How could any mother live with the knowledge that she resented the infant's claim against her own life? These are horrors beyond the horror of death itself. In retrieving the shawl Rosa retrieves the moment before all of this horror descended upon her and "stole" her life.

Even though Peter Brooks takes his key concept of "fore-pleasure," with its implications of fetishism, from Freud's essay "Creative Writers and Day-Dreaming" (1985a, 153), he "deliberately [leaves] aside" those aspects of Freud's essay, both at the beginning and the end, that have to do with the "person" of the writer and the reader (Brooks 1994, 28–29). In other words, he jettisons the old Freudian paradigm, the idea that the literary text exposes something about its characters and about the real people in the real world who write and read the text. To read Holocaust fiction *only* in terms of its "fore-pleasure," as detached from the "persons" of its author and readers, would be also to treat survivors as somehow distinct from their private, personal psychobiographies. And that would make of their texts fetishes: objects of worship, like Rosa's shawl. Indeed, such readings would replicate the incomplete mourning that is the source of Rosa's own fetishizing of the shawl. It would signal the incompleteness of our mourning of the victims of the Holocaust and, worse, our conversion of them into something else.

It is the inevitable fact of the "person" of the reader or writer of historical or fictional texts that is crucial to the kind of mourning that a text like *The Shawl* requires of Rosa and of the reader, although as we shall see in a moment the novella does not quite fulfill the terms of its own considerable moral, psychological, and literary insights. It is only by acknowledging the ways we are personally implicated in the interpretations we make and the opinions we express that any of us can even begin to achieve genuine understanding of other people and their stories. Only by recognizing how our own historical and psychological profiles influence our perceptions can we avoid using other people's narratives in order to serve our own psychological needs.

Fiction, in particular historical fiction, is a powerful instrument, not simply in representing the complexity of other people's experiences but also in educating the reader about his or her own subject position. Literary fictions produce doubts. They raise questions. By producing doubt about Rosa's account of how Magda died (as in raising the question, without answering it, of Magda's paternity), Ozick's *Shawl* reclaims, both for Rosa and for us readers, the space of serious play that D. W. Winnicott calls "the intermediate area of *experiencing,* to which inner reality and external life both contribute" (1971, 2; italics in original). This makes of the text something like Winnicott's transitional object, more like Magda's shawl than like Rosa's, which is a fetish and not a transitional object. Ozick's novella is more like a transitional object than the fetish, although the situation of the literary text is more complicated. As Adam Phillips puts it in *Promises, Promises,* because literary language is not "propaganda" and is linked to something called "not-knowing," it can "resist fetishization" (2002, 20, 27). Nonetheless, as Brooks points out, literary texts might invite fetishism as well: the erotic "fore-pleasure" of literature, Brooks suggests, "implies the possibility of fetishism, the interesting threat of being waylaid by some element along the way to the 'proper' end, taking some displaced substitute of simulacrum for the thing itself. . . . Fetishism indeed seems to be characteristic of literature, especially . . . where objects, details, metonymies, and synecdoches predominate" (1994, 30). The question concerning Ozick's novella is the degree to which, through its incorporation of dubious scenarios and interpretations, it resists the fetishism that it so clearly identifies in its protagonist, and perhaps in us as well, and to what degree it yields to the fetishism that may be inherent in the literary object and perhaps inevitably in relation to the Holocaust as subject as well. This question is inseparable from another troubling possibility that Ozick's text raises: the possibility that the text is producing a redemptive history, the type of history that Saul Friedländer, following the lead of Walter Benjamin, so ardently cautions us against. As Bernard Harrison formulates Berel Lang's objection to writing Holocaust fiction, it might "impose a structure, of plot and denouement on the events it describes . . . invit[ing] the reader to see those events as instantiating some general pattern inherent in human life" (2006, 80–81).

Rosa herself is clearly producing such redemptive history. Raised as she has been in a Christian rather than a Jewish milieu, Rosa experiences her suffering through Christian rather than Jewish tropes. Therefore, the redemptive history that she pursues is more Christian than Jewish. By recalling the "mystery" of immaculate conception, which Rosa assures us she believes in, and by thereby invoking the resurrection of the divine child, Rosa is able to simultaneously deny not only the daughter's death but also her conception in sin, whether Magda's father was Rosa's Christian lover or a Nazi who raped her. Magda is the product of an immaculate conception, a genealogy that moves directly from Rosa's father to her daughter: "she had begun to resemble Rosa's father" (Ozick 1990, 65). Through the Christianization of Magda, Rosa is also able to secure the child from the violence meted out to the Jews in the Holocaust.

"I don't believe in God," Rosa tells Magda (and us), "but I believe, like the Catholics, in mystery" (41). This is not very far from the idea of magic, as in the magic shawl. Mystery for Rosa is primarily the "*fact* of motherhood," but motherhood very specifically defined: "the physiological fact. To have the power to create another human being, to be the instruments of such a mystery. To pass on a whole genetic system" (41). In defining motherhood this way, as bypassing the biological father altogether, Rosa eliminates "the other strain" in Magda (65), which represents Magda's real father, whom Rosa experiences as "dangerous" (65) whether that father was a German or her Aryan fiancé. Rosa's language here exposes her "perplexity" (65) regarding Magda's paternity. It expresses her wish that Magda be a "pure" product of her mother's unadulterated body, hence Rosa's thinking about this other strain just after she has noted how much Magda resembles Rosa's own father. It is as if the child were conceived without benefit of sexual relations through Rosa's paternal line—much like Christ as God's son, delivered without admixture, through the woman's body.

In this line that goes directly from father to daughter to granddaughter, Rosa is the "Virgin" and Magda the "Child," (41), her "beloved" (69), which in the New Testament is often a way of referring to Christ. Lest we miss the Christian context of all this, the story has Rosa insist to Persky: "I'm left. Stella's left. . . . Out of so many three" (59), constructing a somewhat unholy trinity of aunt, niece, and the Holy Ghost. On the one hand, this Holy Ghost, what in a Jewish reading we might think of as the *shekinah*, is her mother's "Soul's Blessing" (39). On the other hand, because of the other strain in her—which, try as she might, Rosa cannot wholly exorcise—Magda is also "ghostly," a "dangerous" "phantom," like the electricity in the fence (65). Thus, the name Magda hints at the other Mary in the Christ story, who is no virgin, suggesting something of Rosa's own unconfessed self-knowledge here. On some level Rosa knows that Magda is only an ordinary child conceived out of wedlock. If she is a ghost at all, she is an everyday-variety ghost and no more divine than that. This knowledge puts Rosa's story, as her language reveals, under considerable "strain."

It is clear what Rosa has to gain from the Christian mystery her drama enacts, and certainly in the larger context of Ozick's critique of assimilated and specifically anti-Zionist (40) Jewry, both in Poland before the war and in the United States afterward, the representation of Rosa's unabashed Christianity serves an important function in the novella. Rosa's mother, we are told by Rosa, "wanted so much to convert" that "she let the maid keep a statue of the Virgin and Child in the corner of the kitchen" (41) Rosa's mother even writes Christian poetry, the words of which infiltrate Rosa's own fantasy of the resurrected daughter, Magda: "Mother of God, how you shiver / in these heat-ribbons! / Our cakes rise to you / and in the trance of His birthing / you hide" (41–42). It is no accident that Rosa should remember, of all her mother's poems, this one, occasioned as it is "by heat coming up from the stove, from the Sunday pancakes" (41). For Rosa Christianity supplies a solution to the incineration of the Jews and the death of her beloved child (albeit by the heat of electrocution rather than the ovens). It promises resurrection, everlasting life, and a reprieve from the sense of sinfulness, shame, and guilt that Rosa feels in relation to her daughter's birth and death: the magic shawl (the shroud) that protects Magda for the period of three days and three nights, which corresponds to the time that Christ spent in his tomb and Jonah in the whale, signals hope not only of redemption for the mother but also of resurrection for the beloved child, who will bring that redemption.

Yet Ozick's reason for having Rosa indulge in a specifically Christian fantasy of resurrection is at odds with Rosa's. This moves us from the assimilationist, anti-Zionist aspects of Rosa and her family, which Ozick wishes to expose, to the text's own (possibly) equally problematical pro-Zionist affiliations. "My father was never a Zionist," Rosa informs Magda (40). She also feels that her niece should be eternally grateful to her for saving her from being "shipped . . . with a boatload of orphans to Palestine, to become God knows what, to live God knows how. A field worker jabbering Hebrew" (40). "It's only history," the text tells us, somewhere between Rosa's voice and her father's, "that made the Zionist answer" (40). Yet the narrative pulls away from Rosa's and her father's anti-Zionistic position so hard that it produces dangers in the opposite direction.

In "Cynthia Ozick's *The Shawl,* the Akedah, and the Ethics of Holocaust Literary Aesthetics," Joseph Alkana suggests that "The Shawl" reads "like a female version of the Akedah" (the binding of Isaac) and cites numerous correspondences between the two stories in defense of this claim (1997, 971). What emerges most powerfully from this strange paralleling between the two texts, suggests Alkana, is the dramatic, moral, religious difference between them. "In the Akedah, the power over life and death ultimately resides with God, while in the camps a human power prevails" (973). The result is that the human sacrifice avoided in the Old Testament text becomes the primary event in Ozick's novella. This human sacrifice is, of course, internal to the Christ story itself. It is what for many commentators differentiates Judaism from Christianity from the start, what makes the crucifixion of Christ the antitype of which the Akedah is only the type. In Christian typology the Akedah prefigures the crucifixion of Christ, which, in its fulfillment, cancels the old law of justice and retribution and brings into being the new law of grace. Isaac does not die; Christ, the antitype, like that other "beloved" in Ozick's story, does, as does another Isaac in Ozick's earlier fiction, who also loses the thread of his Jewish identity, Isaac Kornfield in "The Pagan Rabbi."

Ozick's use of the Akedah in a story overburdened with Christian imagery draws our attention to the very different endings of the type and the antitype of the sacrifice of the child. It places infanticide firmly within Christian rather than Jewish history. Yet by thinking of the Akedah and the sacrifice of Christ together, and by putting this trope into the very unsanctified hands of the Nazis and into the thoughts of a very human mother who wants nothing more than that her daughter should be resurrected, the narrative itself strains against itself. It is next to impossible for the reader to think of the Jewish imagery of this text without thinking of the Christian imagery, and vice versa. The Jewish direction of the imagery is as problematic for Holocaust memory and commemoration as the Christian slant.

For example, in the Christian dimension of the story, Magda's "shawl" is like "a piece of the True Cross," in Stella's words (34), a relic through which, in fulfillment of a Christian scheme of redemption and salvation, Rosa would "save" her daughter. That same shawl, however, also recalls the Jewish prayer shawl, which the blue and white stripes of the Israeli flag are also meant to recall, thus adding to the Jewish implications of the shawl a Zionist politics as well. Nor is this the only image in the text that works this way. Magda is constantly referred to by her mother as a lioness. The lion of Judah, like the word "beloved," is also a reference to Christ (the lion in C. S. Lewis's *Chronicles of Narnia* is, as a messianic figure, a reference to this Christ image). The lion of Judah, however, is also the symbol of modern-day Jerusalem, and indeed it appears on another flag: the Jerusalem city flag. The story's Jewish associations pull away from Christian history and back into Jewish history, making *The Shawl* a super-supersessionist text. The story, it seems, would free Jews of Christian history and its persecution of them. And yet the super-supersessionist move inadvertently, perhaps inevitably, replicates many of the problems of supersessionism itself. It discovers logic, meaning, even a teleology in the events of a history that most of us agree had no redemptive or redeeming value.

For Rosa a way out of the insoluble dilemma of making sense of the senseless massacre of European Jewry is that electric current in her brain. For us this is the source of her disabling delusion. For her it is the power that enables her to translate the instrument of Magda's death into the source of her resurrection. That electric current may also have an Old Testament origin, which reclaims the text as Jewish and simultaneously exposes it to further distortion and abuse. The word "*hashmal*," which is the modern-day word in Hebrew for electricity, originates in an untranslatable "*hapaxlegomenon*" in the book of Ezekiel and in the commentary on that text in the Talmudic text Hagigah. It is associated, in Moshe Greenberg's translation of Ezekiel, with the "fire" and "radiance," the burning coals of fire, torches, lightning, and sparks; also the color amber, "a yellow, translucent resin." "As it belongs to the heart of the vision of the Majesty (vs. 27), hashmal later came to be regarded as endowed with holy and dangerous properties" (1983, 37–38, 43). If Magda is a figure for the beloved of Christianity in Rosa's text, in Ozick's imagining of her she is, through her yellow hair—if we wish to stay with the lion imagery—nothing less than an image of God, and a fiery God at that, a God whose essence is, in modern terminology, electricity. Further drawing the link between Magda and God, one of the four faces of the chariot of the Lord in Ezekiel is that of a lion.

Since the book of Ezekiel, through its exhortation to the Jews, is one of those biblical texts promising the redemption of the Jews in a Jewish nation, the imagery of the golden electricity is, like the lion itself, a figure of redemption. Many of the images in the Ezekiel narrative, such as the fire, drought, famine, and even the sexual abuses through which the divine wrath is heaped upon the Jewish people, find counterparts in Ozick's novella. In the one Talmudic reference to hashmal, there is even reference to a holocaust. As Moshe Greenberg is describing the qualities of hashmal, he directs our attention to "the anecdote of the child burned up by fire from *hashmal* [Hagigah 13a]." This reference occurs within a discussion of who is and who is not permitted to perform the type of sacrifice to God referred to in the text as "holocaust" (Chagigah 1891, 1): "All are bound in the case of a holocaust except a deaf man, a fool, and a child" (in this context we might recall that Rosa thinks that Magda might be deaf). Not only are children not permitted to be sacrifices—as is evidenced by the Akedah—but they also are disallowed from participating in such sacrifices.

The phrase that is translated as "holocaust" in Chagigah (1891) is "*olat riiah*," meaning "burnt offering." This is the way the word "holocaust" is generally understood (1). In *Merriam-Webster's New Collegiate Dictionary* (1977) the definition of holocaust as "a thorough destruction esp. by fire" only follows the primary definition, which is "a sacrifice consumed by fire." It is for this reason that many scholars have preferred the Hebrew term "*shoah*" to "holocaust." To imagine the Jews as a sacrifice is anathema. But the alternative term "shoah" is also problematic. For the Nazis the Holocaust was indeed a holocaust: it sacrificed the Jews to the greater glory and survival of the German nation. Similarly, for some Jews the shoah did represent divine retribution, on the way toward redemption in a national homeland. In both cases nationalism has something to do with the interpretation of the Nazi genocide of the Jews as holocaust or shoah.

For many Jews, Israel was the natural and inevitable consequence of the devastation produced by the Holocaust. Hence the stunning culmination of the exhibits in Yad Vashem: a picture-window-framed view of the Jerusalem hills. To be sure, Zionism has a history that long precedes the Holocaust. It is indeed part of the Jewish liturgy that calls for the return of the people to their homeland. Zionism as a political movement responded to the centuries-long persecution of the Jews, which reached a fever pitch toward the end of the nineteenth century, well before the Holocaust. For all its uniqueness, the Holocaust is in some ways only a magnified version of the disenfranchisement and murder of Jews throughout Europe for centuries. Yet the clear association, both political and emotional, between the Holocaust and the establishment of the State of Israel, even for those who would not be so foolish as to claim that the founding of Israel justified in any way whatsoever what the Nazis did to the Jews, is real, palpable, and extremely problematic for the ways it seems to construct a teleological and redemptive history out of the slaughter of the Jews. Ozick's *The Shawl*—wittingly or not—enters into this fantasy. It is not necessary that we locate the consciousness of the real author in reading out this aspect of the text's dynamic. One great advantage of fiction over other forms of writing is precisely this lack of identity between the author and the text. Yet the novella does put us readers in mind of this teleological assumption, which, especially if we are ourselves Israeli readers, we might share, thus constructing for us the problem that Friedländer defines as writing redemptive history. In James Young's formulation, such redemptive history, as I have already noted, might have to do with the "inexorable logic of narrative itself" (2000b, 44). It might also be an inevitable consequence of the fetishistic quality of literature: the way in which the literary text is always subject to becoming a fetish.

All narrative is in danger of implying a teleological, redemptive logic. All literature is in danger of becoming fetishistic. A historical fiction like Ozick's *The Shawl* piles danger upon danger. Is *The Shawl* any less a fantasy projection than "The Shawl"? Is either the novella or the short story any less fetishistic than the shawl through which Rosa resurrects her dead daughter? Does the narrative manage to steer clear of the redemptive possibilities implied in the resurrection of the State of Israel from the ashes of European Jewry?

The final scene of *The Shawl* partially and temporarily restores Rosa to her world while leaving the reader to wonder about his or her own:

> The shawled telephone, little grimy silent god, so long comatose—now, like Magda, animated at will, ardent with its cry. Rosa let it clamor once or twice and then heard the Cuban girl announce—oh, "announce"!—Mr. Persky: should he come up or would she come down? A parody of a real hotel!—of, in

fact, the MARIE LOUISE, with its foundations, its golden thrones, its thorned wire, its burning Tree!

"He's used to crazy women, so let him come up," Rosa told the Cuban. She took the shawl off the phone.

Magda was not there. Shy, she ran from Persky. Magda was away. (Ozick 1990, 70)

In accepting Magda's disappearance, do we, the readers, accept as well what preceded it: her existence? And if so, what does our acceptance of her existence mean? How does Magda exist for us? As history or as fantasy? And of what value is such a question for us as real persons in the real world?

Rosa claims that the power to make history—to tell, to explain, to retrieve, to reprieve—is the power to lie. In "Rosa" the text itself does some very precise work of telling, explaining, and (especially in the final passage) retrieving, recovering through the repetition of key words and images the scene of Magda's death. But it does so in words that resist the "lie" and make of this text instead a "truth." However, this "truth" cannot be fully contained by its words. Just as the "maaa" of the electric fence delivered Magda's first word into an inarticulate scream that her mother, for all her apparent eloquence, could only endlessly repeat, so the ardent clamor of the phone also reproduces the inarticulateness of sound as what best, most mimetically, conveys the unspeakableness of this story. But this time sound yields to language as well: within the text, the conversation between Rosa and the receptionist and later between Rosa and Persky. For us there is the text itself. The shawl in the final scene is no longer absent. Rather, like the transitional object as Winnicott defined it, it is intentionally removed: "not forgotten" and "not mourned," the transitional object, Winnicott explains, "loses meaning, and this is because the transitional phenomena have become diffused, have become spread out over the whole intermediate territory between 'inner psychic reality' and 'the external world as perceived by two people in common,' that is to say, over the whole cultural field" (1971, 5). Just as it is emptied of significance for Rosa, at least for the moment, by Persky's presence, so for us *The Shawl* becomes a reprieve, through language: through the ability to manipulate reality, not magically, but within a shared cultural field of discourse. A reprieve, we should note, is, by definition, a *temporary* relief or deliverance, not a permanent one. It is a kind of transitional space. The story comes to an end; we put the text away for the time being.

Indeed, while we are reading the story we are in some sense away, in the *as if* world of the story itself. In this way fiction is a transitional phenomenon. The difference between a lie and a fiction is not in the fact of storytelling. "Telling tales" is just another term we have for fibbing, lying. Nor is the difference between a lie and a fiction in the quality of the story told, its linguistic skillfulness or narrative coherence. Rather, the difference between a fiction and a lie is that a lie deceives, whether intentionally or inadvertently or whether it deceives others or ourselves. A lie, we might say, is a kind of fetish in that it comes to substitute for something it conceals and will not confess. A fiction, on the other hand, is a way we have of exposing something, of telling a truth. Fiction is the construction of an *as if* reality, outside of and irrespective of actual truth. In this fictional world Magda has as real an existence as Rosa, and we can accord Rosa's relationship to her every bit of the reality Rosa ascribes to it. We can be with Rosa, "hold" her, in Winnicott's vocabulary (as defined in *Holding and Interpretation* [1987]). And yet because this is a text, and a fiction at that, we register the *as-if*-ness of this holding even as we consent to its claims.

Through our entry into the *as if* world of the text, the shawl becomes not a fetish, but rather an instrument of communication with the nonmaterial world, for us as much as for Rosa. It is restored to its status of transitional object. It reclaims its fictionality as "the intermediate area of *experiencing*, to which inner reality and external life both contribute" (Winnicott 1971, 2; italics in original)— hers and ours. Because a fiction declares itself fictional, it self-consciously also acknowledges the existence outside itself of something that is *not* fiction (namely, the world itself) and that leads us back through the fiction to the world of natural law and historical facts. *Historical* fiction in particular is the *as if* retrieval of specific past events (the ghosts of the past, let us say), not through enactment or corporeal materialization (as through the fetish), but through the self-conscious and inadequate, partial and temporary, and sometimes inarticulate (re)constructions of language. This, it seems, is as good a definition as any of the psychoanalytic conversation and is something that psychoanalysis might rediscover in historical fictions like *The Shawl*.

A Postscript

I cannot say that my interpretation of Ozick's *The Shawl* is correct. It does not really matter, however, whether it is correct or not. The very fact that it is possible for me to doubt Rosa's story without doubting Rosa's suffering and pain and without withholding my compassion takes me beyond a certain kind of judgmentalism in relation to Rosa's experience. Does the fact that I am a mother who lost a child, or was, for the fifteen years before his death, the mother of a handicapped child, influence my reading of Ozick's text? Am I projecting onto Rosa sentiments that belong to me and not to her? In fact, I did something very similar to what Rosa did: I "resurrected" my deceased son. I did so with full consciousness (more or less) of what I was doing. That is, I didn't cut off my relations with others (my other children, for example, or my husband) during this process. Nor did I believe for a moment that my son, who I imagined as a little angel sitting on my shoulder, was actually there. But I experienced him bodily, in both his body and mine.

There is no way my own subject position does not influence my reading of Ozick's novella, both in relation to its major event and in response to its Zionistic leanings (which I share, but which I can recognize as perhaps pulling away from the moral clarity of the text). But if I did not have this subject position, I would surely possess another, and that is my point. We need to interrogate the position from which we interpret a text and to discover both the benefits and the limitations of that position in order to read the text's characters' stories and the text itself with the fullest possible empathy and concern. Perhaps my experience enables me to see something others do not see in the text. Perhaps it only produces in me a wish to fantasize a similarity between my experience and Rosa's. Like Anne Frank, Rosa evokes terrors and desires that I cannot separate from my analysis of the text. I can, however, interrogate my interpretation and try, as much as is humanly possible, to return the story to her.

2   Forced Confessions

Subject Position, Framing,
and the "Art" of Spiegelman's Maus

In cynthia ozick's *The Shawl* (1990) subject position is framed in two different ways. While there may be individuals who are wholly disinclined to listen to the story of the Holocaust for whatever reasons, there are also individuals like Dr. Tree, who actively invite listening to victims' stories. Against such individuals (like us readers, perhaps) the story levels the implicit accusation that to some degree an overly avid interest in the camps, especially in the humiliations and violations suffered there, can well verge on voyeurism. Like everything else that concerns human beings, Holocaust interest is galvanized by psychological forces: wishes, fantasies, terrors, and the like. This is not to say that the investment in keeping alive the knowledge of past events, or even in commemorating victims of violence and cruelty, is not also ethically grounded. Nonetheless, by forcing readers to interrogate their own subjectivities when their hear or read stories like Rosa's, the novella suggests that in order to be good listeners and good historians we might need to separate out our own needs in relation to the events of the past from the responsibility we have to hear other people's stories of pain and to keep alive the histories of catastrophic events.

By the same token, the inability to listen fully to a survivor's story, to entertain interpretations of the story that might perhaps go counter to what we are willing to hear or what we feel we are capable of sympathizing with, might well prevent us from hearing the full extent of another individual's human tragedy, with all of its psychological and historical implications. This is the second way Ozick's novella constructs the problem of subject position. Even without wishing to do so, we might well come to read historical events in terms of some redemptive meaning. We might fit them into our social, political, or religious agendas. By framing Rosa's subjectivity, by making the reader see how she may have repressed elements of her own story, the story implicates us in the kind of inadequate hearing that cannot go the distance of sympathizing with the genuine suffering being expressed even by an ambiguous and moral unsettling narrative. Insofar as Nazism might be understood to evidence how easily humans can separate themselves from the pain of others, such a lack of depth on the part of the reader would indicate how readily we fall into the very position we are hoping to oppose through keeping alive the story of the Holocaust. (This topic recurs in section 3 of this book in relation to narratives of German suffering during the Holocaust.)

What is clear is that Rosa's narrative, as Ozick constructs it, not only informs us about a survivor experience not so different from that of other survivors, but it also expresses the feelings of deep sexual shame and guilt of this particular human being (which may or may not also pertain to other survivors). The challenge that the novella presents is for us to read both the "common memory" of the Holocaust, which in Saul Friedländer's words, "tends to restore or establish coherence, closure and possibly a redemptive stance," and its "deep memory," which remains "essentially inarticulable and unrepresentable" (quoted in Young 2000b, 12–14). The further challenge is to apply that "deep memory" to ourselves and our own subjectivity. To produce a reading of Rosa's experience that experiences her pain at its most profound depths, which just might be our most profound depths as well, we have to be able and willing to interrogate our own psychosexual fantasies as regards her story.

The framing of the narrative process and of the reader who gets drawn into that process becomes even more convoluted and complicated in Art Spiegelman's *Maus: A Survivor's Tale*, first published as two separate volumes in 1986 and 1991, later published as a single volume titled *The Complete Maus* (2011a), hereafter referred to simply as *Maus* (the 2011 edition is also divided into two volumes). As a graphic novel produced in comic book format, *Maus* literally frames the survivor narrative it is telling. Or, rather, it frames the *two* survivor narratives it is telling, for *Maus* is as much about the son of the survivors, who survives his parents' parenting, as it is about the survivor himself. There are no few than three storytellers in *Maus*, each of whom are story-listeners as well: Vladek Spiegelman, the Holocaust survivor, who is, through the text, telling about his life in Poland before and during the war; his son Artie, who is shown in the text as transcribing his father's experiences for the book we are now reading; and, finally, the artist Art, who is both the son and the artist, and who is implicated in but also exceeds his alter ego's storytelling and story-listening. It is Art (rather than Artie) who is the author of the graphic novel titled *Maus*. Art, in other words, frames all of the narratives, including his own, artistically and psychologically, without exempting himself from the criticisms he levels at his younger self. Simultaneously (as is the way of true art), he also exceeds the human limitations of all of his subjects, including himself. In other words, Art is simultaneously a character named Artie within the book, listening to and transcribing his father's story, and also the artist outside the tale, listening to and drawing not only his father's story but also the story of his younger self in relation to the father's story. In this way Art Spiegelman is also producing the narrative that emerges between the lines of those other narratives. This final narrative is the story of the artistic, narrative process itself (the story of Art), which belongs specifically to this storytelling/story-listening situation and also exceeds it. This story serves, among other things, to put the reader into the tale as one more listener, who may also have her own tale to tell about the events narrated in the text. My own reading of *Maus* can be considered such a narrative. The brilliance of Art's novel is that the structure of *Maus* in and of itself emphasizes how the external listener always has her own interpretive perspective. That perspective needs to be taken into account, even in relation to fictional writings that seem addressed to no one in particular and therefore to the world at large.

Of course in the case of *Maus* neither the primary story of Vladek Spiegel-man nor the essential features of his son's recording of his father's story is fiction-al. Both Vladek and Artie tell historical, autobiographical narratives. Therefore we need to bring a genuine sympathy to each of their tales of suffering and pain. Yet as a graphic novel in which people are represented as animals (the Jews as mice, the Poles as pigs, and the Germans as cats), Art Spiegelman's *Maus* is as much a fictional construction as it is a historical document. After all, neither Artie nor Vladek is a mouse. Therefore, the book can sustain all of the critical interventions that we normally bring to bear on fictional writing, even if we need to hear both Artie and Vladek compassionately. Ostensibly Artie's reasons for wanting to hear his father's autobiography are straightforward and aboveboard. Like many an artist working in any one of a variety of media, Artie is looking for a subject. The subject he chooses is the Holocaust, and the direction he moves in with that subject is to produce a documentary text that will presumably represent these events as accurately and as factually as possible. Artie the mouse draws the world mimetically. He draws himself as a mouse, albeit as a stick figure, which is to say he produces a text that is more like a written narrative than a photo-graphic album. His intention seems, simply enough, to introduce the story of the Holocaust into the public record and into public consciousness. That his chosen medium is a comic strip testifies to his wish to reach a wide popular audience, and not necessarily a Jewish one at that. Yet there is a major difference between Artie's work of documentary art and Art's full-fledged work of literary creativity (in one of the interviews included on the CD-ROM in *MetaMaus,* Spiegelman [2011b] says explicitly that he was not interested in producing a history lesson). By representing all of the characters in the book, including Artie and Vladek, as animals, the literal author Art Spiegelman is placing one more frame around his text: a vividly heightened artistic frame.

One achievement of Spiegelman's methodology is to raise the important philosophical questions that artists like Primo Levi have also raised: What is a human being? And how do we know another human being when we see one? That we recognize in these stick figures of mice real human beings (indeed, that we recognize in the stick figures real mice, who then stand for real humans) makes us wonder how the Nazis, looking at real people, could have seen anything other than human beings, although of course the very process in which we as readers engage, by which we so easily see one representation as standing for something else entirely, suggests how effortlessly we humans might also slide from seeing people as people to seeing them as rodents. Spiegelman's graphic representation of people as animals also illuminates the difference between traditional religious anti-Semitism, which often had as its intention the Jews' conversion to Christianity, and the racial anti-Semitism of Hitler's Third Reich, in which Jews were perceived as genetically, biologically degenerate and venomous and therefore deserving of extermination. Mice cannot convert themselves into humans, or, for that matter into cats or pigs. They are forever rodents. The racist emphasis of Nazism is also drawn into focus in *Maus* (as it is in *The Shawl*) through the Jewish survivor's own racist assumptions about others: in the case of Vladek, his prejudice in relation to African Americans. Suffering, as I have already suggested, does not make human beings more moral. Racism is not a problem that disappeared after the Holocaust. Indeed, in Spiegelman's own accounting of his artistic process in *Comix* (1998), *Maus* was conceived within the context of telling a story about race and racism in relation to African Americans. Spiegelman felt better qualified to talk about Jewish history than black history.

By drawing his characters as mice and pigs and cats, Art achieves for his text the status of art rather than history. As a work of fictional prose the text permits us to interpret it not only in terms of those "definite facts" that Rosa too would present in her narrative but also in relation to how those facts come to inform the personalities of Artie and Vladek Spiegelman. As I have already suggested, Artie, as represented by Art, is just one more Jewish mouse writing about other Jewish mice. Therefore, Artie is producing nothing more and nothing less than a mimetic, historical text. Indeed, while Artie and Vladek share a species category (they are both mice), Art and Vladek do not, even though Art and Wladyslaw (Zeev) Spiegelman—Vladek's real name—do. Indeed, insofar as "Vladek" is the diminutive of "Wladyslaw," in the same way that "Artie" is the diminutive of "Art," both Artie and Vladek are clearly marked in Art's text as childlike figures in a (comic book) text. Although Art and Artie clearly merge with each other at various moments throughout the text, and while the boundaries between their textual performances are blurred at best (as when Artie asks his wife how he might draw her, or on the occasions when we see the mouse mask slipping to reveal a human figure beneath), still we can experience Artie's art as different from Art's. Artie's narrative remains within the conventions of historical, autobiographical, and documentary writing. This includes realist fictions that attempt to produce more or less transparent representations of the real world outside the text. Artie could have published a graphic novel about the Holocaust and his father's experiences that would not have contained the external frame that gives us Artie's reception of his father's story or his other interactions with Vladek; his wife, Françoise; and Vladek's second wife, Mala. These features of *Maus* exist only in the novel produced by Art Spiegelman. Since Artie is working in a graphic medium, in which he is not translating people into mice, but drawing mice like himself as they are, he is being even more literal (graphic), more accountable to historical detail than if he were producing a verbal narrative (or a graphic novel such as his author is producing). For most of the book we exist in a world of pictures, not words, and of mice, cats, and pigs, not human beings.

Artie is repeatedly represented by Art as selfish, spoiled, lazy, and immature. Therefore, we might say of the stick figures in which the text is drawn—stick figures and not real mice, such as would have required of a mouse like Artie a certain artistic sophistication to draw—that they too reflect Artie's childishness and his lack of artistic sophistication (note that I say Artie, not Art). The text has Vladek pick up on this when he associates Artie's work with the tradition of Disney animation. We may well laugh along with Artie at Vladek's naiveté in not understanding the difference between Disney and the serious comic book tradition in which Art Spiegelman and his wife, Françoise, write. Yet we need to keep in mind that Vladek may not be entirely wrong in his estimate of Artie's productions, especially if we count in evidence Artie's early foray into the genre, *The Prisoner on the Hell Planet,* which is a less mature, less self-consciously framed work of art than *Maus.* At the very least, Artie's exposing his father to ridicule (as his therapist, Pavel, points out), especially in the context of the Nazis' ridiculing of both Disney and the Jews, reveals what is problematic about Artie's rendering of his father: Artie is forever critical and even contemptuous of him. If nothing else, we (and Artie) might use Vladek's comment to understand something important about Vladek that Artie misses. The Disney cartoon world has value for Vladek. From Vladek's point of view his story has a "happy, happy ever after" (Spiegelman 2011a, 296) ending, a phrase that the reader (like Artie) might feel better suits a fairy tale than a narrative of the Holocaust. But Artie has asked Vladek to tell *his* story, not Artie's, and Vladek's choice of vocabulary matters.

Art Spiegelman objected to his book being classified as fiction rather than nonfiction (1998, 16). Art, I suggest, moved too quickly here to close the distance between his comic book and that of his character Artie. While Artie's text is nonfictional, Art's is emphatically not. And it is precisely its literariness that makes it both available to our psychoanalytic investigation of it as Holocaust fiction and, as importantly, enables it to reflect back to us readers what it means to listen to and interpret narratives such as Vladek's and Artie's. As the author Art Spiegelman sets up and frames his narrative of their interactive narratives, what emerges most strongly in relation to both Vladek and Artie is the element of unexamined psychological fantasy in both major characters. These fantasies prevent them from hearing each other in meaningful ways. They produce in Artie a decidedly biased rendering of his father's experiences and of their father-son relationship.

Framing the Story, Fixing the Father: Artie's Revenge Narrative

The fundamental problem with Artie's storytelling, as Dominick LaCapra has put it, is that "Artie has an insistent and pervasive preoccupation with recording his father's story, which is dangerously close to becoming the master narrative of his own life. But he nowhere sits himself down and asks about his own motivations and reasons or directs at himself the dogged scrutiny to which he subjects his father. Indeed, in certain ways, he becomes a Jew or assumes a Jewish identity . . . through his concern with the Holocaust—a concern that nonetheless escapes sufficient critical examination" (1998, 177). James Young shares a similar point of view (2000b, 12–41). Artie's storytelling is almost like an un-self-reflective psychoanalytic performance: uncensored and full of fantasy and projection. This might be fine in the psychoanalytic or psychotherapeutic setting, such as the text depicts for us in volume 2 of *Maus*, but as history it is highly problematic. As LaCapra has argued about the task of the historian dealing with catastrophic histories like the Holocaust, "Transference is inevitable to the extent that an issue is not dead, provokes an emotional and evaluative response, and entails the meeting of history with memory. When confronting live issues, one becomes affectively implicated" (1998, 40). Therefore, what is needed by the historian, LaCapra advises, is a form of "working-through." Such working-though

> requires the recognition that we are involved in transferential relations to the past in ways that vary according to the subject-positions we find ourselves in, rework, and invent. It also involves the attempt to counteract projective reprocessing of the past through which we deny certain of its features and act out our own desires for self-confirming or identity-forming meaning. By contrast, working-through is bound up with the role of the problematic but significant distinctions, including that between accurate reconstructions of the past and committed exchange with it. (1994, 64)

As LaCapra suggests, the necessity for "working-through" is as important for a son-of-survivors historian such as Artie as it is for the professional historian. Indeed, since many of us are inheritors of this same past that so preoccupies Artie, Artie is as much a stand-in for the reader as he is the narrator of the tale. Many of us (especially, in the case of the Holocaust, Jews) are to lesser and greater degrees victims of what Nicholas Abraham and Marie Torok (1994) describe as *encryptment*. *Encryptment* defines the psychological situation in which what are repressed within the self are not simply the individual's own traumatic experiences, but the secret traumas and repressions of others. These are inherited unconsciously. "What haunts are not the dead," writes Abraham, "but the gaps left within us by the secrets of others" (171). They are "the tombs of others" (172). "Thus, the phantom cannot even be recognized by the subject" (174), since it is "the formation of the unconscious that has never been conscious—for good reason. It passes . . . from the parent's unconscious into the child's. . . . The phantom's periodic and compulsive return lies beyond the scope of symptom-formation in the sense of a return of the repressed; it works like a ventriloquist, like a stranger within the subject's own mental topography" (173). In order to understand his own traumatized youth as the son of survivors, Artie feels that he must come to understand not only his private, personal experience of his father but also what his father's behavior in that experience encodes—namely, his father's sufferings during the Holocaust. A question *Maus* raises is whether Artie or, even more pertinently, any of us need to know the details of the survivor's ordeal in order to understand ourselves, and what price we are willing to make others pay for our acquisition of this knowledge.

Artie, it seems clear enough, has an agenda in relation to his father, which everywhere biases and distorts the story he tells. You are "the REAL survivor," Artie's psychotherapist, Pavel, tells him, perhaps unwisely, since this becomes that master trope that LaCapra refers to, which controls Artie's narrative, at least until the brilliant end of the text (Spiegelman 2011a, 204). Ostensibly Artie intends his text to make a contribution to telling the story of the Holocaust. Nonetheless, from beginning to end it is also clear that Artie's is a revenge narrative. He is out to "frame" and "fix" his father—to use two of the text's own loaded tropes. Artie is witness for the prosecution; he is also judge and jury.

Even before the book represents Artie as failing to "listen" properly to his father's story (16), it provides a bit of back history in the form of an episode from Artie's childhood. Art Spiegelman could not give us clearer instructions on how to read Artie's narrative, and, to some degree at least, his own. In the opening frames of the book Artie's skate has broken and his friends have gone off without him. He comes for consolation to his father, who is busy fixing something. Vladek will not extend comfort to his son; he will not try to fix what ails him. Vladek, it would seem, would fix everything in sight, except his son. Indeed, throughout the book we always see Vladek fixing something, or counting the pills that will fix him, or riding nowhere on his stationary bike in order to fix his heart condition. In thus representing his father this way, the son is not simply erring on the side of accuracy. He is also getting even with his father: keeping his father fixed in position, a broken man fixated on his medications, who can no more fix himself than he could his son. "I've got it," Artie says to Françoise at the very beginning of the second part of *Maus*, proposing what we might take as a second opening to *Maus*: "Panel One: My father is on his exercycle. . . . I tell him I just married a frog. Panel Two: He falls off his cycle in shock" (172). The second opening parallels the first. Once again Art is reminding the reader that Artie is forever framing his father in his text, skating over his text, setting him up to take the fall for the unhappiness of his own life. "Depressed again?" Françoise asks Artie a few frames later (174), and Artie confesses that he is.

What Artie will not do—even or especially through the book he writes—is to fix anything, including his relationship with his father. As we are nearing the end of the first volume of *Maus,* Artie receives a phone call from Vladek's second wife, Mala, telling him that Vladek has been on the roof doing one more repair job and is now feeling dizzy. Vladek wants Artie to come help him "fix his roof." Artie's refusal not only reflects poorly on Artie the son, but it also calls into question Artie the artist as well. "Even as a kid," Artie tells his wife, "I hated helping around the house. . . . He made me completely neurotic about fixing stuff. . . . One reason I became an artist was that he thought it was impractical—just a waste of time . . . it was an area where I wouldn't have to compete with him" (96–97). That art is for Artie not only impractical and a waste of time but also the very opposite of fixing anything casts doubt on the entire worth of Artie's narrative enterprise, whether we think of its value as bringing Artie and his father closer together, or as making the Holocaust more accessible to the reading public, or even as self-psychotherapy for Artie himself.

From the very beginning of their narrative conversation, Artie coerces his father into telling him a story that his father has no wish to tell. "It would take many books, my life, and no one wants anyway to hear such stories," he tells Artie. But Artie insists, "I want to hear it, about your life in Poland" (12). Primarily out of fatherly love, Vladek complies with his son's request. But Artie clearly does not want to hear what his father wants to say. Right at the start Artie directs his father where to begin his narrative and then almost immediately interrupts his father when he catches him in what he thinks is an error. "Start with Mom," Artie instructs his father. "Tell me how you met" (14; on the tape Art/ie can be heard interrupting his father routinely, although his father barely pays any attention to his son's interruptions). This is Artie the son, not Artie the historian or artist, wanting, like any child, to hear primarily about how he came into the world. He wants his father to tell him how he met his mother. When Vladek chooses to begin elsewhere, Artie objects. "But, Pop, Mom's name was Anna Zylberberg" (does Artie imagine for even a moment that his father doesn't know this?), to which his father aptly responds: "All this was before I met Anja—Just listen, yes?" (16; this can be heard as well on the taped conversation included in Spiegelman's *MetaMaus* [2011b]). Just listening is apparently harder for Artie to do than he imagines. Several chapters into Vladek's narrative, Artie once again stops his father in order to have him clarify another, even more loaded narrative detail having to do with the birth of the Spiegelmans' first-born son, Artie's deceased brother, Richieu. Richieu, Artie realizes, had to have been conceived before Anja and Vladek were married. Here is a family secret, hardly suitable for publication, and very much the stuff of childhood fantasies about parental intimacy and the family romance. Artie unabashedly launches into presenting this detail of his father's life to his reader.

What story is Artie inadvertently or unconsciously telling us here about Anja, Vladek, Richieu, and, most importantly, himself? The details of Richieu's conception and birth have even less bearing on the documentary text Artie wishes to produce than the story of his father's previous romantic relationships. Therefore, out of simple discretion, not to mention disciplinary rigor, he might have chosen to ignore this part of his father's story. "Such private things, I don't want you should mention," Vladek admonishes his son, who is, of course, at this very moment in the text mentioning these things to the reader, despite his promising not to (25). Artie impugns his own integrity as witness and writer right from the start of the book. What we see throughout the exchange between father and son is not only that the story Artie wants to hear is not at all the story his father wants to tell but also that the son needs to redress grievances against his father that as we begin to realize rather early on have to do with his psychological survival of his psychologically limited parent. What emerges more gradually and more profoundly during the course of the narrative is that Artie fears as well for his literal, physical survival in a world in which even as capable a father as his own is not able to save his son from death. This is what also emerges through the father and son's exchange about the dead child Richieu.

To some extent the rather piquant detail about Richieu's birth does no more than perform a bit of sibling revenge against the presumably preferred older brother, much like the acts of retribution that the text launches against his father. There is nothing noteworthy in Artie's suffering from sibling rivalry, albeit in his case it is "sibling rivalry with a snapshot" of a dead sibling (175). This makes of Richieu the "ideal kid" who never "threw a tantrum or got into any kind of trouble" (175), even though Artie knows this isn't true. Earlier in the text Artie draws Richieu misbehaving and his mother reprimanding him for it (76). This moment could be read as another moment of his getting even with his brother, but it also might suggest to the reader that Art (behind Artie) knows full well that whatever Artie thinks, his brother was neither ideal nor idealized by his parents. After all, Vladek doesn't seem to provide Artie with this detail of the dinner table. One feature of the graphic novel that Art exploits here is its capacity to represent two different things at once, and what is being narrated in words might be very different from what is being depicted in the drawings. What Art knows may be different from what Artie knows, and whose hand is drawing here is far from clear.

Artie's exposing the family secret about Richieu's premature birth combines the ordinary psychosexual motivations of the child-sibling rivalry and fantasies of the parents' bedroom with the special strains placed on childhood development by the facts of the Holocaust. Artie is jealous of this brother, whose photograph hangs in his parents' bedroom, where his does not. Other eyes than his own, it seems to Artie, have known the intimacy between the parents, from which he is barred. By revealing the secret of Richieu's birth, Artie also subtly implies that even if Richieu is the more beloved child, he is not the more legitimate one. All of this falls well within the boundaries of ordinary sibling tension. But in Artie's relationship to the photograph of Richieu there is another, even deeper tension that is also, like the question of Richieu's place in the family, related to the basic psychological wiring of human beings as it goes haywire under the pressure of the Holocaust: the matter of Artie's own literal survival in a terrifying world. "I can't even make any sense out my relationship with my father," Artie says to Françoise toward the beginning of volume 2 of *Maus*. "How am I supposed to make any sense out of Auschwitz?" (174). The link between the relationship with his father and his understanding of the Holocaust certainly has something to do with understanding his father's neurotic behaviors. But it goes far deeper than that, into Artie's fears, not for his survival of his father's rather bad parenting of him, but for his survival pure and simple. And for this terror we cannot but extend to Artie our own sympathies.

This is the conversation between Artie and Françoise in somewhat skeletal form as they are driving up to the Catskills to see his father:

> When I was a kid I used to think about which of my parents I'd let the Nazis take to the ovens if I could only save one of them. / Usually I saved my Mother. . . . / I wonder if Richieu and I would get along if he was still alive. . . . / My **ghost** brother . . . I didn't think about him much when I was growing up. He was mainly a large, blurry, photograph hanging in my parents' bedroom. . . . I **never** felt **guilty** about Richieu. But I did have nightmares about S.S. men coming into my class and dragging all us Jewish kids away." (174–76)

Artie's question about which of his two parents he would save serves to reverse and also thereby bring into focus the sibling question: if my parents had had to make a choice between my brother and me, which child would they have saved? It also reveals Artie's deeply disturbing anxiety that his father would likely not have been able to save either one of them. Vladek, for all of his remarkable abilities to fix things and to survive—which seems throughout much of *Maus* to be the source of Artie's feelings of inadequacy—was not able to do what in a child's mind may be the single most important thing a parent can do: keep his child safe and alive. Artie is angry with his father for what he perceives as his impotence in not being able to save his son(s) from death. Artie may not feel guilty in relation to his dead brother—although we might suspect that Artie is too quick to come to this conclusion, as the boldface in the text suggests (later his therapist, Pavel, will similarly deny his own feelings of guilt a bit too glibly)—but he does feel "guilt" in relation to his father, *not* simply because, as Artie himself puts it in the same scene, Artie has "had an easier life than [his parents] did" (176), but because of the (illegitimate) anger he feels toward his father for a powerlessness he also knows was not really his father's fault. Hence his fantasy of saving only one of his parents: he would punish his father by not saving him, by letting him share the fate of the older child, which could have been his own fate as well. "They didn't need photos of me in their room," Artie explains to Françoise. "I was **ALIVE**" (175). The word **ALIVE** in boldface suggests how precarious Artie's sense of his aliveness is and always has been. That the photograph of Richieu is blurry and, in Françoise's view, looks a lot like Artie captures Artie's own sense of the fragility and vulnerability that the two brothers share.

No wonder, then, that Artie cries out, childlike, for his mother toward the beginning of chapter 2 of volume 2 of *Maus*: "I want . . . I want . . . my **MOMMY**" (202). Artie is a multiply abandoned, multiply orphaned child, and he always has been (at this point in Spiegelman's composition of the text his father is dead). Neither his mother nor his father has seemed capable of saving him, any more than they were able to save Richieu. Thus Anja's suicide, which he perceives as her unwillingness to remain in the world to mother her second son, serves to confirm for Artie a larger world picture that begins in the photo of Richieu. Artie is not only a "prisoner" of his parents' unresolved issues—in particular their complicated mourning for Richieu—but in his own view of things he is a "murder" victim as well. Indeed, he is a victim of infanticide: "You murdered me, Mommy, and you left me here to take the rap" ("Prisoner on the Hell Planet," in *Maus*, 105). When Artie calls his father a "murderer" for having destroyed Anja's diaries, we might hear in this accusation Artie's sense that his father was also an infanticide and not only Richieu but Artie too was the victim (161; the word "murderer" closes volume 1). Certainly Anja and Vladek seem to have thought of themselves as infanticides, thus making Artie's condemnation of them a quotation of their own condemnations of themselves.

Like Stella in *The Shawl*, Artie is the victim of his parents' incomplete mourning over the death of their first child: "After the war," Artie explains to Françoise, "my parents traced down the vaguest rumors, and went to orphanages all over Europe. They couldn't believe he was dead" (2:15). Because *The Shawl* centers primarily on Rosa, we do not pay much attention to Stella and to her relationship to Magda's death. Yet our responses to Stella, that other survivor (even more authentically a survivor than Artie), must be brought under the same ethical logic as our responses to Rosa. Part of what makes Stella into the very unlikable person she is, is Rosa's inability or unwillingness to be a mother to her surviving "daughter." Stella is only a child when Magda dies. How do we hold her responsible for anything at all, let alone the cannibalism Rosa ascribes to her, which, as I have suggested, likely tells us more about Rosa's imagination than about Stella's? In *Maus* we get a fuller picture than we do in *The Shawl* of the consequences of such incomplete mourning for the surviving sibling. As the son who is born after the death of his brother, Artie (like Stella in relation to Magda) lives in the shadow of his "ghost brother," the "ideal kid," who, like Rosa's Magda, would (in Artie's imagination) have grown up to be a doctor (Spiegelman 2011a, 175). It is not irrelevant in this context that what Vladek needs at the moment more than anything else is medical help, which the surviving son knows he cannot provide him through his art. Art doesn't fix things that way.

The Holocaust experiences of both of Artie's parents undoubtedly produce a complexity to their relationships with each other and with Artie that differentiates the Spiegelman family from non-survivor families, even if to some degree all Jews born during and after the Nazi genocide are its survivor-victims. When all is said and done, how could Vladek and Anja not have been deeply marked by their catastrophic experiences? In many ways, however, Vladek is also a father like every father, a man like every man, and his son Artie is a son like any son. In the same way that many of Rosa's personality traits can be traced to her prewar life, so too the Spiegelmans suffer from, in Vladek's case, tendencies toward vanity, narcissism, and haughtiness and, in Anja's case, depression. These conditions might have been exacerbated by the Holocaust, but they are not produced by it, as the back history provided in *Maus* more than amply demonstrates. Indeed, such aspects of their personalities build on inherent psychological tendencies that as much as their other ordinary non-traumatic experiences make Vladek and Anja who they are. We are all constructed as human beings under the dual pressures of inner drives and outer satisfactions (or the lack thereof). For that reason we are also always the survivors of our childhoods, which is to say of our parents and of their psychological struggles to survive. Artie has to be seen in just this light. Artie's bedroom fantasies, as focused through the photo of his dead brother, expose not only Artie's Holocaust-inflected experience of his parents but his very normal, natural psychological nature as well. Is it "normal"? Artie asks Françoise about his choice to save his mother rather than his father, to which Françoise aptly replies, "Nobody's normal," meaning that everybody is and is not normal in different ways (174). In one view of psychological development, choosing the mother over the father is extraordinarily normal. *Maus* is not a book that shies away from the Oedipal tensions that characterize the child's relationship with his or her parents. Artie's relationship with his parents is, among other things, a paradigm of how every child brings to that relationship a set of impulses that (depending on who we are and how well we function in the world) may or may not need addressing in our adult lives.

Vladek's Story: The Survivor as Hero

In order to hear the story that Vladek wishes his son to hear and that Art ultimately does hear (even if Artie does not), we must remember that Vladek has no wish to tell his story to his son. Nor is there any perceivable benefit to Vladek in telling his story either to Artie or to us. Vladek may be a difficult person, with all sorts of behaviors we disapprove of. Some of those behaviors may even be attributable to, or at least have been exacerbated by, his Holocaust experience. Vladek, and Anja too, may well, like Rosa, be suffering from incomplete mourning. Indeed, because Anja commits suicide, we might feel she needed to tell her story to someone who could have listened with a therapeutic third ear, even a professionally untrained one, such as Simon Persky provides for Rosa in *The Shawl*. Nonetheless, while we see the imprint of the war not only in Vladek's words but also in his everyday behaviors (hoarding, fixing, distrusting, although, of course, we need to constantly remind ourselves that we get this view of Vladek only through the optics of his son), it is not at all clear that Vladek needs fixing. When all is said and done, Vladek is a reasonably resourceful, functioning, and competent human being. Indeed, there is something exceedingly gentle and loving in his voice on the interview tapes included in the *MetaMaus* CD-ROM (Art is also softer than the Artie of the text). If there is a deep sadness in his life, it is as much owing to the suicide of his beloved wife, Anja, as it is to the Holocaust experience and the loss of his elder son. And if he is disgruntled, it is also because of his medical disabilities, not to mention his son's rather flagrant disregard of his filial obligations. We may want to attribute Vladek's attitudes and behaviors to his Holocaust years, but at best they are indirect expressions of that experience, more akin to Artie's secondary trauma than Vladek's own primary experience of the camps.

There is a tendency to categorize all experiences of the Holocaust as traumas. Yet trauma is a very specific psychological condition in which there is a failure either to integrate the affective and conscious aspects of an experience or to enter an experience into conscious memory such that only the affective consequences of the event remain. Although there are clearly traumatic aspects to Vladek's experience (as evidenced perhaps by certain of his repetitious behaviors), it is not clear that Vladek suffers from trauma. Indeed, Vladek seems extremely conscious of what happened to him during the war. Even Vladek's occasional lapses in memory (as when he cannot remember the orchestra at Auschwitz) do not indicate that he is suffering from trauma: who of us, under far more ordinary circumstances, does not forget details from the past? At one moment in the tape-recorded conversations Vladek makes exactly this point about his not remembering a specific detail. And he is quite right. "Trauma" is sometimes a word we employ in order to indicate our respect for the enormity of what an individual has suffered or our inability to put it into words. Yet the word "trauma" can also serve as an excuse for not listening and not understanding another person's story. It may also be a cover-up to justify our invasion of another person's privacy, forcing that individual to confess to what happened to him, so that we can, presumably, better help him to cope with his traumatic memories. Vladek does not need to tell his story. Artie, however, needs him to tell it, and later he needs to tell his own story as well.

The story Artie would have his father tell him, which he would tell of his father in order to produce a Holocaust narrative, is the story of his father's humiliation, suffering, and pain. *That,* from Artie's point of view, is the interesting story. It is the story of the Holocaust, which is also the story readers expect. Most of *Maus*'s readers read the book for the same reasons we read *The Shawl*: we are interested, perhaps too interested, in the Holocaust. In the case of *Maus,* many of us sympathize deeply with Artie. Even if we are not the children of survivors (I myself am not), many of us grew up in the shadow of events that were terrifying as much for their inaccessibility to comprehension as for the literal violence they represented. We have come to accept Artie's claim, expressed also in Israeli author David Grossman's *See Under: Love* (1989), that withholding the story of the Holocaust from the next generation has had pernicious effects, and that those of us who belong to that generation are entitled to be told the truth, in all of its glaring horror. This is a questionable claim at best.

Vladek, who does not think of himself as primarily a survivor in that sense, would tell a very different story. It is much more important for Vladek that his son hears this story than the one that his son is extracting from him and that readers of Artie's generation want him to tell. It is also important to Art Spiegelman for us to hear it as well. For what Art knows that Artie does not yet understand when he first undertakes to tell his father's story is that the survivor is not solely a victim of Nazi atrocities. As Rosa puts it so well in *The Shawl* (the comment takes on extra resonance in the context of Spiegelman's representation of humans as mice): "Consider also the special word they used: *survivor.* . . . As long as they didn't have to say *human being*" (Ozick 1990, 36; italics in original); "the Jews are undoubtedly a race," Spiegelman quotes Hitler on the page facing chapter 1 of volume 1 ("The Sheik"), "but they are not human" (2011a, 10). The survivor, Rosa insists, and Vladek knows this as well, is a person with a unique, personal psychobiography, in which he is in every sense of the word the hero of his story. That Artie cannot or will not hear this story is very much to the point of Art Spiegelman's text.

What Vladek's manner of storytelling tells us about him is already contained in the opening frames having to do with Artie's childhood in Rego Park. It is also contained in a variety of ways every day of Vladek's life in the activities of that life, which Artie largely ignores. Vladek sees himself as competent, self-sufficient, and heroic, capable of performing superbly well in a world of multiple obstacles and hostilities. "I was everything," Vladek tells Artie of his being first a "tin man" (tinsmith) and then a shoemaker at Auschwitz. "And this helped save my life" (Spiegelman 2011b, n.p.). Of course the fact that the young Artie does not understand what his father is saying to him when he refuses to fix the broken skate—and, by implication, the broken boy—is not to be held against the child. Children cannot be expected to understand certain things. They do not "read" texts in the ways adults read them. And children are to be forgiven the narcissism that puts them at the center of every story, whether their own or someone else's. In addition, even if by modern standards Vladek is perhaps to be faulted as a parent for not comforting his son, Vladek is of an age and a culture that would not be critical of his rather curt reply to his son's tears, even if we of Artie's generation object. The adult Artie cannot be let off the hook so easily, especially since, as someone who clearly knows something about the Holocaust other than what his father is about to tell him and who has declared himself an artist capable of telling his father's story, he must be expected to understand precisely the difference between his father's needs and his own. Vladek, who fixes things, has also fixed himself as well as a human being might do this. In his own view of things Vladek is no *Mussulman,* but a maus-man—to apply Art's metaphor.

If Artie had not had his own agenda in place, what might he have heard when his father answered his request to begin with how he met his mother with the story of his years-long relationship with another woman? Why is this where Vladek begins his story? Art Spiegelman titles this section of the book "The Sheik." The artist knows the answer and gives it to us, even if Art's calling his father the "sheik" is not a wholly generous, loving gesture. Obviously Art and Artie do have many things in common. But taking this, for the moment, as it occurs within the world represented within the text: Vladek—the husband, father, survivor, aged refugee-in-America, with one glass eye, diabetes, a bad heart, and barely competent English, who is married to the rather unloving Mala, with whom he does not get along and with whom he is seen arguing in the opening frames over "wooden hangers" (2011a, 13)—begins with himself as the "young, and really a nice, handsome boy," a man "in textiles, buying and selling," who "always . . . could make a living" (14–15; on the tapes, when Vladek deals with his being set up in business by his father-in-law, he is absolutely modest about his business acumen and overawed by his father-in-law's generosity and confidence in him).

Vladek's self-introduction tells us a lot about how Vladek would like to have his son see and represent him in the text that his son is producing. This image of Vladek is the same as the image contained in the photograph that Vladek gives Artie at the end of the narrative, which is the very photo he had sent to Anja after the war. That photograph (which is an actual photograph reprinted in the book, not a drawing of a photograph) is meant to provide Anja with evidence that he is still alive. However, it also suggests how much the dashing young man Vladek still is. In the photograph Vladek is wearing a freshly washed and ironed concentration camp outfit, looking even more handsome than he does as the sheik—in part, of course, because in the photograph he is literally a man and not a mouse. Vladek would not have Anja see him otherwise. He would also have his son and his son's readers see him this way—not as the frail, ailing, dirty "survivor" (a rodent of sorts), to which the Nazis reduced him and as Artie draws him countless times in the text, but as a healthy, virile, successful man. Is it not Vladek's right to insist on this? Is it not his right to present himself to his son not as a dirty animal nor even an ailing elderly man, but as the younger, more vital person he used to be and to claim this as his essential identity?

Yet his son Artie, who is the Holocaust scholar par excellence here, will not permit his father to exit the camps: "Let's get back to Auschwitz," Artie commands Vladek when Vladek begins to complain to him about Mala. "**ENOUGH!** Tell me about Auschwitz" (207). In the pictures recording this exchange we see Art, not Artie, wearing a mouse mask listening to himself and his father on the tape recorder. Art behind the mask of Artie recognizes the degree to which he is issuing orders to his father. "So? . . . Okay, I'll make it so how you want it," Vladek says to Artie earlier on in the narrative (84), and in the very next frame we get the following: "**ORDER**" "All Jews of Sosnowiec must be relocated into the Stara Sosnowiec quarter by January 1, 1942" (84). Represented in the text as endlessly spilling and miscounting his pills and riding nowhere, Vladek is kept by his son's drawings permanently in place, obeying Artie's orders. On some level Artie would have the survivor be a survivor and not a "human being."

In the opening scene of volume 1 of *Maus,* it is clear that Vladek's tiff with Mala over hangers is still hanging over the text (hangers, we might note, are associated with textiles; later Vladek will throw out a jacket Artie is wearing, which he considers too old and worn out). To hear Vladek's story we need to listen not only to the large dimensions of his horrific experiences during the war but also to those small, personal, and very human moments, past and present, that define him as who he is. Once, Vladek knows, he was a really nice man. He knows that he no longer is. Once, too, he made a "living." The word "living" hints at more dire concerns that have less to do with money (he never did "make much," he easily enough confesses) than the two life-threatening heart attacks he has suffered: "Come," he says to Artie after dinner, "we'll talk while I pedal. . . . It's good for my heart, the pedaling" (14). Pedaling has replaced peddling as Vladek's way of living, making a living/keeping him alive. Even if Vladek cannot hear the internal puns, we and Art do; Artie too might have heard them and understood what his father was saying about his desperation and fear.

The story about "Lucia," which immediately ensues, is prompted by Vladek's despair over his health, not to mention his loveless marriage to Mala, which has replaced the truly loving relationship he at one time had with his beloved Anja. Once, he tells us, he "looked just like Rudolph Valentino" (15)—an assertion made startling and also hilariously funny in the text by the juxtaposition of the picture of Vladek the mouse pedaling set against the sheik-mouse dancing with Lucia, who is also a mouse. As I have already suggested, where Artie's ridicule of his father begins and Art's ends constitutes one of those hard calls we need to make, even if we cannot quite draw the line between one and the other. What is clear is that from Vladek's point of view, once upon a time he lived and made a living.

Once upon a time Anja was an event about to happen in a story that, against all odds, Vladek reiterates again and again, had more than one happy ending.

That "happy, happy ending" is a major, constantly repeating motif of Vladek's story. For whatever reasons—and in order to understand Artie we need to come to understand those reasons—Artie cannot hear the happy note his father constantly strikes. Indeed, at one point on the CD-ROM, when Vladek repeats his leitmotif that "I was very happy . . . happy happy," Artie actually interrupts him to ask: "You were happy?" When Vladek responds in the affirmative, "I was happy," Artie tries to supply Vladek with a better word. "Fortunate?" he suggests. Vladek accepts Artie's correction in the following way: "Fortunately happy." Vladek will insist on that word "happy," and while Vladek surely misuses English throughout his narrative, the word "happy" might be a word Vladek understands. Vladek was once a teacher of English in Poland, and in fact he survives the camp partly because of his knowledge of English. Vladek is entitled to that word "happy." It is his choice.

In his father's associating his son's comic book art with the Disney tradition, Artie might have heard the subtext of the fairy tale that determines Vladek's self-understanding. From beginning to end Vladek constructs his story as a Disney movie, which is going to have a happy ending. The son might have taken this as a hint as to the kind of comic Vladek would have Artie draw. Thus, throughout the second volume, in the midst of the Auschwitz and post-Auschwitz experience, the word "happy" (also "joy") recurs with such frequency that it is difficult for us to miss it. It is as if Vladek is working very hard to get Artie to hear above all else that he, Vladek, was a "happy" man (2011a, 187), "amazing well-off!" (193), and "lucky" (186, 194). In some ways he still is. Most dramatically the word "happy" appears three times on the last page of the book. These are almost the last words Vladek speaks to Artie in the text: "More I don't need to tell you, we were both very happy, and lived happy, happy ever after" (296). Earlier in the text Artie had insisted to his wife, Françoise, that "**NOTHING** can make [Vladek] happy" (172). Ironically this pronouncement comes just frames before Spiegelman records Vladek as saying to Artie and Françoise: "I'm happy I have here you 'kids' to stay together with me" (177). So much for Artie's insights into his father's disposition.

What Artie cannot or will not grant his father is not that he has survived the war, even though Artie and Pavel represent this as being Artie's problem ("No matter what I accomplish," Artie tells Pavel, voicing the complaint of many a survivor's child, "it doesn't seem like much compared to surviving Auschwitz" [204]). Rather, Artie resents Vladek's claims to happiness, especially when that happiness has to do with Vladek's relationship with Artie's mother, Anja. "And she was so laughing and so happy, so happy," Vladek tells Artie about his and Anja's stay at the sanitarium where Anja and he went together so that Anja might recover from her postpartum depression after Richieu's birth; "she approached each time and kissed me, so happy she was" (37). That happy ending with Anja begins with the end of Vladek's relationship with Lucia and the beginning of his love affair with Anja. And love affair it was: we are permitted to make no mistakes about this. What we see about Vladek throughout his self-description is that he was a man with a good sexual appetite and an ability to enjoy himself: hence his joking all the time, even during and after the war. Compared to his father, Artie is not only listless; he is humorless. Artie needs to interrogate the degree to which his melancholy is because of his feeling excluded by the depths of Anja and Vladek's feelings for each other and by the joy they took in each other. Vladek's weeping on Artie's shoulder when Anja dies, crying, "Mother, mother" (103), suggests how much Vladek and Anja were everything to each other—not just husband and wife but parent and child as well. This makes Artie, in Artie's view, superfluous.

In the course of his narrative Vladek reveals many less than noble aspects of himself: his concern with money, which initially fosters his interest in the wealthy Anja; his practicality, which almost leads him to break off the engagement when he discovers pills in her medicine cabinet; his lack of idealism and his selfishness when he refuses to permit Anja to continue to work with the Polish underground; his narcissism; and so on and so forth. There is no dearth of damning self-revelation contained in Vladek's narrative, even if he himself is barely conscious of what he is revealing. There is also a good amount of heroism, self-sacrifice, and love that is revealed there as well, some of it less than modestly presented, some of it the sincerest kind of expression of a human consciousness involved in a life-and-death struggle not only for himself but for the people he loves. One very affecting bit on the CD-ROM involves Vladek's conscription into the Polish army, where he kills a German soldier. "Who am I," he asks these many years later, "to kill people?" Vladek then goes on to describe how he tried to save the life of the man he killed. At another point he describes his and Anja's efforts after the war to locate the camp inmate who had helped deliver Vladek's notes and extra pieces of bread to Anja.

This is a whole human life that Vladek is narrating, in all of its aspects. This is a multifaceted human being. If we hear anything less than all of that, we have not heard Vladek at all. But for much of his book Artie hears only what he wants to hear. He hears the factual dimensions of the story and records them with precision and in detail. He does not hear his father's sense of his life as enchanted, a fairy tale in which he is most decidedly a prince charming (the sheik) and his Anja the princess he saves. In the same narrative sequence in which Vladek describes his shooting the German soldier, he evidences his capacity to produce narrative art, especially of the fairy-tale variety, when he describes how a "tree started running" and a "bicycle flying" (the tree is a camouflaged soldier, the bicycle the result of a bridge blowing up). Like his son Artie, Vladek knows how to tell a story. In fact, Vladek can also use an impersonal voice in narrating his story so as to help provide his son with the kind of narrative material his son needs in order to make his story public. Thus, Vladek refers to Anja or Anna as "Mom" or "Mother" only after Artie does. Otherwise he calls her "my wife." Similarly, he refers to Richieu not by name but as his "previous son."

We might not want to fault Artie for not being a psychotherapeutic listener. He is, after all, the son, not Vladek's psychiatrist. Nonetheless, once he undertakes his narrative project, he is obliged to listen with a sympathetic lack of self-concern to the story his father is telling him. At the very least, he might have had the patience to hear his father out, to try to understand why his father did not begin with Anja but with another woman. Instead, the ever competitive Artie jumps in to correct what he hears to be Vladek's mistake. What is clear is that Artie objects to his father's telling his own story rather than the one Artie would have him tell. Perhaps he objects to Vladek's description of himself as a lady's man. Or perhaps he only objects to Vladek not putting his mother first. Or maybe it's the opposite: maybe he wishes to imagine that his father does not and never did put his mother first, not the way that he, the son, did. The only real photograph of Anja presented in *Maus* is one of Anja with Artie, not with Vladek, although we see in *MetaMaus* that Spiegelman has lots of photos of his parents. That Artie cites his mother's name formally and in full as "Anna" Zylberberg rather than "Anja," which is what Vladek calls her, suggests the distance Artie is maintaining from his father and his father's intimacy with his mother. (He also represents his father in "Prisoner on the Hell Planet" as calling Anja "Anna.") Artie's selection of his father's words suggests the competition for the mother in which they are engaged. A major question raised for Artie by his mother's suicide, which should neither surprise nor disturb us, though it must pain us as it pains Artie, is why he could not make his mother happy, when it is so clear that Vladek and Anja made each other happy, albeit not happy enough for Anja (who had depressive tendencies to begin with) to refrain from killing herself.

Artie also has no place in his mental world for Vladek's expressions of his good luck and his hopefulness. Luck, Artie knows, and he says so to Pavel, played a big role in who lived and who died in the camps. It is made to seem in that interview between Artie and his therapist that Artie suspects that something more than luck was involved in his father's successes. That fact contributes to his resentment of his father: "I know there was a lot of LUCK involved [in surviving]," he says to Pavel, "but he WAS amazingly present-minded and resourceful" (205). By capitalizing the word "LUCK" Artie reveals that he also resents that his father was lucky, that Vladek felt himself to be blessed, as perhaps he was.

For Vladek luck serves an important function in his narrative, which has little to do with the more commonplace and logical point that Pavel is making about survival: that it was, in Pavel's word, "RANDOM" (205). We see again and again in Vladek's narrative that he precisely does not consider his survival, or anything else in his life, random. From Vladek's point of view it is lucky that he meets Anja and gives up Lucia. It is lucky that he marries her. Neither of these events is random. Neither is his survival, which picks up on and carries forward his luck in relation to Anja. Vladek's luck begins with the fact that his concentration camp garb fit him (186), and it proceeds from there: "I was worn and shivering and crying a little," Vladek confesses to Artie as he describes his first moments in Auschwitz. "But from another room someone approached over. 'Why are you crying, my son?'" a priest asks him. "Should I be **HAPPY**? Am I at a carnival?'" to which the priest replies, "Let me see your arm":

> "Hmm . . . your number starts with 17, in Hebrew that's 'kminyan tov.' Seventeen is a very good omen. . . . It ends with 13, the age a Jewish boy becomes a man . . . and **LOOK**! Added together it totals 18, that's 'chai,' the Hebrew number of life. I can't know if **I'll** survive this hell, but I'm certain **YOU'LL** come through all this alive!" I started to BELIEVE. I tell you. He put another life in me. And whenever it was very bad, I looked and said, "yes, the priest was **RIGHT**! It totals eighteen'" (188). [The number on Vladek's number is 175113, and the sum of those digits is 18.]

Artie manages a meager, perhaps ironic, response to this. The priest, he says, was a "**saint**," the boldface indicating irony, perhaps (188). And then he lets the moment drop; for him it is not of serious significance to Vladek's story of his survival. However, it is important for Vladek, whose happiness follows the course of his good omens.

Artie is similarly unimpressed by the earlier moment of which this later moment is a repetition. This earlier moment occurs in volume 1 of *Maus* when Vladek is in a prisoner-of-war camp and has a dream in which his grandfather appears to him and assures him, "You will come out of this place—**FREE**! . . . on this day of parshas truma" (59). This is indeed what happens. "You mean your 'parshas truma' dream actually came true?" Artie asks him, and Vladek waxes eloquent: "I checked later on a calendar. It was this parsha on the week I got married to Anja. . . . And this was the parsha in 1948, after the war, on the week you were born! . . . And so it came out to be this parsha you sang on the Saturday of your Bar mitzvah!" (60). This is a magical moment for Vladek, but Artie has nothing more to say on the matter, even though asking the question *why* this constitutes a part of Vladek's narrative and what that story is saying about Vladek's sense of his being chosen might have helped Artie to see something profoundly important about his father. As David Mikics (2003) has pointed out, Vladek is a Jacob figure. He is both a trickster and a recipient of blessings. And those blessings are important to Vladek. In order to understand the survivor experience, we may also need to understand a man like Vladek's sense of being chosen and blessed and lucky. Certainly for Artie to have understood his father's self-conception and not merely what the Nazis did to him might have helped Artie both to understand his father better and to clarify his own resentments about what his father believed and felt.

Psychoanalysis and the Story of Art

As I announced early on in this study of Holocaust fiction, my intention is to read texts psychoanalytically, employing strategies of listening that involve both self-conscious self-reflection and a non-self-referential willingness to be with the narrator in his or her suffering, however that suffering expresses itself. My claim about Art Spiegelman's *Maus* is that by the end of the narrative Art has displaced Artie as the recipient of his father's story and that the text Art produces is a work of psychoanalytically informed art of the highest level. Indeed, the book presents a theory of art as necessarily psychoanalytically invested, which therefore requires a similar kind of psychoanalytic hearing on the part of the reader.

Maus proceeds to this position vis-à-vis transcribing and telling stories of the Holocaust (whether of one's own experience or the experience of others) through its very self-aware rendering of Artie's own experience with psychoanalysis, or at least psychodynamic psychotherapy (which is an abbreviated form of psychoanalysis). Here, more than almost anywhere else in the book the identities of Art and Artie become blurred, although it is still, I maintain, Art and not Artie who is in control of the text and its representations. Artie's failed psychotherapeutic intervention does not succeed in helping Artie (though it might have aided Art) in deciphering the depths of the fantasy that is controlling his life. Through Pavel the analyst, who should know better, the book provides us with another failure of subjective perception to recognize and regulate itself. The book does so in a way that suggests both how psychoanalysis depends on the skill of the analyst and how that skill is much like that of the artist, who must simultaneously be both in her text and neutrally outside it. *Maus*'s rendering of Art/ie's psychoanalysis brings the real author, Art Spiegelman, into his text in a very clear and marked way.

One of the few places where Art shows a human figure wearing a mouse mask is in this scene of psychotherapeutic intervention. This scene follows another such rare moment, when Art/ie is half man, half mouse, at his drawing table, drawing the graphic novel itself. It is this earlier scene that prompts the conversation with the therapist, Pavel. The scenes, in other words, are multiply linked and draw our attention to that linkage. What we know about Art from this earlier scene in volume 2 is that writing *Maus* has not been the least bit "cathartic" for him (Spiegelman 2011a, 202). I suggest that this is not simply because, as Pavel suggests, he has "exposed [his] father to ridicule" (204), among other things, but, rather, because if the picture is to be believed, his costume or disguise is slipping. This is to say that on the one hand he cannot yet remove the mask, yet on the other hand he can no longer keep it in place. That Art draws himself in the therapist's office as Art wearing a mouse mask that, as in the previous scene, is slipping puts the artist firmly in his text in a very self-conscious way. In other words, by the logic of the scenes his analytic failure may be traced to his therapist, Pavel, although by the same logic Art's success as a writer, able finally to come out from behind the mask, might in a contrary way be taken as testimony to the skill of Art's analyst, whoever he was.

As Art reminds us through representing Pavel and Artie as humans wearing mouse masks, psychoanalysis is not an ordinary, everyday conversation between two people in the real workaday world. As the text quite accurately depicts it, it is something more like a narrative performance, the construction of a text, such as Art is producing in *Maus*, hence the linking of the scene of psychotherapy and the scene of Art/ie drawing the book. In the psychodynamic psychotherapeutic or psychoanalytic drama, two individuals (the patient and the therapist), each of them playing a role (wearing a mask, as it were) mutually construct the story. This storytelling enactment is intended to unmask to the patient certain of his psychological processes. The goal of dynamic psychotherapy or psychoanalysis is, in the first instance, to bring the patient to the point where he can see the mask that he himself has thrown over the therapist. This is the mask that the therapist has consented temporarily to wear so that he can become an actor in the patient's internal psychobiography (playing the role, say, of the patient's father or mother). By unmasking the therapist in the patient's internal drama, the patient then also unmasks himself. This is the goal of the drama: to make visible to the patient those forms of behavior or enactment that are otherwise invisible to the patient in terms of what inner psychological narrative those behaviors are expressing. In this dialogue between analyst and analysand, the therapist must be careful to preserve a double consciousness throughout. He must remain aware that the role he is playing is being imposed by the patient, and that the enactment is going forward for one purpose only: for the patient's self-illumination.

Artie's therapist does open up a certain perspective on what ails Artie, which contains some solid psychological observations about children generally and the children of survivors in particular. "EVERY boy, when he's little, looks up to his father," Pavel tells Artie, which is likely true enough but does not provide a particularly useful insight. More to the point, although not a useful psychotherapeutic intervention, is Pavel's observation: "Maybe your father needed to show that he was always right—that he could always SURVIVE—because he felt GUILTY about surviving" (204). This observation fails on two counts: first because the therapist and not the patient is doing the interpreting, and second because he is interpreting the father and not the patient. Ultimately Pavel serves in the text as one more reflection of the habit of unexamined subject position, which produces bad listening, bad analysis, and, finally, the production of bad texts (whether written or oral).

The Pavel who is drawn as Artie's therapist is not necessarily an accurate picture of Art's therapist. He may no more be Art's real therapist than Artie's Vladek is Art's Wladyslaw (or either Artie's Vladek or Art's Wladyslaw is the person whom Vladek/Wladyslaw understands himself to be). Our perceptions of other people always belong to us. They contain our projections and interpretations, our subjectivity and not that of the other person. This fact bears a special relationship to psychodynamic psychotherapy and psychoanalysis. Even if the represented Pavel were an accurate portrayal of the real therapist, this therapist would still be a representation of his patient's construction. That Art/ie casts Pavel in the role of the father (note how the name Pavel recalls the name Vladek) and that Pavel consents to play this role is all to the good. The problem is that Pavel loses himself to the role (in technical language, fails to check the countertransference) in significant ways. Pavel is also significantly confused about his relation to Art/ie and about whose Holocaust obsession is the object of the therapy.

Art/ie opens the conversation with his therapist by saying he is "completely messed up," even though "things couldn't be going better with [his] 'career' or at home." "Mostly," however, Art/ie tells us, he "feel[s] like crying." "I'm totally BLOCKED" (203). The narrative frames surrounding Art/ie's litany of self-contradictory statements and complaints (the graphics seem literally to block him in) tell us not only that his therapist is himself a Holocaust survivor but also that the therapist's office is "overrun with stray dogs and cats." "Can I mention this, or does it completely *louse* up my metaphor?" Art asks us, the readers, not Pavel. He then shows us a "framed photo of [a] pet cat. Really!" thereby reaffirming that in the therapist's office we are in the real world of Art's life (2:43; italics added). Art/ie's internal dialogue, not expressed to his therapist, but addressed to us, says something about what Artie is not willing to say to his therapist, which he probably should have shared with him. Artie needs to express to Pavel his feeling that the disorder of the therapist's office, overrun with animals, is somehow contributing to Artie's feeling that he is "messed up," feeling "lousy," and being "overrun" by his therapist's (as by his own) metaphoric displacements of the issues that are bothering him. The framed photo of the cat situates itself nicely as a stand-in for the other framed photo that dominates volume 2 of *Maus,* the photo of Richieu, to whom the volume is dedicated and which graces the opening page. That the drawing of the photograph depicts a real cat and not a cartoon figure further strengthens the association between the two photographs. Like the photo of the dead son, the photograph of the cat is a fetishistic object. It also embodies Pavel's deeply ambivalent relation to human beings. Pavel suffers from a basic distrust of people, and whether he intends to or not, he is communicating that distrust to his patient.

In keeping with the psychoanalytic theories of the day, Pavel is quick to ascribe Vladek's behavior to survivor's guilt: Vladek, he tells Art/ie, in the above quoted passage, "felt GUILTY about surviving." The passage then continues, providing Art/ie with one of Art/ie's several unexamined tropes: "And he took his guilt out on YOU, where it was safe . . . on the REAL survivor" (204). Yet as quick as Pavel is to attribute such guilt to Vladek, he is equally quick to deny feelings of guilt within himself. To Art/ie's question as to whether he too feels guilty, Pavel says no, he feels only "sadness," only to reveal to us, through Artie's rendering of the scene, how guilty he indeed feels: "It wasn't the BEST people who survived," Pavel explains; "It was RANDOM. / *Sigh*." Not only does Pavel self-punishingly not count himself among the best, but his claim for randomness flies in the face of what follows. Art/ie has expressed to Pavel his technical problem, now that his father is dead, in describing his father's work in a tin shop, whereupon Pavel immediately provides the necessary information, accounting for his know-how by saying he worked in a tool shop before the war. That Pavel then abruptly ends their session in order to walk the dog suggests that he wants to avoid further questions about how he might actually have acquired his tool-man's skills and how those skills might have contributed to his not so random survival. The best people were not the ones who necessarily survived, and those who survived did not always survive purely by reason of randomness.

Pavel thus simultaneously exposes and pushes away from his own story, acting out in the psychotherapeutic session. He also expresses his discomfort with Holocaust storytelling altogether. "Look how many books have already been written about the Holocaust," Pavel says to Art/ie. "What's the point? People haven't changed. . . . Maybe it's better not to have any more stories" (205; "It's enough stories," Vladek will say to Artie at the end of the book [296]). Even though Pavel assures his patient, "I'm not talking about YOUR book now," he has called into serious question Art/ie's entire artistic enterprise. No wonder Pavel has surrounded himself with pets, *lousing up* Art's metaphor, or perhaps exposing part of what informs that metaphor: the animals that play the roles of humans in *Maus* are not at all capable of doing what the humans they represent have done. When Art/ie counters Pavel's wish to silence him (another odd signal for a therapist to give his patient) by saying, "Samuel Beckett once said 'Every word is like an unnecessary stain on silence and nothingness [but] [o]n the other hand, he SAID it," Pavel agrees with Art/ie, only to violate the therapeutic relationship in one more way. He articulates his own fantasy of coauthoring Art/ie's book with him: "Maybe you can include it in your book," he advises Art/ie, which, of course, is advice that Art/ie is now taking (205).

By the time we get to the scene between Art/ie and Pavel, Artie is dealing not only with his father but with his "father's ghost" as well (203), adding a rather Hamlet-like dimension to an already Oedipal drama. Insofar as the father's ghost now doubles the other ghost in the story—the "ghost brother," Richieu—and insofar as both of Art/ie's and Richieu's parents are now dead, it is as if there is a complete and intact ghost family that has excluded, perhaps even expelled, the now literally orphaned Art/ie, who as the second volume opens is on the verge of producing a family of his own. How, then, shall Art/ie become a father? How shall he constitute a new family, and how will he not repeat the repetitions of the past? One route to the kind of art Spiegelman produces in *Maus*, which it turns out is also the art of living a productive and moral life, is contained in learning how to hear another person's story, including one's own. In this process both Vladek and Pavel have contributed importantly, and Art's telling us the story of his psychotherapy is one more avenue through which we as readers are being drawn into the listening process: if we see all too clearly how Artie is framing his father, and if we are thereby tempted to sympathize more with Vladek than with Artie (simultaneously attributing this construction of self-critique to Art), here we are invited to hear Art/ie's story more compassionately. We are asked to sympathize with Art/ie: to hear the wounded voice of the man who needs to imagine himself as a mouse in order to come to terms with the major narrative of his and his father's lives. The novel achieves on a level that the psychoanalysis cannot the psychological knowledge that can both heal the person—enable her to listen and forgive—and be productive of the creativity we witness in *Maus,* in which we ourselves are asked to participate as readers. Just as Pavel and Vladek finally figure in the final construction of Art, so does Art/ie himself.

In their volume of essays titled *Testimony: Crises of Witnessing in Literature, Psychoanalysis, and History,* Shoshana Feldman and Dori Laub (1992) suggest that witnessing the survivor's story serves to validate and thereby make real those experiences that seem to the victim implausible and phantasmagoric. As I have already suggested, Artie is not a witness of this sort. His father does not actually need validation, and in any event the son does not give it. Indeed, Vladek is, if anything, re-traumatized—or perhaps, more accurately (since it is not clear Vladek suffers from trauma), traumatized—by his son's ventures into witnessing his historical past. Only at the end of the text does Vladek slip and call Artie by the name of his dead son, Richieu (his "previous son," as he refers to him on the tapes). We are given a miniature version of the problem of the text as a whole within the text itself in the form of the son's earlier venture into comic book history, when he publishes the story of his mother's suicide and his father accidentally comes upon it. Reading the son's account of his mother, the father is sympathetic to the son's need to tell this story, just as he is sympathetic to his son's entire oral history project. Nonetheless, he is deeply pained by what he reads: "I saw the picture there of Mom, so I read it . . . and I cried. . . . It's good you got it outside your system. But for me it brought in my mind so much **memories** of Anja" (Spiegelman 2011a, 106). Artie is so much not on the side of his father's greater mental health in all of this that at one crucial moment in the text, to which I've already referred, he actually questions the accuracy of Vladek's claim that there weren't orchestras at Auschwitz, as if Vladek's memory lapse matters (214).

For this reason Artie is more like a witness for the prosecution than a witness of his father's testimony. Throughout the text he accuses his father of crimes against himself to which he himself testifies and finds his father guilty. Artie not only frames his father, frame after painful frame; he also convicts and incarcerates him. If anything, Artie is bringing false witness, framing his father for crimes he has not committed. When Artie calls his father a murderer for having destroyed his mother's diaries, we might feel, even if we sympathize with the son's wish to know his mother's story, that Vladek has demonstrated a respect for his wife's privacy of which his son is wholly incapable. At many moments in the text, as when he is ordering his father back into the camps, Artie is much more a patricide than his father is a murderer.

If Art Spiegelman's relationship with his father is any different from Artie's, it begins with the way his work of art *Maus* witnesses and frames his own testimony. It is clear from the start of *Maus* that Art Spiegelman knows a lot about the Holocaust. He also reveals, right from the beginning, in that opening section about the skates, that his father has hardly been silent on the topic. Vladek is not like the father in Anne Michaels's *Fugitive Pieces* (1998) or in David Grossman's *See Under: Love* (1989), who refuses to say anything whatsoever about what happened to him in Europe. Vladek's Holocaust experience is present and active in his consciousness, and he doesn't keep silent to his son. If Art needed to talk to his father about his wartime experience or, for that matter, their relationship, he could have done so at any time. He did not have to commit that conversation to print. A question we need to put to Art is what motivates him to tell this story, not simply of the Holocaust survivor, but of the survivor and his son.

As Freud understood, it takes two to witness the unconscious. Hence the job of psychoanalysis is largely to provide an external witness to the internal processes of the mind, which the subject himself may not be able to perceive. According to Freud's theory of the dynamic unconscious, the precipitates of that unconscious mind manifest themselves in our everyday lives in various thoughts, feelings, and actions that we do not consciously identify or comprehend. The job of psychoanalysis is not to make the unconscious conscious: the unconscious is just as the word suggests, *un*conscious. Rather, psychoanalysis is intended to help bring into conscious awareness those precipitates of the unconscious so that the individual is enabled to witness himself and in this way confront and surmount the compulsions, obsessions, and anxieties produced by repressed, unconscious materials. This is the psychotherapeutic role Pavel fails to play properly for Artie. And it is the role that Art the artist plays quite well to his less self-knowing younger self. He does this by insisting on the absolute neutrality of himself as analyst toward the unconscious materials of the patient, who is also himself. This means that Art is unrelenting in his detachment, objectivity, and criticism about his younger self, Artie—so much so, perhaps, that he represents his younger self as being of another species altogether (one more way of understanding Spiegelman's methodology). That there might be limits to this distance from himself of which Art is not fully conscious we need to recognize as well. Repression is a feature of the human psyche that no amount of psychotherapy is going to "cure." Indeed, repression is necessary to our survival as humans. (Mice probably don't need to repress anything.) What psychotherapy and psychotherapeutic art can do, however, is to replace less well functioning repressions with better functioning ones. They can free the individual from enslavement to dysfunctional behaviors that hinder the achievement of the individual's fullest psychological satisfaction. In the case of the stories of other people's lives, they can also enable us to more fully comprehend and sympathize with the pain and suffering of others.

What occurs in the final frames of *Maus* is that Artie becomes Art, and Art evidences the ability lacking in his less well developed alter ego not only to hear his father's story but to enter into and entertain his father's fantasy of the fairy tale that was his life. Indeed, by the end of the book, Art literally signs on to his father's story, by writing in script after the final frame of the narrative: "—art spiegelman 1978–1991." The lowercase letters indicate both humility and submission. Because this signature appears under the drawing of his parents' double tombstone, which is partially inside the frame and partially outside, Art's affixing the dates of the text's composition to his name, mirroring the appearance of his parents' dates on the tombstone itself, hints at resolution and acceptance, at least for the period of time it has taken him to write the book. So does Art's hearing, without murmur or objection, his father calling him by the dead brother's name. These are the concluding words of the text: "So . . . let's stop, please, your tape recorder . . . I'm **tired** from talking, Richieu, and it's enough stories for now." What immediately follows are the tombstone and signature.

This is not to say that there isn't a grimmer way to read the ending of the book (Bosmajian 1998). The end might still express Art/ie's anger and hostility toward his father. Indeed, we might read the end of the book as a repetition in mirror reversal of the picture of Artie earlier on, when he is narrating his text over the bodies of the slaughtered Jews. In this final frame Artie is being buried beneath the weight of his parents' lives and their death. In that case we might read the son's signature in small print and script as a kind of faint reminder of the parents' monumental status in his life and the trailing off of the Spiegelman family line into the tale (tail) of little art spiegelman. Perhaps there can never ever be a really happy, happy ending for this son, who, by some peculiar logic of his father's mind as it is pictured here, is never even born. The Spiegelmans do not display his picture in their bedroom. It is as if he never existed.

Mature acceptance can never exist apart from such further repression and resistance. A bit earlier in the book Art gives us an almost literal picture of what repression looks like, especially when aesthetically dressed up and displayed. He prints that extraordinary photograph (a real photograph, not a drawing) of his father, which is surely one of the oddest documents in the text, in anybody's reading of the book. Even Spiegelman himself, on the CD-ROM, refers to the photo that Vladek had taken shortly after the war as "troubling." "I passed once a photo place what had a **camp** uniform—a new and clean one—to make **souvenir** photos," Vladek explains to his son (294). And indeed the photograph shows Vladek looking young and handsome, very military, in neatly starched concentration camp garb. Indeed, the photograph vividly captures one aspect of what most defines Vladek, which is also what defines his narrative to Artie, if only we have ears to hear it (which is surely why Spiegelman places the photograph here in the volume): his defiance of everything that has been done to him and his wish to transform humiliation, filth, disease-ridden incarceration, and dehumanization into their opposites. This photo is decidedly of a man, not a mouse. Vladek, of his own free will, dons his prison uniform and makes himself into the hero of his story, the author of his own destiny.

But the photo is "troubling" nonetheless because what we also see pictured in the photograph is that what determines Vladek's choice of costuming is the degradation and humiliation he is now eternally compelled to resist. In anticipation of his numerous repetitive, compulsive behaviors, such as riding endlessly nowhere on his exercise machine and counting the pills that are always getting away from him, the photo freezes Vladek permanently in that position of the individual who can never free himself from his past experiences. It is through that past that he now asserts his identity. His every behavior bespeaks the suffering he cannot quite get past. Thus, the photo (especially as it is contextualized by Spiegelman's text) is a portrait of repression. Because the photo is embedded in the story of his life, we can also glimpse that repression from within as well, from behind the eyes that look out at us blankly and without emotion from the photo. We realize that the moment Vladek survived, his identity as survivor was issued to him like a camp uniform. Fortunately, this new uniform fits, for he will wear that identity for the rest of his life. The souvenir photo, which is modeled on a genre of such photos, in particular of soldiers, helps us to feel the force of social convention as well: the images by which we would assert who we are as a person are most often issued by culture. Vladek's freedom, from this perspective, consists only in his being his own captor. He will remain free only so long as he can maintain this pose.

In a similar way, the photograph also offers a commentary on the problem of documentary evidence, which genre presumably defines Artie's text, albeit not, as I have been arguing, Art's. Accompanying the reproduction of the photo is a drawing of Anja receiving the photo and, or perhaps as, the news of Vladek's survival: "And here's a **picture** of him!" she says. "My God—Vladek is really alive" (294). Anja immediately grasps what is surely a major part of Vladek's motivation in having the photo taken: the photo reveals the unbelievable fact of his having survived. *Here I am*, the photo announces, *alive and well, a heroic survivor*. (This may be a reason for many such souvenir photos of military personnel: it asserts their survival in the face of what was unrelentingly the possibility of their imminent death.) Thus, the photo is a paradigm of witness testimony. It documents or evidences the historical events that, having transpired, bear witness to Vladek himself as much as to his family of his own harrowing experience. Presumably Art/ie's inclusion of the photo serves a similar purpose for the reader. Like the tape recordings of his father, the photograph constitutes documentary witness proof. But what the photo also evidences, in both Vladek's use of it and in Art/ie's, is the fictionality of all evidences, even those of documentation and photography. This photo is *not* of a camp inmate.

Primarily, the souvenir photo evidences for Vladek the real possibility of what he thinks of as the happy, happy ending to his story. And this is the other side of the photo, the side we need to see in order to see Vladek clearly, in his three-dimensionality. In one aspect of its being, and wholly in keeping with the idea of manufactured fantasy images of reality, the photo threatens to make a lie of every detail of the story that Vladek has just narrated and his son has transcribed. It erases, sweeps away, and cleans up the horror, degradation, filth, and suffering that have been depicted frame after narrative frame of the book. It is pure fiction. If there is any full-fledged condemnation of the fictionalizing imagination, and thereby of the book itself, this photograph would seem to be it. And yet the photograph also demonstrates the value of such fantasy and belief. Having produced a cartoon version of one of history's most appalling human chapters, in which the fictionalizing imagination of the artist confesses in many ways over and over again its self-serving and fantasy motivations in telling the story of the past, Spiegelman produces the artifact itself: the father's narrative in the father's own language, unprocessed by the son except, of course, by its placement in the text. Even if the photograph is the height of fictionality; even if it as subjective and psychologically slanted as any tale the son tells, the photograph is the truest image we have of Vladek: the man who heroically survived and was, from the beginning to the end of his life, in his own view of himself, a hero, a sheik. It demonstrates that against all rhyme and reason happy endings do occur, however compromised and painful they are.

Imre Kertész presents a similar idea quite beautifully at the end of *Fatelessness* (1992). Kertész's narrator/alter ego is by no means deluded about the complexities of continuing his "uncontinuable" post-Holocaust "life," especially in relation to that "happiness [that] lies in wait for me like an inevitable trap." Yet happiness, Kertész's narrator recognizes, is also a part of the human condition and was so, even in the camps:

> Even back there, in the shadow of the chimneys, in the breaks between pain, there was something resembling happiness. Everybody will ask me about the deprivations, the "terrors of the camp," but for me, the happiness there will always be the most memorable experience, perhaps. Yes, that's what I'll tell them the next time they ask me: about the happiness in those camps.

If they ever do ask.
And if I don't forget. (190–91)

It is as if at the end of *Maus* Art finally thinks to ask his father, How do you *feel*? How do *you* see the story of your life?

Vladek is not wrong about his happy ending. In defiance of Nazism's intentions to the contrary (and it is the Nazi regime, we must remember, that is so dismissive of Mickey Mouse and the idea of the happy ending), he is reunited with Anja, they do go off to begin new lives in the United States, and they do have another child: the artist who is telling us their story. Who is to say for someone else what constitutes his or her happy ending? Or how much repression it is permissible for a happy ending to incorporate before it becomes madness or hallucination? By the strange, perverted logic produced by the Holocaust, even to be united in death or to have a tombstone (and imagine, a tombstone shared with one's beloved) is, like survivorship itself, a new definition of what constitutes a happy ending. That Richieu is there in his mind until the end also gives Richieu a burial place and—through his son Art's book, which is dedicated to Richieu—a memorial.

By permitting his father to address him as Richieu, Artie accepts the place that Richieu occupies in his father's consciousness, right up until the end of his life. As a new father, who dedicates the volume not only to his ghost brother but also to his infant daughter, Art has a new perspective through which to understand fatherhood. Indeed, in letting his father's last address to Richieu to stand uncorrected, Spiegelman incorporates into his already dual tale of father and son a double audience that multiplies exponentially the dynamics of the text: although his parents' lost child will, till the end, shadow Art/ie's own existence, making him forever not only the second child but the survivor child, Art comes to accept that the story his father has told him (both in a lifetime of actions and now, finally, in more explanatory words) was being told simultaneously, perhaps even primarily, to the other son as well, much as Rosa is telling her story less to us or to Persky than to Magda. For Vladek it is Richieu, if anyone, who deserves an explanation. At the end of the narrative Art acknowledges that his father's efforts to speak through the medium of art to the ghost child have not been in vain. The narrative stands as the father's testimony to the dead son. At the same time, however, Art couples that address by his father to the past with his own address to the future: to his newly born (and yet-to-be-born) children. On the other side of the spectrality of the past, which despite its lack of substance cannot be simply disbelieved and disregarded, is the equally unknowable, ungroundable future, which also cannot be denied. Between the two is perilously suspended the speaking voice of the present, mediating between the two. That is Art.

3 Aryeh Lev Stollman's
The Far Euphrates
Re-Picturing the Pre-Memory Moment

CYNTHIA OZICK'S *THE SHAWL* is not primarily about the problem of subject position. Yet it frames that problem in ways that open up the subject of Holocaust fiction to dazzling new scrutiny. In Art Spiegelman's *Maus* the problem of subject position moves to the center of the text. Frame after frame as the novel unfolds, and frame within frame as we read each of the storytellers/story-listeners enfolded within the other, we experience the profound impact of every listener's fantasies and fears concerning the stories being told. Each of these subject positions in turn gets expressed in the stories each listener turned narrator tells. In both *The Shawl* and *Maus* the exposure of the characters' subjectivities within the texts and of the author outside it frames our own reading. It holds up to us the mirror of the characters' (and sometimes the authors') failures to examine or deal adequately with their own fears and fantasies about the Holocaust. These fantasies and fears reflect not only their conscious thoughts about the Holocaust but also their largely unconscious motivations and incentives to think and behave in certain ways.

Aryeh Lev Stollman's *The Far Euphrates* (1997) explores this problem differently. Like Spiegelman's *Maus* and Roth's *Ghost Writer*, *The Far Euphrates* is a *Künstlerroman* (artist's novel). It tells the story of the artist not only as a young Jewish man but as a homosexual man as well. Aryeh Alexander is Stollman's Zuckerman, Art's Artie. The story is less eventful than contemplative and psychological. It has to do with how events that happen to others in the world, both in the present and in the past, have an impact on Aryeh Alexander and how other people's sadness and suffering come to construct the writer's sense of self, world, and God. Alexander's immediate environment consists of his parents: his father, a rabbi and scholar studying the far Euphrates, and his mother, Sarah, who is suffering her inability to have more children, not to mention her concerns about

Alexander; their best friends and next-door neighbors, the cantor and Berenice Seidengarn, who cannot have children and therefore are second parents to Alexander; the cantor's twin sister, Hannalore, who, like the cantor, is a Holocaust survivor and who now works at the Henry Ford estate as a maid; and a series of local events, such as the deaths of two young children, as well as of the young girl Marla, and of Sarah's institutionalized brother, who is suffering from an unnamed neurological disease. The novel also involves the protagonist's gradual coming into awareness of his homosexuality and of the demands of art. Through his temporary withdrawal from the world, in what the text calls his *"Tzimtzum"* (147; italics in original), the writer in this text—who is both the literal author and his protagonist (who carries his name into the text)—takes the horror of the Holocaust into the realm of writing. There, spirituality, religiosity, and morality, while by no means ever free from the dangers of our projections and fantasies, find a way to convey the story of other people's suffering that respects the integrity and autonomy of other people and their narratives.

Since Stollman is younger than either Ozick or Spiegelman, he writes in a later generation of post-Holocaust Jews. Stollman is therefore less concerned with the discovery of the Holocaust as a subject than with its recovery from the proliferation of facts, images, and projections that have already inundated the post-Holocaust imagination. The overly present Holocaust, the text suggests, might well have dulled our ability to experience and respond meaningfully to victims' stories. Stollman's concern, in other words, is with how we might have become desensitized to stories and pictures that have become nothing less than the backdrop of our lives, not to mention the screen onto which we project our own fantasies. The novel therefore works its artistic, psychological, and ethical magic in order to shock the reader into a new apprehension of the horrors of the Holocaust, which, it insists, happened to other people and not to us (unless, of course, we are survivors). In the novel's most dramatic scene—the unveiling of the gravestone of Hannalore—Stollman does nothing less than launch a physical assault on the reader's consciousness. He produces a controlled quasi- and mini-trauma that might just be capable of shocking the reader into a renewed consciousness of what occurred during the Holocaust.

Indeed, Stollman wishes to return his reader to the position of the generation that was contemporary with the Holocaust, which could barely fathom what was going on in Europe. He does this so that his reader might once again be capable of experiencing the profound shock of these events and the trauma-like impairment of sensibility that the Holocaust produced on an unprepared public. I say trauma-like because, as I have argued in relation to Vladek, not all survivors suffered from trauma in the technical sense of the word. Certainly, neither for those who were contemporary with the events nor for readers of Holocaust writings is there trauma per se. Rather, there was likely something more like shock:

a weakening of the conscious faculties and a loosening of rational thinking. That condition of impaired comprehension is for Stollman a prerequisite for understanding Holocaust narratives. More important, it is essential to moving on to a more deeply rational *and* affective comprehension of Holocaust experience, which might also permit the listener/reader to maintain a proper respect not only for what is unknowable in other people's suffering but also for the privacy of their experiences of humiliation and shame (the "pain in the loins," as Ozick's Rosa puts it). By linking the subject of the Holocaust with the issue of the narrator's coming into sexual (and intellectual) maturity as a homosexual male, Stollman expands the Holocaust subject into important new ground. In doing so Stollman risks alienating readers who, like myself, were trained to see the Holocaust as sui generis and not to be compromised by becoming a metaphor for something else. Stollman's achievement, therefore, is not only to keep the reader on the side of his protagonist but to make our difficulty in negotiating the homosexual theme a part of the process by which we renew and resharpen our sense of what happened in the Holocaust as well. Neither the Holocaust nor homosexuality is a trope for something else or for the other. Rather, Stollman's novel makes us confront how the underlying causes of both homophobia and the Holocaust have everything to do with a lack of respect for the inner lives of others and their differences from ourselves, and the degree to which human choices and experiences must be respected as private matters that are not to be subjected to public interrogation and judgment.

Repetition, Mind, and the Production of Material Consciousness

The Far Euphrates, I have suggested, is more a psychological novel than it is a dramatic novel. It is as much about the construction of human consciousness as it is about anything else. For Stollman, human consciousness turns out to be nothing less than our link with the divine. Therefore, what we think and feel about things is no trivial matter. Throughout the novel the imagery is informed by the idea that the material universe of objects, people, words, sounds, and even ideas is a manifestation of the immaterial universe of God. "My father," the narrator-protagonist, Alexander, tells us, "told me, to my great amazement, leaning across the dining room table, how God's sweet letters were also the powerful tools whereby He created light and everything in the universe: establishing the earth, suspending the sun and moon in the firmament for signs and for seasons, for days and for years" (1997, 3). That Alexander is told this over the dining room table is not a casual detail. In this universe of divine manifestations, human beings replicate divine processes physiologically, in their bodies. In a reversal of this, they also convert matter into idea. "Eat some music, *Alexandre*," our narrator-protagonist is instructed at the beginning of the text as he is passed cookies in the shapes of musical notes (2; italics in original), shortly to be followed by "sugar cookies in the shapes of those transmuting and buoyant letters that drifted down to us from the seafaring Phoenicians" (3). Stollman (who is by professional training a medical doctor, specifically a radiologist) is giving us a picture here of how the human body takes in the objects and images of the world and converts them into bodily matter. Insofar as this body includes the brain, impressions and experiences from the external world produce nothing less than mental consciousness itself.

To some degree all fictions work through structures of repetition in which the ultimate reach of such doubling or duplication extends to the relationship between the reader and the text. It is the possibility of such correspondences between the world within the text and ourselves that permits us to read fiction self-referentially, as somehow pertinent to us. In Stollman's *Far Euphrates,* however, the doubling of characters and events is so persistent and so pervasive as to claim our attention as a matter in their own right, in the same way that the graphics in *Maus* assert themselves as something worthy of our consideration. If as a graphic novel *Maus* implicitly poses the question of how we *see* or *picture* the events of the Holocaust, *The Far Euphrates* directs our attention inward to the neuropsychoanalytic processing that produces, and perhaps is even synonymous with, consciousness. How, the book asks, do we become conscious of other people's suffering, whether in relation to the Holocaust or anything else? The novel's network of repetitions and duplications produces a verbal picture of mental process as it pertains both to the book's characters and, ultimately, to the reader. This pattern of repetition, which produces a picture of mind, also extends beyond our physical reality to the realm of God. In the final analysis *The Far Euphrates* is more than a highly astute historical novel that recovers historicity as mental inscription in the physical brain. It is also a work of specifically Jewish art, in which the world we record in our minds is a world that originates in the mind of God.

Yet the repetitions through which we perceive the world and construct both our relation to that world and to other people carry with them the serious danger that we will forget the difference between the objects, persons, or events outside us and their relocation in the brain and that we will therefore blur together other people's experiences with our own vicarious experiences of those events. Even more than in the psychoanalytic view, in the neurobiological view of mental process, as Stollman is presenting it here, the events of our lives, which include our hearing or reading other people's stories, are, in the mind's terrain, physical inscriptions that produce immaterial precipitates. Considered as physical substance, from the mind's point of view there may be little difference among mental inscriptions, such that our transcriptions of other people's experiences may on some organic level be indistinguishable from the transcriptions of our own lived experience. Certainly our reception of other people's stories will become in the brain's recording of them mental experiences like all others. In *The Far Euphrates* the protagonist's mother fears for her son's sanity because he is, in her words, a "day-dreamer" (21). In the book's view, as articulated by Stollman's gypsy character, we are all daydreamers. We live as much within the world that the mind dreams as within anything we might determine to be an external, material world. Inner events repeat external events; we are mirrored in the replications of other lives that are reflections of our own, and somehow, in order to preserve sanity and logic, on the one hand, and, on the other (and just as important), to preserve the integrity and autonomy of others, we must derive ways of differentiating among different sorts of mental realities. In other words, we must separate out other people's stories from our own in order to prevent ourselves from being overwhelmed by other people's stories while remaining sensitive to and respectful of other people's experiences, which, we need to acknowledge, we can only (begin to) imagine.

To simply cite some of the more prominent of the novel's repetitions: the protagonist Alexander's mother, Sarah, and her best friend, Berenice, the cantor's wife, are frequently referred to as twins (the "Bobbsey Twins" [5] as Alexander's father the rabbi calls them). Although they are physically dissimilar, these twinned women choose to dress and behave in nearly identical ways. That these two women are also married to the rabbi and the cantor of the town expands this pattern of doubling, making the rabbi and the cantor also twins of sorts. There is also the doubling of the protagonist Alexander, who suffers from ear problems, with the young girl Marla, who is dying of heart failure, and the replication of aspects of both of them in Alexander's uncle, who has been institutionalized for some undisclosed degenerative disease and who, like Marla, dies before the end of the novel. There is also the odd reference to a maid at the estate of Henry Ford who is "almost identical in appearance" to the cantor's sister, Hannalore, who is, of course, the cantor's twin (18). And there is a gypsy woman there as well, who is also in some ways Hannalore's double: both Jews and gypsies, we are made to recall, suffered at the hands of the Nazis, most especially in relation to the medical experiments of Josef Mengele, of which both Hannalore and the cantor were subjects. Insofar as Aryeh Alexander carries a part of the author's own name into the text, there is a doubling here as well between author and protagonist (in the manner of Spiegelman's *Maus*), which receives further emphasis within the world of the text through the repetition of parts of Aryeh Alexander's name in the names of other characters as well, all of them dead. That homosexuals (like the novel's protagonist Alexander) were also targeted by the Nazis serves to broaden the historical reference contained in the twinning of gypsy and Jew. It also reinforces the link between the protagonist and the author, suggesting the author's own special and double vulnerability: he is a *Jewish* homosexual.

The most important twins in the novel, of course, and the ones toward which the other repetitions are insistently pointing are the cantor and Hannalore. Both of the text's most dramatic moments occur in relation to the Seidengarn twins, and both of these moments direct our attention not to what doubles duplicate but to the differences we must distinguish and respect, most especially between ourselves and whatever seems to replicate us in the text or in the world. The first dramatic moment involving the Seidengarn twins is when Berenice shows Alexander the photograph of the cantor from which the portion containing Hannalore's image has been cut away. The second and even more startling moment is the unveiling of Hannalore's tombstone, which is also, excruciatingly, the unveiling of her biological gender: "Hannalore Seidengarn," we discover with a shock (perhaps a shock of recognition if we have been paying enough attention to the clues), was born "Elchanan ben David," which our narrator quickly translates into English for us, lest we miss the force of this: "Elchanan, *son* of David" (191; italics added). The tombstone contains both of Hannalore's names in utter contradiction to each other, and the effect is mind-boggling, to say the least. Is Hannalore a man or a woman? Are the cantor and his sister identical male twins or not? How, then, do we picture them, as doubles or as radically different individuals?

What Stollman is doing in this scene (among other things) is staging a moment of frightening revelation in which we are not so much witnesses of as participants in the shocking disclosure. This is jarring at best, quasi-traumatizing at worst. If trauma is by definition a gap or absence in consciousness where affect displaces intellect or the two fail to inform each other in a meaningful way, the incomprehensible information that the scene of the unveiling throws at us produces what we would have to call a readerly trauma. Even if Hannalore has not been traumatized by her horrific experience—and, like Vladek in *Maus,* it may be the case that this survivor has not suffered from trauma per se—the reader of this text may well find that she has been psychically wounded, at least momentarily and partially, by the text's climactic unveiling of the gruesome facts of Hannalore's biological wound. The hysteria expressed by the narrator's mother at this moment in the text can stand for our own: "No one ever told me about Hannalore! No one ever told me! It's too much . . . it's too much. . . . I thought she was—" (193).

What we know about the cantor and Hannalore until this moment is that both of them are Holocaust survivors. We also know that they were victims of the infamous Mengele medical experiments on twins, which, as Berenice tells Alexander much earlier in the novel, have left the cantor and Hannalore unable to conceive children. Since Mengele experimented on fraternal as well as identical twins, there is no necessity for us to suspect that Hannalore had been born a man, although, obviously, identical twins were more easily identified and therefore constituted the larger population of Mengele's victims. There is an inherent affinity suggested in Stollman's novel between the physical mark of circumcision, which made Jewish males especially vulnerable to detection, and other physical attributes of Jews, which, like the attributes of identical twins, exposed or unveiled them as Jews. Jews are to some degree marked and very often identified by physiological differences, which inspired fear and anxiety in non-Jewish others. Indeed, by invoking Mengele's medical experiments, Stollman's novel points to the nature of anti-Semitism in Germany as being more racial and biological than religious (something *Maus* brings into focus as well through its animal imagery). The medical experiments on Jews can be understood as the Nazis' attempt to prove beyond a shadow of a doubt what they also knew was *not* the case: that the Jews were not human beings. Indeed, the inherent contradiction in the murder of the Jews is exposed in the medical experimentation on them: the Nazi doctors would discover through the mutilation of Jewish bodies universal biological features of human beings while simultaneously making of the Jewish body a nonhuman thing. Hannalore's humanity as a woman is testimony to the Nazi failure to prove the Jews nonhumans. Her gender shift suggests how insignificant even physical markers (in this case, a penis) can be in the definition of who is a human being.

That Jewish physiognomy disproportionately exposed Jewish men to harm has special pertinence to the protagonist of the novel. That both Aryehs are also homosexuals further strengthens, although it also complicates, the apparent linking of Jewish male vulnerability, circumcision, and castration. We must be very cautious here *not* to fall back on anti-Semitic and homophobic equations of Jewish or homosexual men with castrated males. As Alexander tells us very early on in the novel, whatever his mother's irrational fears for him, they have nothing to do with her suspecting he might be homosexual: "I was not effeminate; I did not lisp or play with dolls" (2).

Of course there are many clues throughout the text as to Hannalore's biological gender, which some readers (especially those who are well versed in Holocaust studies) might have picked up on, especially given (as noted) the greater likelihood of identical twins being identified as such. Hannalore, we are told, is a "weird creature" (101) with a "husky" voice (10). She is "Ugly. Ugly. Ugly" (33). She is also "a different woman from either [Alexander's] mother or Berenice" (9). And in what is perhaps the most telling clue of all, she is, in her own description of herself, "the twin without *anything* at all" (12; italics in original). That in the photograph of the cantor, which Berenice shows Alexander halfway through the novel, the image of Hannalore has been cut away by her own hand with "unsharp scissors" (86) provides another suggestive clue. Hannalore, we are told by Hannalore herself at the beginning of the book, has secrets that she will not disclose. Throughout the text we are being tempted to guess at those secrets, to see something in the novel's portrait of Hannalore (as in the photograph shown to Alexander) that we don't quite grasp and that also (rightly or wrongly, as is the case regarding Magda's paternity as well in Ozick's *The Shawl*) sparks our curiosity. Alexander's mother's incomplete exclamation, "I thought she was—" (193)

may suggest our own unconfirmed, albeit vague, suspicions, not to mention our somewhat salacious curiosity about Hannalore, indeed about survivors in general. The problem that the text raises is what we do with such questions, and with the answers.

It is Berenice, the wife of Hannalore's twin brother, who is given to articulate the text's wisdom:

> Finally Berenice caught my mother in her arms and for a moment shook her roughly, then slapped her, as if to say, It was not you who suffered so! It was not you who was dragged into the living darkness, into a living hell! And then Berenice held my mother tight as if she were a baby. . . . "Sarah, Sarah. They did terrible things to Hannalore, Sarah. Unspeakable. Worse than what happened to the Cantor. But even so, she was strong and used all her strength to make a new life. She wanted it to be secret while she was alive, and the Cantor promised her. Let her be our Hannalore. Let her be Hannalore." (193)

But Sarah cannot let her be Hannalore, and while we object to that, we have to concede that aspects of Sarah's response are not totally without merit. "My mother, exhausted, turned pale," we are told. "She opened her mouth wide and cursed God" (193). She curses her best friend, Berenice, as well, not for withholding Hannalore's secret from her but, rather, for having revealed this information to Alexander: "When you turned sixteen," she tells her son, "you went into your room and stayed there for a year. Just like a zombie. . . . Didn't you ever hear of the subconscious? You did what you did at the same age that the Cantor and Hannalore were first taken away" (195–96).

Alexander adamantly denies that the knowledge imparted to him by Berenice affected him this way. Nonetheless he is "shaken by this bit of information" (196), just as he had been earlier when Berenice first imparted the story to him: "I had to sit on my hands," he tells us at that point, "because they had begun to shake uncontrollably" (87). It would be a mistake, therefore, for us to dismiss Alexander's mother's observations as unfounded, despite her overly hysterical and deeply offensive responses to Berenice and her son. Both of Alexander's responses, first to the photograph and then to his mother's interpretation of his state of mind, take the form of somatic rather than intellectual responses, quite like his mother's reaction in relation to the tombstone unveiling. Even if Alexander's homosexuality is not to be explained by Hannalore's castration, his withdrawal from the world (so like Hannalore's withdrawal from the photograph and from her biologically determined gender) probably is. Berenice, we might feel, had no right to tell these things to a teenage boy. Some atrocities are too gruesome for even adults, let alone children, to assimilate: Yad Veshem has an age requirement for children entering the museum. In any event, however we might feel about Berenice's showing the photograph to Alexander or Alexander's mother's response at the unveiling, that unveiling is likely as shocking to readers as it is to Alexander's mother, and that shock replicates Alexander's experience earlier in the novel when Berenice first tells him (and not the reader) the story of Hannalore.

It is the renewal of the moment of shock, I suggest, that is precisely the purpose of the scene of the unveiling. In the unveiling Stollman would do several things at once. He would construct a moment of fright for the reader. He would also produce in the present moment a repetition of what was likely for the reader an earlier moment when the reader first became conscious of what had happened to the Jews of Europe. And, finally, he would suggest how that first exposure might have concealed (and continue to conceal) as much as it exposed. Just as in the scene of the unveiling Alexander's mother stands in for the reader, so in the earlier scene Alexander enacts the moment when most of us first confronted images of camp survivors and heard their stories. In that moment Alexander experiences a terror so powerful that he has to sit on his hands. So too we likely suffered such an experience of terror. Fright, Freud stresses in *Beyond the Pleasure Principle* (1973; first published 1920), is a primary requirement for the formation of trauma. Thus, in the scene of the unveiling Stollman's text would (re)produce in the reader something akin to that earlier potentially traumatizing fright. Why does Stollman need to wait to produce the reader's moment of virtual trauma until near the end of the text? In other words, why can't he make us privy, along with Alexander, to Hannalore's story earlier in the novel; why in this novel of so many repetitions does the text repeat also the moment of fright?

There are several important answers to these questions. That we do not hear Hannalore's story along with Alexander earlier in the text and do not see (except in its description) even the half picture shown to Alexander says something about how, at the moment of our coming to hear and see such things for the first time, there were many things we did not hear and did not see. Like Alexander, we never heard or saw more than half the story, and that half was only a poor and partial image of what was absent from the story, which continued to remain largely invisible to us. Yet we somehow imagined that the single image did tell the whole story. Since the missing half of the photograph that Berenice shows to Alexander presumably contains a duplicate of the image of the cantor, it also stands for the way we imagine one image to stand for every other image, multiplied by six million. But the missing half of the photograph also tells a somewhat different story. Hannalore's half of the photo also exposes aspects of the narrative contained but concealed in the picture of the cantor as well. The absent half of the photo is a better picture of what happened to the cantor than the picture of the scrawny but intact survivor. That we cannot see Hannalore's half of the picture—that, technically, we cannot see the photograph at all, because it is not reproduced in the text but, rather, only described—says something about how the best image of what happened to the camp inmates is the image that is not there, that cannot be brought into graphic consciousness except by reference to another image and through the highly distorting lens of the viewer's/reader's imagination.

The problem of the image's (or images') incomprehensibility is exacerbated, of course, by the fact that, like Alexander, many of us came to these images too young to absorb them. And, also like Alexander, many of us may well have suffered a form of fright made worse by the fact that we did not confide our fears and anxieties to anyone else. Berenice enjoins Alexander to secrecy, just as Alexander's mother enjoins Berenice to secrecy in relation to Alexander's uncle. Yet as Alexander is told by the gypsy woman on the Ford estate, "all secrets contain the seeds of death" (22). The book seems to concur with her on this. Even without his promise to Berenice, it is hard to imagine that Alexander would have confided this knowledge to his parents. Keeping secrets is a natural occurrence in Alexander's world. This is a world suffused with death and suffering—two children killed by a skidding car, Alexander's uncle, Marla—events that affect him deeply yet none of which he feels he can discuss with his parents. While *The Far Euphrates* is very clearly about the rights of Holocaust survivors like Hannalore to maintain their privacy, it is also keenly aware of the costs to the individual psyche of keeping secrets: the secret of homosexuality, for example.

Even more pertinent, however, to Stollman's purposes in *The Far Euphrates*, we readers are not told the story and not shown the photograph along with Alexander, because the picture of the "skeleton in striped rags with a dark, knotlike face" (86), "taken when he was liberated" and after "he had almost starved to death" (87), is an image that by now is so familiar to us that there is a true doubt whether, if we were literally shown the photograph, we would see it any more clearly than the half of the photo that is actually missing. We know this story of the starvation and liberation of camp survivors all too well. These images of survivors have become non-images (like the nonexistent other half). They have in their surfeit vanished from view. The pictorial arts (including photography) have had their own responses to this problem of the image glut, as Monica Bohm-Duchen (2003) and Carol Zemel (2003) have pointed out. *The Far Euphrates* is a literary version of painting's and photography's attempts to revitalize an image that is threatening to dissolve before our very eyes.

In *Family Frames: Photography, Narrative, and Postmemory,* Marianne Hirsch (1997) describes the post-Holocaust condition that, according to Stollman's novel, we all occupy and (in the text's view) must therefore dislodge if we are to truly see images of the Holocaust. "Postmemory," Hirsch explains, "characterizes the experience of those who grow up dominated by narratives that preceded their birth, whose own belated stories are evacuated by the stories of the previous generation shaped by traumatic events that can be neither understood nor recreated" (22). Postmemory, which is captured in *Maus* in the photograph of Artie's ghost brother as it is, in Stollman's novel, in the photograph of the cantor, is what we might think of, following the work of Nicholas Abraham, Maria

Torok, and Nicholas Rand (to which I've already referred), as *inherited trauma* (1994, 165–69). It is a bypassing of conscious knowledge, which we can never hope to restore to such consciousness, because it belongs to someone else's experience. For this reason its origins are literally and eternally invisible and absent—much like the missing half of the photo. The traumas to which we are exposed do not originate in us but elsewhere. They do not belong to us. And this, according to Stollman's novel, is a fact we need to recognize and respect.

The scene of the unveiling is an effort to bypass two interrelated phenomena in our contemporary relation to the events of the Holocaust. One is the consequences of such "postmemory," which has affected us in ways we literally cannot access. The traumas of the past belong to others and are at best only to be partially glimpsed by us, even in the most graphic and realistic representations, such as (half) a photograph. The other consequence is the glut of Holocaust images and narratives, which have no less than swamped our contemporary world and have resulted in our being desensitized to these same images that have produced our postmemory condition. It is as if we have become inured not only to the traumas of others but to our own wounded state as well. And that, for Stollman as for Dominick LaCapra, makes us poor instruments for the transmission of Holocaust memory and history. Thus Stollman would stage two different scenes of post-Holocaust awareness: the one concerning Alexander in which we retrospectively read in our own earlier and primary experience of exposure to images of the Holocaust; and the unveiling, when we recover the shock that we felt then but are perhaps no longer capable of feeling in relation to those historical facts.

The photograph of the cantor is from the start only half the story. Yet we come to realize that it is also a whole story and, in terms of the cantor (not Hannalore), the only story. The two halves of the photograph—the one omnipresent to the point of vulgarity, the other absent, invisible, terrifying in hints and clues we genuinely do not wish to bring to conscious mind—do replicate each other as much for what they don't show us as for what they do. Within the scene in the novel Alexander simultaneously does and does not see the image of Hannalore (after all, she and the cantor are identical twins). We, not seeing the photograph at all, see it in our mind's eye, since the image of the "skeleton in striped rags with a dark, knotlike face" is already emblazoned in our brains. Whatever image we do or do not see, however, the historical events that the photograph records exist quite independent of our perceiving minds. What we see is only the dim reflection as a mental event of what others experienced literally in their bodies. It is an impression that is also susceptible of dissolving into a generalized psychological condition of anxiety and fear, as it does for Aryeh Alexander, whose response to the terrifying effect of the photograph is to go into withdrawal from the world.

The text also refrains from giving us an actual photographic reproduction in the text, because the physicality of the represented image of the cantor might distract us from the far more important missing half of the photograph: the story that we do not know and that is more horrifying than we can imagine, the story that is closer to the invisible imprint of the story in our unconscious minds than a feature of our conscious intellects. The literal material photograph might become for us, or come to be for us once again, a fetish rather than a source of mourning and grief. It might become a way of preventing ourselves from putting the past to rest decorously and with dignity. To some degree all photographs are fetishistic objects, because, as Hirsch (1997) reminds us, they partake of two different epistemological fields: not only the unreal of representation but also the "real" of the quotidian world. In this way photographs differ from written texts, even though as we have seen, texts can also, become fetishes. "The photograph," writes Hirsch, alternately paraphrasing and quoting Roland Barthes's *Camera Lucida,* is

> a physical, material emanation of a past reality; its speech act is constative: it authenticates the reality of the past and provides a material connection to it. Reference, for Barthes, is not content, but presence. . . . The photograph [is not] a "copy" of reality, but . . . an emanation of *past reality: a magic* . . . evidentiary force, and . . . its testimony bears not on the object but on time. From a phenomenological viewpoint, in the Photograph, the power of authentication exceeds the power of representation. (6)

Hirsch continues, first quoting Barthes and then moving into her own voice:

> "The photograph is literally an emanation of the referent . . . light, though impalpable, is here a carnal medium, a skin I share with anyone who has been photographed." But it is precisely the indexical nature of the photo, its status as relic, or trace, or fetish—its "direct" connection with the material presence of the photographed person—that at once intensifies its status as harbinger of death and, at the same time and concomitantly, its capacity to signify life. (19–20)

For Berenice the photograph is a fetish of this sort. Otherwise, why would she carry it around in her purse? It is hardly the sort of photo most of us would want to show or be shown. For Berenice the photograph of her husband enables her to cope with the major disappointment and frustration of her life, which is not having children. Indeed, it is her saying to Alexander that she and the cantor cannot have children and that "God is blessing" (86) his mother by giving her a baby that prompts her to show the picture to Alexander in the first place. This aspect of the photograph as fetish also serves to recall the problematical fetishizing of the Holocaust (as in, say, a shawl that merges with a shroud, on the one hand, and, on the other, with a national flag) on the parts of certain individuals for whom Holocaust images become sacred in ways that are neither decorous, useful, nor particularly respectful of survivors or victims.

The book's criticism of Berenice in no way intends for us to dismiss her as a pathologically or even neurotically dysfunctional person. On the contrary, Berenice is a loving human being who is devoted to the cantor and capable of taking on his suffering in extraordinary ways. She certainly does not deserve to be treated the way Alexander's mother treats her after the unveiling, which might stand as a warning to us readers how not to respond to Berenice. Nonetheless, she occupies a certain relation to the Holocaust that is not so dissimilar from the relation that many of us bear. Insofar as she eventually goes to live with her brother in Israel, the book might even be suggesting a problem in the Israeli relation to the Holocaust as well. The sanctity of images, Stollman understands, can all too easily come to substitute for the sanctity of lost human lives, which cannot be represented either in words or pictures, and which we need to mourn rather than to hang on to, as we might a photograph or a book.

Trauma, Fetish, and the Rights of Repression

Berenice's photograph of her husband is not the only fetishistic object in the novel. But whereas Berenice's photograph belongs to a non-survivor and reflects other such images throughout the culture, the cantor's palm trees and Hannalore's crucifix occupy a wholly different status of response. Whether or not these objects suggest repression or trauma, insofar as they enable these individuals to cope with unimaginable suffering and loss, they are mechanisms that we need to respect, even if we see through them to what they displace.

Like Rosa's shawl the cantor's trees substitute for the children he cannot have. They are reminders of the loss he has suffered in terms of not only his procreative but his creative abilities as well. The cantor would have been a musician. The war put an end to that, just as it put an end to Rosa's dreams of intellectual fulfillment, which she projects onto the illustrious careers of her resurrected daughter. When the cantor's "beloved palms" (92) are destroyed in a tropical storm, "for the first time," Alexander tells us, "I saw a man—a man who once looked like a skeleton with a knotlike face, a man whom evil people had operated upon without anesthetic so he could never have children, a man who wrote the most beautiful melody I ever heard—I saw this man cry" (94). Like Vladek in *Maus*, collecting trash that might one day come in handy and having himself photographed in a concentration camp outfit, Cantor Seidengarn will forever incorporate into his identity traces of his camp experience. This is not to reduce the cantor to an automaton. The cantor's trees and his music express a beautiful creativity. Nonetheless, they continue to express the desires thwarted by the war, and they do so in ways that are largely unconscious to the cantor. Most of us do not name our trees, whether for musicians or anyone else. The challenge for us, as it is for Berenice, is to appreciate the cantor for who he is.

The case of Hannalore is more difficult than that of the cantor, and therefore it is more central to the workings of the novel. It is Hannalore who focuses the ethical demands being placed on the reader by the novel. After all, the cantor is a highly functioning member of his community. Whether or not Hannalore's injuries are more severe than her brother's (Berenice says they are), she responds to them in a more radical way. Since Stollman's narrative is not rendered through Hannalore's mind and since we do not get much information about her experience of the war, I do not want to speculate as to whether Hannalore's mental condition is technically, medically, to be defined as trauma or whether she suffers instead from a repression so severe that it borders on trauma. Within the technical psychoanalytical literature there is a question as to the degree to which repression and trauma are wholly autonomous phenomena or, instead, mark positions on an ascending scale of response to various kinds of experiences. There is, however, no reason to suppose that Hannalore is not fully conscious (emotionally as well as intellectually) of what has happened to her in the camps. As Freud had already pointed out in *Beyond the Pleasure Principle,* victims of catastrophic events who bear the physical scars of their experiences may suffer less from trauma than those who do not bear such visible evidences (which is not to say that such individuals do not suffer as much, just that they suffer differently). Even without her wound to remind her of what happened, Hannalore has the physical presence of her (once identical) twin brother to remind her of who she was and what she has lost. By labeling the experience of a survivor like Hannalore a "trauma," the listener or reader may be doing something similar to what Dr. Tree is doing in *The Shawl:* lumping survivors together and diagnosing them as all suffering from the same syndrome, thereby declaring, by contrast, our own mental health. In other words, the term "trauma" might describe our incapacity or unwillingness to imagine the experience of the survivor. Thus, it might facilitate our placing the survivor's experience outside our need to give tangible substance to it, because the story does not seem to be constituted by knowable features. Understood this way the designation of Holocaust experiences as "trauma" constitutes an evasion of a genuine confrontation with the survivor's suffering. The term might just seem a kinder, more sympathetic way to label the otherwise inexplicable behaviors of a character such as Vladek in *Maus* or Hannalore in *The Far Euphrates*.

Whether or not Hannalore is suffering from posttraumatic stress disorder, she does repress aspects of her experience. The most dramatic physical manifestation of this, aside from her re-designation of herself as a woman, is the cross she wears around her neck, *not,* I must stress, because conversion to Christianity is necessarily a symptom of anything at all, but, rather, because of Hannalore's denial of the significance of the crucifix. (Conversion, no more than homosexuality, is a symptom of disease in Stollman's novel, even if both human choices tell stories.) *"Oh, Rabbi!"* Hannalore says, almost flirtatiously, *"C'est juste un jouet— ein Spielzeug sozusagen!* It means nothing, absolutely nothing to me! It is just two silly toy sticks hitting each other over their heads. Click! Clack!" (11; italics in original). Yet early in the text, in a moment of stress, we see her clutching at the crucifix and crossing herself (32–33). And later her final request to the rabbi is to be buried with her cross around her neck. Hannalore's conversion to Christianity is as total and fully intended as her conversion to the female gender. This is ratified by the text, subtly but firmly, by the cantor's palm trees, which already have a Christian connotation, and which, during the storm, are seen to have "fallen over each other like sticks, so that they made a cross like the golden crucifix Hannalore wore" (93–94). The question the text is raising is to what degree we humans are entitled to our repressions and our conversions. Hannalore's decision to become Christian is also one more way that Stollman's text, like Spiegelman's, marks the difference between traditional Christian anti-Semitism, which, while certainly not treating the Jews kindly, never culminated in a Holocaust, and the racial anti-Semitism that produced genocide. Christianity is not the enemy in this book; Nazism is.

Donning the cross, like ripping herself out of the photograph, is a material action that displaces internal pain onto an external, objective correlative. In terms of the photograph, Hannalore's action essentially reenacts her wounding, but in such a way as to give her some measure of control over the pain she suffers. She does this at the cost of destroying a part of her biographical past, including the close identity she shares with her brother as well as her identity as a Jew. Yet wearing the cross provides a physical substitute for what has been lost: both the penis and the child that Hannalore (like her brother) might have fathered. As she herself puts it, Hannalore is "practically, deliciously invisible. A happy and contented ghost" (11). The cross around her neck marks the tombstone that is her living body. Insofar as the cross also remains a constant physical reminder of what has happened to her body, it provides the same kind of mechanism of control exhibited when she cuts herself out of the photo. Her cross is literally the cross she bears, which expresses, in order to limit, the otherwise limitless horrors of her injury. In this way the cross is like Rosa's shawl and the photograph of Richieu. If the shawl and the photograph keep the dead child alive, the cross, in a bizarre way, keeps alive the child who will never be born. Like so much else in this novel, the term "conversion" in reference to Hannalore's decision to become Christian and a woman is more than a mere metaphor. It describes the psychological, biological process by which human beings may convert horror and fear into something else. This something else is equally physical and also not entirely rational nor conscious. Yet it is somehow healthier than other reactions might be. The repressions that characterize Hannalore as well as the cantor and Berenice also extend to us readers, especially through the figure of Berenice, who, like most of Stollman's readers, is not a survivor. Repression is not always a symptom to be treated. Sometimes it is a sign of mental health.

Hannalore offers the book's major imaginative as well as moral challenge to the reader: How do we picture Hannalore? Do we see her as a castrated man or as a woman; as a Jew or as a Christian? And what does it say about us that we choose to see her one way or another? Throughout the novel Hannalore is presented as a woman. Another reason that Stollman does not let us in on Hannalore's secret until the end of the book is that he needs time for us to establish her gender in our minds as female. In order for us then *not* to see her as a woman, we have to violate that image we have of her. We have to un-castrate her. And when we do that, *if* we do that, we become, in imitation of the Nazis, the violators of her personal, bodily integrity. We yield to racial (biological) rather than spiritual definitions of the human. In its incompleteness the photograph pictures not only what cannot be told but also what it is that we recipients of the photograph cannot fathom or accept: how we are not a part of the picture and therefore how we cannot put ourselves in the place of the victim. We cannot imagine the unimaginable. Therefore, we do well *not* to violate Hannalore's privacy by trying to picture her at all. We need to accept the image that she has constructed for herself and by which we have come to know her.

Similarly, by the end of the book we may well need to see the cross as more relevant to Hannalore's identity than the Hebrew name inscribed on her tombstone. Hannalore's burial in the Jewish cemetery could (like the Spiegelmans' tombstones) seem the final triumph of Judaism over the Nazis' attempt to obliterate the Jews. However, it could also serve as the final evidence of everyone's unwillingness to let Hannalore be whoever she determines she is. That would be the triumph of a sort of fascism—different, to be sure, from the Nazi fascism that tortured and mutilated her, but nonetheless an attempt to impose ideological absolutes on the victim. Like Vladek in that photograph of him in concentration camp garb, Hannalore has worn a "disguise" for all of her post-Holocaust life (10), which conceals and expresses her repression. Yet it is Hannalore's right to picture herself as she wishes herself to be seen and to assume her identity, even if—like the tattoo on her arm—it will forever carry with it the imprint of the Nazis.

Tzimtzum and the Creation of Post-Holocaust Jewish Art

The cantor is not Hannalore's only twin in the novel. Her other twin is the protagonist-narrator, Aryeh Alexander, who, by carrying the author's name into the text, also doubles the writer Aryeh Lev Stollman. It is through his year of "isolating" himself and "withdrawing" into himself—his *tzimtzum*—that Aryeh Alexander becomes the author who produces the object we call art. "I knew that at Creation, God performed *tzimtzum*," Aryeh Alexander explains to us. "He withdrew into Himself, contracting His very being, and made within Himself an isolated place in which to set His universe—an infinite creation within an even greater infinity. There He organized all the attributes of His being in harmony. . . . This was something I then felt I needed to do for myself" (139–40; italics in original). Tzimtzum grants to the created universe a measure of freedom from

God's divine omnipotence. It constitutes a kind of withdrawal (a form of coitus interruptus on the large cosmic scale), which, precisely in its incompleteness, is progenerative. Tzimtzum is not intended as a permanent abandonment of the world. Rather it is a way of making space for and permitting authority, potency, and fertility, albeit on a human scale, to human beings. It is a part of a creative process, the process of creation.

Viewed from one perspective Alexander's tzimtzum is indeed a not so conscious reaction to and reenactment of Hannalore's mutilation. It duplicates the withdrawal from active saying and doing, which is simultaneously (for Hannalore and Alexander both) a withdrawal from a certain idea of masculinity. In this way it bespeaks a form of repression, verging on hysteria. Yet Alexander's withdrawal is only a temporary contraction out of the plentitude and fullness of his life, to which Aryeh Alexander returns in order to speak not only his own words in this text but also, and even more compellingly, in the scene of the unveiling, Hannalore's words, which, of course, become a part of his text. Not accidentally, it is to attend Hannalore's unveiling that Alexander withdraws from his withdrawal.

In *Representing the Holocaust* Dominick LaCapra reminds us that even if "there is a sense in which silence may indeed be the only way to confront a traumatic past"; nonetheless, "this contention does not justify a specific silence concerning something that can be said or with respect to the problem of attempting to say what can be said in the face of the risk that language may break down in a more or less telling manner" (1994, 122–23). The breakdown of language is part of what in Michael Rothberg's view constructs a "traumatic realism," as his 2000 book is titled. "Memory," writes Geoffrey Hartman, "especially the memory that goes into storytelling, is not simply an afterbirth of experience, a secondary formation: it *enables* experiencing, it allows what we call the real to enter consciousness" (1996, 158–59; italics in original). For Hartman, this potentially mediating and distancing function of memory is the achievement of literary language, which produces distance and the possibility of conscious reflection: "a massive realism which has no regard for representational restraint, and in which depth of illusion is not balanced by depth of reflection, not only desensitizes but produces the opposite of what is intended: an *unreality effect* that fatally undermines realism's claim to depict reality. . . . Art creates an unreality effect in a way that is *not* alienating or desensitizing. . . . It also provides something of a safe house for emotion and empathy. The tears we shed . . . are an acknowledgment and not an exploitation of the past" (157; italics in original).

Stollman's novel brushes up against the limits of articulation. That torn photograph, for example, picturing what could not be pictured in the first place is one expression of the struggle for representation. The virtually indecipherable, multilingual tombstone inscription at Hannalore's unveiling is another and more complex image of the same effort to put into speech what cannot fully be spoken, which is articulated, finally, by Alexander. Here is the climactic scene of the novel in its entirety:

> When the cover was withdrawn from the stone, I read the inscription. Hanna-lore's name was carved on top in English. As I read it I heard her own voice whispering, reading out her name to me. "Hannalore Seidengarn!"
>
> . . .
>
> I thought it funny to hear Hannalore speak her name now that she was dead. . . . I realized the voice might have come from within me. Perhaps her soul had even entered mine. . . .
>
> And while she spoke I looked underneath the English lettering to the small Hebrew inscription that contained the same honeyed letters that God used to create His universe in seven days: *Ud mutzal m'aish.* "An ember saved from the fire."
>
> Then I read Hannalore's Hebrew name: "Elchanan ben David." Elchanan son of David.
>
> . . .
>
> I see quickly the full words, a man's name, the son of another man. . . . But at that time it seemed I was reading everything slowly, letter by individual let-ter, until the ember spared from fire floated before me, burning brightly, phos-phorescent like the letters I used to imagine at Creation. The name itself be-came a little holy universe suspended before me, containing the components of my own name as well. (190–92; the component of his own name contained in the tombstone inscription is, presumably, *ben,* meaning *son*)

This is a mystical moment, when parallel universes collide: one that is the mate-rial, biological universe of parent-child descent, the other that is the spiritual creation of God: not only His physical world but the immaterial, textual universe of names and letters as well. When Alexander says that the letters on the stone are "like the letters I used to imagine at Creation," he intends not only the sim-pler, literal sense of that statement, that these letters remind him of his childlike imaginings of the divine Creation, but also that the text at this moment speaks as if in the voice of God, when at the Creation God imagined the world into be-ing through letters: these are the letters I used to imagine the world into being at Creation, says God through Alexander. If Hannalore is the "ghost" haunting this text, she is also its *shechinah,* or holy spirit, a designation of her being that is simultaneously Jewish and Christian.

Tzimtzum, Alexander tells us at the very beginning of the novel, before we understand its significance or even have seen the term, is "withdrawal and in-ternal realignment, a painful but necessary rearrangement of the hierarchy that exists in every breathing soul, the structure that mirrors the mystical shape of the living God Himself" (9). What Hannalore's holy spirit gives birth to through Aryeh is nothing less than an image of God. In other words, Alexander's tzimtzum, as now enacted in relation to Hannalore by making room inside him for her voice to speak, is divinely conceived. And it is penultimate and preparatory. It is not, nor was it ever, a final surrender to silence, but a moment on the way to speech of another order: the order of art (divine art), which in this scene literally speaks in the voice of another person. Such art maintains its humility before someone else's story of suffering. It acknowledges that no one else can ever truly know or understand someone else's experience, because it belongs to that person and not to anyone else. This art respects the silence of the sufferer. Aryeh Alexander will not force Hannalore to speak. He will not reinsert her into the torn photograph she has crafted as a picture of her pain. We might say that Hannalore's tearing herself out of the picture is her own version of withdrawal, of tzimtzum. It is her silent speaking, to which the text grants her full title. And it is progenerative: at one moment, at least, she will speak, through the author, her voice becoming literally the voice of the text as the text becomes no less than the voice of God. God, we might remind ourselves, is neither Jewish nor Christian.

Alexander's tzimtzum, both before Hannalore's death and at her unveiling, is not, then, so much an acting out as it is a creative response to what he comes to read as Hannalore's similarly creative act, her self-enabling self-representation, with its important excision/contraction, a secret she keeps, which he respects her right to keep. In this way art abjures projection, which makes of other people's suffering the stage on which we play out our own fantasies and fears. In the image of tzimtzum we also get a model of Stollman's idea of a specifically Jewish art. This is art that will preserve the memory of the Holocaust for future generations, despite the potential of the event to traumatize and render us silent, and without sacrificing the sense that these events belong primarily to others, whose secrets we are also obliged to keep.

Jews, Homosexuals, Others: A Postscript

To read *The Far Euphrates* as exclusively about an Oedipal complex writ large (even if only in relation to the protagonist) would be both simplistic and reductive. Nevertheless, the fantasy that shadows this text, in terms of the two Aryehs' self-conceptions and self-representations (reminiscent of the two Arts in Spiegelman's *Maus*) and in terms of the reader's responses, cannot be summarily dismissed. Indeed, what the novel has to tell us about the Holocaust and homosexuality has everything to do with fantasies of gender designation and bodily harm, both during and after the Holocaust. I do not think that Stollman is primarily, like Lev Raphael in *Dancing on Tisha B'Av* (1990) or like Lesléa Newman in "A Letter to Harvey Milk" (1988; in the collection by that name), simply reminding us that Jews were not the only victims of the Holocaust, that whatever the Nazis feared in relation to the Jews, they feared in relation to gypsies, homosexuals, and the handicapped as well. Gypsies, homosexuals, and the handicapped all figure in Stollman's novel. His purposes in including them, however, go deeper. One thing Stollman is insisting on is that fears of different others have not subsided in what is still a homophobic, anti-Semitic, and racist world. This world is none too kind to the handicapped either, nor to someone like Hannalore, whose gender is beyond our capacities of definition. Such fears as govern our attitudes to other people in our own world might characterize our responses to Holocaust victims and writers. That is, as readers we might ward off certain kinds of characters and subjects.

For example, in relation to *The Far Euphrates,* we might want to dismiss the homosexual subject as irrelevant to the major subject of the text: Jews and Jewish history. This, I think, would be a mistake. Like Ozick in *The Shawl,* Stollman is inviting both our discomfort with certain issues and our voyeurism in order to have us interrogate them, to ask ourselves what we fear, and why, and what it means that we read and interpret texts without a careful comprehension of our own subject position in relation to what we are responding to. One of the first awards Stollman's book received was from the Lambda Society for homosexual, lesbian, gay, and bisexual literature. For us to evade this aspect of the novel would be to not rise to the occasion of acknowledging Alexander's homosexual choice as an important component of novel. This would be like our failing to accept that Hannalore, whatever her biological definition at birth, through her own self-designation is now a woman. Berenice speaks for the book when she pleads with Sarah to "let her be Hannalore." Accepting human beings for what they are, irrespective of gender choice or sexual preference, is one imperative of this text.

Yet to read the novel as primarily a homosexual bildungsroman and therefore as *not* about the Holocaust, or, for that matter, not as Jewish fiction, would be equally absurd. Reviews of the novel, its critical interpretation, and its inclusion in syllabi on Holocaust fiction suggest that this book is quintessentially a Holocaust novel. Our refusing to see the novel as Holocaust literature would just be one more duplication in this novel of doublings of our refusal to see there the homosexual subject, as would, for that matter, our refusing to credit the text's decidedly Christian bent, which is likely also distressing, at least to some Jewish readers. The text has more in common with the Christian fantasies of *The Shawl* than meets the eye. This does not make the novel any less Jewish or any less a Holocaust novel. To read the text with a third ear, nondefensively, in order to hear what else there is to hear is the challenge of Stollman's text. To hear others in the same way is the challenge of our lives in a human world of indecipherable others.

SECTION II

GOLEMS, GHOSTS, IDOLS, AND MESSIAHS: COMPLICATED MOURNING AND THE INTERTEXTUAL CONSTRUCTION OF A JEWISH SYMPTOM

AT THE CENTER of my discussion in this section I address a set of interrelated texts, all of which express versions of the same symptom already introduced in relation to Cynthia Ozick's *The Shawl,* Art Spiegelman's *Maus,* and Aryeh Lev Stollman's *The Far Euphrates.* This is the symptom known as "complicated" or "incomplete" "mourning." My intention is to show how the texts themselves display the symptom that they expose in their characters and how we as readers might be similarly afflicted by this symptom. In the end, both the text and the reader might find themselves in possession of instruments by which they are enabled to convert "incomplete mourning" into genuine mourning. They would then be able to get on with the important work of remembering and commemorating. Nonetheless, in the first instance what the texts represent in their characters as an obsession with the murdered past to some significant degree characterizes the texts themselves.

Since the books I discuss here are authored by Jewish writers, perhaps the symptom expressed by the text is a Jewish symptom, or at least a symptom to which Jews in the post-Holocaust world are particularly susceptible. And perhaps that means that Jewish readers (like myself) must take a particular kind of caution in their relation to the subject of the Holocaust, which I have tried to do by interrogating my own interest in Holocaust fiction, not to mention how I read a particular text. Non-Jewish readers, of course, will need to guard against other potential interferences in their relation to the Holocaust. That is my subject in section 3 of this study. Obviously, I can only comment on the non-Jewish subject position from my own Jewish one, and therefore I must be aware of potential defensiveness on my own part, which I will need to resist. All inheritors of history, all readers of texts, if they are to engage the object of study fairly and with respect, cannot do less in terms of self-skepticism and self-interrogation.

To recap what I said in my first chapter in relation to the symptom I am calling incomplete mourning: incomplete, complicated, or blocked mourning involves the internalization (introjection) of a lost loved object who cannot be properly mourned because of ambivalences and unresolved issues in the relationship between the bereaved individual and the deceased. Incapable of mourning properly, the mourner attempts through various means to keep the dead person alive. Therefore, the deceased person remains a virtual entity within the mourner, producing the condition that Freud defined in "Mourning and Melancholia" (1973b; originally published 1915) as melancholy. In Ozick's *The Shawl* the dead baby's shawl becomes for the mother the fetishistic object, the idol (as Rosa's niece unkindly labels it), which in the book reveals the mother's inability to mourn in such a way as to lay the dead child to rest. It is because of this complicated mourning that Rosa persists in conjuring her dead daughter and entering into conversation with what we understand to be not the living child but that part of Rosa's own consciousness that preserves the child as a living presence within her. Rosa would finish her unfinished business with her daughter, a virtually impossible and highly exhausting psychological task. It is a task that prevents Rosa from getting on with her life until Persky becomes the listener who might finally hear Rosa's pain sympathetically and without judgment.

Incomplete mourning characterizes Vladek and Anja Spiegelman in *Maus* as well, and their incapacity to mourn the death of their first child, as of their many relatives, suggests how the incomplete mourning of one generation can spill over or (to use a comic book term) bleed into the life and narrative of the next generation. Artie is infected by his parents' melancholy. This is especially apparent in the second volume of *Maus,* written after Vladek has died and subtitled *My Father Bleeds History.* So does Artie, and neither Artie's nor his father's bleeding is ever wholly cauterized, even at the end, when Art/ie (as I have tried to suggest) seems finally to mourn his parents' deaths. "Bleeding" technically refers in graphic novels to the way colors or images run from one frame into another. This describes exactly the configuration of the final image of the Spiegelmans' tombstone. It is impossible to determine wholly whether Artie has finally buried his parents emotionally as well as physically or whether their wounds continue to bleed into his. Indeed, Spiegelman's graphics throughout *Maus* might be understood as one more venue through which the author exposes his own tendencies toward object fixation, fetishism, and iconographic idol worship, at least as characterized in his younger self or in that part of himself that will always remain the son rather than the artist (who of us does not have such a self?). If the parents' photograph of Richieu is, like the photo carried by the cantor's wife in *The Far Euphrates,* a fetishistic object, so (potentially) is Artie's graphic art, which is also a picture and which we also see inherits unawares his father's talent for diagramming. Art always contains its fetishistic dangers. That does not in the least diminish its power as art. Insofar as art speaks to the readers' own deepest fantasies (as Freud argued in "Creative Writers and Day-Dreaming" [1973a]), its fetishism is necessary in order for it to communicate to us, especially when it comes to our own fetishistic inclinations. Graphics will return as a major trope in many of the texts I discuss in this chapter.

In order to understand how the symptom I am calling "incomplete mourning" does not necessarily have to signal either pathology or severe neurosis and therefore how it can describe a literary or graphic text, I need to expand upon what I mean by the term "symptom." As Slavoj Žižek defines it, the symptom is

> the way we—the subject—"avoid madness," the way we "choose something . . . instead of nothing" . . . through the binding of our enjoyment to a certain signifying, symbolic formation which assures a minimum of consistency to our being in the world. . . . In the real of [the] symptom is the only support of [an individual's] being. . . . The symptom is not only a ciphered message, it is at the same time a way for the subject to organize his enjoyment.

Of special pertinence to reading literary texts is Žižek's further assertion that the symptom "not only can be interpreted but is, so to speak, already formed in view of its interpretation. . . . There is no symptom without its addressee" (1991, 206–208).

By the term "enjoyment" Žižek means what Freud means in "Beyond the Pleasure Principle" (1973d) by the term "pleasure." Freud's essay is indeed the text that prompts Žižek's thinking in this matter, as it does Jacques Lacan's before him. Pleasure for Freud has to do with how we human beings maintain our mental stability in the face of everything that threatens to disrupt it. Such forces of disruption include ordinary, everyday matters from infancy on. However, they also include more dire matters, such as what is the key topic in the Freud essay and a major trope and topic within much Holocaust writing as well: trauma. An underlying contention in psychoanalysis, as formulated by Freud, which the terms "pleasure" and "symptom" bring into focus, is that human behavior makes sense. This is *not* to say that a person's behavior is rational, that it makes sense according to some external standard of reason. Nor does someone's behavior necessarily make sense to others or even to the individual herself, from a conscious, rational perspective. Saying that a person's behavior makes sense is also not to claim that such behavior is ethical or that it necessarily serves the individual's best interests. From some internal, unconscious point of view, however, the behavior does make sense. It tells a story, which both the individual and anyone attending to her might want to understand.

My reason for applying a psychoanalytic perspective to Holocaust fictions is not to diagnose pathologies or neuroses in persons or texts. Rather it is to discover what additional sense we can glean in the written or enacted stories of both characters and texts, and how that meaning-making sheds light on our own meaning-making as readers. To what degree do the "symptoms" that characterize the fictions' characters or the fictions themselves pertain to us? And therefore what might we want to understand about those human or textual symptoms in order for us, as recipients of other people's histories and stories, to find better, more ethical, and more useful responses to the suffering of others? Many of us, especially Jews like myself, are inclined to mourn the victims of the Holocaust, whether or not they were close relatives. This seems like an ethical obligation, and I believe it is. Yet we must ask ourselves to what degree do factors other than sadness for the deaths of others get in the way of that mourning so that we become melancholic rather than mournful, fixated, or otherwise obsessed with the Holocaust rather than engaged in meaningful intercourse with it? Mourning is a process that comes to an end. It yields to remembering and memorialization. Melancholy is not mourning; rather, it is the condition of mourning unresolved. It stymies both conscious contemplation and fruitful communication with the past. It permits us to conflate the living and the dead and to assume positions that might be in the interests neither of preserving the memory of the dead nor dealing with the living realities of the present.

As I have already begun to argue, the texts that interest me in this section all represent—in two senses of the word "represent"—the same complex processes of complicated mourning that occur in *The Shawl, Maus,* and *The Far Euphrates,* even if by the end they also produce at least implied models of mourning, often based on the Jewish ritual of sitting shivah (the seven days of mourning following the death of a family member). In the first instance the texts represent incomplete mourning as a condition that characterizes aspects of the characters' (survivors' or children of survivors') responses to loss and bereavement. The texts also, however, represent such mourning in their own narrative structures. In other words, the consciousness of the text—whether we wish to identify that consciousness with the real author (which I prefer not to do) or to take it as a fictive construct informed by unconscious elements of the writer's psyche—also displays the symptoms of incomplete mourning that the text simultaneously exposes and criticizes vis-à-vis the characters in the text's created world. The consequence of the two parallel lines of incomplete mourning is that both the characters in the texts and the texts themselves become involved in forms of conjuring and idol worship, escapist fantasies, and the production of golems and messiahs. Their mode of interaction with the world is one of melancholy, which may well correspond with the reader's own melancholic position, at least while reading the text. Such mirrored and endlessly re-mirroring melancholy can leave the reader in the same position as the texts' characters: endlessly mourning. Or it can produce self-illumination and self-consciousness such that the reader can come to mourn (which is to say also to read) in a healthier, more productive way.

Indeed, as I have been suggesting, insofar as some of us have chosen the study of the Holocaust as an academic project, the texts may permit us to glimpse how the Holocaust has become for us an idol of sorts or a fetish that blocks rather than expresses mourning. And we might thereby discover how to conduct our academic project in such a way as to return us to mourning and to its eventual culmination in memory and commemoration. I conceive my project in this book as just that. As I have indicated, just as Anne Frank figured in my early development as an icon of sorts, so I also know firsthand something about the tendencies toward incomplete mourning that will once again concern me here. There are aspects in my responses to these texts that I needed to examine and clarify to myself to the best of my ability and, if I am to produce meaningful scholarship, expose to my reader as well.

4 Bruno Schulz, the Messiah, and Ghost/writing the Past

THE INDIVIDUAL WHO in most of the texts I discuss in this section (although not all of them) figures as the object of the characters' and texts' incomplete mourning, and whom both the texts and their characters idolize and resurrect, is the murdered Polish Jewish writer Bruno Schulz. In *The Modern Jewish Canon*, Ruth Wisse (2000) laments not having discussed Schulz in her book, and she astutely asks:

> Has any writer exerted greater influence on emerging Jewish literature than the enigma from Drohobycz . . . ? In what must be the highest form of literary appreciation, the American Cynthia Ozick made a lost manuscript by Schulz the centerpiece of her novel *The Messiah of Stockholm* (1987) at almost the same time that the Israeli writer David Grossman animated his deathless spirit in the novel *See Under: Love.* (347–48)

Schulz's influence on recent literature, I suggest, is even broader and deeper than Wisse and others, such as Naomi Sokoloff (1988), and David Goldfarb (2011) have observed. Indeed, it has become something of an obsession. Wisse's own reference to Schulz as a "deathless spirit" might suggest how she, too, has succumbed to the power of this resurrected ghostly idol. In addition to Ozick's *Messiah* and Grossman's *See Under: Love,* I include in this legacy of direct inheritance of Schulz (in chronological order of composition): Aharon Appelfeld's *The Age of Wonders* (first published, in Hebrew, in 1978; English translation in 1981); Philip Roth's *The Prague Orgy,* the fourth in the Nathan Zuckerman novels and the culminating piece in the publication titled *Zuckerman Bound: A Trilogy and an Epilogue* (1985); Michael Chabon's *Amazing Adventures of Kavalier and Clay* (2000) and his *Final Solution: A Story of Detection* (2005); Nicole Krauss's *History of Love* (2005); and Jonathan Safran Foer's *Tree of Codes* (2010b). Another novel that might be added here is Danilo Kiš's *Peščanik* (1972; later published in English translation as *Hourglass* in 1990). Since Kiš is a Serbian writer, he is somewhat outside my area of expertise, as is Aleksandar Hemon (from Sarajevo), whose

The Question of Bruno was published in 2000. It is to be noted, however, that Kiš's Jewish father died in a concentration camp and that the novel, like Schulz's writing and like many of the texts I discuss in this chapter, is obsessed with the father and his ghost. Several texts that do not directly engage or evoke Schulz that I nonetheless include in my discussion are Anne Michaels's *Fugitive Pieces* (1998); Dara Horn's *The World to Come* (2006), which is also not a Holocaust novel; and Krauss's *Great House* (2010). I include these books because they, too, express the dominant features of incomplete mourning in relation to Jewish history that are suggested by the other texts in this intertextual nexus. They resonate deeply with the Schulzian texts.

All of this rewriting and evocation of Bruno Schulz is quite remarkable given how slender a canon Schulz produced: a mere two volumes in Polish. Indeed, had it not been for the attention focused on him by these American and Israeli authors, Schulz might otherwise have disappeared from the literary landscape, at least within Western European, Israeli, and American literature. Indeed, interest in Schulz is initiated through the efforts of one of the writers in this group of authors, Philip Roth. In 1977 Roth facilitated the republication in English of Schulz's *Street of Crocodiles* (1963; published in Polish in 1934) as a part of his Writers from the Other Europe series (the series that also published Tadeusz Borowski's *This Way to the Gas, Ladies and Gentlemen* in 1976 [originally published in Polish in 1959] and also Kiš's *Hourglass*). This is the same year that saw the publication for the first time in English of Schulz's other novel, *Sanatorium under the Sign of the Hourglass*. Cynthia Ozick dedicates her *The Messiah of Stockholm* to Roth, a favor Roth returns by specifically alluding to Ozick's novel in *The Prague Orgy*, in which the Writers from the Other Europe project is directly invoked. Nor is it mere coincidence that it is in an interview with Roth in 1988, only a year after the publication of Ozick's and Grossman's novels, that Aharon Appelfeld explains that although Schulz came to his attention too late to be a major influence on his writing, he experienced a profound affinity with his work (1994, 63–65). Not only do these writers share an obsession with Schulz; they are cognizant that their adoration of the dead writer is shared by others in their field.

Because Schulz was killed by the Nazis, he comes to stand in these texts for a whole generation of Jews slaughtered in the Holocaust. For this reason, Schulz rather than Kafka is the Jewish writer whom these texts consciously or unconsciously resurrect. Kafka may have foreshadowed, even prophesized the Holocaust, but he was not one of its victims. As Roth puts it in "'I Always Wanted You to Admire My Fasting'; or, Looking at Kafka," Kafka "died too soon for the holocaust" (1975, 89). Therefore, he can be assimilated into both Jewish and non-Jewish literary history in a fairly traditional way. Not so the murdered Bruno Schulz. Since Schulz was also a Kafkaesque writer, he does double duty in these texts. He serves to incorporate both Kafka and himself in the processes of complicated mourning that the texts represent. Schulz helped his fiancé translate Kafka's *The Trial*, and his writing does bear a deep affinity to Kafka's.

In addition to these factors Schulz emerges as a central figure in these texts because he is rumored to have authored a now lost (perhaps never written) text titled *The Messiah*. Therefore, Schulz also represents the Jewish art that was also lost in the Holocaust, as well as the texts never written because of the murder of the artists who would have produced those works. The texts I discuss in this section all deal one way or another with lost, forged, or perhaps never written documents or manuscripts, a feature that makes these texts recall several other precursor texts: a short story by Isaac Bashevis Singer, for example, titled "The Manuscript" (in Singer 2011) and two short stories by Cynthia Ozick: "Envy; or, Yiddish in America" (1971) and "Usurpation (Other People's Stories)" (1976). As Ozick puts it in "Usurpation," "Occasionally a writer will encounter a story that is his, yet is not his" (131). The texts that I discuss here seem to concur. Whether in imitation of Schulz's perhaps apocryphal text or as themselves acting to save or recover that text, many of these fictions also deal with resurrections and with messianic figures, as does Ozick's short story. The Jewish messiah that emerges in these Schulzian texts has everything to do with the incomplete mourning they express in relation both to dead Jews and lost Jewish art works.

Since part of my intention in this section is not only to put several texts into dialogue with one another but also to produce a sense of the obsessive, compulsive whirl of repetitions and fixations these texts create when this dialogue ensues (not to mention how that whirl might catch the reader in its violent vortex), let me take a breath and briefly summarize the texts that feature most prominently here, in particular as related to the figure of Bruno Schulz. Several of them deal directly with the real Schulz. Ozick's *The Messiah of Stockholm*, for example, creates a child survivor now living in Sweden who fantasizes that his father is the dead author Schulz and who conceives his primary mission in life as recovering his father's lost manuscript, *The Messiah*. That manuscript does or does not make its way into his hands, depending on how you interpret the evidence of the story. Whether genuine or not, however, the manuscript recovered in Ozick's novel winds up in ashes, like the many Jewish artists who perished in the Holocaust, although not Schulz. In *See Under: Love* David Grossman constructs an equally Holocaust- and Schulz-obsessed character—not a survivor, but a child of survivors—in Israel, who, like Artie in *Maus*, believes he needs to know his parents' story in order to get on with his life. Momik fixes on Schulz as the muse who might secure for him both emotional sanity and artistic creativity. Grossman devotes an entire section of the novel to producing a surrealistic, phantasmagoric portrait of Schulz; and he places his protagonist Momik in direct conversation with the dead writer. He also imports the story of Schulz's death into the biography of another of the characters in the book, thus creating two Schulzes (Michael

Chabon in *The Final Solution* [2004] also splits Schulz into two characters). This other Schulz is Momik's great uncle Wasserman, who is also a writer and who died in the Holocaust. It is Wasserman's story that Momik would really like to tell but believes he is incapable of doing.

In *The Prague Orgy* Roth projects Schulz's story onto an Eastern European Jewish writer named Sisovsky, whose manuscripts Nathan Zuckerman is commissioned by the writer's now ex-patriot son to smuggle out of Prague. As in the first novel in the trilogy, to which *The Prague Orgy* is the epilogue, Zuckerman here plays out his conflicted Jewish identity: his wish to be a reputable member of the community, especially in his father's eyes, and his desire to be an artist in his own right. The recovery of another writer's Jewish manuscript would, for Zuckerman, serve an ethical purpose. However, it might also put to an end to or at least overshadow his own creative career. That Zuckerman fails in his mission to smuggle out the manuscripts might have to be understood as his signaling to the reader that he has succeeded in his other more important mission: to be a writer rather than a rescuer of others' texts.

Prague is, of course, the home of the famous Golem, who is thereby also alluded to in Roth's story and who becomes a central figure in another of my intertexts: Michael Chabon's *The Amazing Adventures of Kavalier and Clay* (2000). In Chabon's novel one of the two major characters escapes the Holocaust along with the Golem in the Golem's coffin, which returns at the end of the novel at the survivor's door. Joe Kavalier's graphic art, which puts us in mind of Schulz's other career as an artist, has everything to do with getting past his unceasing mourning for his parents, his brother, and his teacher (who is actually described in Schulz-like terms). Eventually Joe will produce a Jewish comic book about the Golem, and he will be reunited with his wife and son, whom he had abandoned because of his grief over the death of his little brother. Like Aryeh Stollman's Alexander, the other graphic artist in *The Amazing Adventures* is homosexual, and Chabon's novel is as much concerned with Sam Clay's coming to terms with his sexuality as with Joe's finding a way to mourn the past. Clay, we discover in the novel, also suffers from incomplete mourning, in relation to his father, the Mighty Molecule, who abandons him and his mother when Sam is still a child. The "river-clay" (119) out of which the Prague Golem was made, which arrives on Joe's doorstep, becomes in Clay the dynamism and vitality (the mighty molecules) of life in the United States, which offers new creative artistic and life possibilities, especially for Jews.

Appelfeld's engagement with Schulz is similarly indirect, even though his major character is actually named Bruno. In *Age of Wonders* Appelfeld is primarily concerned with the crisis of Jewish authorship produced not only by the Holocaust but by the anti-Semitism that preceded it, especially in European intellectual circles. Like Grossman's Momik, Appelfeld's Bruno is an Israeli writer who is stymied in his authorial career. His father was a writer in the tradition of Kafka, Zweig, and other Jewish writers, all of whom are cited in the text and all of whom were condemned as degenerate by the Nazis (as they are by the communists in *The Prague Orgy*). Bruno travels back to his childhood town as part of a project concerned with republishing his father's writings. What he discovers there is not only the ghost of the Jewish community but the ghost of his father and his father's authorial ambitions as well. Since the story of the father in the years leading up to the Holocaust is recorded in the first part of this two-part novel, we might take the first part of the text as authored by Bruno and therefore as evidence of Bruno's eventual artistic recovery as he repairs his relationship to the Kafkas, which is also to say, the Schulzes, of his past. There is certainly a Bruno Schulzian quality to the novel as a whole, proving Appelfeld's declared affinity with Schulz's writings.

In Krauss's *Great House* the link is not to Schulz directly, but to the recovery of a desk, an object closely enough affiliated with writing to stand in for a lost manuscript. In this novel of multiple narratives, the desk is the possession (by which many of the characters are possessed) that circulates among the protagonists of the novel, many of whom are authors, thus linking their stories together. What they are thus linked to, however, is for one of the characters in the novel nothing less than a figure of obsession. It is the fetish that is the symptom of the character's blocked mourning for his murdered father. For the antiquities dealer George Weisz the desk is the last item he needs to recover in order to reassemble in Jerusalem his father's study, which was destroyed by the Nazis in Budapest. The obsession with the desk brings pain and suffering until, like the "great house" of Yochanan ben Zakkai, the desk recovers its proper place as a spiritual link rather than a literal object. Just as Jewish learning comes to substitute for the destroyed temple in Jerusalem, so the desk becomes what Bruno Schulz in *The Street of Crocodiles* called "The Book," in this case a book titled *Great House*.

The literal recovery of a lost object is also the major motif of Dara Horn's *The World to Come*, in which the protagonist steals from the Jewish museum a work of art that used to hang in his parents' home. The painting turns out to conceal a Yiddish manuscript as well. That double object, painting and manuscript combined, must also discover its continued existence in its dissemination and translation over continents and time—that is, into a world to come, which is not the hereafter but the here and now as transformed by our willingness to let the past go. In Anne Michael's *Fugitive Pieces*, Ben, a son of survivors, is set on a similar quest of discovery in which the object is the poems and letters of another Jewish writer, Jakob Beer. Beer is the survivor, who must himself get past his complicated mourning, in particular for his sister, and who finally does so both through his writing and through the love of a very special woman, not coincidentally called, in this novel by Anne Michaels, Michaela. Like Krauss's *Great House*,

Michaels's *Fugitive Pieces* replaces the literal with the literary. Ben must inherit Beer's own insights into this displacement of the literal by the literary in order to get past his own emotional troubles. Since the difficulties of Ben's parents mirror the incomplete mourning suffered by Jakob in relation to his dead sister and parents, the poet's life and work serve to illuminate for Ben his own need to get past the condition of incomplete mourning, which, as in Grossman's and Spiegelman's works, is inherited rather than acquired firsthand.

The evocation of Bruno Schulz in Chabon's other novel, *The Final Solution: A Story of Detection,* is more direct, even though Schulz himself does not appear in the book, except, as in Appelfeld's *Age of Wonders,* through the use of the name and, as in *The Prague Orgy,* through the imposition of Schulz's story onto one of the characters, a strategy in Grossman's *See Under: Love* as well. Here Bruno is a parrot who is the object of an investigation by a Sherlock Holmes–like detective, who is trying to arrive at a final solution as to why the bird has been kidnapped and how he can retrieve it. To other characters in the novel, the bird, who is the sole companion of a mute Jewish refugee child, seems to hold the key to unlocking either German war codes or a Swiss bank account. To the reader, however, he seems to somehow decode that other Final Solution to which the book's title also, obviously, refers. Bruno Schulz is evoked as well, and more directly, in the novel through the story of the child's father, a psychoanalyst, who is initially kept alive by a German officer in the same way Schulz was kept alive and for the same sorts of reasons: in order to help the German who is his rescuer. This is the story of Bruno Schulz that circulates in *The Final Solution, See Under: Love,* and *The Prague Orgy,* as formulated by Jonathan Safran Foer in his afterword to his own Schulzian "die-cut book by erasure" (2010b, 138), *Tree of Codes*—the title of which is extracted from "[S]tree[t] of C[r]o[co]d[il]es":

> Felix Landau, a Gestapo officer in charge of the Jewish labor force in Drohobycz, became aware of Schulz's talents as a draughtsman, and directed Schulz to paint murals on the walls of his child's playroom. This relationship brought Schulz certain privileges, most importantly protection. Like a modern Scheherazade, he was kept alive for as long as his creation continued to please his captor.
> But on November 19th, 1942, Landau killed a Jew favored by another Gestapo officer, Karl Günther. Soon after, Günther came upon Schulz, on the corner of Czacki and Mickiewicz Streets, and shot him in the head. "You killed my Jew," he is said to have later told Landau, "I killed yours." (138; Schulz's wall paintings still exist.)

Jonathan Safran Foer's is the most inventive of these Schulz-derived novels, even if it is not a Holocaust text, although Foer's status as a writer of another important Holocaust novel, *Everything Is Illuminated* (2002), helps put one in mind of the Holocaust while reading *Tree of Codes.* What Foer does in this book is literally to rewrite Schulz's *Street of Crocodiles.* He does this by physically cutting out words from the original, such that the words of the old text hang together in a new way and a new text emerges. Like *The Street of Crocodiles*, this text is not a narrative per se. It does not tell a story. Rather, it is a text of vignettes about the narrator's mother and father and the ghostly, haunted world they inhabit as perceived by their son, the narrator. Like Krauss's *Great House*, Foer's *Tree of Codes* would replace the literal object or manuscript with the textual tradition of allusions, adaptations, erasures, and revisions, the Great House of Yochanan ben Zakkai. Hence Foer's own reference to the Western Wall of the Temple in his afterword to the book. And yet Foer's own text is a literal object, resurrecting another literal object, in an extremely material way. His book resurrects a book authored by Bruno Schulz in the same way others of the books I am discussing resurrect Schulz.

Krauss's *The History of Love* is the most deeply Schulzian of all the books I examine here. Krauss's Bruno is an actual person, and, like his historical counterpart, he is a writer. Like Schulz, Krauss's Bruno is killed by the Nazis in Poland, albeit in 1941 rather than in 1942 (the date as well of the death of Roth's Schulz-derived character in *The Prague Orgy*). Recalling Roth's strategy in relation to Anne Frank in *The Ghost Writer* and Kafka in "'I Always Wanted You to Admire My Fasting'; or, Looking at Kafka," Krauss's Bruno appears in the present moment of the text as alive and as much part of the action as any other character in the novel. Only toward the end of the novel do we come to realize, with something of a shock (reminiscent of the shock delivered in *The Far Euphrates*), that Bruno is dead and has been for decades. Therefore, the Bruno we have been meeting in the course of the narrative is a ghost conjured and materialized by one of the text's two major characters.

The History of Love tells two interconnected stories, each one of which produces its own connections with and among not only the other characters and events but with Schulz as well. One of these intermeshing narratives involves a Yiddish writer, Leo Gursky, who writes a book with the same title as Krauss's: *The History of Love*. With the war advancing he entrusts this manuscript to the care of one of his best friends, Zvi Litvinoff, who carries the text off to South America, where he publishes it in Spanish translation under his own name. Eventually Gursky's lost manuscript finds its way home to Gursky, but in an English translation that has been commissioned by Gursky's son, Isaac, who is born to Gursky's sweetheart and his muse, Alma, after her escape to America. Gursky does not know that Alma is pregnant with their son when she flees. He does not know that he has a son until after he arrives in New York City and discovers that Alma is married to another man. Nor does Isaac know who his real father is until shortly before his (Isaac's) untimely death.

The English translation of Gursky's *The History of Love* is the most direct link (literarily) between the two parallel and intersecting stories, the second one having to do with Alma Singer, who is named by her parents for the Alma in

Gursky's novel (in Spanish translation) and whose mother is hired by Gursky's son to translate the book into English. Throughout the novel, manuscripts—lost, plagiarized, translated, found—link the characters to one another and reveal the secrets of their true relationships. The only word or name in Gursky's text not translated from Yiddish to Spanish and then from Spanish to English is the name Alma, which, conveniently and somewhat prophetically, means spirit or soul in Spanish. The spirit remains, whatever the terms used to convey it, itself untranslatable and in no need of translation. The spirit of Gursky's Alma must come to be understood by him to be just that: a soul of one departed, not a living person. But since the word "alma" can also mean soul in the sense of a living person (as in the English word "soul"), Alma is also not a ghost but, in the form of Alma Singer, a very real girl who needs to be freed from the incomplete mourning of her mother, and, for that matter, Leo Gursky. It is very much to the spirit of Krauss's text that both Almas—the living and the dead—are present at the text's end. There, as we shall see, each is securely placed in its different realm of existence.

Even though not all of the texts I discuss here deal as directly with Bruno Schulz as Krauss's, they all concern lost and forged manuscripts, resurrected authors, pen names, and other evidences of unreliable, illegitimate, or lost authorial attribution. All of them to some degree ghost/write the precursor texts they conjure. They recover through their own authorship the lost texts of the past, for which their own writings come to substitute. They also conjure dead authors like Schulz, who in Krauss's text, as in Ozick's, is recalled in such a way as to figure not so much as an object of mourning as an idol or fetish, or a golem or a messiah. These creatures promise redemption, but they also threaten the health and sanity of the novels' major protagonists and finally of the texts themselves, at least until the end of the book. The texts therefore almost remain as stuck in a stultifying repetition of a horrific and deathly past as do their characters.

The convergence of interest in Schulz on the parts of such prominent and talented contemporary writers might suggest only what Philip Roth as early as *The Ghost Writer* referred to as the "family resemblance" among Jewish authors and their texts, though even that idea takes on haunting possibilities in light of the title of Roth's novel (1995, 47). But the fascination goes further, I suggest. By Krauss's own admission, Schulz and three other members of this family of authors (Roth, Appelfeld, and Grossman) are among her favorite writers (Q & A 2010 and Estrin 2011). Schulz's *Street of Crocodiles* is Foer's "favorite book" (2010b, 138), to which he returns again and again. Indeed, the book he writes becomes something of an idol, idols being very much a recurring motif in Schulz's own writings. *Tree of Codes* is a physical resurrection or replication of another text, and what is an idol if not that? It is this quality of Schulz as idol that I highlight in these texts.

Jewish authors, it would seem, are nothing less than haunted by one another. They reincarnate one another. This is evidenced already in *The Ghost Writer*. The text not only links real writers such as Isaac Babel, Bernard Malamud, and Anne Frank to one another, but it links them as well to the novel's fictive authors: I. E. Lonoff, Felix Abravanel (the name Abravanel being itself an allusion to a famous fifteenth-century rabbi), and Nathan Zuckerman, blurring the distinction between literal authors and made-up ones. Insofar as Zuckerman is a thinly veiled figure for Roth, Roth too becomes a part of this family of real and imagined, living and dead writers. The intertextual family of Jewish authorship is even more insistent in Krauss's *History of Love,* which, like *The Ghost Writer,* is a novel about art and authorship. Alma Singer's brother, Emanuel Chaim Singer (called Bird), is named "Emanuel Chaim after the Jewish historian Emanuel Ringelblum, who buried milk cans filled with testimony in the Warsaw Ghetto, and the Jewish cellist Emanuel Feuermann, who was one of the great musical prodigies of the twentieth century, and also the Jewish writer of genius Isaac Emmanuilovich Babel, and her uncle Chaim, who was a joker, a real clown, and made everyone laugh like crazy, and who died by the Nazis" (52). Grossman produces a similar compendium of dead Jews in *See Under: Love* as does Dara Horn, even more insistently, in *The World to Come.* Bird also recalls the Rothian nexus in that Bird's father's nickname for him was Manny, which is Lonoff's nickname in *The Ghost Writer.* Babel is also referred to in Roth's book, as he is in *The Prague Orgy.* Krauss even adds an additional strand to this already Gordian knot of Jewish authors through Bird's and Alma's family name. Isaac Bashevis Singer, whose wife's name was Alma, is a writer who is as important to Ozick and Roth as he is to Krauss. In a similar vein, the naming of Leo Gursky's son, Isaac, and of Isaac's half-brother, Bernard, reinforces the novel's links to Lonoff/Malamud, not to mention to Roth's Abravanel, whose historical antecedent was also an Isaac. That Gursky's beloved muse is Alma makes Gursky, the Yiddish writer, also a figure for Singer in the novel. As I have already noted, Singer himself wrote a famous short story about a lost manuscript (titled, simply, "The Manuscript"), which was finally burned by the author's mistress, something similar to what happens to Gursky's manuscript at the hands of his friend Zvi's wife, Rosa (the name Rosa, which recurs in Chabon's *Amazing Adventures* and Horn's *The World to Come* [Rosalie], might be a nod in the direction of *The Shawl*).

Insofar as Krauss's Bruno is not only, for the duration of the novel, a figment of Gursky's memory but, perhaps, an invention of his imagination as well—in Gursky's words Bruno is *"the friend I never had," "the greatest character I ever wrote"*—he might signify Krauss's self-conscious awareness of the tradition of Schulz-incarnating fictions in which her own participates (382; italics in original). This is the tradition in which a Schulz who is not necessarily Bruno Schulz himself but a phantasm or phantom fabricated for literary purposes is both inherited and passed on as an obsessive, intertextual trope or symptom of the characters' and texts' melancholy and incomplete mourning in relation to the past. The wish to resurrect or reincarnate someone from the past, then, motivates

Krauss as well as her Leo Gursky, both of them in relation to a Bruno and, for the character Leo, in relation to the woman who had been the love of his life and his muse, Alma. Insofar as the name Alma recalls Schulz's similarly named object of adoration, Adela, we are invited to see here an additional thinking together of Leo and Schulz. This means that Schulz's Adela is also reincarnated in Leo's Alma for readers of the text, as that Alma is also reincarnated—for Leo and for us—in the young Alma Singer, who is named by her parents for the same beloved Alma. Reading these texts, one has the eerie sensation that perhaps there is only a single Jewish author and a single Jewish text, which, in some breaking of the vessel, has shattered into fragments, each retaining its reflection in and of the others. And the author of authors, who wrote the original "Book," is Bruno Schulz, albeit in Schulz's own book *The Street of Crocodiles* "The Book" already exists as an object of reverence, if not idol worship.

The history of love, it would seem, is a history of resurrections and reincarnations reaching back before the Holocaust and extending well into the contemporary period. It is no coincidence that Alma Singer's mother suffers, like Leo, from severe melancholy. In the case of Mrs. Singer this melancholy has to do with the death of Alma's father, David, who, not incidentally in this novel about the history of love and the Jewish people, is an Israeli. We need to recall here that when Leo first sees her, Alma Singer is wearing her father's old sweater, which she refuses to take off. Inhabiting her dead father's clothing (wearing what is tantamount to a kind of shroud, reminiscent of the baby Magda's shawl in the Ozick story), Alma is doubly a figure of reincarnation. On the verge of becoming an artist, she also doubles Gursky in relation to his resurrections of Alma and Bruno, which is to say Bruno Schulz's in relation to his father as well as his Adela: Bruno Schulz's father is a major figure in his fiction. In the first instance Alma Singer fashions herself as the visible form that her father's immaterial soul now takes in the physical world; later, we might project, she will produce vivid portraits of her dead father, much as Dara Horn's heroine Sara does of her dead father in *The World to Come*. Alma becomes not just an artist but a graphic artist, like Artie, Clay, Kavalier, Sara, and Schulz himself. Not incidentally Gursky first glimpses Alma Singer in her art class. Art, as we see in others of these books, can well become an instrument of fetishistic preservation. It can produce messiahs and golems and resurrected saviors, even though, obviously, it can, and does, do other things and more as well.

Through Alma, who thus keeps alive the spirits of both her father and of the Alma of Leo Gursky's book, Leo's melancholy is linked to that of Mrs. Singer, and both of these instances of complicated mourning thus intertwined assume significance beyond that of local narrative details. Melancholy, it would seem, is a general affliction of Jews in the modern world. Perhaps it is no surprise, then, that it is Freud who defines melancholia for contemporary society. Although Freud might have distanced himself from his Jewish origins in many ways, through his

various experiences of Jewish mourning he had clearly internalized the significance of such periods of mourning for the psychological health of human beings.
Whatever alternatives to melancholy either Freud or Jewish tradition propose,
melancholy is pervasive in Krauss's novel as it is in the other novels I am examining—for example, in Michael Chabon's *Amazing Adventures of Kavalier and
Clay,* which is also a novel of incomplete mourning.

In Chabon's *Amazing Adventures* it is the escape artist Harry Houdini who
stands in for Bruno Schulz and who is one of the objects of Joe Kavalier's incomplete mourning. Houdini's "inverted triangle" face, "brow large, chin pointed,
with pouty lips and a blunt, quarrelsome nose," recall Schulz's facial features
(2000, 3). That Chabon imagines Schulz as an escape artist in his novel links
his text with Grossman's, which has everything to do with Schulz escaping (as
a fish), not to mention with Roth's *Ghost Writer,* in which Kafka's "little sister,
his little lost daughter," Anne Frank, is also imagined as escaping (1995, 170).
Houdini stands behind Clay's and Kavalier's comic book character the "escape
artist," as the first section of the novel is titled. This escape artist incorporates Joe
Kavalier's expertise in escape along with the fact of his actual escape from Prague
in the coffin of the Golem of Prague. From the beginning of Chabon's novel, the
Golem, it seems, who is a savior figure within the Jewish tradition and in that
sense one of several messiahs to emerge in this set of texts, is an escape artist,
who leads another Jew to safety. We must observe that in the Jewish scriptures
the word "messiah" does not primarily mean a savior in a transcendent sense.
Rather, the word more nearly refers to one who has been chosen or anointed by
God as a leader, with all of the historical and political implications of nation and
community intact. As Gershom Scholem has put it, "Judaism, in all its forms
and manifestations, has always maintained a concept of redemption as an event
which takes place publicly, on the stage of history" (1971, 1). This is not to dispute
the messianic traditions within Judaism that veered toward the mystical and the
spiritual, as Scholem also makes very clear and as many of these novels suggest:
all of those conversions of plot in Krauss's novels are hardly logical and rational;
Joe's escape in the Golem's coffin and the return of that coffin at the end of the
novel are mysterious, if not mystical. There is a divine alma at work here. Nonetheless, in these and others of the books I am discussing, there is another way of
looking at what the idea of a messiah might mean in the context of the Jewish
Bible (what Schulz calls "The Book"). And that idea might have to do with history, in the literal sense of the word, including the history of death and devastation of pogroms and Holocausts, as well as the history of love. When, in the texts
we have been examining here, Jewish writers and their Jewish protagonists try to
undo the rush to death of other Jews—to detain "the man in the long black coat
… hurrying … hurrying and hurrying toward the chimneys," as Ozick describes
him in *The Messiah of Stockholm* (1987, 144)—through acts of conjuring, rescue,
translation, and resurrection, they are employing a practice that is reminiscent

of Christianity in order to reverse or undo the consequences of Christianity's efforts to obliterate the Jewish world. By this I mean both the destruction of the textual traditions of Judaism and the murder (finally through the Nazi genocide) of literal communities of Jews who both practiced and did not practice those traditions. Judaism, however, has its own modes of practice, which the texts and their readers might come to recognize and employ.

This idea of the Jewish messiah/golem as an actor in this world also suggests something about the history of comic book action figures (Superman et al.) that Chabon's novel invokes: "In June 1938, Superman appeared. He had been mailed to the offices of National Periodical Publications from Cleveland, by a couple of Jewish boys who had imbued him with the power of a hundred men, of a distant world, and of the full measure of their bespectacled adolescent hopefulness and desperation" (2000, 77; the points of historical convergence between Chabon's novel and the actual story of Superman's creators can be verified through reading Larry Tye's study *Superman* [2013]). The superheroes aren't deities; they aren't gods. They are men, albeit of super (golem-like) strength, and they are dedicated to human issues within an ongoing human world. They are also masters of disguise, which, when you think about it, is also a form of escape. This escape through disguise also reflects an aspect of their Jewish creators, who hide behind their comic book heroes. "*See you in the funny papers,*" Joe says to his family as he is about to flee Prague; "jaunty, he reminded himself, always jaunty. In my panache is their hope of salvation" (2000, 19; italics in original). Joe's line can been taken as a coda for American Jews, in their jaunty concealment of their Jewishness within the cultural media, whereby they not only survived but flourished. Needless to say, our author Michael Chabon is also a part of this Jewish American culture. Like others, he might be felt (even by himself) to be a bit too cavalier about his Jewish identity.

It is through his relationship to the American comic book industry, and specifically through his telling the story of the Golem, that Joe Kavalier is finally able to free himself of the ghosts of Europe and enter into a creative and procreative life in America. But this only happens at the end of the novel. Before that time, both Joe and his cousin and cowriter, Sammy Clay, are struck in places of complex mourning from which they cannot escape, no matter how many action heroes they draw. For Sammy the prison from which he needs to break free is his own unconfessed homosexuality. Sammy's marrying Rosa when Joe disappears, Joe comes to realize, is "not a merely gallant gesture but a deliberate and conscious act of self-immurement" (581). "I didn't want to, well, be a fairy," Sam tells Joe (580). Sam's immuring himself in Joe's abandoned love relationship cannot be separated from Sam's unceasing grief over his father's abandonment of him. Sam sees his father as "the World's Strongest Jew. . . . He was all muscle. No heart. He was like Superman without the Clark Kent" (119–20). It is no accident, then, that Sammy should come up with "a costumed hero whose power would be that of impossible and perpetual escape" (120). Escape is very much what Sammy desires. It is also what his father has done to Sammy and his mother, which, in repeating as fiction, Sammy comes to control. Nor is it odd that Sammy's superhero the Escapist has a heart, which his father does not. Clay and Kavalier's Escapist "doesn't just fight" evil; "he *frees* the world of it. He *frees* people" (121; italics in original). He is Sammy's wish fulfillment pure and simple, his father with a heart. What Sammy must become, for a while at least, is such a father to Tommy.

Such self-denying self-entrapment and wish fulfillment are even more decidedly the keys to Joe's psychological condition. It is for Joe's brother, Thomas, that the comic book character Tom Mayflower, who is found in "an orphanage in Central Europe" (134), is named. In similar fashion, the "Ogre" in the comic strip, Professor Alois Berg, is named for "Alois Hora . . . from the Circus Zeletny" (52), in whose clothes Joe and his teacher, Kornblum, dress the Golem of Prague, while the maestro himself is Kornblum. "Stop wasting your life. . . . You have the key," Joe writes into the comic (132). That key—the "Golden Key" (133)—will be, for both Sammy and Joe, Tommy, who is also named for Thomas. Tommy is Rosa's and Joe's son. However, insofar as he is raised by Sammy, whom Tommy is led to believe is his father, Tommy is Sammy's son as well (a feature of disguised paternity the novel shares with Krauss's *History of Love*; Chabon's book could also be titled "A History of Love"). But Sammy and Joe have to learn to use the key they have been given, which is also to be understood as what the world of comics has opened up to them, if they can only see it, as finally Joe comes to see that Tommy is his son. Tommy is both the comic book Tom made real and Thomas reborn in the new world. Therefore, he is the link between the comic book world and the world of human beings. He is also neither Tom nor Thomas but Tommy. In other words, he is a subject in his own right, thus resisting the claims and desires of both fetishism and reincarnation. He has two fathers. He has a history different from theirs and from the comic book characters that his two fathers created.

The condition of complex mourning that characterizes Sam characterizes Joe even more severely and in a more politically embedded and complex way. In the course of the book Joe not only escapes from the Nazis, but he also suffers the loss of his entire family, and "because he had not been taken from them, they could not seem to let him go" (489). This, we shall see, is very much the situation of Anne Michaels's protagonist Jakob in *Fugitive Pieces*. "[Joe] didn't really have a home to come home to. . . . His family in Europe. . . . All dead" (499). Joe's teacher, Kornblum, early on recognizes the quality in Joe that, with the death of his family and Kornblum, finally comes to overwhelm him:

> He had never had so naturally gifted a student, but his own discipline—which was really an escape artist's sole possession—had not been passed along. . . .
> What he . . . privately believed [was] that Joseph was one of those unfortunate boys who become escape artists not to prove the superior machinery of their bodies against outlandish contrivances and the laws of physics, but for

dangerously metaphorical reasons. Such men feel imprisoned by invisible chains—walled in, sewn up in layers of batting. For them, the final feat of autoliberation was all too foreseeable. (37)

"Forget about what you are escaping *from*," Kornblum tells him, "reserve your anxiety for what you are escaping *to*." This is a bit of wisdom that stays with Joe throughout his travels (21; italics in original), even if, melancholic that he is, he cannot quite implement it until the end of the story.

Because he is escaping from rather than escaping to, what Joe discovers in America is a trap from which he cannot spring himself without help, even after he has returned from his period of self-imposed exile (slightly reminiscent of Alexander's tzimtzum in *The Far Euphrates*) in order to reclaim his wife and child: "I didn't know how to come back to you," he says to Rosa, "I was trying for years, believe me" (572):

> Joe loved his comic books: for their inferior color separation, their poor-ly trimmed paper stock, their ads for air rifles and dance courses and acne creams, for the basement smell that clung to the old ones, the ones that had been in storage during Joe's travels. Most of all, he loved them for the pictures and stories they contained, the inspirations and lucubrations of five hundred aging boys dreaming as hard as they could for fifteen years, transfiguring their insecurities and delusions, their wishes and their doubts, their public educa-tions and their sexual perversions, into something that only the most purblind of societies would have denied the status of art. Comic books had sustained his sanity. . . . Having lost his mother, father, brother, and grandfather, the friends and foes of his youth, his beloved teacher Bernard Kornblum, his city, his history—his home—the usual charge leveled against cosmic books, that they offered *merely an easy escape from reality,* seemed to Joe actually to be a powerful argument on their behalf. . . . *That* was magic—not the apparent magic of the silk-hatted card-palmer, or the bold brute trickery of the escape artist, but the genuine magic of art. (575–76; italics in original)

For that reason, even though "he had returned to New York years before, with the intention of finding a way to reconnect . . . with the only family that remained to him in the world," he had "instead . . . become immured, by fears and its major-domo, habit, in his cabinet of mysteries on the seventy-second floor of the Empire State Building. . . . Like Harry Houdini, Joe had failed to get out of his self-created trap" (556). "Merely an easy escape from reality" is not sufficient a purpose even for a comic book. But "now the love of a boy had sprung him, and drawn him at last, blinking, before the footlights" (556). "Only love," Kornblum had once told him, and the text repeats this twice, "could pick a nested pair of steel Bramah locks" (532, 535). Like Krauss's characters, Chabon's have to travel an arduous route to return to love. This route includes mourning for the death of other loved ones and, finally, putting those dead loved ones to rest. Just as "the Golem must be spirited from its hiding place" (15), so must Joe. The word "spirited" is not lightly chosen. Joe must return to the world of living souls. The Golem, who once saved him and now obsesses him, must be laid to rest along with the rest of the murdered Jews, transmuted from material object to cultural form. This transformation of the physical savior to an immaterial presence inspires Nicole Krauss's *Great House* as well.

In conjuring the ghosts (and golems) of the past, in ghostwriting the stories of the ghost writers of the past, the authors in this group of texts write a Jewish phantasmagoria much like Schulz's own (Ozick [1983c] titles her essay on Schulz "The Phantasmagoria of Bruno Schulz"). In so doing they make themselves as authors into ghostly, somehow phantasmagoric, and therefore (to introduce a key term in Ozick's *The Messiah of Stockholm*) somehow "illegitimate" presences. They illegitimately assume the identity of others. They illegitimately conjure dead writers and lost fictions. Finally, they produce texts that are in one way or another illegitimate, at least from a Jewish perspective, either because they produce or resurrect idols or because they claim a transcendent messianic function for their writing. Jews, it would seem, do not easily accept the world of demons and ghosts, golems and messiahs, which they themselves are tempted to conjure. At the very least they recognize the danger of such phantasmagoria, especially in relation to their Judaism. And yet they indulge in just this sort of necromancy nonetheless, even if to finally put an end to it.

Take Ozick's *Messiah of Stockholm,* for example. As if in a frenzy to recover or resurrect the dead author Bruno Schulz and his text, Ozick imagines not one but two heirs to and inheritors of the murdered Polish writer. Or, more precisely, she creates three heirs, since it is her book and not the manuscript that Schulz's illegitimate daughter in the text professes to have found that is the only extant text of *The Messiah* (albeit of *Stockholm*). Ozick, we might say, sets herself up as another of Schulz's illegitimate children involved in his rescue or at least of his text. In this context we might note that it is possible to interpret the birth of the original messiah as an "illegitimate" birth. Christ is not the son of his mother's husband, Joseph, who is actually the biological descendant of the Davidic line. (This is likely a Jewish take on the matter.) A similar kind of illegitimacy pertains to Leo Gursky's son, Isaac, who is not the son of Alma's husband. And we might even extend this pattern to Alma Singer herself, not within her literal biological family but within the family constructed by Gursky and his Alma, in which Alma Singer becomes the daughter they never had. Her brother, Bird, fantasizes that his father is not Alma's father, hence that she is illegitimate, lending a certain credence to the more metaphorical reconstruction of family in the novel. Tommy Clay (Kavalier) is also, as I have noted, an illegitimate child. Insofar as Jewish culture (at least as represented by Yiddish literature) is left orphaned after the Second World War, we might imagine Ozick's and the other Schulz-inspired texts in this group as, like Lars in Ozick's novel, seeking to establish legitimacy and paternity (or maternity) against all reason and odds, trying to reconstruct the devastated Jewish family by any means possible.

As if to draw our attention to the fact that Ozick's own *Messiah* text is itself an act of resurrection and displacement, Ozick (like Krauss and Grossman later) not only incorporates themes and images from Schulz's fiction into her own (blurring the boundaries between her text and his), but she also produces a plot summary of what Schulz's lost manuscript was (or, more precisely, might have been) about. Through this device the frame narrative (*The Messiah of Stockholm*) merges with the tale-within-the-tale (Schulz's *Messiah*). It assumes the place of and displaces or succeeds that precursor text. Because that precursor text likely never existed, Ozick's *Messiah* becomes the only *Messiah* there is or ever was, until, perhaps, Krauss's novel comes upon the scene, similarly professing both its validity and illegitimacy as Gursky's/Schulz's lost text: who is the author of *The History of Love*? Nicole Krauss? Leo Gursky? Or Zvi Litvinoff, whose Spanish translation sets the entire narrative into motion?

It is in Ozick's novel's move not only to inherit Schulz's *Messiah* but to resurrect it, to become the incarnation of that lost, possibly never written text, that *The Messiah of Stockholm* makes itself a participant in the odd family romance of thwarted mourning and idol worship, which is also an aspect of the plot of the novel and an object of its critique. For a story in which, as Lars puts it, "there's no room . . . for another child" (1987, 53), Ozick has made room for even one child more: herself. Furthermore, all of these descendants of Schulz are "illegitimate" not only in the common sexual meaning of the word but also, and more importantly, in the sense of their being literary forgeries or fakes, a subject that takes center stage in Dara Horn's novel. There were rumors concerning Schulz himself having had illegitimate offspring. Ozick is likely playing off these rumors in her text. Ozick as author doubles the fake illegitimate daughter, Adela, whose name is taken from Schulz's published works and which is recalled in the names of Krauss's doubled female protagonist(s). She also doubles the similarly fake illegitimate son, who is also Adela's double. Finally Ozick also doubles Heidi's husband, Dr. Eklund, who is both Lars's "psychological twin" (95) and the father (perhaps illegitimately so) of Adela. Does so much reproduction of illegitimate births produce a line of legitimacy after all, albeit of a literary or textual rather than a literal nature?

Like Eklund's *Messiah* within the novel, Ozick's *Messiah,* which is the novel, is a forgery in the sense that it is *not* the text of Schulz's *Messiah*. Or is it? Ozick lets drop the tantalizing possibility that the manuscript of Eklund, who claims to have known Schulz intimately and who was born Eckstein (and if born Eckstein, why not born Schulz?) may be authentic. Perhaps Eckstein is Schulz. By the same token, Ozick's text may truly be *The Messiah*. In fact, it is. That is the book's title. Who is to say who or what constitutes a false *Messiah*/messiah, or a true one? Who can say which is the true text, which the forgery? To complicate things even more, who can say what gender the messiah or the author of *The Messiah* might be? Gender turns out to be not an incidental detail in this story of illegitimate inheritance and the production, or reproduction, of literary tradition. "It was being *saved*," Adela says to Lars of the found manuscript, "for the daughter" (79; italics in original). This introduces the question whether the author of a text named *Messiah* might not be a woman—say, like Ozick herself. Thus Ozick creates a female Golem in her 1997 novel, *The Puttermesser Papers*. "Maybe it was supposed to be female," Chabon's Josef Kavalier suggests to Kornblum when they notice that "there was only a smooth void of clay" in the Golem's "crotch," where a penis ought to be. To this Kornblum replies: "Not even the Maharal could make a woman out of clay. For that you need a rib" (2000, 61), or perhaps a poke in the rib, which Ozick achieves in *The Puttermesser Papers*. In *The Messiah of Stockholm*, the female Jewish writer is also the new progenitor of a tradition, although in this case, in order to become a part of that tradition, she, like its other members, finds herself conjuring the dead male writer and making him into an idol of sorts.

This would explain Nicole Krauss's strategy in *The History of Love* in permitting the female child Alma to share the role of messiah with her younger brother, Bird. According to the novel, Bird is a self-declared messiah. By the end of the novel he has indeed served a messianic function, not in some cosmic sense but, in relation to both Gursky and his two Almas, in the very human and Jewish sense of saving human beings in the here and now, that other world to come, which is *this* world, as Dara Horn suggests in her novel. Insofar as Krauss's text is, like Ozick's, one more version of Schulz's *Messiah*, Krauss too (like Ozick) becomes a female savior, albeit of an authorial kind. Krauss's novel could have been titled "The Messiah [of New York]," since it signals its relationship to Schulz in more ways than one. The excerpts from Gursky's books (written, of course, by Krauss) are highly reminiscent of Schulz's writing style. Like Grossman, who replicates sections of Schulz's texts in *See Under: Love,* and like Jonathan Safran Foer, who, as noted, literally reproduces Schulz's words, Krauss rewrites Schulz. Several times in the course of the novel there is also direct reference to Schulz's *Street of Crocodiles,* which Alma reads at the suggestion of Gursky's son, Isaac, whose own writing style, in the same way as it reflects his father's, can be understood to be Schulzian as well. Indeed, toward the end of the book, as the final climax of discovery and restitution is hurtling toward its culmination, Alma recovers *The Street of Crocodiles* (long overdue at the library) in a pile of Bird's clothing. Birds, we need to add here, flit about convulsively in Schulz's fiction. Indeed, Grossman's transformation of Schulz into a fish in *See Under: Love* partakes of the dynamics not only of Kafka's "Metamorphosis" (alluded to in Roth's *Prague Orgy*) but also of Schulz's own obsession with animals and with blurring the lines differentiating between and among animal kingdoms, an aspect of Spiegelman's undertaking in *Maus* as well. Indeed, if, as Adam Gopnik (1987) has suggested, Spiegelman's strategy in *Maus* bears some relationship to the bird head illustrations of the Jews in certain ancient Haggadoth, as has been argued, Krauss's, I suggest, does too.

The discovery of Schulz's book among Bird's (the "messiah's") laundry serves to do more than reinforce the already pervasive allusions to Schulz's lost, perhaps never written masterpiece, *The Messiah*. Both Schulz's manuscript and Gursky's *History of Love* are also texts that have been discarded (as if in someone's laundry or trash) and recovered. They are fictions that travel countries, continents, and languages. Bird's name is one more instance of haunting convergences verging on an obsession in Krauss's book not only with Schulz himself but with the authors in the tradition that descends from and also tends obsessively to memorialize Schulz. Bird's nickname conjures for us a famous Roth story. Not accidentally this is also a story about the Jewish relation to the messiah. In Krauss's novel the child's name originates in his flight out of a window, an event reminiscent of the major event in Roth's "Conversion of the Jews," where the child protagonist threatens to jump off the roof of the yeshiva if the rabbi will not admit that an omnipotent God can clearly produce a child through immaculate conception.

Like Roth's text, and Schulz's, and like other works in this family of texts, Krauss's novel seems to be investigating the degree to which Jews believe in saviors, and, if so, saviors of what sort: immaterial presences, holy spirits, and ghosts (as in the Christian tradition) or more concrete entities like reincarnated ghost writers or golems (the subject of Chabon's *Amazing Adventures of Kavalier and Clay,* and of Ozick's *Puttermesser Papers* and Thane Rosenbaum's *Golems of Gotham* [2002]). Krauss's novel might have been titled not simply "The Messiah" or "The Messiah of New York," but "The Messiahs of New York," since Bird's role is, as noted, doubled by that of his sister, Alma, who, in addition to being a messianic figure, is also a figure of reincarnation. She reincarnates both Leo Gursky's lost love, Alma, and her own father, David (not an incidental name in a story of the messianic house of David). Indeed, in crossing gender lines in relation to her messianic figure, Krauss also replicates another feature of Ozick's *Messiah.*

All of this Jewish interest in messiahs and ghosts is very odd at best. As Ozick herself (1983a, 1983b) makes very clear in several of her essays, Jews do not generally believe in idols, however tempting even Ozick herself finds both paganism and Christianity to be. In keeping with the dominant subjects and tropes of Schulz's published writings and certain of his comments concerning his lost manuscript, the encapsulated version of Schulz's *Messiah* in Ozick's *The Messiah of Stockholm* is all about idols: "No human beings remained . . . only hundreds and hundreds of idols. . . . Then . . . the Messiah arrived. . . . More than anything else . . . he resembled a book—The Book" (1987, 108–10). Even though "The Book" suggests that the messiah resembles the scriptures—this seems to have been

Schulz's meaning—it is possible to entertain the idea that he only resembled an ordinary "book," more like Ozick's own, or Grossman's. For Grossman's narrator-protagonist Momik in *See Under: Love*, Schulz's *Street of Crocodiles* was "The Book for me in the sense Bruno had yearned for *that great tome, sighing, a stormy Bible, its pages fluttering in the wind like an overblown rose—*" (1989, 99; italics in original). We might extend that definition of The Book both to Momik's writing and to that of his author, David Grossman, whose inclusion of these comments in *See Under: Love* could be taken as self-referential. The Book might even be a comic book, such as is produced by the two protagonists of Michael Chabon's *Amazing Adventures of Kavalier and Clay*.

As we have seen, just as literature can come close to a form of fetishism, it may also constitute a form of idolatry, especially given the use of figuration or even in some books (such as in Schulz's own texts, as well as in *Maus* and *The Final Solution*) actual graphic representations. The Book as messiah is an idol. And yet "a Jew," Ozick says adamantly, "is someone who shuns idols (1983b, 188) not to mention messiahs: "*The Book of Creation* has been returned to the Creator," Ozick quotes Isaac Bashevis Singer as writing. "Messiah did not come for the Jews, so the Jews went to Messiah" (1983a, 221). For Jews who remain Jewish, however, there is no Messiah, and for them at least (as presumably for Christians as well) idol worship went out with Abraham. Yet Ozick herself, like Schulz, manufactures idols, even though she also sees through them and smashes them. She is like Harold Bloom as she describes him in her essay "Literature as Idol" (1983b). She is both Terach and Abraham. Her messiah in *The Messiah of Stockholm* is also similarly self-destructing, which may be a principal feature of Jewish messiahs and golems, such as Ozick also produces in *The Puttermesser Papers* or Chabon creates in *The Amazing Adventures of Kavalier and Clay*. Jewish messiahs and golems dissolve. They disappear. Like Chabon's Golem at the end of *The Amazing Adventures*, they return to the clay out of which they were fashioned. That Schulz's masterpiece, *The Messiah*, might well be apocryphal adds still further support to the idea that such Jewish messiahs as exist are firmly transient creatures of the human imagination. Like golems, they image only fantastic possibilities of escape and salvation, hence, Chabon's idea of the Golem as a superhero rather than a transcendent god. Eventually the Golem must finally die, not to be resurrected, although perhaps to be mourned. The novels and stories by Ozick, Roth, Grossman, Appelfeld, Chabon, Horn, and Krauss that I have discussed here, like the fiction of Kafka and Schulz before them, are haunted by the phantoms or ghosts of dead Jews, who cannot be properly mourned and who therefore cannot be properly buried. For this reason they pop up in the world of the fiction as idols, golems, and very material, visible ghosts, sometimes (as in the case of Horn's novel) reincarnated spirits. Yet even as these ghosts and golems promise salvation, they threaten disaster.

5   A Jewish History of Blocked Mourning and Love

Roth's *THE PRAGUE ORGY* has everything to do with the same problematic idolization of art and of dead (especially Jewish) writers. This is Roth's subject in *The Ghost Writer* as well. For the American Jewish public in *The Ghost Writer,* the idol that needed to be served (and, from Roth's point of view, seen through) is Anne Frank, whom Zuckerman (but also Roth) resurrects from the dead in order to authorize or legitimate (to pick up the language of *The Messiah of Stockholm*) his own Jewish loyalty (Anne is another female messiah in this gender-crossing tradition). The idolization of Anne is repeated in the young Zuckerman's similar reverence for the Jewish writer Lonoff (read: Babel, Malamud, and I. B. Singer). Zuckerman's reverence for Lonoff itself emulates Lonoff's reverence (which is also Roth's, not to mention Ozick's as well) for Henry James. This possibility of self-serving idolization of the great authors of the past is exposed in its full folly toward the end of *The Prague Orgy,* in which Anne Frank once again figures, albeit this time as the character in the play. Through playing the role of Anne, the non-Jewish actress who is one of the major female protagonists of *The Prague Orgy* acquires a pseudo-Jewish identity that subjects her to prejudice and finally to exile. Even the vicarious inhabitation by a non-Jew of the dead Jewish soul can signal disaster.

Roth's Schulz in this novella is a Czechoslovakian writer named Zdenek Sisovsky, who, according to his son, is a "Semite-obsessed" "Jew writing about Jews" in "the Yiddish of Flaubert," an "elliptical," "humble," and "self-conscious" style, "all . . . his own" (1985, 716, 720). Sisovsky, in his son's account, is killed in 1941 and the story he tells of his father's death recalls that of the real Bruno Schulz. Befriended to play chess with a local Nazi, who becomes so enraged with another Nazi that he kills this other Nazi's Jewish dentist, Sisovsky is murdered in return: "'He shot my Jew, so I shot his,'" writes Roth (718), and he repeats this later in the text (757). This is the refrain that in slightly altered form comes to dominate the Bruno section of David Grossman's *See Under: Love:* "On November 19, 1942, on the corner of Czecskyk and Mizkewitz Streets, Karl Gunther shot Bruno and, as the story goes, went to Landau and said, 'I killed your Jew.' To which Landau replied, 'In that case, I will now kill your Jew'" (1989, 100); "I killed your Jew. In that case, I will now kill your Jew" (115). The refrain "I killed your Jew. In that case I will kill your Jew" forms a leitmotif, or perhaps more accurately a stutter in the novel. As we have seen, Jonathan Safran Foer directly cites this story in the paratextual materials at the end of *Tree of Codes*.

Both *The Messiah of Stockholm* and *The Prague Orgy* evoke aspects of Henry James's 1888 *Aspern Papers*. Like James's novella they issue in a critique of the un-examined psychosexual motives that lead some writers (or critics) to turn other writers into idols or gods. In Roth's text the plot conforms more closely than Ozick's to James's original text: Nathan Zuckerman courts Olga, the abandoned wife of the refugee writer, who sets Zuckerman on his quest to acquire his father's manuscripts, which are now in her keeping. Sisovsky's son (also named Sisovsky) even sets up his instructions to Zuckerman in such a way as to recall the James story. He tells Zuckerman that if he (Zuckerman) were "to visit Prague, and . . . meet Olga and Olga were to fall in love with [him], she would even give" him the papers (1985, 721) by way of "dowry" (767), as Zuckerman finally puts it, complet-ing the allusion to *The Aspern Papers*. The obsession that Zuckerman finally takes on as his mission is the younger Sisovsky's own "obsession . . . with this great Jewish writer that might have been," the man who "in America . . . would have been a celebrated writer. . . . He would be something more now than just another murdered Jew" (720).

In the end we discover that Sisovsky's story is a "lie." "It happened to another writer," Olga tells Zuckerman, "who didn't even write in Yiddish. Who didn't have a wife or have a child"—in other words, we might fill in for Olga: it hap-pened to Bruno Schulz. "Sisovsky's father was killed in a bus accident," we are told; "Sisovsky's father hid in the bathroom of a Gentile friend, hid there through the war from the Nazis, and his friend brought him cigarettes and whores" (757). Sisovsky's desire to tell his father's "story," then, like Lars's motivation in *The Messiah of Stockholm*, is to recover a father. It is also to assuage his Holocaust guilt and to establish for himself a place within a sacred, sanctified heritage of Jewish authorship. Indeed, Sisovsky so much desires to become a part of this lin-eage that he teaches himself to read Yiddish. It is no accident that of his father's stories the one Sisovsky cites is called "Mother Tongue" and that it is associated in his mind with homelessness. "Kafka's homelessness," he tells Zuckerman, "was nothing beside my father's" (Roth 1985, 719), and we might well hear: his own. Homeless, Sisovsky would recover his identity as a Jew in America by writing in what Ozick once called the "New Yiddish" (1983d): English.

Zuckerman in the story is equally motivated by guilt, and he knows it. "*Why am I forcing the issue?*" he asks himself concerning his pursuit of the papers.

> *What's the motive here? Is this a passionate struggle for those marvelous stories or a renewal of the struggle toward self-caricature? Still the son, still the child, in strenuous pursuit of the father's loving response? (Even when the father is Sisovsky's?). . . . Would it be so hard to convince myself that I am stupidly endowing these stories with a significance that they can't begin to have? . . . Think of all that his stories will be spared if instead of wrenching his fiction out of oblivion, you just turn around and go . . . [sic] Yet I stay. In the old parables about the spiritual life, the hero searches for a kind of holiness, or holy object, or transcendence, boning up on magic practices as he goes off hunting after his higher being, getting help from crones and soothsayers, donning masks—well, this is the mockery of that parable, that parable the idealization of this farce.* (Roth 1985, 766–67; italics in original)

Just as the author of *The Messiah of Stockholm* comes to double both the murdered author of *The Messiah* and those heirs who would resurrect their idol and thus become the author of his text, so Roth comes to replicate both the Yiddish writer and his ex-patriot writer son, even if he writes his legend of the Jewish quest as farce.

Already in his first conversation with Sisovsky, Zuckerman believes his troubles with his American critics cannot hold a candle to the censorship and exile the ex-patriot half-Jewish writer has had to suffer. Jews are privileged in America, even Jewish writers like Zuckerman, who are the target of public censure—hence, perhaps, Roth's own participation in the Writers from the Other Europe project, which succeeded in putting Schulz and others on the literary landscape. The text exposes the problem of potential self-interestedness directly when Olga hurls at Zuckerman the following accusation, which cannot so easily be dismissed: "So *that's* what you get out of it! *That's* your idealism! The marvelous Zuckerman brings from behind the Iron Curtain two hundred unpublished Yiddish stories written by the victim of a Nazi bullet. You will be a hero to the Jews and to literature and to all of the Free World" (770; italics in original). Roth is nothing if not honest, both about his characters and about himself. By implied extension, of course, Eastern European writers are also not suffering what Jews and Jewish writers suffered in the Holocaust—hence, the invention of the Eastern European Sisovsky's Jewish, Yiddishist father, murdered by the Nazis.

The frame narrative is also revealed here to be a cover story for the ever Jewish Zuckerman's/Roth's inner plot, which is the obsessive and guilt-ridden post-Holocaust rescue (as in and by Ozick's *Messiah* or Dara Horn's *The World to Come*) by Jews of Jewish texts. This is the Jewish subtext, perhaps, of Roth's own involvement in the Writers of the Other Europe project, which by no means dealt exclusively with Jewish writers. In *The Prague Orgy* Zuckerman discovers his lost homeland (he will make this discovery again in the 1987 *The Counterlife*), not in Israel, but in the destroyed alleyways of Kafka's and Schulz's devastated Europe:

This is the city I imagined the Jews would buy when they had accumulated enough money for a homeland. . . . What was to betoken a Jewish homeland to an impressionable, emotional nine-year-old child . . . was, first, the overpowering oldness of the homes, the centuries of deterioration . . . the leaky pipes and moldy walls and rotting timbers and smoking stoves and simmering cabbages. . . . Second were the stories, all the telling and listening to be done, their infinite interest in their own existence, the fascination with their alarming plight, the mining and refining of *tons* of these stories—the national industry of the Jewish homeland, if not its sole means of production. . . . The construction of narrative out of the exertions of survival. (760–61; italics in original)

Hurrying at the end of the story, with a "candy box full of Yiddish manuscript" (771), recalling the NJF (National Jewish Federation) collection box of his youth (760), Zuckerman is like "the man in the long black coat, hurrying with a metal garter box squeezed under his arm, hurrying and hurrying toward the chimneys" toward the end of Ozick's *Messiah of Stockholm* (1987, 144). The man in the long black coat who is ever hurrying toward the chimneys is not a particular individual but the Jewish collective. Jews hurried then, even before the Holocaust, and they hurry now, afterward. The interest in the fiction of younger American Jewish writers such as Horn and Nathan Englander in European pogroms and the Stalinist purges—specifically the evening of the murdered poets in 1952—recognizes that persecution and decimation are the essential conditions of Jewish history (see both Horn 2006 and Englander 1999, "The 27th Man," *For Relief of Unbearable Urges*). It is this line of Jewish dead about which Bruno Schulz had written and to which he belongs, hence his reincarnation in both Ozick's and Roth's texts. This "Hurrying hurrying" toward an escape that will be only another form of what Roth identifies throughout "'I Always Wanted You to Admire My Fasting'; or, Looking at Kafka" as "entrapment" (1975, 256) is Zuckerman's (and Roth's) Kafkaesque/Schulzian inheritance. Writes Roth in "Looking at Kafka": "[Kafka] died too soon for the holocaust. Had he lived, perhaps he would have escaped. . . . But *Kafka* escaping. It seems unlikely for one so fascinated by entrapment and careers that culminate in anguished death" (248; italics in original).

Like Kafka, Roth's inability to escape is linked to the ties of family, specifically to the father. In "Looking at Kafka," Roth attributes to Kafka no fewer than three fathers (253). Kafka is truly the Rothian hero writ large, not just K. from Kafka's *The Trial* (1925), but K. with paternity issues. Toward the end of *The Prague Orgy* Roth becomes that Kafka, just as the elder Sisovsky becomes Schulz. Zuckerman, the story writes somewhere between its own voice and Zuckerman's, *"awoke one morning from uneasy dreams [and] found himself transformed in his bed into a sweeper of floors in a railway café"* [1985, 778; italics in original]. This is a version not only of Kafka but also of a statement Roth includes in "Looking at Kafka," which ties the two texts together and both of them to Kafka and the issue of the father: *"As Franz Kafka awoke one morning from his uneasy dreams he found himself transformed in his bed into a father, a writer, and a Jew"* (255; italics in original).

To be sure, Roth is a far less anguished writer than Kafka, but the bid to be admired for taking on Jewish suffering characterizes not only Zuckerman's fantasy in *The Ghost Writer* and *The Prague Orgy* but Roth's fantasy as well in these and others of his writings. By the end of the story, which is also the end of the collection *Zuckerman Bound*, Zuckerman has "lost that astonishingly real candy box stuffed with the stories I came to Prague to retrieve" (they are confiscated by the authorities), and for this loss Zuckerman is truly regretful. "One's story," he says, "isn't a skin to be shed—it is inescapable, one's body and blood. You go on pumping it out till you die, the story veined with the themes of your life, the ever-recurring story that's at once your invention and the invention of you" (1985, 782). Entrapment in Jewish history is Roth's lot. Humor and irony (farce) are his way of coping, his way of releasing the spring and freeing the subject from the prison of the past—to use terminology that is pertinent in relation to Chabon's *Amazing Adventures,* in which escape (including through humor) is precisely what the fiction is aiming at. Already at age nine the narrator of "Looking at Kafka" feels "guilt" about the "'Jews in Europe,'" whom he believes he personally must "save" (Roth 1975, 259). Yet "comic" that he is, he also knows that to dub the famous writer "Doctor *Kishka*" (258; italics in original) and to produce a story like *The Ghost Writer* is not only to spoof but also to humanize a Jewish martyr. And humanize he will. "'Zuckerman the Zionist agent," says the passport official to Zuckerman at the end of *The Prague Orgy* as he returns Zuckerman's passport to him (a minor detail in the story that also relates to Schulz is that the passport officer is dressed in an "hourglass" suit [1985, 783]). And the book ends with these words: "Now back to the little world around the corner" (784), which is Roth's literary realm, the kitchen table in Newark, as he refers to it in *The Counterlife.*

It is also the lot of David Grossman's protagonist in *See Under: Love* to find himself a prisoner of Jewish history, from which Grossman (through his narrator-protagonist, Momik) nonetheless imagines an escape, if only into fantasy, heroic quest, and, finally, literature. Like the protagonist of Ozick's novel, like Ozick's novel itself, and like Roth and Appelfeld and their characters in *The Prague Orgy* and *The Age of Wonders* (1981), respectively, Grossman's Momik sees the contemporary world through the "murdered eye" of the dead father, to quote a recurrent phrase from *The Messiah of Stockholm* (1987, 3). In the case of Momik (who is of a different generation than either Lars or Ozick, Roth or Zuckerman, Appelfeld or Bruno), this father is a grandfather named Anshel Wasserman, who coexists in Grossman's text with an actual Bruno Schulz and also partakes of some of Schulz's qualities. Thus Grossman produces two Schulzes in his text. *See Under: Love,* we might say, is doubly obsessed with Schulz. Indeed, it is because the protagonist Momik is having trouble telling Wasserman's story—the actual story of the Holocaust—that he turns to the figure of Schulz, thus suggesting why others of the writers in this group also turned to Schulz. Schulz may be a victim of the Holocaust, but he is not a victim of the camps. Wasserman, on the other hand, is a survivor of Auschwitz, and the reality of the camps is a much more difficult reality to write about. Like the historical Jakob Wassermann, who was a Jewish-German writer and novelist (Appelfeld refers to him in *The Age of Wonders,* alongside Stefan Zweig and Arthur Schnitzler [1981, 108, 151]), Grossman's Wasserman is a Yiddish modernist. Insofar as the real Wassermann's first novel is titled *Melusine* (1896)—referring to the legendary, folklorist female spirit of sacred waters—there is reason to suspect that Grossman took his fantasy of Schulz as a fish from the link to Wassermann (the name Wassermann also refers, of course, to water: water man). Jakob is also the name of Schulz's father, both in biographical fact and in the represented world of his fiction. It is the name as well of the poet in Anne Michaels's *Fugitive Pieces.* Extending this pattern of intertextuality, Krauss names the protagonist of the English translation of the Spanish version of Gursky's *History of Love,* Shlomo Wasserman. There is also a second Leo Gursky in *The History of Love,* who, like Grossman's Wasserman, is a writer of children's books.

The child protagonist, Momik, of Grossman's novel is the reincarnation of a long line of Jewish dead who are locked away from grieving and thus locked into dysfunctional grief. Like the child character Bird in Krauss's novel, Momik's name is a litany of murdered and martyred Jews. "His full name, it should be mentioned, was Shlomo Efraim Neuman, in So-and-so's and So-and-so's memory. They'd have liked to give him a hundred names. Grandma Henny did it all the time. She would call him Mordechai Leibeleh, and Shepseleh and Mendel and Anshel and Shulam and Chumak, and Shlomo Haim, and that's how Momik got to know who they all were" (1989, 26). But despite his researches into the dead Jews that he in his own person resurrects, he cannot tell their story—the story of the Holocaust—directly, either through telling the story of Anshel Wasserman or through compiling a documentary history of the Holocaust:

> For many years after Grandfather Anshel's disappearance I used to hum his story to the German. I tried to write it down a couple of times . . . with no success. . . . I had reached an impasse with the story of Grandfather and Herr Neigel, so I decided to go after documentary materials, quotations from books about the Holocaust, excerpts of the victims' testimony, psychological profiles of the murderers, case notes, etc. . . . [My] own life became more and more circumscribed. . . . I [was] trapped in Zeno's paradox. (101–105)

Grossman's Wasserman ("Anshel Wasserman-Scheherazade" [194]) is the "Scheherazade" (20) of this text, who engages in what Roth, in *The Prague Orgy,* labels the "national industry of the Jewish homeland": "the construction of narrative out of the exertions of survival" (1985, 491). Foer in *Tree of Codes* (2010, 138) deals similarly with this. For this reason Wasserman cannot die, even though he would very much like to. If Grossman's Momik (and perhaps Grossman himself) cannot let Schulz rest in peace, in the novel Wasserman/Schulz cannot let himself rest in peace. He is eternally enduring, forever self-resurrecting. For this reason he becomes a philo-Semitic retrieval of an anti-Semitic trope: the wandering Jew Ahashverus, who is caught between life and death. Even though others think Wasserman is speaking "gibberish," Momik knows he is "telling a story" (1989, 19): a story of the Jewish uncanny—that place between life and death, language and silence that Jews seem always to have inhabited and that, rushing, rushing, they inhabit still. Momik also knows that for him to tell that story (or for Grossman to tell it), "a new grammar and a new calligraphy had first to be invented" (89), one that Anshel Wasserman, as a writer more similar to the more popular lineage of Yiddish and Hebrew writers than to Kafka and Schulz, does not himself write—hence Momik's (not to mention Grossman's) recourse to Schulz himself. Like Lars in Ozick's *The Messiah of Stockholm*, Momik sets out to recover Schulz's *Messiah*. Like Ozick's novel, Grossman's becomes a version of that lost masterpiece.

But Momik goes further than Lars in pursuing the dead author's text. Momik makes himself literally into the instrument of Schulz's creative genius. As I have already noted, for Momik, Bruno Schulz's *Street of Crocodiles*

> was The Book for me in the sense Bruno had yearned for *that great tome, sighing, a stormy Bible, its pages fluttering in the wind like an overblown rose*—and I believe I read it as such a letter deserves to be read: knowing that what is written on the page is less significant than the pages torn out and lost; pages so explicit they were expunged for fear that they would fall into the wrong hands. . . . [*sic*] And I did something I haven't done since I was a child: I transcribed entire paragraphs in my note book . . . to feel the words streaming out of my pen and collecting on the page. (99–100; italics in original)

Thus, in a kind of tzimtzum, Momik "vacate[s] [himself]" to "serve as his [Schulz's] writing hand, or even more than that: who could say what he would demand of me in return for re-creating his lost work, *The Messiah*?" (108). "For me," Momik continues, "Bruno is the key: an invitation and a warning. And I quoted his stories from memory" (109). Even more than Ozick, Grossman establishes himself, through Momik, as the true and only author of the *Messiah*, which the novel suggests had never actually been completed by Schulz. Whereas Ozick's Lars only wishes to recover the lost manuscript, Grossman's Momik (like Zuckerman in relation to *The Diary of Anne Frank*) makes himself the literal ghostwriter of the earlier text. He makes himself into "the vessel, the writing hand, the weak link through which [Schulz's] stifled energy could flow" (99). In this way he associates also himself with "Kafka and Mann and Duer and Hogarth and Goya and the others gracing his notebook. A fragile network of weak links across the world" (91). Although Momik includes Edvard Munch in this list of weak links, Munch (the non-Jew) does finally escape the dynamics of the Jewish symptom. He produces the kind of art that might have actually exorcised the ghosts of the past for these Jewish writers, the kind of art that Grossman himself may be thought to have produced in *See Under: Love*. But Momik, as Momik puts it, is "trapped."

Even more literally (if also literarily), Jonathan Safran Foer establishes himself as Bruno Schulz's amanuensis in *Tree of Codes*, which, like *See Under: Love* (and other books in this group) is a ghostly rewriting of Schulz. In this way Foer himself becomes a reincarnation of sorts of Schulz, producing Schulz's "Book" as ghost/written by himself. Schulz's fiction, we might note, is itself ghostly. As much a consequence of its mode of production as anything else, Jonathan Safran Foer's book is even more haunted than Schulz's. This is the case not only because we know that the words on the page we are reading are literally Schulz's words, not Foer's, but also because of the technology whereby the "die-cut book by erasure" is produced. Foer's book is created through the literal cutting out of words on the page to produce the new text. This means that words from subsequent pages inevitably peer up at us through the holes in the page we are trying to read, whatever page we are on. Like Spiegelman's graphic novel *Maus*, Foer's presents material difficulties in reading it. We might insert a blank sheet to separate the pages, or we might use our hand to block interference. Either way, however, we inevitably glimpse words from beneath that interrupt our reading and very often add resonances that are not quite applicable to the text we are at that moment perusing. Furthermore, insofar as we the readers must insert either our hands or blank sheets into the text, we are made into coauthors of the text, replicating an aspect of Foer's relationship to Schulz's text. Thereby we are forced to conspire in the conjuring of ghosts, the ghostwriting of the text. The blank sheet is reminiscent of something Appelfeld does in *Age of Wonders* when he inserts a blank sheet in the book to divide the pre-Holocaust section of the novel from the post-Holocaust section, making of the Holocaust itself a kind of blank page in and interrupting human history. In order to read Jonathan Safran Foer's book we also replicate a feature of Appelfeld's strategy, in a sense, then, conjuring and rewriting Appelfeld as well. Also, for the same reason of its material, graphic construction and our physical manipulation of it, *Tree of Codes* becomes, like *Maus*, a physical object as much as a literary text. In the case of *Tree of Codes* this material object literally reincarnates another material object, another text, even if in the process Foer produces a text of his own. This is conjuring and ghost worship at its very best. Foer exhibits the symptoms of his predecessor and of those other writers who similarly worship and idolize Bruno Schulz, such as David Grossman, whose novel precedes Foer's into print by several decades. To reintroduce

Ruth Wisse's words, Schulz's timeless spirit (his alma) cannot die. It animates Foer's text, which becomes in its own right a superbly ghostly, ghastly, and haunting text.

As novels by younger authors who have not experienced the Holocaust firsthand, both *Tree of Codes* and *See Under: Love* make explicit the consequences of the Holocaust for later generations, especially of readers. *See Under: Love* is typical of that genre of Holocaust novels that we met in *Maus*: the child-of-survivors narrative, such as discussed by Alan Berger (1997). Like Thane Rosenbaum's *Second Hand Smoke* (2000), Anne Michaels's *Fugitive Pieces*, and *Maus*, it deals with the child for whom "Over There" and the "Nazi Beast"—as Grossman's novel refers to Europe and the Nazis—is all the more terrifying because its horrors remain nameless, unspoken, and thereby still very much present in the world. Like these novels and like Art Spiegelman's *Maus*, not to mention Krauss's *Great House*, *See Under: Love* is a classic study in inherited trauma. Nor do the devastating consequences of such inherited trauma end with the child: Momik's dysfunctional fathering, born of his parents' dysfunctional parenting, threatens to perpetuate this inheritance. Thus Momik, like Lars, discovers himself unable to parent the future except in the most minimalist and compromised way. "On account of this father," *The Messiah of Stockholm* records, "Lars shrank himself. He felt he resembled his father: all the tales were about men shrinking more and more into the phantasmagoria of the mind" (1987, 5). In this way he acquires "the face of a foetus; it was as if he was waiting for his dead father to find him, and was determined to remain recognizable" (6). The (male) child Lars would un-birth himself in order to father himself; he would virtually *become*—that is, reincarnate—his own father. So would Momik un-birth and rebirth himself. His major fantasy in the Bruno section of the novel has to do with a return to the womb-like sea, which is the Schulz-accented maternal presence that might give birth to a new creative and procreative son—namely, the author Momik—not to mention the writer whose text this is: Grossman. Is the feminized name Momik a way for Grossman the author to rid his own name both of its grossness and its masculine claims (gross man)? The name Wasserman, echoing Grossman, would also associate the male author with the female sea rather than the more masculinist earth.

In this way Grossman's text, like Ozick's, has much to do with female messiahs and the procreative future of the Jewish people. "What are we to think," writes Ozick in her essay on Singer, "of the goblin cunning of a man who has taken his mother's given name—Bashevis (i.e., Bathsheba)—to mark out the middle of his own? . . . Does the taking-on of 'Bashevis' imply a man wishing to be a woman? Or does it mean that a woman is hiding inside a man?" (1983a, 218). The identification of Yiddish with the *mamaloschen* or mother tongue features prominently in Ozick's story "Envy; or, Yiddish in America" (1983d; "Mother Tongue," we recall, is the title of a story written by Sisovsky's father in Roth's

Prague Orgy; I take this as Roth's nod to Ozick). This idea of the mother tongue takes a new turn in Grossman's Israeli novel. Here the more masculinist Hebrew language is made to recover its relationship not only to the story of the Diaspora Jew (which story the Hebrew literary tradition had all but squelched, except in writers like Appelfeld) but to the feminine aspects of the mamaloschen as well. The name Momik recalls the term of endearment whereby a child (irrespective of gender) is dubbed in Israel a *mommy,* in this way wishing the child not only long life but a procreative future. "Goblin cunning" is not unrelated to an idea of golem-making, and golem-making involves not only "saving" the Jewish people but also the procreative act of birthing (generally a male golem by a male conjurer), by which that rescue might be accomplished.

Remaining recognizable—maintaining what Roth calls the "family resemblance"—is the inner burden of this family of texts, for if these Jewish protagonists and writers do not back up out of time and if they do not recapitulate in their own being the murdered fathers (and, we might add, mothers), how, then, will their parents know them in order to give birth to them again? How will their dead parents be remembered? (The scene at the end of Dara Horn's *The World to Come* seems to resonate with such questions.) The survival through literature, as Roth suggests, is the Jewish homeland: telling the story is survival itself. And yet as Kafka made so clear, and as Roth echoes him as knowing, literature is not a form of escape. It is instead further entrapment in the very condition the writer would flee. It is a symptom that, like an idol (which is the form the symptom might take), refuses to acknowledge death and mourn the dead. Grossman, Ozick, Appelfeld, Roth, Chabon, Michaels, Foer, and Krauss share a fate and a homeland. The story the Jewish storyteller finds herself telling is just that story of doomed and detested survival, which does not so much exhaust itself in the telling as drain the teller of all energy and life: "Zeno's paradox," always approaching and never arriving.

Michael Chabon's *The Final Solution: A Story of Detection* (2004) is another contender in the competition to inherit Schulz. Once again Schulz plays the role of (false) messiah or idol who needs to be discarded and yet who haunts, even to the point of obsession, the novel itself. Like the other texts I am looking at here, *The Final Solution* is a multiply intertextual text. It establishes both a lineage for itself and a potential inheritance for the murdered Schulz. Yet Chabon's novel also acts to discredit the very intertextuality through which it claims its relationship to this tradition. In keeping with its postmodernist moment, it discovers that disentangling intertextual allusions, like decoding clues (which is the expressed subject of the novel), does not solve any puzzle worth solving, especially not the Holocaust. Through the figure of Dupin/Holmes, Paul Auster's *New York Trilogy* (1994) is an intertext here (the trilogy consists of *City of Glass* [1985], *Ghosts* [1986] and *The Locked Room* [1988]). Nor is it irrelevant to the intertextual conversation initiated by Chabon's *The Final Solution* with Auster's *New York Trilogy* that the trilogy is made into a graphic novel in 2004 with an introduction by Art Spiegelman, or that illustrations by Spiegelman are contained in the 2006 deluxe edition reprint of *The New York Trilogy* (the name Spiegelman occurs, as I noted, in Chabon's *Amazing Adventures*). Auster and Chabon are agreed that no kind of detective work can solve the puzzle of the Holocaust, or, for that matter, colonial imperialism, which, according to a reading by Stef Crap and Gert Buelens (2011), is the parallel abomination toward which Chabon's *Final Solution* novel is pointing.

Like the language of the unnamed detective's beloved bees and like the numbers ("a series of uncanny noises, savage avian utterances devoid of any sense") spouted by the parrot, literature (to apply the words of the novel's detective) "mean[s] nothing" (2004, 5, 63). This does *not*, however, "imply, not in the least, that [it] ha[s] no meaning" (63). The bees can be taken to stand for the alphabet itself [i.e., b's]), not to mention that other "B" who is prominent in the text, Bruno the parrot, who represents one of the text's two Bruno Schulzes. The bird Bruno's numbers as well mean nothing but are hardly without meaning: the numbers, we come to realize, refer neither to the numbers of a Swiss bank account nor to Nazi encryptments, but to the numbers on the trains transporting the Jews to the camps. These Jews include the parents of the young Jewish boy Linus Steinman. The numbers, in other words, refer directly to Hitler's Final Solution, and they offer no final solution to the meaning of the Holocaust. Neither does Chabon's novel, despite all of its intertexts and correspondences. Indeed, the bird Bruno's uninterpretable language recalls the virtual impossibility of fully deciphering Schulz's own writings. Whatever it will mean to read Schulz, to rescue him from murder as the bird Bruno is rescued, it will not mean to make comprehensible his incomprehensible language, an insight that is of paramount importance in reading Foer's *Tree of Codes,* which is similarly difficult to decode. This is part of what makes Schulz the extraordinary writer he is. There is no mathematical equation here, no sum of all events, no translation into other words or other texts that can provide the final solution to what things mean and how or why they occurred. The spirit of things remains untranslatable, like the name Alma in Gursky's manuscript.

If Bruno Schulz is one major figure evoked in this text, initially through the name of the parrot Bruno, who is the encoder of mysteries in this book (recall again Schulz's fascination with birds), another figure is none other than Freud himself: the founder of psychoanalytic "detection" in Western culture. Freud is the decoder of the kinds of encrypted dreamlike meanings produced by Bruno Schulz in his writings. Indeed, Schulz and Freud are interpolated in the figure of Dr. Julius Steinman, the father of Linus Steinman, whose parrot, Bruno, goes missing in the story (is the name Linus a nod to another Schultz, who produces a comic strip with a character named Linus?). Julius Steinman, who bears the name of a character in the Nabokov novel *Pale Fire* (1962; a text that deals with lost and forged manuscripts) is, in *The Final Solution,* a psychoanalyst living in Vienna, whose temporary respite from deportation brings into the novel the dominant lore surrounding Bruno Schulz as we have already met it in Grossman's *See Under: Love,* Roth's *Prague Orgy,* and Foer's *Tree of Codes.* Dr. Steinman's Nazi captor, we are told, "held on to his personal Jew doctor for as long as he could" (2004, 68). Thus Dr. Steinman is one more figure for Schulz. It is Dr. Steinman's residence with this Nazi officer that gives Bruno the bird access to those cryptic, perhaps encrypted, numbers that everyone is trying to fathom, thus doubling the association between the psychoanalyst Steinman/Freud and the writer Schulz.

Steinman's vocation as a psychoanalyst is not the novel's only link to Freud, nor is the Schulz-Freud connection the only way Chabon's novel raises questions about "detection" and "final solutions." As almost all readers of the novel quickly recognize, the book's detective, with his proverbial pipe, automaton-like behaviors, and somewhat autistic personality (25, 53, 83), is a barely veiled version of Sir Arthur Conan Doyle's Sherlock Holmes. That Chabon's detective has no name further encourages the reader to assign him this name, if not literally, then at least literarily, or to assign him the equally plausible name Auguste Dupin. For behind Conan Doyle's Holmes is Edgar Allan Poe's Dupin, which is to say that behind Chabon's detective are at least two detectives, or rather three, since Paul Auster's detective in *The New York Trilogy,* named Paul Auster/William Wilson (William Wilson being the name of another Poe character) is also a descendant of Dupin and Holmes.

Chabon has several reasons for producing an American alongside the British context for his detective, which is reinforced through his naming one of the characters Shane (Shane is a famous American cowboy figure). America's relation to the Holocaust is very different from that of Europe, or even England. Primarily, however, Chabon wants Poe in his novel because Poe's detective fiction, like other of his stories of psychopathology and of conscience and revenge ("William Wilson," for example) directly anticipates key features of Freudian psychoanalysis as Freud develops them and as a critic like Marie Bonaparte (a close friend and protégé of Freud) interprets them in relation to Poe. Bonaparte writes one of the first extended interpretations of Poe and the first Freudian interpretation of his writings. Like Poe before him and like Auster later on, Chabon emphasizes the phenomena of doppelgängers and mirror images that Poe introduced into the literary tradition. By the time these doubles arrive in the writings of Auster and Chabon they produce only a funhouse of horrors that transverses several continents and imprisons all of the characters and their authors in murderous, deadening, almost meaningless patterns of duplication. In the end these doublings arrive nowhere but back at the self, as self-reflection. "In the end," Chabon's *Final*

Solution comments about the work of "detection" (announced as the book's subtitle), "their trade boiled down to purest mirror work: inversions and reflections, echoes. And there was always something dispiriting about the things one saw in a looking glass" (2004, 70). The puzzles of the world cannot be solved in any satisfactory way, even by the most astute detectives, and in the final analysis, even such detectives as Dupin, Holmes, Auster, or our nameless detective in *The Final Solution* will detect only themselves reflected in the final solutions at which they arrive. In the context of the Final Solution in its historical meaning, this means the detective will discover only himself as the source of evil and villainy he seeks. (In this context we might wonder if the character Kalb, whose name becomes reversed as Black, doesn't import Bernhard Schlink's detective Selb into the novel, producing a German turn of the screw; "*Selb*" in German means "self," and Schlink's detective series includes *Selbs Justiz, Selbs Betrug,* and *Selba Mord.*) Pertinent to such a reading of Chabon's novel is the interpretation cited above, in which the Holocaust story is itself a mirror of the story of colonial exploitation. The self-reflexivity of the book, its emphasis on doubles, also inevitably points to the author himself, who is also obsessed with conjuring and decoding, and from the author to the reader, engaging in a piece of literary interpretation.

One might say that the most one can expect in the way of solutions is a "seven-per-cent solution," to allude to the title of a novel by Nicholas Meyer (1993) that preceded Chabon's into print by several years. Given the popularity of Meyer's novel, it is difficult not to hear an echo of it in Chabon's title. At very least *The Seven-Per-Cent Solution* reminds us of the same links between the father of psychoanalysis and the art of detection that are being drawn in Chabon's *Final Solution*. Meyer gets at the essence of the parallel between psychoanalysis and detection as developed through the line of Dupin/Holmes/Auster through the same device that emerges so prominently in the other writers of the fiction in this line: the doppelgänger. In these novels detective fiction and psychoanalysis are doppelgängers of each other, while within each work characters serve as doubles of other characters. Thus in *The Seven-Per-Cent Solution* Holmes and Freud are as much doubles as are Watson and Holmes or (for that matter) Meyer and Watson, while the initial villain of the novel (from Holmes's drug-induced and neurotic perspective) is Dr. Moriarity, Holmes's "evil genius" and "his nemesis," hence a mirror image of Holmes (1993, 23). The description of Dr. Moriarity that follows could as easily fit Poe's Minister D- in "The Purloined Letter," who is a double for the protagonist Dupin: Dr. Moriarity "had been born into a good family and had had an excellent education, being endowed by nature with a phenomenal mathematical faculty. At the age of twenty-one he had written a treatise upon the Binomial Theorem, which had enjoyed a lengthy European vogue. . . . But the man possessed hereditary tendencies of the most diabolical kind, crossbred with his incredible mental prowess. . . . He is a genius, a philosopher, an abstract thinker"

(23–25). Not accidentally, Moriarity's field of expertise is mathematics, the same field of expertise as Dupin's nemesis the Minister D-. Nor is the crime that this "Napoleon of crime" (24) is guilty of unrelated to Poe's "The Purloined Letter": just as the Minister D- catches on to the queen's adultery, so is Moriarity guilty of the crime of adultery, with none other than Holmes's mother. The nature of Holmes's delusion thus matches that of the other villain of the piece in Meyer's novel, the baron's son, who kidnaps and tortures his father's bride not only for the material gain involved but in order to avenge his mother. Both Freud's neuroses and those of the sons of the baron are aptly analyzed for us in Meyer's novel by Freud himself. The "atrocities" that Holmes believes Moriarty is guilty of are only the ordinary violations of domesticity that, with Oedipal tensions gone wild, Holmes imagines as international conspiracies (25). Yet as Holmes and Freud go racing around in pursuit of their solution in a Europe that Holmes predicts will quite soon be ravaged by war, we readers become aware that looming on the even more distant horizon of the Second World War are genuine "atrocities" to be perpetrated by another "evil genius" of a different order altogether. These atrocities will far exceed the more personal and familial concerns of a Dupin or a Holmes, and they will remain impervious to deduction. These are the atrocities that move to the center of Chabon's own tale of detection, *The Final Solution*.

What the Poe/Freud or Dupin/Holmes/Freud line reminds us in Chabon's novel is that repetition in the form of doppelgängers is the *prima mobile* of this fictional tradition. Chabon's novel might well have been titled "The Purloined Parrot." Chabon's Dupin/Holmes detective; the young son of "Freud," Linus; and the parrot, Bruno, we readily come to see, all represent versions of each other. Not only do they all seem, at least to others in the book, significantly "incapable of speech" (25; the boy, we are told, is as "dumb as a mallet" [15]), but they are also adjudged to be "*non compos*" (25), either because they are too young, too old, or too animal to understand anything. Throughout the text the detective is described in animal imagery, as having "canine aplomb," being a "great bat" and "hawk moth" (88), a "lean, dank dog" (90) who huffs and "grunts" (29), and mutters and nods, "carrying on one half of a conversation" (30). Of the boy Linus we are told: "The density of his silence suggested something more than unwillingness to speak; the old man wondered if the boy might be rather less German than mentally defective, incapable of sound or sense" (6), "a mute . . . something wrong with his vocal apparatus" (8). Of course, this "mute nine-year-old boy whose face was like a blank back page from the book of human sorrows" (12; we've met that blank page before), is speaking what is, from some points of view, the only proper language vis-à-vis the Holocaust: the language of silence, as Sara Horowitz (1997) has so eloquently presented it in relation to a range of Holocaust novels. Insofar as his closest alter ego, the parrot, speaks the language of facts, like the encyclopedia that concludes Grossman's *See Under: Love*, what we have represented here are two equally possible and equally inadequate varieties of linguistic expression that mirror each other in their inability to say. No language, Chabon's book suggests—not the language of silence, not the iteration of facts, not even the rational language of detection—can offer even a "seven-per-cent solution" to the mystery of the Holocaust. "Tell me how you came to be so very far from home," our detective asks the young boy when first they meet, to which the parrot replies, "*neun neun drei acht zwei sechs sieben* (2004, 8–9; italics in original). Even after we come to see that these numbers actually do answer the detective's question, albeit obliquely and in code, they still remain what they seem to be from the start: "only . . . a series of uncanny noises, savage avian utterances devoid of any sense" (5). What, after all, do the numbers of the trains—any more than any of the historical and archival research into Nazism and its methods—tell us about the Holocaust? If the detective, bird, and child figure muteness and animal incomprehension, they are shown to mirror us, the readers, who also do not understand and cannot say.

What can be said of the language of the bees can be said of the language of the parrot and, finally, the language of the text: "The bees did speak. . . . The featureless drone, the sonic blank that others heard was . . . a shifting narrative, rich, inflected, variable and distinct as the separate stones of a featureless gray shingle. . . . It meant nothing, of course . . . but this did not imply, not at least, that the song had no meaning." But if the bees' song "was the song of a city" (63), the parrot's song is of something else again: it is the song of devastation. The paradox at the heart of this text, like the paradox at the heart of that paradox Bruno Schulz, is that even if the world has meaning it means nothing. It is this nothing that Chabon's novel so exquisitely expresses.

Even though Dara Horn's *The World to Come* (2006) does not deal directly with the Holocaust or with Bruno Schulz, I am including her novel here, since it resonates so well with the other books I am discussing. Also, Horn both multiplies the number of lost manuscripts and doubles the image with a lost painting. The novel's major protagonist, Benjamin Ziskind, who steals back the painting that had once belonged to his family and that had housed lost stories by the Yiddish writer Der Nister (who died at the hands of the Soviets rather than the Nazis), is clearly suffering, like Lars, Momik, and others in this line, from complicated mourning:

> Lately it had begun to seem to Benjamin Ziskind that the entire world was dead, that he was a citizen of a necropolis. While his parents were living, Ben had thought about them only when it made sense to think about them. . . . But now they were always here, reminding him of their presence at every moment. He saw them in the streets, always from behind, or turning a corner, his father sitting in the bright yellow taxi next to his, shifting in his seat as the cab screeched away in the opposite direction, his mother—dead six months now, though it felt like one long night—hurrying along the sidewalk on a Sunday

morning, turning into a store, just when Ben had come close enough to see her face. (2006, 9)

And later, when he actually visits the Jewish Museum to see "the exhibit of Marc Chagall's Russian Years," "he saw that the other people . . . were little more than walking ghosts: his mother, his father, preserved in other people's skin" (11). Added to Benjamin's inability to mourn his parents' death is his sense of himself as *"a freak, a relic, a generational error, a leftover shard from a broken world"* (12; italics in original). For Benjamin the Chagall painting and its hidden manuscripts are more real than the present world he inhabits.

Insofar as Benjamin reincarnates his grandfather Boris Kubak, whose Hebrew name is Benjamin and to whom the painting is initially given by Chagall, Benjamin is in many ways even more its rightful owner than his mother, Rosalie (Raisa), who carries it out of the Soviet Union with her. Rosalie is an author and illustrator of children's stories that translate into contemporary English idiom stories from the Yiddish folk tradition: stories (according to Horn's notes) that, like various episodes in the novel as well, originate in works by Der Nister, Moyshe Nadir, Mani Leyb, I. L. Peretz, Nachman of Bratslav, Sholem Aleichem, and Itsik Manger. Like Krauss's novel, Horn's is a graveyard of resurrected ghosts/writers, who haunt her novel in various ways throughout the story, making the book itself a replica of Rosalie's books within the novel: telling Yiddish stories in that new Yiddish, English. The book also becomes an act of recovery and restoration like Benjamin's when he steals back the family painting. Not for naught is Benjamin given a twin sister in the novel: Horn, like Ozick in *The Messiah of Stockholm,* twins her male protagonist, and women seize the day. "My mother rescued all these stories that were buried in library vaults and that no one would ever read again," Benjamin explains to the curator of the Jewish Museum, Erica, who discovers that Benjamin's mother has plagiarized the stories: "When she tried to publish them with the dead authors' names, nobody wanted them . . . and when she decided to publish them under her own name, her greatest dream was that someone would notice that they weren't hers, because that would have meant that someone finally cared" (2006, 206–207). The basis for Benjamin's relationship to Erica is that she is "the first person in fifteen years to care" (207). Rosalie's rescue of dead Yiddish authors parallels her rescue of the Chagall painting that was in her father's possession when he was arrested by the Soviet secret police. Her father is betrayed by his upstairs neighbor, an art thief, who himself eventually steals back the Chagall, only to have it rescued (once again) by Benjamin himself.

Horn is a younger writer than Ozick, Roth, or even Grossman. Her characters are therefore as much plagued by non-Jewish history (the Vietnam War, for example, where Benjamin's father, Daniel, loses a leg) as by Jewish history. Insofar as Jewish history nonetheless pertains, this history has more to do with the

Soviet Union, both past and present, than with the Holocaust. Benjamin's twin sister eventually marries and has a child with a Jewish refugee from the Soviet Union, while the central Jewish catastrophe of the novel, involving Der Nister, is the Night of the Murdered Poets, when thirteen Jews, five of them Yiddish writers who (like Der Nister) were members of the Jewish Anti-Fascist Committee, were executed in 1952 (Der Nister was not killed in this particular execution). The characters in Ozick's and Grossman's novels, and Leo Gursky as well, who are Holocaust survivors, have endured much more recognizable forms of bereavement and dislocation than Horn's Benjamin. For this reason Lars's fantasy that his father is the dead author Bruno Schulz, like Momik's weird games and obsessions in *See Under: Love,* or Leo's delusional conjuring of his dead friend, Bruno, may seem to us less neurotic symptoms we wish to cure than understandable and forgivable—if desperate—fantasies. Yet these fantasies do not serve these protagonists' best interests any more than Benjamin's do. Like hysterical symptoms (which, of course, they are, however much we might understand and sympathize with them), these fantasies keep the characters (and often their families) pinned in the place of devastation and loss, unable to grieve properly and hence unable to move on. Krauss's doubling the melancholic survivor Leo in Alma's melancholic mother, who still has two young children to raise and who is not a Holocaust survivor, suggests the dangers of getting trapped in the kind of complicated mourning that afflicts these characters. It is a significant moment in Krauss's novel when the daughter says to her mother that she needs her to be less sad. Alma needs and is entitled to a less dysfunctional mother. Similarly, Horn's Benjamin needs the promise of a "world to come" in this world that will be informed by but will not necessarily suffer the symptoms of the past.

6 See Under: Mourning

IN RESURRECTING BRUNO SCHULZ or other figures from the murdered Jewish past, Ozick, Roth, Grossman, Appelfeld, Chabon, Krauss, Horn, and Foer ghost/ write that past. In fact, they golem/write it, producing idols in and as text. "You lovers of literature. You parasites," Elsa/Adela hurls at Lars at the end of Ozick's *The Messiah of Stockholm* (in a line that echoes the auto-anti-Semitic and anti-Semitic definition of the Jewish writer in Appelfeld's *Age of Wonders*); "you should ask yourselves if *you* exist" (Ozick 1987, 141; italics in original). It is an accusation, I suggest, that the text hurls at itself. Like Roth's *The Prague Orgy*, Ozick's *Messiah of Stockholm* impugns its own motives. The text is on some level aware that it is as obsessed with Bruno Schulz and the Jewish history he represents as is its protagonist Lars. How could Jews not be obsessed this way? For the writers I have been discussing, the demons of the past are captured in Ozick's image of "the man in the long black coat . . . hurrying . . . hurrying and hurrying toward the chimneys" (1987, 144); they hurry around and through us as well. To deny this current of Jewish history would be to evade and bury the past in oblivion. To be swept along by it would be to see the world through a murdered eye that can see only what has been and is now destroyed. "That roasting in the air," writes Ozick, somewhere between her voice and Lars's. "His own sweat. The exertion. His legs like gyros. O the chimneys of armpits, moist and burning under wool" (18). The imagery repeats throughout the text. In fact, the imagery *is* the text, and that is my point.

And yet on occasion and despite the persistence of the great rush of symptoms of Jewish history, we can do something else: "Yet it happened on occasion— not very frequently—that Lars grieved for his life." And in the text's final sentence, simply, "he grieved" (143–44). In the final analysis, against the powerful temptation that they embody to surrender to idols, golems, and messiahs to save themselves and the Jewish people, these texts *do* grieve. In grieving they open up for themselves and their readers the possibility of a future homeland that is not merely an entrenched, reincarnated, reconstruction of the past and its sorrows and traumas but also a place of mourning and finally of life—even, as Krauss puts it, of love. Thus Ozick writes of her protagonist in *The Messiah of Stockholm,* when he reads through the manuscript he believes to be the lost text of Schulz's *Messiah:* "Lars fell into the text with the force of a man who throws himself against a glass wall. He crashed through it to the other side, and what was there? Baroque arches and niches, intricately hedged byways of a language so incised, so *bleeding*—a touch could set off a hundred slicing blades. . . . Lars did not resist or hide; he let his flesh rip" (105; italics in original). The expression of grief in Ozick's text (captured in the squawking of the parrot Bruno in Chabon's novel) is finally a kind of scream that can neither be squelched (as Rosa squelches it in *The Shawl*) nor decoded (as everyone wishes to do with Bruno's squawks in *The Final Solution*). It certainly cannot be transformed into an idol or golem or messiah.

What Jewish tradition has instead of a messiah is mourning, sitting shivah for the dead. This is implicit in Aharon Appelfeld's *Age of Wonders,* which is it-self (like many of Appelfeld's novels) an act of mourning for Europe's dead Jews, including the tradition of Jewish authorship that died with them. This act of mourning is available to the characters in the book, but they do not avail them-selves of it, making first Father and then his son, Bruno, victims of incomplete mourning. The novel's titling of the major character, Bruno, and its constant ref-erence to the tradition of Kafka, Wassermann, Zweig, and Schnitzler suggests the book's own placement of itself within the same lineage that characterizes father and son. Yet, like Ozick's *The Messiah of Stockholm* and the other novels I have been discussing, *The Age of Wonders* exceeds, even while it participates in, the characters' torments. Indeed, the book's ability to acknowledge in a straightfor-ward manner the great German-speaking Jewish writers (as well as the Polish Schulz) reverses the father's obsessive, self-hating disowning of these writers (as of himself). "Once they would allude to his Jewishness indirectly," we are told of Bruno's father's critics. "Now they spoke openly about the alien elements, the germs of decadence, sown in all his sentences. . . . And he was thus ready to admit that neither he nor Wassermann nor Zweig nor even Schnitzler had attained any real standing in art" (1981, 107–108). "Perhaps he really is guilty of something," David Grossman has his Bruno Schulz think. "Of looking as he does. Of being the Jew he is. Of writing as he does" (1989, 95). It is this view of the literary tra-dition of Kafka and Schulz that the minister of culture expresses in *The Prague Orgy,* where communism substitutes for fascism: modernist art, Jewish art, is art produced by "sexual perverts," "alienated neurotics," "bitter egomaniacs," "malcontents and parasites and outcasts. At least their blessed Kafka," he finally exclaims, "knew he was a freak" (Roth 1985, 777). Kafka remains immune to Fa-ther's condemnation of Jewish artistic genius (Appelfeld 1981, 92–93 and 44), but Kafka is not enough to sustain him in his belief in his own Kafka-like, which is to say Schulzian, art, which might be another reason Appelfeld names Father's son Bruno: Bruno Schulz stands in for Kafka, who is the one Jewish writer who survives the anti-Semitism and Jewish self-hatred of the Nazi era. Yet, as I have already suggested, as a victim of the Holocaust, Bruno Schulz also imports into Appelfeld's story the murder of the Jews in a way Kafka cannot.

Like his father before him, Bruno is compelled by an "alien force" that takes "possession" of him as it once did his father (67). By transforming him into his father, it deprives him of independent action and desire:

> Coming back had not been his idea. Something stubborn and abiding inside him had sealed off whole sectors of his emotions. In the course of the years he had learned to live without them, as a person learns to live with a paralyzed limb. The two letters suddenly coming from far away had stirred the old scar into a new pain: his father. His father. The disgrace he had not dared to touch, sitting silently all these years like pus inside a wound. . . . In recent years, perhaps because he himself was already approaching his father's age, he felt the old, wretched shame swelling inside him in a different way, no longer hatred but a kind of distance and even wonder. . . . His father, his father. The wound that never healed. (209, 266)

Although "reincarnation" is associated in the text with the character Brum, the Jew who metamorphoses into an Austrian before the war and thus survives, it is Bruno who is presented as reincarnating the past. Because he is stuck in the past, he returns to his hometown as his father's ghost to a world unchanged except that almost no one remembers him or the father whom he reincarnates. Do not "stir up evil spirits," Brum tells him, repeating the words "evil spirits" from part 1. "Nothing in your character has changed, I see," he says to Bruno, "the same old Jewish impudence" (267). Bruno's response to Brum, which is to beat him up, brings him no solace. Bruno gets no further in his progress toward self-acceptance of himself as a Jew and a Jewish author than his father had. As he leaves his town of birth, Bruno's words, we are told, are still not his own, and as he was at the beginning of his journey, he is "empty of thought [and] feeling" (270). Like his child-of-survivors wife, Mina, he has been "bequeathed . . . too much suffering" (265). He is wracked by guilt. He has experienced his father as a disgrace, and he would make up to his father both for what he (the son) has felt and for what his father has lost. Like the son in *The Prague Orgy,* he would make his artistic goal to secure the publication of his father's writings, thus resurrecting his father through himself, becoming his father's reincarnation.

By the end of the novel Bruno is as much an automaton as his father had been at the beginning. In both cases the characters' psychological dysfunction is associated with their hostility to Jews and Jewish tradition. "Even now Father clung to his illusions," the text tells us in part 1. "He wrote, polished his manuscript feverishly. All his rage was turned inward against himself, against the flawed creations of his spirit. He shut himself in his room and worked day and night, struggling against the evil spirits that had not stopped beating on our door since the summer" (154). Those "evil spirits" (24, 26, 39, 75, 140, 141) are not only the anti-Semitic powers that be, who will put an end to Father's career and eventually to his life, but also the forces of Jewish self-hatred that haunt prewar Austria, both in relation to what are perceived as petit bourgeois Jews (45, 54) and "the *Ostjuden*" (24), the Eastern European Jews, who were (from Father's perspective) "infesting Austria like rats, infesting the whole world, to tell the truth" (133), picking up sentiments expressed earlier in the text as well (61). Bruno is similarly repulsed by the religious Jew he meets on the train heading back into Austria.

It is no surprise, therefore, that Bruno and his father should resist Jewish rituals, including the one ceremony that might actually have put some closure to the devastation caused by the Holocaust: mourning, sitting shivah for the dead. Toward the end of section 1, Mother's sister, Theresa, dies, and the novel gives us the scene of "mourning" (119, 120) that Father earlier refuses when his aunt Gusta dies:

> We were left with the task of burying her according to the customs of her forefathers, which she had written down in a notebook before she died. Father brought some Jews from the provincial capital. They spoke in an unintelligible language and scurried about the rooms kicking up a racket. It was ugly and shameful, but since it was her last wish we did everything mutely and submissively. (85–86)

When Theresa dies, however, Bruno's mother does sit shivah for her sister, and she mourns. The backdrop to this scene of Jewish mourning is the decision of Father's friend Kurt, who is only half Jewish, to take on Jewish identity and be circumcised. Father is as little pleased with Kurt's decision to become an identified Jew as he is with his wife's observance of the customs of mourning. "'Why take this trouble on yourself, Kurt?'" he asks his friend. "'You're a free man. . . . Your artistic heritage is one of freedom . . . and you want to exchange this health, this freedom, for an old, sick faith'" (120). What Father feels in relation to Kurt's decision is "naked pain" (121). This is what he might have felt in relation to what his Austrian compatriots have done to him and his family. Yet Father cannot express naked pain, and his dismay in relation to Kurt's choice leads him down an old familiar trail: he further rails against his "incurable literary defects" as defined by his anti-Semitic critics. "Only the dispassionate French artists," Father finally concludes, "only they were the true artists" (120). Dispassion rather than the expression of pain, sorrow, or outrage becomes for Father the defining characteristic of art. Father will bequeath to his son not only "too much suffering" (265) but the dispassion, which is to say repression, denial, and refusal of pain, that also afflicts Bruno's wife, Mina, as it once characterized Bruno's father. Father and Bruno will not rail against what comes to seem to them not injuries and assaults against them, but disgraces and flaws that they possess. They will not grieve, but will turn their anger inward and convert it into "depression" and "gloom" (133–34).

To invoke the image from the beginning of the "Bruno" section of *See Under: Love,* which Grossman takes from the paintings of Edvard Munch, neither Bruno nor his father will utter the scream—so much like the parrot Bruno's squawk, so much like the shrill scream of Schulz's own fiction—that might pierce through the dispassion that afflicts them. Neither will mourn, and in failing to mourn they condemn themselves to obsessively repeat the disgraces they have suffered at the hands of others. As we have seen, in *See Under: Love* Momik imagines Schulz as entertaining the idea that Munch too is one more weak link in the chain of artists with whom Momik identifies. Yet Munch, as he emerges in the Bruno section, is a different sort of artist altogether. It may be significant that Munch is *not* Jewish:

> They displayed Munch's painting in the farthermost corner of the gallery (so disturbing was it to them). . . . It was cordoned off, with a sign in Polish and German saying: DO NOT TOUCH. . . . Idiots. They should have protected the public from the painting, not the other way around. . . . Kissing it there in the gallery, Bruno felt infected. Or perhaps the kiss had brought a latent infection to life. . . . The moment Bruno saw *The Scream* at the Artus Hopf Gallery, he knew: the artist's hand must have slipped on the canvas. Munch could not have planned such perfection. He would not have dared to. . . . The kind of perfection Munch discovered was either a mistake or a case of serendipity. . . . Munch turned traitor. He allowed himself to be unraveled, and the scream burst rudely into your midst. And now it is here, so quickly patch the hole. . . . DO NOT TOUCH." (Grossman 1989, 89–90)

The question for the writers of post-Holocaust Schulz-obsessed fiction is how to utter this scream within their fictions without obliterating the history of events or the history of love. The question is how to mourn the Jewish dead, for to mourn is not to forget. It is not to make the dead disappear; rather it is to place the deceased in a vital, life-sustaining relation to the living. It is to make them present in a way that neither possesses nor paralyzes the present. So as not to remain stuck, in melancholy, in the place of death and loss, the protagonists of these texts—indeed the texts themselves—must learn, like Lars does (at least on occasion), to "grieve." They must learn to mourn. They must permit the dead to die.

This is what Joe Kavalier in Chabon's *Amazing Adventures* learns at the end of the novel. For Joe the healing process only begins with his writing his comic book fiction about the Golem of Prague, who is the very Golem who saved him and whose image, reconfigured as a comic strip, begins the process of his recovery from grief:

> He immersed himself ever deeper into its potent motifs of Prague and its Jews, of magic and murder, persecution and liberation, guilt that could not be expiated and innocence that never stood a chance—as he dreamed, night after night at his drawing table, the long and hallucinatory tale of a wayward, unnatural child, Josef Golem, that sacrificed itself to save and redeem the little

lamplit world whose safety had been entrusted to it, Joe came to feel that the work—telling his story—was helping to heal him. (2000, 577)

But

by 1953, when Tommy Clay had stumbled upon him in the magic shop, Joe's ability to heal himself had long since been exhausted. He needed Rosa—her love, her body, but above all, her forgiveness—to complete the work that his pencils had begun. The only trouble was that, by then . . . it was too late. He had waited too long. The sixty miles of Long Island that separated him from Rosa seemed more impassable than the jagged jaw of one thousand between Kelvinator Station and Jotunheim, than the three blocks of London that lay between Wakefield and his loving wife. (578; "Wakefield" is an important intertext for Paul Auster in *The New York Trilogy*, which, as I noted earlier, forms an intertext for Chabon's *The Final Solution*; Chabon uses the words "wonderful escape" from "Wakefield" as one of two epigrams in *Amazing Adventures*.)

"Something paradoxical had occurred in the five years he had worked on *The Golem*: the more of himself, of his heart and his sorrows, that he had poured into the strip—the more convincingly he demonstrated the power of the comic book as a vehicle of personal expression—the less willingness he felt to show it to other people, to expose what had become the secret record of mourning, of his guilt and retribution" (578–79). This, Rosa fears, is "'survivor's guilt'" (562), and until Joe can grieve for his losses, it is just that.

It is only after a visit to "Machpelah" (606), where Houdini is buried (the word *machpelah* referring in Hebrew to the cave where Abraham is presumably buried), that Joe can mourn and go home to his wife and son. "He wondered what he would have put on his own parents' tombstones had he been given the opportunity. Names and dates alone seemed extravagance enough" (607). The moment recalls the final drawing in Spiegelman's *Maus* of his parents' tombstones, together with their names and dates, when Art signs on to Vladek's idea of the happy, happy ending of his life with his beloved Anja. Here the moment signals Joe's acceptance of the fact that his family is really gone. As soon as he associates Houdini's tombstone with that of his parents, Joe has a vision in which he sees Bernard Kornblum, whom he also must accept is dead: "*Lieber Meister,*" he addresses him. "What should I do?" "Go home," the ghost of Kornblum tells him (608), and he does, to the only home left to him: Tommy and Rosa. It is because before this moment Joe had not given up his hope that someone of his family might have survived that he is reluctant to use his considerable savings to buy Empire Comics. Now he will go home, and he will purchase the comic book company so that he and Sam can begin anew. For Sam beginning anew will mean leaving for California, for the new Jewish entertainment industry. "[Sam] had no choice," we are told, "but to set himself free" (651). In leaving Rosa and Tommy, Sam will reverse the direction of Leo's action in Krauss's novel. He will give the child back to his biological father, though he will also, like Leo, relinquish his own parental authority. For Joe beginning anew will mean staying and taking on the responsibilities of paternity (as Grossman's Momik and Appelfeld's Bruno cannot do). It will mean realizing his dream (like Benjamin's mother in *The World to Come*) of translating Jewish tradition into popular images that an American public, even a child, can read. Joe would do what Chabon is doing in the novel: produce literature.

Not accidentally Joe's arrival home after his revelation at the cemetery occurs simultaneously with the arrival of the box containing the Golem of Prague, with whom Joe had begun his journey to the "Statue of liberation," as his brother, Thomas, had called the Statue of Liberty (59). "Prague," says Rosa, reading the address off the coffin. "What do you know," which is immediately followed by Tommy's saying, "He's home. . . . Rosa didn't understand what he meant until she heard the sound of the Studebaker in the drive" (599). Both Joe and the Golem (conflated in the word "he") arrive home together, not to Prague but to Rosa and Tommy. The box, Joe tells Tommy, contains "chains"—not the iron chains Tommy imagines, but the invisible chains that have bound his father to a past that he must finally let go. "It was strange, Joe thought, that the box should weigh so much more, now, than it had when the Golem was still intact. He wondered if other dirt, extra dirt, had come to be added to the original load, but this seemed unlikely. Then he remembered how Kornblum . . . had quoted some paradoxical wisdom about golems, something in Hebrew to the effect that it was the Golem's unnatural soul that had given it weight; unburdened of it, the earthen Golem was light as air" (611). Thus the box is filled not with "dirt," as Tommy surmises when the lid comes off, but with "ashes." These ashes are not only of the "silty bed of the Moldau," out of which the Golem was formed, but, of course, of the murdered Jews, including Joe's parents. "Possibly there [was] more than one lost soul embodied in all that dust, weighing it down so heavily, Joe thinks to himself" (612). Indeed, the one object Tommy finds in the ashes is Joe's father's calling card. "Every universe, our own included, begins in conversation," Joe explains to Sammy. "Every golem in the history of the world, from Rabbi Hanina's delectable goat to the river-clay Frankenstein of Rabbi Judah Low ben Bezalel, was summoned into existence through language, through murmuring, recital, and kabbalistic chitchat—was, literally, talked into life" (119), or perhaps more accurately for Chabon's book, drawn into life. And drawn into life, as text, the Golem draws his artist Joe into life after him, the dead souls of the Jewish dead and the dead soul of the Golem made clay again, to be replaced by the living soul of the artist, the "alma" of this text.

The recovery of a lost text that has the power to draw a melancholic character out of his melancholy and back into life is a central feature of Anne Michaels's *Fugitive Pieces* as well, which, like the other novels we have been looking at, also features a protagonist locked into a state of unending mourning for his murdered family. Indeed, it features two such protagonists, the second of whom is called, like the hero in Horn's *The World to Come*, Ben. Like Horn's Ben, who is poised at the end of the novel, ready to enter "the world to come," which is not the world beyond this world, but this world itself, so Michaels's Ben must step into the world to come, which is also, simply, the world that exists. He does this through the recovery of a manuscript. This is a manuscript written by a person who, like Rosa in *The Shawl*, is unable to enter the world to come until the end of his life and to love until he (like Joe) produces the text that heals his sorrow.

The child survivor Jakob Beer never has children, although his wife, Michaela, is pregnant when they die. Like other Holocaust fictions (*The Far Euphrates*, *The Age of Wonders*, Rebecca Goldstein's *The Mind-Body Problem* [1983], and Imre Kertész's *Kaddish for a Child Not Born* [1997], for example), *Fugitive Pieces* multiplies the murdered six million by the millions of others who will never come into the world as a result of the Holocaust. But from the book's perspective Jakob Beer is also not the right vehicle for the reproduction of the Jewish people. As his name suggests, Jakob Beer belongs to the Jewish past: he is the coffin (bier) in which that past (like the Golem of Prague) can be buried, even if his story cannot be forgotten and abandoned. Jakob's relationship with the woman who teaches him to love (Michaela) is what begins the process that undoes not only Jakob's complicated mourning but also, and more to the point of future generations, Ben's. It is for Ben, the survivors' son, to bring the process of regeneration to fruition through the recovery of Beer's manuscripts.

"*To remain with the dead is to abandon them*," Beer realizes. "All the years I felt Bella entreating me, filled with her loneliness, I was mistaken. I have misunderstood her signals. Like other ghosts, she whispers; not for me to join her, but so that, when I'm close enough, she can push me back into the world" (Michaels 1998, 170; into the world to come, to apply Horn's title; italics in original). "My son, my daughter: May you never be deaf to love. Bela, Bella: Once I was lost in a forest. I was so afraid. My blood pounded in my chest and I knew my heart's strength would soon be exhausted. I saved myself without thinking. I grasped the two syllables closest to me, and replaced my heartbeat with your name" (195). That internalization of the dead sister Bella, like the introjection of the dead child Magda for Rosa, saves Beer, but at the cost of perpetuating the mourning that prevents Jakob's recovery from the horrific losses of his childhood. Hence Jakob's advice to his unborn son or daughter Bela/Bella, which becomes (through his writings) his advice to Ben as well, is not to stay with the dead, but, rather, to remember and commemorate them and to let them go:

> Child I long for: if we conceive you, if you are born, if you reach the age I am now, sixty, I say this to you: Light the lamps, but do not look for us. Think of us sometimes, your mother and me. . . . Light the lamp, cut a long wick. . . . I pray that one day in a room lit only by night snow, you will suddenly know how miraculous is your parents' love for each other. (194–95)

The lamp that Jakob would have his son or daughter Bela/Bella light can be identified with the *yartzheit* (memorial) candle that Jews light immediately following the death of a loved one and every year thereafter on the anniversary of the death. Jakob would have his children mourn in this specifically Jewish way: ritualistic, moderated, and a part of a continuity of acts of mourning, and thus not in the service of death but of life. And he would have them also let in the light of the "night snow" (195), the light of nature that shines through darkness and death. It is this light that is shining on the snowy night when we last see Ben on his way home to his wife, recollecting his father "in the snow-blue kitchen" and his mother stroking his father's hair (294), thus recalling his own parents' love for each other.

Insofar as Jakob's rescue from the Nazis is itself an image of rebirth (he is pulled out of the ground by the geologist Athos), the book configures recovery from the horrors of the Holocaust, whether as primary traumas for victims or secondary traumas for the children of victims or, for that matter, for the rest of us, as a sort of historical or evolutionary process. It occurs over time, which is the only route by which either an individual or a community can come to assume a posttraumatic self. Victims are not to be viewed as sacrifices, which is how Rosa views Magda: as a Christ figure. The Jewish dead do not bring redemption to anyone. They are not messiahs in that sense. Nor are the dead meant to be a temptation to suicide. Committing suicide would affirm the idea that the Jews were not meant to survive. Mourning is rather a multigenerational process, which has as its objective a mediated and protected relationship to the dead.

A similar dynamic of grief and mourning characterizes Nicole Krauss's *Great House,* which, like another of Aharon Appelfeld's novels, *Iron Tracks* (1998), records one man's rescue of the material artifacts of murdered European Jewry. In Appelfeld's novel the child survivor Irwin, now a fifty-year-old man, follows the iron tracks of a double obsession. He intends to recover lost items of stolen and abandoned Judaica (which, by selling, he secures his livelihood), *and* he plans to avenge the murder of his father, with whom he had a complex, somewhat ambivalent relationship (somewhat reminiscent of Bruno's relationship to his father in *The Age of Wonders* or of Bruno Schulz with his father). Indeed, Irwin pursues the rescue of Jewish possessions in order to accomplish his revenge on his father's murderer. By the end of the novel, Irwin's two obsessions have become synonymous, and what we are witnessing is a man who is so incapable of mourning that he has become possessed by his obsessions. Insofar as Irwin carries the author's name into the text (Appelfeld's original name was Irwin), and insofar as many of the objects Irwin recovers are "manuscripts" and "books" (1998, 183), the Jewish writer (whether self-reflexively as Appelfeld himself or Jewish authorship generally) is implicated in the iron tracks of an obsession-compulsion such as typifies many of the other authors and characters we have examined thus far: Lars in Ozick's *Messiah of Stockholm,* for example, and Bruno in *The Age of Wonders.* Irwin's obsessive-compulsive quest brings no more solace to him than to the other Jewish non-mourners we have met. Not only has he sold all of the objects he has recovered, but also his murder of his father's murderer only makes him more acutely aware of his despondency and his obsessive-compulsive traits. The book ends thus: "It was clear that my life in this place had burned up and come to an end. If I had a different life, it wouldn't be happy. As in all my clear and drawn-out nightmares, I saw the sea of darkness, and I knew that my deeds had neither dedication nor beauty. I had done everything out of compulsion, clumsily, and always too late" (Appelfeld 1998, 195).

Krauss's *Great House* has a somewhat less grim conclusion, although, as is the case with other texts we've been examining, it is not necessarily the characters who resolve their issues so much as the text itself. In the case of Krauss's novel, as of Dara Horn's, recovery from the Jewish past is put in the hands of heretofore unborn generations, to whom is bequeathed the "key" to Jewish survival (the key to the migrating desk being reminiscent of the key in Chabon's *Amazing Adventures*). Like *The History of Love*, *Great House* is told in multiple voices, producing multiple histories and perspectives, all of which come to converge by the end of the novel through the single object—the desk—that travels throughout the text, from character to character, and over time and geographical distances. Since many a text is written at this desk, it obviously becomes a figure for authorship writ large. The major narrators of the different sections are Nadia, the New York writer who opens the text and who writes the two sections titled "All Rise"; the father of "Your Honor" (Dov), the man to whom Nadia is narrating her life story as contained in those sections, after she has accidentally run him down with her car while she is visiting in Jerusalem (the father's two sections are titled "True Kindness"); an English professor named Arthur Bender (two sections titled "Swimming Holes"), whose wife, Lotte Berg, is the owner of the peripatetic desk before it is given to the Chilean poet (eventually killed by the regime in Chile) Daniel Varsky, who in turn gives it to Nadia in New York, who then gives it to the daughter of a collector of lost Jewish possessions (like Irwin in Appelfeld's novel) named George Weisz. This story is told, first, by Weisz's son Yoav's girlfriend, Isabel (Izzie), in "Lies Told by Children" and then, in the concluding chapter, by Weisz himself (the final section of the novel is titled simply enough "Weisz"). It is Weisz's daughter, Leah, who retrieves the desk from Nadia, which is the event that sends Nadia fleeing to Jerusalem in pursuit of the desk, with which she has developed her own obsessive relationship: "I'm not going in order to claim back the desk," Nadia tells her psychotherapist, which is good evidence that that is indeed why she's going (Krauss 2010, 45). As Nadia's ex-husband puts it, "You're lost in your own world, Nadia, in the things that happen there, and you've locked all the doors" (38). It is on the trip to Jerusalem that Nadia hits Dov with her car and inadvertently reveals to Weisz that his daughter has indeed rescued the desk, the desk with a locked drawer that will finally begin to unlock all of Nadia's as well as Dov's and the Weiszes' locked doors.

Leah Weisz gains possession of the desk by claiming to be Daniel Varsky's (illegitimate) daughter, hence the legitimate (but also illegitimate) owner of the desk. Of course, as the daughter of the man, or, more precisely, the granddaughter of the man, to whom the desk belongs (the desk originally belonged to Weisz's father), Leah is in fact the legitimate owner of the desk. Since Bender (Lotte Berg's husband) imagines that Daniel is his wife's son (later he'll think Weisz is the father of her illegitimate child, whom he already knows is not Daniel), we have in this book, as in Ozick's *Messiah of Stockholm*, lines of imagined and perhaps illegitimate descent. We also have the reconstruction of family along nonbiological lines. Characters double each other as if they were indeed relatives of each other. Thus, when Nadia first meets Leah, she sees her as the spitting image of Daniel Varsky, who is, of course, not her father. Similarly, she sees the man she picks up in Jerusalem as Varsky's double. Like the lost manuscript of Schulz's *Messiah* in Ozick's novel, Jakob Beer's writings in *Fugitive Pieces*, or Gursky's in *The History of Love*, the desk organizes the otherwise unrelated individuals in the novel into a family of sorts, a Jewish, post-Holocaust family founded on loss and desire rather than biological reproduction. By the end of the novel, Nadia, who has no offspring of her own, is also put in a familial relationship with Dov. The hospital staff understands her to be his wife or girlfriend, and by sitting at his side till his father arrives, she indeed takes on that role. Dov had also wanted to be a writer (like Nadia), but he became a judge instead, taking on his father's profession, albeit in England rather than in Israel. This is also a multinational family: Dov and his family and the Weiszes are Israeli; Nadia and Yoav Weisz's girlfriend are American; Lotte and Bender are British (although Lotte is a refugee); and Daniel Varsky is South American. In contrast to, but also as a reflection of, these manufactured familial ties is the hope of the actual marriage between Yoav Weisz and his American girlfriend, which we assume will take place after the book ends and which in Weisz's view promises to bear offspring, thus finally producing some biological descendants to this complicated and very sad Holocaust-scarred community. These descendants represent the world to come, who will inherit the desk not as a fetishistic object of blocked mourning, but as containing the enduring secret of Jewish existence: the Great House of Jewish learning, which is a figure for the immaterial transmission of Jewish learning and Jewish texts.

Of all the characters in the novel, Weisz is the most deeply entrenched in melancholy, depression, and the obsessive-compulsive pursuit of the past, with its devastating consequences for his children, a feature of father-child relations that to some degree is replicated in the relationship of Dov and his father. Weisz, we are told, suffers from a "hereditary disease" (286), and like others in the Jewish family, he passes it on. Weisz's fetishistic relationship to objects of the past dooms his children to an inherited trauma of repetition compulsion and despair. His profession (like that of Appelfeld's Irwin), on the surface of it, is reasonable enough: he recovers remnants from people's former lives. But Weisz's profession is hardly innocent.

As he describes his pursuits in his conversation with Bender:

> a little child's bed or the chest where he kept his toys. . . . I can't bring the dead back to life. But I can bring back the chair they once sat in, the bed where they slept. . . . They can hardly believe it, as if I'd produced the gold and silver sacked when the Romans destroyed the Temple two thousand years ago. The holy object looted by Titus that mysteriously disappeared so that the cataclysmic loss would be total, so that there would be no evidence left to keep the Jew from turning a place into a longing he could carry with him wherever he wandered, forever. (275)

Weisz would undo the totality of the loss, but to do that he has to become, like Chabon's Josef Kavalier, a conjurer, a magician. Therefore, Weisz sometimes produces the object "out of thin air." This, he suggests, is not "cheating" (276). Rather it is charity. It brings solace to souls in pain, permitting closure and an end to suffering to those who are willing to accept substitute objects in place of the originals, despite their initial inklings that the objects before them are *not* the original pieces. In so doing Weisz trades in necromancy and the dark arts.

Such magic, however, is less dangerous than what Weisz does with the desk. Unlike his customers, Weisz cannot be deceived. He cannot receive the gift of substitution, the magic of "thin air," that will ultimately be revealed as the desk's mystical secret. The desk, which had belonged to Weisz's father, is for Weisz the fetishistic object pure and simple. He may be able to pass off to others his quest (like Irwin's for revenge) as being of a piece with his other missions, but he cannot deceive himself. Nor can he fool himself as to which desk is the authentic desk. He will not accept anything but the selfsame object. Indeed, the desk is the culmination of his attempt to replicate in full in his study in Jerusalem his father's study in Budapest:

> He had searched for and repossessed every . . . piece of furniture in that room, the same pieces that had sat in own father's study in Budapest until the night in 1944 when the Gestapo had arrested his parents. Another person would have considered them lost forever. But that was what set her father apart. . . . In the years after the War, when Weisz returned to Budapest, the first thing he did was knock on [the] neighbors' doors and, as the color washed out of their faces, entered their apartments with a small gang of hired thugs who seized the stolen furniture. . . . Later, in his business, Weisz hired others to do such work. But his own family's furniture he always appeared to claim himself. (114)

Our narrator in the section titled "Lies Told by Children," Yoav's girlfriend, Izzie, tells us that "at the time" that she lived with Yoav and his sister in London, "I didn't know anything about Weisz's study in Jerusalem, and so the poetic symmetry of the [London] house's nearness to Freud's was lost on me":

> When Freud fled Vienna almost all of his belongings were crated up and shipped to the new house in London, where his wife and daughter lovingly reassembled, down to the last possible detail, the study he'd been forced to abandon at 19 Berggasse. . . . Maybe all exiles try to re-create the place they've lost out of fear of dying in a strange place. . . . I was often struck by the irony that Freud, who shed more light than anyone on the crippling burden of memory, had been unable to resist its mythic spell any better than the rest of us. After he died, Anna Freud preserved the room exactly as her father left it. (110–11)

Whether or not Freud's suffering from the same neurosis as Weisz lessens our sense of Weisz's dysfunction, his daughter, Leah, distinguishes herself from Freud's daughter by resisting her father's obsession with replicating the past, *"as if by putting all the pieces back together he might collapse time and erase regret"* (116; italics in original). *"The only thing missing in the study on Ha'Oren Street,"* Leah writes to Izzie in the letter in which she also asks Izzie to return to Yoav:

> *was my grandfather's desk—where it should have stood, there was a gaping hole. Without it, the study remained incomplete, a poor replica. And only I knew the secret of where it was. That I refused to hand it over to him was what tore our family apart in the year when you lived with us, a few months before he killed himself. And yet he refused to acknowledge it! I thought I'd killed him with what I'd done. But it was just the opposite. When I read his letter . . . I understood that my father had won. That at last he found a way to make it impossible for us ever to escape him. After he died, we went home to the house in Jerusalem. And we stopped living.* (116; italics in original)

Yet in her resistance to her father—what her father calls her "denying" him (288)—Leah, in her father's view, "could not have invented a more fitting end. . . . She found a solution for me," Weisz explains, "though it was not the one either of us had intended" (288). Leah does not cause her father's death, at least not in the way she imagines. As is the case of Wasserman in Grossman's *See Under: Love* and, as we shall see, for Leo Gursky in *The History of Love*, Weisz needs permission to die. Speaking of himself in the third person, as one of his customers rather than as himself (which itself suggests something of Weisz's alienation from himself), he says to Bender in London: "And I understood then that he could not die until I found the desk. That he wanted to die, but he could not. I became afraid. I wanted to be through with him. What right did he have to burden me with this? With the responsibility of his life if I didn't find it, and his death if I did?" (Krauss 2010, 277).

The absence of the desk is what keeps Weisz alive, in pursuit (like Gursky and Wasserman) of what he needs in order to die. By being prevented from actually bringing the desk to Jerusalem, Weisz is forced to stay alive, but the visit by Nadia, to whom he had traced the desk and from whom his daughter had received it, only to hide it in a warehouse in New York, finally does put him in possession of the desk's whereabouts. He is then able to go to the desk, sit at it for an hour, and having fulfilled his quest, return home to commit suicide, *without* relegating the desk to a permanent place in his Jerusalem apartment. Leah had left her address in Jerusalem with the New York writer, suggesting that to some degree she has anticipated and contributed to the ending without being fully conscious of what that ending is supposed to be. Let's say this is an assisted suicide, in which Leah extends to her father the act of mercy that he has spent a lifetime extending to others, albeit not to himself. This culminates in her brother's finally being able to get on with the business of marrying and producing a new generation of children, a new *house* that is located neither in New York nor in London, in Chile or even in Jerusalem, but in the idea of the Jewish people, although the book does bring its major protagonists to Israel and imagines their future there.

Here is the story that Weisz's father once told him, which Weisz tells Bender in London (and which Foer recalls at the end of *Tree of Codes*) and which provides Krauss's novel with its title. It concerns "the first-century rabbi Yochanan ben Zakkai," after he fled Jerusalem following the destruction of the temple and his construction of the Great House, which is not a physical structure but a spiritual one:

> In his agony, he thought: What is a Jew without Jerusalem? How can you be a Jew without a nation? How can you make a sacrifice to God if you don't know where to find him? In the torn clothes of the mourner, ben Zakkai returned to his school. He announced that the court of law that had burned in Jerusalem would be resurrected there, in the sleepy town of Yavne. That instead of making sacrifices to God, from then on Jews would pray to Him. He instructed his students to begin assembling more than a thousand years of oral law.
>
> Day and night the scholars argued about the laws, and their arguments became the Talmud. . . . They became so absorbed in their work that sometimes they forgot the question their teacher had asked: What is a Jew without Jerusalem? Only later, after ben Zakkai died, did his answer slowly reveal itself. . . . Turn Jerusalem into an idea. Turn the temple into a book, a book as vast and holy and intricate as the city itself. . . . Later his school became known as the Great House. (278–79)

The Great House is an idea. It is like the "thin air" out of which Weisz produces artifacts for his clients or the "gaping hole" that remains in Weisz's replica of his father's study after all the objects have been assembled there except his father's desk or the empty drawer within the desk itself. This absence or empty space recalls the kabbalistic idea of the divine tzimtzum that is so important, as we have seen, to Aryeh Lev Stollman's novel *The Far Euphrates*. "When I was a boy," Weisz tells Bender in a self-description that recalls Alexander Aryeh's self-portrait, "I wanted to be in two places at the same time. It became an obsession of mine. . . .

My mother laughed, but my father who carried two thousand years with him wherever he went . . . saw it differently. In my childish desire he saw the symptom of a hereditary disease" (286). One of the reasons for Weisz's attraction to his wife is that "she was the only woman I'd ever met who didn't want to bring the dead back to life" (284–85). In this she is very different from Lotte Berg, who, like Weisz and Nadia, cannot leave the past behind. Says Bender of the desk, "We all lived in its shadow. As if death itself were living in that tiny room with us" (27–28).

The key to the desk's meaning is twofold and involves two literal keys: one is the key to the drawer that Weisz locked when he was still a little boy; the other is the key to the warehouse where the desk now resides, bequeathed to his grand-child and locked away until the time is ripe for it to be retrieved. "One day," Weisz explains, "a child will be born," not a Christ child, but, along similar lines,

> a child whose provenance is the union of a woman and a riddle. One night as the infant sleeps in the bedroom, his mother will sense a presence outside the window. At first she will think it is just her own reflection, haggard in her milk-stained robe. But a moment later she will sense it again, and suddenly afraid, she will switch off the lights and hurry to the baby's room. The glass door of the bedroom will be open. On top of the pile of the child's tiny white clothes the mother will find an envelope with his name, written in small, neat handwriting. Inside the envelope will be a key and the address of a storage room in New York City. And outside, in the dark garden, the wet grass will slowly straighten up again, erasing my daughter's footsteps. (289)

The "riddle" that will father this offspring is what opens the Weisz section of the novel:

> A RIDDLE. A stone is thrown in Budapest, on a winter night in 1944. It sails through the air toward the illuminated window of a house where a father is writing a letter at his desk, a mother is reading, and a boy is daydreaming about an ice-skating race on the frozen Danube. The glass shatters. . . . At that moment the life they know ceases to exist. *Where does the stone land?* (283; italics in original)

The stone's literal trajectory turns out to be less important than the way it travels: through the shattered glass in Budapest, the broken window in Bender's apart-ment in London, and, finally, the open window in the house on Oren Street in Jerusalem, where the key to the desk's location and its meaning will be placed. Like the "torn clothes of the mourner" that ben Zakkai wears when he creates his Great House, or like "the Baroque arches and niches, intricately hedged byways of a language so incised, so *bleeding*—a touch could set off a hundred slicing blades" (105; italics in original) that Lars discovers in Schulz's language, so the shattered glass in Krauss's novel will eventually give way, not to the substance of the solid desk, but to the empty space where a desk once stood and where it may one day stand again, albeit (like the messiah in Jewish thought) not yet and never in a material way, as an actual thing. The violence of that first shattered window (recalling *Kristallknacht*), which itself recalls the destruction of the temple in Jerusalem, is still too recent, too fresh, for the desk to be recovered. It is too soon to rebuild the temple in Jerusalem. The messiah has not come for the Jews. Nor will he. Nor should he.

The locked drawer within the desk, which Weisz had locked when he was four years old and which is and always has been "empty," already incorporates the desk's deepest meaning, which the child intuitively grasps: "In my mind I went over my most prized possessions again and again, but all of them suddenly seemed flimsy and grossly insignificant. In the end I locked the empty drawer and never told my father" (284). So long as Weisz tries to physically repossess the literal desk, his children will remain "prisoners . . . locked within the walls of their own family" (113). The key to unlocking this prison is the key to the secret of Jewish survival over the centuries: the Great House of Jewish learning, which is not a physical "possession," but a spiritual one; not salvation, but a place of study. In order to enter the Great House, Weisz, like ben Zakkai, has to mourn. Like Lars, he has to "grieve":

> The tremendous desk stood alone, mute and uncomprehending. Three or four drawers hung open, all of them empty. But the one I locked as a child, sixty-six years later was locked still. I reached out my hand and ran my fingers across the dark surface of the desk. There were a few scratches, but otherwise those who had sat at it had left no mark. I knew the moment well. How often I had witnessed it in others, and yet now it almost surprised me: the disappointment, then the relief of something at last sinking away. (289)

This is where the stone lands; this is also where it finally sinks away. Jewish mourners typically place stones on the gravesites of their dead. Weisz's father has had no such place of burial. And Weisz (like Josef Kavalier) has had no place to mourn. When he recovers the desk, only for an hour, he finally experiences the relief that will release him and his family. The desk is mute, its drawers empty, no one has left his or her mark on it. That is the way with material "possessions," as Weisz so long ago knew. But one of those empty drawers has *not* been emptied. It was empty to begin with, and locked. Therefore, it has maintained its emptiness over time, which is to say it has resisted the destructive forces of the material world (including those human forces of violence and also despair), remaining an un-violated, inviolate space of faith and of a child's, but also a man's, belief in the future. The stone disappears. The Jews do not. "In the torn clothes of the mourner ben Zakkai [had] returned to his school" in Yavne, there to produce the Great House of Jewish learning and prayer (279).

Krauss's two novels record what she calls in the first of the two "the history of love." The books would insist that love is as much a part of the history of Judaism as of Christianity, which through the advent of the messiah sought to have displaced or superseded what it saw as Judaism's insistence on retribution and revenge. Krauss would remind us that love is not a Christian invention. Love informs the Jewish scriptures: the love of God for His people and of His people for God and, perhaps even more important, the love of people for each other: of a father, say, for a son named Isaac, whom he does not in the end sacrifice. In *History of Love* Gursky plays this retreat from the sacrifice perfectly: he wants to identify himself to his son, but he decides not to. He decides not to interfere in his son's life; he does not claim what is his by rights: his biological son. He is a figure of Abraham in the purest sense in that he is willing to sacrifice, out of love, his only son, not to kill him but in order to enable him to live. The "angel" of God, who is and is not Alma Singer, as she appears in the final sequence of the novel, further suggests how Jewish history bypasses the literal enactment of the sacrifice of the son (or daughter), opting for life instead of death. In her role as the angel of God, Alma Singer also saves herself and her family in a specifically Jewish sense.

One inevitable problem for any Jewish author who wishes to incorporate biblical themes and imagery into his or her fiction is that most of the central tropes and figures of the Old Testament text have already been co-opted by Christianity. Hence, were a Jewish author to stage an *Akedah* (the binding of Isaac), in the mind of the contemporary Western reader it would quite effortlessly metamorphose into a scene of crucifixion. This means that Jewish writers must either avail themselves of lesser known biblical figures and motifs, or they must employ some mechanism by which to reclaim the Jewish type from its antitypical usurpation by Christianity. In other words, the literary text must somehow recover the antitypicality of the Jewish scriptures, its originality, and its originating force within Judaism itself. For most of us who have grown up in the Western literary tradition there is one and only one individual to whom the term "messiah" refers, and that is Jesus Christ. He is the antitype of which the biblical Isaac is the type (recall we have several Isaacs in Krauss's and Roth's texts). Yet the messiah is not a figure unique to Christianity any more than the history of love is. Indeed, Christ himself is descended of the Israelite House of David. He is the culmination of Jewish history, the last and final incarnation in a long line of Jewish messianic figures who lead their people, golem-like, to survival, only then to disappear and return to the clay from which they have emerged.

It might have been more effective and Jewish for these characters and their authors to have sat shivah instead of trying to undo death and resurrect the dead—in other words, to have genuinely mourned in an authentically, genuinely Jewish way. And perhaps such an idea of shivah—the Jewish idea of mourning that likely informed Freud's own ideas on the matter—does inform these texts (Bernard Malamud's "The Mourners" (1955) might be an intertext here for Krauss). Not for naught does Krauss include a scene of shivah in *The History of*

Love. In fact it is Gursky's visit to the house of mourning when his son, Isaac, dies that provides him with the knowledge that his son probably did know of his existence after all, thus cauterizing one very painful wound. Nor is it accidental that in the last scene of Krauss's book Leo and Alma Singer are sitting together on a bench, a typical seat of mourning, both of them, each in their own way, mourning their dead. To some extent Krauss's *History of Love* can be read as a kaddish (the prayer of mourning), both for the individual characters of the text (including Gursky, who, it seems to me, dies in the last scene) and for the six million murdered Jews whom Gursky and others in her novels and in other Jewish texts represent. The kaddish is a prayer, not to the dead, but to God, to restore to the world some of the life that has just gone out of it. Thus, the very last document in *The History of Love,* an obituary notice of Gursky's death, is written by Gursky himself when he was still a young man, before he fled to America, and it is preserved by his friend Zvi in order to keep Gursky alive rather than to announce his death. The obituary, in other words, is a document of life, not death—until the end of the novel. If for the duration of Krauss's novel, and in others of these novels, characters fail to mourn their dead, thus preventing the dead from dying, Krauss concludes her own work of art with something between an obituary and a kaddish, simultaneously declaring death and praying for the continued life, not of the dead, but of the living.

In the service of this declaration of life, Krauss dedicates *The History of Love* to her four grandparents, "who," she tells us in the dedication, "taught me the opposite of disappearing." The opposite of disappearing turns out to be something quite different from attaining to immortality, like the dead child in Rosa's fantasy in *The Shawl* or Bruno in *The History of Love,* like either the fish Schulz or his Wasserman counterpart in Grossman's novel, or like a golem. "I try to make a point of being seen," Gursky tells us toward the beginning of *The History of Love*: "Sometimes when I'm out, I'll buy a juice even though I'm not thirsty. If the store is crowded I'll even go so far as dropping my change all over the floor, the nickels and dimes skidding in every direction . . . I'll go into the Athlete's Foot and say, *What do you have in sneakers?...* I never actually buy. All I want is not to die on a day when I went unseen" (Krauss 2006, 4–5; italics in original). It is for this reason that Gursky signs up to be a "'*NUDE MODEL FOR [A] DRAWING CLASS $15/HOUR*' It seemed too good to be true. To have so much looked at. By so many" (5; italics in original). Deeply melancholic, Gursky will no less than strip himself bare in order to be seen. He will do this, it turns out, not so that he might live, but so that he might (recalling Wasserman's wish in Grossman's novel and Weisz's in *Great House*) be permitted to die.

Alma Singer is one of the students enrolled in that class who makes Leo Gursky not unseen on the day the novel begins. Alma will also make him not unseen on the day of his death some months later. It is Alma who permits him to die. From the start of his post-Holocaust existence, it has been the other Alma

(Mereminski) who has kept Leo alive. "In the summer of 1941," we are told, "on a bright, hot day in July they [the Germans] entered Slonim. At that hour, the boy happened to be lying on his back in the woods thinking about the girl. You could say it was his love for her that saved him" (18). It is that love for Alma that drives Gursky to America, that compels him to find her, and that finally determines he must let her and his son go out of his life, not, however, without his becoming obsessed with both of them. Leo's conjuring of Bruno, as I have already suggested, is one figure for that complicated mourning, which will not let the past go. His muse, Alma, is another. But Gursky needs to let the past go, and he needs to die. He needs to be buried, and he must also himself be mourned in proper fashion. And this the other Alma accomplishes for him.

Sitting on the park bench with her, his heart surging, the conversation between Leo and Alma Singer gradually metamorphoses into a conversation between Leo and the "angel" of death, who is Alma Mereminski. The language of tapping has been the language of Leo and the ghost/fictitious Bruno. Two taps means Leo (or Bruno) is alive. Insofar as Bruno is dead, the language of tapping is the language of the dying with the living dead. By the end of the scene with Alma, Leo has "stopped tapping" (384). It is not clear whether his final word, *"Alma,"* spoken three times, is spoken to the living Alma or to the dead one, or whether we are to understand the moment as a transition from the one to the other, the middle *"Alma"* standing as a conflation of past and present (384–85; italics in original). Alma gives the final two taps. They either confirm Alma Singer's being alive (as she surely is) or Gursky's having arrived in the world beyond where his original Alma now resides and where Gursky has joined her, the two of them now occupying the same ontological dimension. The transition from living to dead must keep the dead and the living on opposite sides of the divide.

The novel closes twice (with two taps of sorts, perhaps)—once with Gursky's death, then again with the obituary printed at the end, which was there from the beginning: the obituary that Gursky had written for himself when he was still a young man in Poland and which his friend Zvi had stolen (25) and kept in his jacket pocket all his life:

> [Zvi] read it over and over, mouthing the words as if they were not an announcement of death, but a prayer for life [a kaddish]. As if just saying them, he could keep his friend safe from the angel of death, the force of his breath alone keeping its wings pinned for a moment more, a moment more—until it gave up and left his friend alone. . . . He folded THE DEATH OF LEOPOLD GURSKY in half. And . . . for the rest of his life he carried in his breast pocket the page he'd protected, so that he could buy a little more time—for his friend, for life. (187–88; italics in original)

This is also the obituary that Zvi had appended to the Spanish publication of Gursky's novel, thus signing the translated/plagiarized text with the name of its original author. The obituary has been held in suspended animation from the period of the war to the present moment, and for the duration of Krauss's text. From the beginning of the first chapter of Gursky's novel (titled "The Last Words on Earth"), Gursky and the story he tells have to do with his death, which began with his birth. "Leopold Gursky started dying on August 18, 1920" (387) his obituary begins, and the novel begins: "When they write my obituary. Tomorrow. Or the next day" (3). The book and Gursky's life hang between these two moments. When Alma Singer (the reincarnation of Gursky's Alma) makes Gursky visible on that last day of his life, she also makes him not so much vulnerable to death as finally capable of dying, which is to say of finally rejoining his beloved Alma, that "angel" of God, in death (373).

"*Show me a Jew that survives,*" Gursky tells us, "*and I'll show you a magician*" (211; italics in original). Magic can mean conjuring a child from a shawl, resurrecting a dead writer, inhabiting the body of your dead father, and so on and so forth. The magic in Krauss's book, however, like the magic in *Great House, The Amazing Adventures,* or *The World to Come,* has to do with the magic of literature: with how human beings keep each other from disappearing by keeping each other—imaginatively, through self-conscious fiction and memory—in mind. In the final analysis, the novels by Ozick, Roth, Grossman, Chabon, Krauss, Horn, Michaels, and Appelfeld all work in similar ways. They are also, each one of them in and of itself, an obituary for the six million. For every one of those six million, "the words to say it" (as Gursky titles his second book) will be something analogous to what Gursky's obituary says of himself, no more and no less: "Really, there isn't much to say. He was a great writer. He fell in love. It was his life." A human life is just that: a human life, no more and no less. In order to live that life one has to accept one's death. One also has to accept the deaths of others, let them die and in dying having lived. We mourn, we grieve, but we go on. That is our amazing adventure, of which the great house of literature is our Book.

SECTION III
MOURNING BECOMES THE NATIONS: STYRON, SCHLINK, SEBALD

In this section I examine three novels that were not written by Jewish authors: *Sophie's Choice* (1979) by William Styron, *The Reader* (2008) by Bernhard Schlink, and *Austerlitz* (2001) by W. B. Sebald. I would not label all of these texts, perhaps not any of them, as Holocaust fictions. However, every one of them deals with the Holocaust in one way or another. All of them are serious and skillful works of fiction that clearly intend to fiercely and unequivocally condemn the Nazi atrocities against the Jews. Yet they all deal more with victimizers than with victims: American Southern racists in the case of Styron's novel; Germans in the case of Schlink and Sebald. The novels, therefore, are problematic in one way or another. The story of the Nazi genocide, when told in combination with other stories, cannot but alter the Holocaust narrative itself. It is this aspect of the problematic nature of the texts that I focus on in my readings, especially in relation to the subject position of the text itself, and, finally, my own subject position as a Jewish reader. Let me say up front that I do not think it is illegitimate for non-Jewish writers to write about the Holocaust. I require of such writers what I require of Jewish writers and of Jewish and non-Jewish readers as well: to clarify as much as is humanly possible the reasons for their interest in this subject and to guard against personal agendas that distort or violate the historical events being depicted or evoked. As Alvin Rosenfeld has pointed out in his book *The End of the Holocaust* (2011), in certain hands the Holocaust has become an instrument of nothing less vile than anti-Semitism and a reassertion of just those premises that produced the slaughter of the Jews by fascist Germany. This is decidedly not the case with any of the three books to be discussed here. Nonetheless, when the subject of the Holocaust combines with other subjects, as perhaps it inevitably must, the danger is grave that the Holocaust will come to merely serve or illuminate the other subject and thus be diminished in terms of its own integrity and gravity.

Two of the authors in this group—W. B. Sebald and Bernhard Schlink—are not only non-Jewish writers; they are German writers as well. Therefore, they necessarily bear a particular historical relationship to the events of the Holocaust. This is so even though neither one of them was of the wartime generation. Therefore neither one is in any sense either a survivor or a perpetrator of the events. Indeed, in *Guilt about the Past* (2010) Schlink has written quite directly and effectively about second-generation German responsibility for the Jewish genocide, despite the fact that this generation only inherits its parents' culpability. Since Schlink is a prominent lawyer and teacher of law, his public profile carries significant force. Styron bears a more distant relationship to the Holocaust than that of either Sebald or Schlink. Nonetheless, as an American Southerner he is heir to a travesty that is heinous in its own right and often linked to the Holocaust (as it is in his own novel): nineteenth-century slavery and the racism that succeeded it. The inquiry prompted by these texts is what happens to the story of the Holocaust when it becomes a part of the narrative of a writer who is implicated as victimizer rather than victim, whether of Jews or others, and when he wishes to tell this story of the victimizer, as Jonathan Littell's narrator does in *The Kindly Ones* (2009). The companion question that this question has to inspire is how the descendants of the victims respond to the attempts of the descendants of the victimizers to tell the victims' stories of devastation. One of the texts I want to examine, Bernhard Schlink's *The Reader*, actually stages such a confrontation between the heir of the victimizers and the victim herself. To what degree can such texts augment our consciousness of our own subjective relation to the events of the Holocaust, not to mention other events that are other people's catastrophes, not our own?

7   Blacks, Jews, and Southerners in William Styron's *Sophie's Choice*

I N A N I M P O R T A N T article on Primo Levi that appeared in 1989 in *Memory and Metaphor*, Cynthia Ozick faulted Styron's *Sophie's Choice* primarily for giving us "as the central genocidal emblem of Lager policy . . . a victim who is not a Jew." Ozick is quick to point out that "the suffering of no one victimized group or individual weighs more in human anguish than that of any other victimized group or individual." Nonetheless, as Ozick observes, whereas Catholic Poland still exists, "European Jewish civilization was wiped out utterly" ("Primo Levi's Suicide Note," in Ozick 1989, 43). This is a point with which Alvin Rosenfeld, among other critics, adamantly agrees. To be sure, as Styron himself has put it, and as quoted by Rosenfeld, "To say that only Jews suffered is to tell a historical lie" (2011, 44). Nonetheless, Rosenfeld adds, "The crime was not spread out neatly and evenly among the Jews and Gentiles alike. Most of European Jewry was murdered, and the murderers were European Gentiles, some of whom also died. The extent of the dying and the motives behind the deaths were not equivalent, though, and it simply makes no sense to add up all the corpses without distinction and pile them on to some abstract slaughter heap called 'mankind'" (2011, 44). Irving Saposnik (1982) has argued similarly.

The question I have about Styron's novel is why Styron puts the Holocaust at the center of a novel, which is a rather straightforward *Künstlerroman*, much like Aryeh Lev Stollman's *The Far Euphrates* or, even more to the point, Philip Roth's *The Ghost Writer* (to which Styron's text bears uncanny similarities). For Stollman and Roth, who present the artist as a young Jewish man, making reference to the Holocaust is more or less inevitable. For Styron, however, the "Stephen Dedalus" of his text is a white Anglo-Saxon Southerner with no particular links to Jewish history (1979, 150). There is no obvious reason why either Styron or his alter ego in the text, Stingo, ought to be particularly interested in the Holocaust. Even if the plot of the novel proceeds primarily through Stingo's increasingly intimate relationship with Sophie and her Jewish boyfriend, Nathan, whose mental instability takes the form of an obsessive sensitivity to anti-Semitism, the story of Stingo is the story of the Southern writer. Thus, we are told, Stingo is heir to the legacy of slavery not only by virtue of his being a Southern but through an actual monetary inheritance. He would be a moral person in relation to his past, and he would be a writer, which (ironically) puts him in direct conflict with Jewish writers like Roth, who seem to be taking the day in American literature because of their subject: the Holocaust. Therefore, Stingo's experiences up north as a writer can be taken as a kind of counter-life to the Jewish writer's experience: he does not have to leave Jewish history behind; he has to earn the right to use it. Whatever symptoms Stingo displays they are not Jewish symptoms. Rather, they are more American and Southern, as Stingo struggles to become the writer that his author William Styron has become. Like Roth's Nathan Zuckerman, Styron's Stingo has a lot to do with Styron himself, and *Sophie's Choice* is Styron's *Ghost Writer*: his glance backward at his younger self in the process of confronting ghosts and demons not of his own making.

If for a series of American and American Jewish writers and intellectuals the Holocaust and the historical anti-Semitism that it reflects are the prototype of racism through which antiblack prejudice is to be understood, Styron flips the analogy over such that slavery and racism become the lenses through which the Holocaust might be better viewed and understood. "Wasn't it in Poland," he has one of his Jewish characters ask, "that young, harmless Jewish students were segregated, made to sit on separate seats at school and treated worse than Negroes in Mississippi?" (1979, 438). Whichever of the two—slavery or the Holocaust—is worse in this competition between varieties of atrocity, there is a link here between them that Styron is by no means the first American writer to take note of: as I noted in *Blacks and Jews in Literary Conversation* (1998), Alice Walker in *Meridian* (1976) makes such a link, as does Toni Morrison in *Beloved* (1987). But Styron is the only writer to make this connection a major backbone of his text and thereby to write a Holocaust novel (of sorts), which is also a treatise condemning slavery. It is this double agenda that lands Styron in trouble with the subject of the Holocaust.

One must be very careful here to differentiate between the author and his narrator. Stingo is Styron's invention. He does not necessarily or always speak for the author. Indeed, as in Roth's novel, the older protagonist telling the story of his younger self is also to be differentiated from that younger self. The older Stingo lets slip the detail that at the time he is writing his novel he is already a father, therefore suggesting that his days of bachelorhood and sexual frenzy—which occupy much space in the novel—are behind him. Nonetheless, Styron does invest Stingo with much of his own autobiography, including, most significantly, his own authorial ambition to write on the subject of slavery. Stingo's proposed novel on the historical Nat Turner (which his creator William Styron had already written some ten years before the publication of *Sophie's Choice*) goes to the heart of Styron's intentions as well in writing *Sophie's Choice*.

The subject of the "ole prophet Nat" (148)—a way of referring to Nat Turner that already links him to a religious tradition that also serves to connect him to the Jews—is first suggested to Stingo by his father, who wants to persuade Stingo to return home to the family's recently inherited farm, which, it so happens, is right next to where Nat Turner once initiated his rebellion. This is the place that Stingo, toward the end of the novel, fixes on taking Sophie and her Jewish lover, Nathan, on their travels south. Even closer to the end, after Nathan and Sophie seem to have parted ways, it is where Stingo hopes to marry Sophie and set up housekeeping with her, writing his novels as she tends the farm. Nat Turner is nothing less than a part of Stingo's guilty patrimony in multiple senses of the word "patrimony." If Nat is the source of his guilt, he is also to be the means of expiating that guilt and, in the process, of establishing Stingo's career as a writer. By marrying himself to Sophie (in a logic similar to that of Nathan Zuckerman marrying Anne Frank), Stingo would also expiate his guilt as a Christian in relation to victims of the Holocaust, an expiation Styron hopes to achieve by writing his novel.

As Stingo explains to the baffled Northern Jew Nathan, who is his nemesis but also his troubled alter ego, "Nat Turner was a Negro slave who in the year 1831 killed about sixty white people—none of them, I might add, Jewish boys" (560–61). Nat is the pure subject through which Stingo can clear himself of the moral taint of slavery: "He had appeared out of the mists of history to commit his gigantic deed in one blinding cataclysmic explosion, then faded as enigmatically as he had come, leaving no explanation for himself, no identity, no after-image, nothing but his name. He had to be discovered anew" (561). And that is the task Stingo assigns himself. Of course in 1979, when *Sophie's Choice* appeared, it was no longer the case that Nat Turner was an unknown figure of history, since Styron had already published his *Confessions of Nat Turner* in 1967. Nor, strictly speaking, was that the case even in the 1940s, when the conversation between Stingo and Nathan takes place. Styron's *Confessions* itself is a rewriting of an earlier text with that same title. Styron's *Confessions,* however it fails to achieve its purposes, has to be read as Styron's attempt to replace this earlier text, which was also written by a white man and not by Turner himself. In his *Confessions* Styron would correct for the ethical affront perpetrated by the white man's misrepresentation of the slave hero, although, of course, in being himself the white author of a black man's story Styron cannot but perpetuate the problem of the white enslavement of the black voice.

In order to differentiate his Nat Turner from the Nat Turner of the original *Confessions,* Styron imbues his Nat (as Roth does his Anne Frank) with a deep inner life, including a sexual life, a feature that recurs in his depiction of the highly sexed Nathan and Stingo in *Sophie's Choice.* What Styron does not quite take in is that his sexualization of Nat aggravates even further the problem of his white voice silencing the black voice and thereby black narrative agency. Hence, in 1968, only a year after the publication of the *Confessions* to largely positive reviews, ten African American critics responded no less vigorously against Styron's attempt to write an African American novel than did Ozick and Rosenfeld to his subsequent attempt to write a Jewish one (Clarke 1968).

From the beginning of the novel Stingo has felt the taint of slavery and racism as a personal burden. The money he is using to support himself while he writes his first novel (not on Nat Turner) is a late inheritance derived from the sale of one of his ancestor's slaves, Artiste. And even though earlier in the book Stingo claims that this inheritance "bears only indirectly upon the new life [he is taking] up in Brooklyn," it is, he comes to realize later, of the essence (1979, 40): "Artiste! My grandmother's chattel, source of my own salvation. It was the slave boy Artiste who had provided me with the wherewithal for much of this summer's sojourn in Brooklyn" (559–60). Therefore, when that money is stolen, Stingo feels not only outrage but also a certain measure of relief. Yet he knows that even divesting himself of the monetary benefits of slavery is not enough: the only way he will "*ever* get rid of slavery," he understands, is to write about it: "to make [Nat] mine, and re-create him for the world" (560; italics in original; the word "mine" is loaded, to say the least). "You know something, Nathan," Stingo says to this Jew, whose name—not incidentally, I suggest—recalls that of Nat Turner, "I'm going to make a *book* out of that slave. . . . It'll be my next book, a novel about old Nat" (561; italics in original. This choice of name, obviously, is Styron's, not Stingo's; it is also one of many eerie, uncanny links between Roth's *Ghost Writer* and Styron's *Sophie's Choice*).

As Stingo's own formulation "making a book out of that slave," not to mention his rather unguarded use of the word "salvation," already makes clear, Stingo's ethical position is hardly pure. His morally compromised position is also exposed in his belief that his writing a book celebrating the slave Nat Turner more than frees him of his debt to his family's own slaves: "Years later, I thought that if I had tithed a good part of my proceeds of Artiste's sale to the N.A.A.C.P. instead of keeping it, I might have shriven myself of my own guilt. . . . But in the end I'm rather glad I kept it" (48). Keeping his inheritance becomes ethically justifiable because of the way it enables the writing of Stingo's book. Stingo's lack of self-awareness here may well represent part of Styron's critique of his narrator, or at least the older Stingo's later knowledge of his early failed moral sensibilities. Or it may not. However, even if it is, Styron's choice to write about the Holocaust doesn't seem much of an improvement over Stingo's choice (which was also Styron's) to write about Nat Turner. While Styron does not repeat the error of speaking in the voice of the ethnic other—indeed, *Sophie Choice*'s structure might well have been dictated by a desire on the author's part to avoid that particular problem—he once again treads on the historical ground of another minority group, which doesn't relish his being there and which Styron treats with what he likely imagines as critical candor but which is read by the group in question as blasphemy. In the very same letter that Stingo's father sends him informing him of his inheritance, he chitchats about a family friend who remains unabashedly a racist despite the clearly rising fortunes of the Southern Negro. This friend also "remains an anti-semite," even "after the recent revelations of the horrors of Nazi Germany" (44). Southern racism and anti-Semitism coexist, side by side. For the Southerner, Jews constitute a race, and if they have received better treatment than blacks, it is only because blacks were there to be more despised: "The Jew has found considerable fellowship among white Southerners," he explains, "because Southerners have possessed another, darker sacrificial lamb" (57). This forges a further link in the text between blacks and Jews.

With these features of the text in mind, one might read Styron's novel (not Stingo's) this way: recognizing the degree to which his own existence has been enabled through the crimes of slavery, perpetrated not only by his community but by his own family, Styron (like his protagonist and like a real author such as Hawthorne in *The House of the Seven Gables* [1851]) sought public expiation. It is for this reason that he had decided some years earlier to tell the story of Nat Turner, an experiment that had failed woefully. Therefore, it is not far-fetched to take *Sophie's Choice* (with a Nathan instead of a Nat) as providing an alternative, less dangerous vehicle for Styron's confessions. Furthermore, as a white male Christian, Styron would use his female protagonist to take responsibility in some measure for the sins not only of his immediate Southern past but for the Holocaust and of the history of the oppression of women.

All of these goals are laudable and yet extremely problematic. In a text that announces in its title that it is about a "choice," Styron's own choice to write about the Holocaust has to figure in our interpretation of the text, especially since it significantly reverses Sophie's first choice in the novel. This choice is not the choice that most readers remember from the novel: the choice of which of her children she will designate for extermination during the final selection. Rather it is the prior "choice" as to whether she will put herself on the side of the Jews (endangering both of the children and herself), a choice that she is asked to make by the same character, Wanda, who winds up in Auschwitz with her. "You have to make a choice," the Polish patriot Wanda tells Sophie before their incarceration (496); "you *must* come to a decision" (498; italics in original), to which Sophie responds: "'I have already made my choice. . . . *I will not get involved. I mean this! Schluss!*' Her voice rose on this word and she found herself wondering why she had spoken it in German. '*Schluss—aus!* That's final!'" (498; italics in original). Sophie's language, with its sudden eruption into German, declaring this is the end of the conversation and sliding as it does, in the English sentence, into the word "final," makes her choice her own personal final solution. "I'm not Jewish! Or my children—they're not Jewish either," she tells the Nazi doctor at the camp, once again breaking into German speech. "They are racially pure. They speak German." The doctor replies: "You may keep one of your children. . . . You're a Polack, not a Yid. That gives you a privilege—a choice" (641–42). In addition to linking Sophie's mentality at the moment she makes her first choice to what she shares with the Germans, both in terms of culture and in terms of a latent anti-Semitism, the word "*schluss*," when linked with the intensive "*aus*," already signifies Sophie's German sympathies and her view of Jews. The word "*Ausschluss*" means "exclusion, expulsion, disqualification." There may also be here a reminder of the word "*Einschluss*," which, meaning the opposite of *Ausschluss*, signaled the German takeover of Austria.

Styron's choice to tell the story of the Holocaust would seem to reverse Sophie's choice not to get involved. Unlike Sophie, and in line with the ideas expressed in Bernhard Schlink's *Guilt about the Past*, Styron takes "responsibility" (373) by putting himself on record as the inheritor of not one but two morally compromised traditions: Southern racism and Western anti-Semitism. In this way he disentangles himself from Sophie's anti-Semitism, and Stingo's as well. "She could not wriggle out from beneath the suffocating knowledge that there had been this time in her life when she had played out the role, to its limit, of a fellow conspirator in crime. And this was the role of an obsessed and poisonous anti-Semite—a passionate, avid, tediously single-minded hater of Jews" (293–94). This is Sophie's confession: "All my childhood, all my life I really hated Jews. They deserved it, this hate. I *hate* them, dirty Jewish *chochons*" (470). In a similar way Stingo is also something of a self-confessed anti-Semite. From page 1 of chapter 1, Stingo represents himself as uncomfortable with Jews: a "lean and lonesome young Southerner wandering amid the Kingdom of the Jews" (9), he says of himself; an "ineffective and horny Calvinist among all these Jews" (54). By the end of the novel he and Sophie are, in his own words, just "two anti-Semites, on a summer outing" (471).

Like Nathan and Sophie, "Jew and *goy* in magnetic gravitation" (170), so Stingo and Nathan, within the novel—and, I suggest, Styron and Jewish history outside the novel—are drawn into the inescapable tensions between Christian and Jew. "You Southern white people have a lot to answer for when it comes to such bestiality," Styron's mentally imbalanced Jewish sadist Nathan says to Stingo. "I say this as someone whose people have suffered the death camps. . . . As a Jew I regard myself as an authority on anguish and suffering" (96–98). "Stingo! Oh, Stingo!" says Nathan. "'Put on yo' bathin' *costume*. We gonna hab old Pompey hitch up the old coach-an'-foah and hab us a little picnic outin' down by the seashoah!'" (77; italics in original). Nathan not only mocks Stingo but once again draws the connection between slavery and "*shoah*." In a novel filled to the bursting point with literary allusions, it is not insignificant that this same Nathan also disparages Stingo as a writer: he is, in Nathan's view, a second-rate imitator of

William Faulkner, and, in any case, "Jewish writing is going to be the important force in American literature in the coming years" (157). Even though Stingo will only read such books as *Marjorie Morningstar* and *Goodbye, Columbus* later (229), he has already read Saul Bellow's *Dangling Man*. "I saw myself running a pale tenth," Stingo laments, "in a literary track race, coughing on the dust of a pounding fast-footed horde of Bellows and Schwartzes and Levys and Mandelbaums" (158). No wonder Stingo begins his text with "Call me Stingo" (9). Like the two protagonists in Bernard Malamud's *The Tenants* (1971), Stingo vies for ownership of the American house of fiction as defined by the same Hawthorne and Melville that Roth's Zuckerman cites as his progenitors in *The Ghost Writer*. He aims to oust the competition, many of whom happen to be Jewish writers, including the author of *Goodbye, Columbus* (1959), whose novel landed him in as much trouble with his Jewish readership as Styron's *Confessions* did with his black readership. Both Roth's later novel *The Ghost Writer* and Styron's later book *Sophie's Choice* can be understood as reflecting back on the authors' crises with their audiences. Ironically both books only produce more problems in their wake, for both *Sophie's Choice* and *The Ghost Writer*, as I've already indicated, produced storms of protest, this time from the same readership—the Jews. Styron became more a Jewish writer than he had bargained for.

Since both *Sophie's Choice* and *The Ghost Writer* appeared in the same year, we cannot speak here of influence or allusion, only uncanny similarities. The two books are structurally alike in remarkable ways: both of them deal with their authors' previous bad experiences with their readerships, and both of them fantasize the wedding of the narrator-protagonists to women who will secure them against further such recriminations. In both cases these women are foreign-born survivors of the Holocaust with accents described as "fetching" (Styron 1979, 12, 41, 42; Roth 1995, 28, 125). Furthermore, the two books share a wealth of local details. Both have a Jewish protagonist named Nathan, and Roth's Nathan's last name, Zuckerman, is echoed somewhat in the last name of the owner of the boardinghouse where Stingo lives, which is Zimmerman. Additionally, both Nathans have brothers who are dentists.

The issue that Roth's and Styron's novels put before us replicates the controversy raised between Styron and the African American community in relation to the publication of *The Confessions* and between Roth and American Jewry: who, if anyone, possesses the rights to a particular story of a people's historical suffering? In the case of *Sophie's Choice,* the tension between Christian and Jew within the novel, which Styron might well be understood as framing and thus as exposing his own position as a Christian writer, is very close to the tension produced *by* the novel. This is the tension in relation to the scripting of Holocaust narratives by non-Jewish authors. The convergence of the plot within the novel and the novel's position in the field of Holocaust writing produces discomfort in the reader concerning Styron's objectives or, at the very least, the consequences of his literary strategies. One of the most troubling aspects of Styron's text is its elegiac conclusion, which, in addition to the false comfort it might seem to provide, might also be understood as emerging out of the sacrifice of the tortured Jewish Nathan, who perishes so that a universal and Christian message might once again emerge:

> It was then that the tears finally spilled forth. . . . It was the letting go of rage and sorrow for the many others who during these past months had battered at my mind and now demanded my mourning: Sophie and Nathan, yes, but also Jan and Eva . . . and Eddie Farrell and Bobby Weed, and my young black savior Artiste and Maria Hunt, and Nat Turner, and Wanda Muck-Horch van Kretschmann, who were but a few of the beaten and butchered and betrayed and martyred children of the earth. . . . *'Neath cold sand I dreamed of death / but woke at dawn to see / in glory, the bright, the morning star.*
>
> This was not judgment day—only morning. Morning: excellent and fair. (682–84; italics in original. Since the book has cited as a major Jewish novel *Marjorie Morningstar,* one almost experiences an echo here of that title in the words "star" and "morning," as if the words have stuck in the writer's Jew-obsessed imagination, but perhaps I go too far here.)

The elegiac note Stingo sounds here at the end of the novel is problematic on its own. To find consolation in the Holocaust or, even worse, some sort of redemption, is for most Holocaust authors, as we have seen, anathema. The novel's lyrical conclusion becomes even more troubling, however, when read in relation to the final words of Styron's autobiographical *Darkness Visible: A Memoir of Madness.* These are the final words of Styron's memoir, which incorporate words from Dante's *Inferno* (perhaps not insignificantly an important intertext for Primo Levi's *Survival at Auschwitz* [1947]):

> For those who have dwelt in depression's dark wood, and known its inexplicable agony, their return from the abyss is not unlike the ascent of the poet, trudging upward and upward out of hell's black depths and at last emerging into what he saw as "the shining world." There, whoever has been restored to health has almost always been restored to the capacity for serenity and joy, and this may be indemnity enough for having endured the despair beyond despair.
> *E quindi uscimmo a riveder le stelle*
> *And so we came forth, and once again beheld the stars.* (Styron 1992, 84; italics in original)

That Styron comes out in the same good place in *Darkness Visible* that he had in *Sophie's Choice,* once again beholding the stars, might not be troubling were it not for the fact that in the memoir Styron attributes his descent into psychological hell as partially the consequence of his failure to read his mental landscape as expressed in his many novels. "Until the onslaught of my own illness and its denouement," Styron writes of his near fatal depression, "I never gave much thought to my work in terms of its connection with the subconscious—an area of investigation belonging to literary detectives. But after I had returned to health and was able to reflect on the past in the light of my ordeal, I began to see clearly how depression had clung close to the outer edges of my life for many years. Suicide has been a persistent theme of my books—three of my major characters killed themselves" (78). Two of these suicides occur in *Sophie's Choice* (there's even a third suicide recorded in that text: that of an ex-girlfriend of Stingo). *Sophie's Choice* more than confirms Styron's observation about himself that he never learned to read his own fiction for evidences of his turn of mind.

In *Sophie* Stingo notes explicitly that "in my career as a writer I have always been attracted to morbid themes—suicide, rape, murder, military life, marriage, slavery. Even at that early time I knew my . . . work would be flavored by a certain morbidity" (149–50). Later he takes note of a *"recurring"* dream he has, which is associated with his mother's death (614; italics in original). This is the event Styron eventually comes to see, after his brush with suicide, as formative of his young consciousness. The similarity between the final words of *Sophie's Choice* and the memoir are thus troubling, because it is as if now, at the end of his text about a depression that nearly culminated in his own suicide, he has once again completely eclipsed the insights he might have garnered from his own texts. Suffering like Rosa in *The Shawl* from what Styron identifies as "incomplete mourning" (81) for the death of his mother when he was thirteen, Styron does more or less what Rosa does: he resurrects a figure that occludes the necessity for mourning, both in the form of the female protagonists in his texts who, one way or another, keep his mother alive, and in terms of the upbeat faith that the final words in both *Sophie's Choice* and *Darkness Visible* inscribe. Such words deny the necessity of mourning. Hence they perpetuate the author's melancholy, which culminates in his depression. Indeed, one might even read Sophie's choice as to which of her children to send to the crematorium as incorporating the author's sense that he was both his mother's special favorite but also the child his mother sacrificed through her death.

The final words of *Sophie's Choice* do more than offend the sensibilities of those who may feel that such an expression of faith, especially as it is cast in overtly Christian terms, both belittles the suffering of the victims and repeats the denial of the non-Christian Jewish subject, who was the primary (albeit not the only) victim of the Holocaust. Styron's final epiphany mourns neither the victims of the Holocaust nor of slavery and racism. Because the Holocaust that Sophie experiences is not the Jewish Holocaust but the more general slaughter in which the Nazis engaged (horrific, needless to say, in its own right), it is not the Jewish Holocaust for which Styron is taking responsibility. Indeed, the Holocaust that killed Sophie is not the racially motivated (i.e., anti-Semitic) Holocaust that might be imagined to provide an analogy to the slave experience or to subsequent racism in the United States. In the text's final words, the novel catapults both Jewish and black victims into a specifically Christian teleology of recovery, which, if Styron's personal experience of repetition is any indicator, in no way mediates against the recurrence of such catastrophes in the future.

As is the case with any such text of embedded voices—the character within the text, the character narrating the events after the lapse of many years, and the author outside the text altogether—it is impossible to determine absolutely how much the author is conscious of or is intentionally producing limitations on his narrator's consciousness. Is the Stingo who tells the story aware of how his younger self exploited his relationship with Nathan and Sophie, not to mention Nat Turner? Is Styron self-consciously addressing his own tendencies to project his consciousness onto the historical events of the past, working out his own psychological, aesthetic, and ethical problems rather than address the suffering of other people? Certainly one consequence of the novel can be to make the reader aware of the problem of subjective framing and of something verging on the exploitation of historical materials. That is no mean feat for a text to accomplish, although it depends on our willingness as readers to suspect authorial intentions and narrative voice alongside our own claims against the subject of the text. It is too easy to read *Sophie's Choice* more directly and innocently, and therein is its problem as a text of Holocaust fiction.

8 (Re)Reading the Holocaust from a German Point of View

Bernhard Schlink's The Reader

B ERNHARD SCHLINK'S *THE READER* has occasioned significant criticism
much along the same lines as the charges issued against Styron's *Sophie's Choice*
by the Jewish community or by African Americans in relation to Styron's earlier
novel *The Confessions of Nat Turner* (1966). The Holocaust does not seem like
an appropriate topic for a German writer, especially if he is going to write about
Germans rather than Jews. Schlink actually mentions *Sophie's Choice* (the movie
version) in *The Reader* as one early source of the protagonist's knowledge of the
Holocaust (2008, 148). This might signal Schlink's belief that his own novel can
serve, like Styron's, as a source of general knowledge about the Holocaust. (*The
Reader* will also be made into a movie, thus giving it wider influence than the
book alone might have had.) However, it could also indicate Schlink's anxiety
that *The Reader* is going to land him in the same sort of head-on confrontation
with the Jewish community that *Sophie's Choice* did Styron. In this sense Schlink's nod to Styron could be a defensive gesture intended to protect the author
against the criticism he nonetheless received.

This criticism primarily centers on the plot of the novel: the story of a young
man, Michael Berg, who has an adolescent affair with an older woman who turns
out to have been a concentration camp guard. Many years after their affair, Michael meets up with Hanna Schmitz when she is on trial and he is a law student
witnessing that trial, in which a central mystery concerning Hanna is cleared
up for Michael: Hanna is illiterate. What readers such as Ozick (1999), Donahue (2011), Kahlendorf (2003), and Devereau (2004) object to is twofold: first,
the rather explicit sexuality of the first part of the book, which makes the novel
somewhat sensationalistic, and, secondly and even more problematically, Schlink's seeming to let the Germans off too easily by making the key perpetrator in
his story an illiterate woman, who might be understood not to have known better

or to have been unable to choose another course of action. Not only is the protagonist Hanna a victim of her illiteracy when she signs on to be a camp guard, but her vulnerability is further emphasized when we witness her struggling to process the charges being brought against her during her trial. Hanna cannot read the written documents that testify against her. As a result of her inability to understand the charges against her, other Germans who are at least as guilty as she is get off with lighter sentences than they deserve. Whether or not Hanna should have been sent to prison (there is no doubt from the point of view of the novel that she should have), justice is not served in this novel. Certainly Schlink's heroine and the novel's inclusion of a heady and somewhat inappropriate sexual relationship between her and the novel's young protagonist (who seems to serve as an alter ego to Schlink) are problematical features of Schlink's novel that need to be interrogated, especially if we are to avoid Holocaust pornography. Nonetheless, *The Reader* may be a powerfully honest confrontation with the impossibility of meting out justice to the perpetrators of the Jewish genocide and with the matter of collective guilt. What could justice possibly mean in the context of the Holocaust? And for what should later generations of Germans feel guilty? Indeed, what purpose is served if generations of Germans continue to feel shame (not guilt) for what their parents and grandparents did to the Jews? The difference between shame and guilt is very much to the point of Schlink's novel, even if the distinction pertains to the perpetrators and their descendants rather than to the victims and theirs.

Shame, we must remember, is not the same as guilt. To revisit the distinction, as Ruth Leys (2009) defines it, guilt has to do with our actions; shame has to do with who we are. Thus, "Schlink's concern," as critic Bill Niven puts it, citing work by Aleida Assmann, "is not with Hanna's illiteracy in itself, but with her fear of stigmatization, a fear which binds her into a destructive system of shame and compensation. . . . Hanna's shame finds its correlative in Michael's shame. . . . Schlink's book sets out to demonstrate how irrational, self-negating, indeed destructive a reckless fear of shame can be when the individual makes no attempt to face it" (2003, 382–84, 387–89). Martin Swales (2003) similarly highlights the centrality of shame in the novel. The words "shame" and "ashamed" so punctuate the text as to constitute much more even than a leitmotif. They approach closer to something like an obsession on the part of the narrative consciousness. Does the book itself get stuck in the obsession with shame? Or does it attempt to "read" this shame and do something with it? The shame that Michael feels in relation to Hanna clearly conjures the shame felt by Germans of Michael's and Schlink's generation concerning their parents' generation. Therefore, Michael's shame is the shame felt by the narrative consciousness produced by the book itself.

Insofar as Hanna is significantly older than Michael and her first meeting with him has to do with taking care of him when he is ill, she stands in for Michael's mother. Michael's girlfriend, a psychoanalyst, later diagnoses Michael as having failed to "work through [his] relationship to his mother": "Did it not strike me that my mother hardly appeared in my story at all?" (Schlink 2008, 174). Michael's mother does appear, of course, but through his transference of her onto not his girlfriend, but his surrogate mother, Hanna. Like others of his generation, Michael "condemn[s] his parents to shame"; he puts them "under sentence of shame" (92), even though the only "charge" of which the parents might possibly be found guilty, according to Michael, "was that after 1945 they had tolerated the perpetrators in their midst" (92). That Michael first meets Hanna when he is ill suggests that Michael's generation suffers from what Schlink diagnoses in his book *Guilt about the Past* as the "infection" of collective guilt (2010, 1). It is this infection, he notes, that afflicts second and subsequent generations of Germans, like Michael.

When Michael snubs Hanna just before she leaves the city (he is embarrassed to acknowledge her in front of his friends), he feels, as is appropriate to his behavior, "guilt": "Why hadn't I jumped up immediately when she stood there and run to her!" (83). Since so many Germans were bystanders during the Holocaust, the specific offense Michael offers in relation to Hanna is a significant one. These feelings of guilt (not shame) are made to carry over into the opening chapter of part 2, suggesting the importance of the concept of guilt to what the book is aiming at. The problem for Michael as he reports it at the beginning of part 2 is that "the feeling of guilt that had tortured me in the first weeks gradually faded" (87). Guilt quickly becomes confused with shame for Michael; hence Schlink's representation of the relationship between Hanna and Michael as a sexual one, which could be seen as more likely conjuring a sense of shame rather than guilt. The German word "*Scham*," shame, also means "pubic," thus linking shame specifically with the sexuality of Michael's relationship to Hanna. And these feelings of shame (rather than guilt) are exacerbated when Michael once again confronts Hanna in the context of her trial, where his shame about their sexual relationship becomes confused with his shame about the Holocaust, not to mention her shame about being illiterate. "The worst were the dreams in which a hard, imperious, cruel Hanna aroused me sexually," Michael later reports. "I woke from them full of longing and shame and rage. And full of fear about who I really was." Even though Michael knows that his "fantasized images were poor clichés . . . they undermined my actual memories of Hanna and merged with the images of the camps that I had in my mind" (147).

Clearly for Michael the Holocaust is a field for projections having to do with more personal issues of who he "really was." "If I think about it more, plenty of embarrassing and painful situations come to mind," Michael admits at the beginning of part 2 of the novel. Therefore, he decides "never to let myself be humiliated or humiliate myself after Hanna, never to take guilt upon myself or feel guilty, never again to love anyone whom it would hurt to lose" (88). Michael's resolutions dangerously lop together feelings and responses that have absolutely nothing to do with one another: humiliation, guilt, and love. To never feel guilt represents an ethical response, which is highly problematic, to say the least; to never feel shame is a more psychological attitude, which, if guilt remained an option, might actually indicate psychological health. Love and its avoidance are not necessarily a consequence of either guilt or shame.

As Michael's Holocaust fantasies later on suggest, however, for Michael shame trumps guilt. It also blocks love. In *Guilt about the Past* Schlink supports the idea of assigning collective guilt to the German nation. But in the manner of fiction *The Reader* seems to know otherwise. The mismatching of legal terminology like "condemn," "sentence," and "charge" in *The Reader* with the nonlegal term "shame" suggests the problem Schlink does not address or perhaps even recognize in *Guilt about the Past:* that shame is not guilt. Michael's family is not Jewish, although the name Berg certainly does associate the Bergs with Jews, as do the reasons for the elder Berg's being dismissed from his university job during the war. Berg Senior, we are told, "lost his job as lecturer in philosophy for scheduling a lecture on Spinoza [a Jewish philosopher], and had got . . . through the war as an editor for a house that published hiking maps and books" (2008, 92). Given Michael's own *Odyssey*-like attempts to navigate his way home to German culture (Michael himself mentions the *Odyssey* in his narrative), his father's wartime profession is rather carefully chosen by the author of the text. In any event, the Bergs remain in Germany during the war, at home. They are not exiled or sent to concentration camps, and for this Michael would try to sentence his family—not to guilt, but to shame. Can one do that?

During the course of her trial Hanna poses to the presiding judge the naïve and apparently absurd question, which is the major moral (rather than legal) quandary of the novel: "so what would you have done?" (111). The judge's response that "there are matters one simply cannot get drawn into," "that one must distance oneself from, if the price is not life and limb," can be understood in two ways. It can be taken as his quite appropriate juridical response: I cannot get drawn into this debate; I must distance myself from it, because the issue of this trial is a legal judgment concerning a particular set of events, not whether you or anyone might have avoided them. Or the judge's reply can be taken, as Michael takes it, as a general moral comment "about what 'one' must and must not do" as a moral human being. On this second level the judge's words, as Michael immediately observes, do "not do justice to the seriousness of Hanna's question. She had wanted to know what she should have done in her particular situation, not that there are things that are not done" (112). As the text itself notes, "the judge's answer [comes] across as hapless and pathetic" (112). John E. MacKinnon (2003) has argued that "if we imagine ourselves into Hanna's mind and circumstance . . . we can only conclude that we too would have acted as she did. Our tendency, then, will not be to blame, but to forgive," and that "is symptomatic of a prevailing cultural drift that ought to cause us concern" (3). Yet if "the literary imagination," as MacKinnon (2004) cites Martha Nussbaum as arguing, "is crucial to the principled application of law" (181), then our imaginative extension of ourselves into Hanna's situation can have consequences other than condoning or forgiving her actions. It can produce, not forgiveness of her, but self-reflection and even theoretical condemnation of ourselves as potential criminals like her. We can understand that we too would have to stand trial and take responsibility for our actions. The law, as the judge puts it, cannot get drawn into the "What would you have done?" debate. In relation to this aspect of Hannah's question, he is correct. The law has to judge what individuals do. This does not mean, however, necessarily judging who they are. As Pedro Alexis Tabensky (2004) argues, "Understanding people is incompatible with judging them in a way that involves an ethic of desert, that is, an ethic that allows us to exalt or condemn individuals for their acts." Yet judging actions, he goes on to maintain, remains an ethical option. The point is that condemnation (like exaltation) must be of actions rather than of persons (212). Guilt is not to be confused with shame, nor innocence with saintliness. Even if we try to sentence individuals who are guilty of the horrors that Hanna and her fellow guards perpetrated, nonetheless we have to pose and answer to ourselves the question: Would we have acted differently? Do we now, even if we are not actual perpetrators of violence and genocide, not countenance such violence as a part of our world? We are not necessarily guilty before the law. That does not mean we might not be guilty in another sense.

In his autobiographical memoir *Little Did I Know*, Stanley Cavell (2010) tells the following story about fellow philosopher Kurt Fischer, who fled Vienna in 1938, when he was sixteen years old, after "gentile friends picked him up at his high school and took him directly to the train station to join his mother in leaving for Czechoslovakia, ahead of Hitler's army of annexation." It is Fischer's decision to return to Vienna that occasions the following comments on Cavell's part:

> [Fischer] reported that the middle-aged Viennese couple who owned a modest restaurant in Berkeley—the husband having been a prominent young lawyer in Vienna before the Anschluss—questioned him about how he could think of going back to live in Vienna: "Won't you always be asking yourself, with every new acquaintance, 'Where were you at that time, on that day?'" I seemed to know, without Kurt's supplying an explanation, that he understood the question as years, decades, too late, that he already knew where the ones who stayed had mostly been, namely, getting by, going along, the better among them just wishing to live, the more imaginative hoping they could live without becoming unforgivable. It is knowledge compounded with pity and amusement, a kind of forgiveness in advance at the fate of being alive and damned. It takes an extreme case of oppression, which tore him from his home in his adolescence, to be posing the question every decently situated human being, after adolescence, either asks himself in an unjust world, or coarsens himself

to avoid asking: Where is one now; how is one living with, hence counting upon, injustice? (345–49)

"How one is living with, hence counting upon, injustice": this, I suggest, has to be an integral part of our thinking about our own positions concerning our own behavior as well as our judgments of other people's moral trespasses. And this, I think, is what Schlink's novel knows.

In *Guilt about the Past,* Schlink justifies the idea of collective guilt for the German people on the basis of the fact that those who abided the events and lived their lives in the presence of the perpetrators benefited from what had occurred. Yet by this definition most of us are guilty of some sort of collective guilt, especially given how technological advances have made crimes against humanity committed far away from our literal homes quite accessible to our knowledge and therefore to our intervention. The globe has become our nation of responsibility, our shared neighborhood of crimes against humanity. Doing "justice" to Hanna's question is as pertinent to us as doing justice to Hanna's victims. The law, we might say, has to judge *what was;* literature judges, or, more properly, enables us to judge, *what is,* and not only as it pertains to other people, whether fictional or real, but also to ourselves.

Hanna's question to the judge and his rather evasive answer, which serves to evacuate Hanna's question of its moral thrust, is replicated in Michael's conversation with his father about whether or not he should reveal the secret of Hanna's illiteracy. Because of this replication the court scene cannot be dismissed as inconsequential either to the novel or to the problem of legal versus moral justice. Like the judge, most readers are likely to claim in judgment of the Germans (or others whom we find guilty of crimes against humanity) that there are simply things that human beings cannot permit themselves to do. But what happens to moral logic if we are able to admit to ourselves that even if what camp guards like Hanna did was brutal and unethical in the extreme, we cannot say beyond a shadow of a doubt what we personally would have done? Would moral logic be changed in any way? The judge adds to his statement: "if the price is not life and limb." That is a big "if," and in fact for Hanna and others the price might well have been, or at least seemed like it would have been, life and limb. How, then, do we judge? How do we *not* judge? Morality may require that we act exactly as we would have had we not interrogated ourselves and our own ethical choices, but our relationship to ethics may nonetheless be radically altered and deepened (both theoretically and pragmatically) when we honestly confess to ourselves our own guilt in relation to a shameless, shameful world.

The question that Michael raises as he is observing the war crimes trial, a question that echoes what seems to be Hanna's ignorant and stupid question to the judge (what would *you* have done?), is absolutely pertinent and important to both the second generation of Germans and to those of us who are not Germans at all and may even be descendants of the victims:

What should our second generation have done, what should it do with the knowledge of the horrors of the extermination of the Jews? We should not believe we can comprehend the incomprehensible, we may not compare the incomparable, we may not inquire because to inquire is to make the horrors an object of discussion, even if the horrors themselves are not questioned, instead of accepting them as something in the face of which we can only fall silent in revulsion, shame, and guilt. Should we only fall silent in revulsion, shame, and guilt? To what purpose? . . . That some few would be convicted and punished while we of the second generation were silenced by revulsion, shame, and guilt—was that all there was to it now? (Schlink 2008, 104)

One is reminded of Dominick LaCapra's caution (1994, 123) that even if silence is in some ways the most decorous response to the unfathomable events of the Holocaust, one must not fall silent about things that can and must be said concerning what happened to the Jews of Europe. Silence is precisely what characterized Michael's parents' generation. And such responses or representations of the Holocaust as did exist were silent in a different way: "When I think today about those years, I realize how little direct observation there actually was, how few photographs that made life and murder in the camps real. . . . Back then, the imagination was almost static: the shattering fact of the world of the camps seemed properly beyond its operations. The few images derived from Allied photographs and the testimony of the survivors flashed on to the mind again and again, until they froze into clichés" (Schlink 2008, 147–48). The final word "clichés," in relation to the "images" of the camp flashing on the mind, which end the chapter, picks up the reference some sentences earlier to the "fantasized images" of Hanna, which are also, Michael realizes, clichés. The clichés of sadomasochism put us in mind, once again, of Jonathan Littell's *Kindly Ones* (2009). Shame and desire can make us focus on the wrong objects of scrutiny, whether we praise or condemn them.

Whatever else one might want to say regarding Schlink's novel, the book does not remain silent about things that can and have to be brought into public consciousness. The testimony provided at the war crimes trial that Michael attends and that sentences Hanna to prison by no means exhausts the subject of the Holocaust, but it does provide necessary information about what happened to the Jews of Germany and Eastern Europe. For the postwar generation of Germans, the discussion of the Holocaust is a necessary subject. But so is mourning the loss of German national pride in its cultural achievements, even its system of law. It is only by acknowledging its own national trauma—that is, by acknowledging both guilt and shame and working through the resistance to admitting that shame—that the second generation might come to acknowledge its relationship to the past. In this context Michael's father's final words to him, after he has given him the philosophical wisdom to determine whether or not he has the moral right to reveal Hanna's secret, are extremely pertinent: "I can't say that I'm sorry I can't help you," his father begins. "As a philosopher, I mean, which is how you were addressing me. As your father, I find the experience of not being able to help my children almost unbearable" (Schlink 2008, 144). There are legal issues that the legal system can address, legally. There are moral issues that philosophy can address, philosophically. But the issue Michael needs to resolve in relation to Hanna cannot be resolved either ethically or legally, and the impossibility of such a resolution is, to repeat Michael's father's word, unbearable. It is unbearable because, just like the bond between parent and child (which Michael's relationship to Hanna to some degree replicates), it has to do with love, not logic.

Michael's divorce from his wife (as the Jewish survivor at the end of the novel correctly diagnoses) stands in evidence of how his distancing himself from Hanna (and from the world of his father and mother, which she represents) produces a crisis for the procreative future of the German nation, similar to that evidenced by Momik in Grossman's novel and Bruno in Appelfeld's. Momik and Bruno are also ashamed of their parents. For this reason they also cannot move on with their paternal lives. Michael and his wife produce a child who will be bereft of the benefits of family and the guidance such family might provide. Since Michael himself suffers from a lack of parental direction (his parents, throughout the period of his affair with Hanna, are strangely oblivious to his comings and goings), this is a heavy indictment of the next generation of German families. "We had cheated her of her rights by getting divorced," Michael says in relation to his daughter, "and the fact that we did it together didn't halve the guilt" (174). Since the failure of Michael's marriage has a lot to do with his inability to confess his relationship with Hanna to his wife, the legalistic language of this, having to do with rights and guilt, suggests how shame precedes guilt and produces situations that are better defined in terms of guilt than shame. Since the idea of cheating the child of her rights invokes the context of the Jews in the years preceding the catastrophe, the example of the family breakup has very real and dire historical implications. The acceptance of the bond of love between children and their parents, the book intimates, is vital to the future of the German nation. Loving one's parents, like loving one's children, may not be something that can be made subject to juridical or even rational judgment.

Legally and ethically there may be no choice but to find perpetrators like Hanna guilty of war crimes and punish them accordingly, although it might be hoped that the courts were a bit better at figuring out the nature and extent of every perpetrator's individual guilt. We live by judicial authority. However, that does not mean that any one of us might not have acted the same way in the same circumstances. It might be ethically imperative for us to keep that in mind, especially when we are making such judgments, whether or not the issue is, to quote the judge, one of "life and limb" (112). And that has to be for each and every one of us an "unbearable" truth, and one that will be experienced by each person through his or her very different subject position in relation to the events of the

Holocaust or other, more current events. In this context it is useful to recall the fallacy of moral equivalence to which the text itself directs us. "When I likened perpetrators, victims, the dead, the living, survivors, and their descendants to each other, I didn't feel good about it and I still don't," the narrator tells us. He continues: "Can one see them all as linked in this way? When I began to make such comparisons in discussions, I always emphasized that the linkage was not meant to relativize the difference between being forced into the world of the death camps and entering it voluntarily [as, for example, do lawyers or historians vicariously], between enduring suffering and imposing it on others, and that this difference was of the greatest, most critical importance" (103). This is the meditation that leads into Michael's question "What should our second generation have done" (104)? This question, I have suggested, needs to be taken even more broadly as asking what each and every one of us should do or have done. It is not an illegitimate question. Rather it is *the* question, as the concluding chapters of the novel suggest.

In the final chapters of the novel Schlink introduces two new characters to the Michael-Hanna dyad: the prison warden in Germany and the lone living survivor of the conflagration in the church, for which Hanna takes sole and reckless responsibility, all because of her shame about being illiterate. The positions of the German matron and the Jewish survivor represent two diametrically opposed relations to the events of the past. Neither of them reflects the ultimate wisdom of the book, although the contrast between them does produce something like a glimmer of moral clarity. The prison warden's highly Christian concept of forgiveness and charity is certainly not what the book is advocating, as the scene with the survivor makes clear. In no unconditional terms the prison matron expresses her anger at both Hanna and Michael for Hanna's suicide. She would like to have imagined that Hanna's years in prison, and especially her newfound ability to read (Holocaust works being chief among the many texts she devours) might have reformed her so that she might have gone out in the world to become a useful citizen in it. "Can the world become so unbearable to someone after years of loneliness?" the warden asks somewhat rhetorically, that word "unbearable" harking back to Michael's father's feeling unable to provide the correct paternal wisdom for his son. "Is it better to kill yourself than to return to the world from the convent, from the hermitage?" she asks (208). The matron formulates her question as if Hanna's suicide had nothing to do with the enormity of the crimes she has committed. She reiterates the trope she has already introduced in her description to Michael of Hanna's years in jail:

> For years and years she lived here the way you would live in a convent. As if she had moved here of her own accord. . . . She was greatly respected by the other women. . . . She had authority, she was asked for her advice. . . . Then a few years ago she gave up. She had always taken care of herself personally. . . .

> But now she began to eat a lot and seldom washed. . . . She didn't seem unhappy or dissatisfied. In fact it was as though the retreat to the convent was no longer enough, as though life in the convent was still too sociable and talkative, and she had to retreat even further, into a lonely cell safe from all eyes. . . . No, it would be wrong to say that she had given up. She redefined her place in a way that was right for her. (207–208)

Although we readers are invited to see that her suicide is her last "retreat" and that she had indeed "given up," the prison warden, who, like the other prisoners, basically respects Hanna, essentially validates Hanna's decision throughout her life not to confess her illiteracy. What is important to the prison guard and the other prisoners is Hanna's apparent wisdom and authority: her nun-like qualities in this prison turned religious sanctuary.

Given how many S.S. guards expressed their mission in religious terms, this sanctification of Hanna into a kind of saint does not bode well for the future of German self-interrogation. The world of the prison becomes a mirror of the world outside. This includes the world of the courts, which imagine that legal justice can redress the horrific wrongs of the Holocaust. That legal justice goes astray in Hanna's trial is one condemnation of the idea that there can ever be justice in this matter. That the object of the mis-sentencing at the trial can then be catapulted into a religious figure adds insult to injury, as does the fact that by taking responsibility Christlike on herself and thereby becoming a sacrificial lamb, her equally guilty co-guards get off with lesser sentences.

To the degree that Michael is made to feel guilty for his treatment of Hanna by the prison warden, he participates in the moral failure of the judiciary system and its Christian morality, which both the trial and the prison represent. But Michael's relationship with Hanna does not end with Hanna's death and his conversation with the prison warden, and while Michael's consciousness does not accede to the more powerful wisdom of the text itself, it does go some further distance by the end of the book. Feeling that he has not adequately confronted his relationship with Hanna—which is to say his shame in relation to that relationship *and* the shame for which that shame stands, his shame about being a German—Michael finally decides to deliver Hanna's legacy to the one remaining survivor of the fire. This is a turn away from not only German perpetrator to Jewish victim but also from Christian morality to Jewish morality, at least as that is imagined by the Christian author. In New York City the austerity of the prison cell (which is made by the warden to carry with it the religious connotations of penitence and thus mercy) is replaced with a different kind of "matter-of-fact" "severity" (211): "Her tone was absolutely matter-of-fact. Everything about her was matter-of-fact" (212). This space of Jewish pragmatism correlates with the survivor's refusal to "grant Frau Schmitz her absolution" (212), even to the extent of "using [the money] for something to do with the Holocaust." Such a use of Hanna's money, the survivor tells Michael, "would seem like an absolution to me and that is something I neither wish nor care to grant" (214). Insofar as absolution is a Christian rather than a Jewish concept, and the Jewish God is associated with the severity of the law that Christian mercy would oppose, the Jewish survivor here plays the role of the quintessential Jew against Hanna as the quintessential Christian. The survivor's God is the Jewish God of justice, not mercy—justice, in this scenario, belonging to God and not to the courts. It is the Jewish survivor who has the last word in this book, though not the final moment. That moment, however, is a rather Jewish moment too.

The conversation between Michael and the Jewish survivor stands in painful contrast to what precedes it, in the prison in Germany, and what follows it, which is Michael's single visit to the cemetery to stand beside Hanna's grave. In keeping with Hanna's wishes, Michael wants the Jewish survivor to donate Hanna's money to a charity "for illiterates who want to learn to read and write," as if the problem of Hanna's participation in the war, not to mention the whole shame culture that she and he both represent, were simply a matter of reading the right books after all (including the New Testament perhaps?). "There must be nonprofit organizations, foundations, societies you could give the money to," he says to the survivor, still wanting her to accept Hanna's money after her refusal to do so, even "corresponding Jewish organizations" (214–15). The survivor's refusal is absolute. In pushing "the check and the money back" to Michael, she exposes both his ignorance and even, perhaps, his disingenuousness in making the request. This disingenuousness belongs to him and not to Hanna. The Jewish survivor does not need money (like many Jews, even after the war, she is quite well off), and even though she acknowledges that "if there are organizations for something, then there are Jewish organizations for it," as she states very clearly and firmly, "illiteracy, it has to be admitted, is hardly a Jewish problem" (215). In her view Jews are a charitable lot; they have charities for everything. But they are not in need of charity, and certainly not for illiteracy. In her view, therefore, Michael's plan is downright laughable. "Let's do it this way," she finally says. "You find out what kind of relevant Jewish organizations there are, here or in Germany, and you pay the money to the account of the organization that seems most plausible to you," and then "she laughed": "If the recognition is so important, you can do it in the name of Hanna Schmitz. . . . I'll keep the tin" (215).

Bill Niven quotes Harold Bloom that "reading [even] the very best writers—let us say Homer, Dante, Shakespeare, Tolstoy—is not going to make us better citizens" (2003, 393). Neither reader in Schlink's novel—which is to say neither Michael nor Hanna—achieves clarity of moral vision through reading. But it is after Michael's direct contact with the Jewish survivor and her rejection of him that he performs the one gesture (reminiscent of similar moments in Appelfeld's, Krauss's, and Chabon's novels) that indeed bespeaks moral growth: he goes to visit Hanna's grave, and he mourns. (In the movie this scene is staged with his daughter, a useful if somewhat sentimental addition, I think, to the logic of the scene.) Michael does donate Hanna's money to "the Jewish League Against Illiteracy" (note the league does not specify *Jewish* illiteracy), for which he receives "a short, computer-generated letter . . . thank[ing] Ms. Hanna Schmitz for her donation." With this letter, which being "computer-generated" signifies the opposite of reading and writing, he goes to visit Hanna's grave (Schlink 2008, 218). Germans will have to reconcile themselves to their past and to their parents' role in that past without Jewish forgiveness and with full consciousness of how empty a gesture repentance is to those whose lives were extinguished or mutilated by the Nazi regime. Schlink's having the survivor keep the empty tin is one way of registering how vacant the bid for forgiveness and absolution really is, although her keeping the tin is not wholly ironic. The survivor also needs something to hold on to—an object (even an empty one), a memory, a story, such as the one Michael Berg is now producing in his text. The survivor is the woman, after all, who wrote the story that launched the trial of Hanna and her codefendants. The survivor too is a part of the narrative chain. She too needs to tell the story, however empty a gesture that might be.

By the end of the novel Schlink has brought his protagonist very close to what he would have us understand is his own position in relation to the events of the Second World War. Not only is the Holocaust a set of actions taken against the Jews, but it is also an event that befell the German nation unto subsequent generations. Writes Schlink in *Guilt about the Past:*

> The legal historical perspective shows that the act of not renouncing, not judging and not repudiating carries its own guilt with it. . . . It is equally true today that one becomes entangled in another's guilt if one maintains or establishes solidarity with that person. . . . To not renounce the other includes one in that person's guilt for past crimes, but so that a new sort of guilt is created. . . . Children too become entwined in the guilt of non-renunciation. This guilt sits in wait for them until they become able to recognize the guilt of others, dissociate or not dissociate themselves from it. (2010, 15, 18)

In writing the novel Schlink, like his protagonist, renounces the actions of the past, without removing himself from the circle of community of which he is a part. For this reason it is difficult for Schlink/Michael to write the book. "Maybe I did write our story," Michael says in the penultimate paragraph of the book, just before he tells us about his visit to Hanna's grave, "to be free of it, even if I never can be" (218). To be free of something one can never be free of is precisely the paradox, which is also represented by the empty tin. On the one hand, by accepting an empty box, the recipient empties the gesture. On the other hand, the recipient also accepts that an empty gesture is the only sort of gesture that can be made, and she accepts it. "The path [Michael's] life had taken" and the "written version" of the story, which is the one that "wanted to be written" (216–17), this book and no other, have both a finality and a provisionality to them that bespeak a humility before "unbearable" facts that cannot be altered and the "unbearable" crimes for which there can be no atonement. Any and all gestures will be empty ones. And yet they must be made. And perhaps accepted.

What, then, of the final reader in this text, who is the reader of the text? Like Michael's father and the trial judge, the survivor returns moral accounting to Michael. There can be no ultimate justice. The Jews cannot give atonement. By producing three endings—one within the jail, one in New York City, and one at Hanna's graveside—the book places that burden of moral accounting on the reader of the text. How we read it depends on our own subject positions in relation to the text and the events that it records. What is required is that we recognize the unbearable truth that this subject position belongs to us and that we must take responsibility for it. This includes acknowledging that our subject position is always imperfect, inadequate, and biased.

As is clear from my discussion of *The Reader,* I greatly respect what I take to be the novel's honesty in exposing the deeply experienced ambivalences and shame of postwar-generation Germans and in asking complicated and not always "politically correct" questions concerning what the younger generations of Germans should "do" in relation to their parents' generation. Implicit in that question, especially as it plays off of Hanna's question to the judge during the proceedings, is what ordinary, average Germans should have done during the war. This implies the question to *the reader* (the reader of the text, that is), which is, What would *you* have done? The answer to that question may in no way change the implementation of legal justice or of ethical judgment. But it may force a more honest confrontation with what it means for any of us to ask that question of others. It also may suggest something about our own implicit impropriety in relation to the Holocaust subject. Hanna's taking young women out of the transports to read to her has seemed to some readers to imply sexual impropriety. Yet we readers know full well that Hanna's need to be read to trumped her need for sexual intercourse in her relationship with Michael. So this other thought involving sexual impropriety, like the questioning of Magda's parentage in Ozick's *The Shawl,* functions as evidence of our own somewhat salacious curiosity about sexual matters in the camps. Why do we immediately suspect sexual foul play when Hanna wants to be read to? The explicit sexuality of Michael's relationship with Hanna—which occupies the whole first part of the book (almost half of it) and which has nothing whatsoever to do with the Holocaust, either in our perception of it or in Michael's (we don't know about what Hanna is thinking, but likely she too would not have associated her relationship with Michael to anything that happened in her previous history)—further reinforces how thinking about the

Holocaust may become a temptation to dwell on illicit sexual matters. Michael, after all, is the narrator and de facto author of this text, who chooses to begin his narrative this way. Of course, that Schlink also begins his book this way might indicate his similarly indulging in such psychosexual fantasies of the Holocaust. However, it might represent his self-conscious framing of his narrator's tendency toward fantasy—which is, I think, what Littell does in relation to Aue's narrative in *The Kindly Ones*. Since the text everywhere, except at the very end, exposes Michael's lack of insight, the evidence of the text suggests that Schlink himself is not to be implicated in the sexualization of the Holocaust. We, however, are.

From beginning to end *The Reader* is about how we read and what we do with what we read. The English translation of the book's title obscures the difference marked in the German title between, one the one hand, *Der Vorleser* (the German title of Schlink's book), which means someone who recites or reads out, much as a sentence is read out in a court of law or as a letter might be computer-generated, and, on the other hand, *des leser,* which would refer to someone who reads in the sense of reading a book, like this one. Michael and the young women in the camps are readers in the more technical sense of reading out a written narrative. The last time Michael sees Hanna before the trial, he tells us that he cannot "read her expression," and lest we miss the point, he repeats: "her face was turned towards me but with an expression I cannot read at all—that is another picture I have of her" (80). Michael is *der Vorleser,* in life as much as in his relationship to Hanna. Hanna, however, when she finally learns to read is *"des leser."* Hanna learns to read in the fullest sense of that word. That Michael refuses to write letters to Hanna, even after he realizes she is no longer illiterate, suggests the degree to which he will not submit himself to the requirements of reading, which is to say as well the requirements of writing, since reading is always, insofar as we internalize and interpret language, a form of writing. Until Michael consents to become an author, he will only passively and with detachment record other people's words and read them out loud, as in a court of law. To read this novel, to read history, can be as meaningless as reading out the words on the page, reciting or parroting (to bring in the image from Chabon's book) what we think is the moral burden of the text or its violation of that moral burden. To read a text (*lesen*)—this or any other text—we must make sense of it. This means we have to permit the text to produce words in us to which we subscribe and that come to narrate our personal relation to the story.

9 Mourning and Melancholia in W. G. Sebald's *Austerlitz*

"IN THE SECOND half of the 1960s I traveled repeatedly from England to Belgium, partly for study purposes, partly for other reasons, which were never entirely clear to me" (Sebald 2001, 3). Thus begins Sebald's extraordinary novel *Austerlitz,* in which a nameless narrator records his repeated encounters with the mysterious and elusive Jacques Austerlitz, a Jewish survivor from Czechoslovakia who arrives in England on the *Kindertransport* and grows up without knowing the story of his origins. The novel unfolds through the narrator's retelling of Austerlitz's narrative as Austerlitz comes to understand more and more about his own story. In odd and discomforting ways that story becomes the narrator's own autobiography, both in the present moment of the narration and, more profoundly, in terms of his history as a German, not a Jew.

Austerlitz, we very quickly realize, is the narrator's uncanny doppelgänger. Not only do they meet unexpectedly at the most fraught junctures in the narrator's life, but they also are so in tune with each other that they can seamlessly resume conversations begun years earlier. Thus, concerning their initial meeting the narrator writes: "When I finally went over to Austerlitz . . . he was not at all surprised by my direct approach but answered me at once" (7–8). Or later in the book: "On this second meeting, as on all subsequent occasions, we simply went on with our conversation, wasting no time in commenting on the improbability of our meeting again in a place like this, which no sensible person would have sought out" (28). And even later on, in what proves to be their most significant encounter:

> As I was watching all of this I suddenly noticed a solitary figure on the edge of the agitated crowd, a figure who could only be Austerlitz, whom I realized at that moment I had not seen for nearly twenty years. . . . As far as I remember, I was overcome for a considerable time by my amazement at the unexpected return of Austerlitz. . . . Without wasting any words on the coincidence of our meeting again after all this time, Austerlitz took up the conversation that evening . . . more or less where it had last been broken off. . . . Oddly enough,

said Austerlitz . . . he had been thinking of our encounters in Belgium, so long ago now, and telling himself he must find someone to whom he could relate his own story . . . for which he needed the kind of listener I had once been in Antwerp. . . . Contrary to all statistical probability, then, there was an astonishing, positively imperative internal logic to his meeting me here in the bar of the Great Eastern Hotel, a place he had never before entered in his life. (39–44)

While the narrator's reasons for traveling to Belgium are never made explicit, it is at this juncture in the novel that the story of his double, Austerlitz, begins to become very clear indeed, both to the narrator and to the reader, not to mention to Austerlitz himself.

As a child survivor, wrenched from his home in Prague and thrust into a new language and a new culture in Wales, Austerlitz comes only now, as an adult, to confront his past and recall his childhood. When he does so, the dimensions of that story become glaringly, painfully clear. Austerlitz's story is a fairly familiar Holocaust narrative. Indeed, according to Sebald himself, it is based on a historical narrative he heard on television. Nonetheless, the story is skillfully, affectingly, and lovingly told by the narrator in a narrative that is often presented (as if) in Austerlitz's own words. This story is also told in the accompanying photographic materials that appear throughout the text, some of which are also attributed to Austerlitz. In what might be understood as the ultimate humility, the narrator would not tell the Jew's story for him (as would Styron for the African American or the Jew); he would have the Jew tell his story by himself. Of course it is a German narrator who is actually narrating the story as it is a German author writing the novel. As the term "doppelgänger" suggests, the relationship between the narrator and his double might not be as smooth and untroubled as we might wish. A doppelgänger isn't simply a double or twin; rather it is often a detested, rejected, aspect of oneself, the reviled conscience, for example, as in the fiction of Edgar Allan Poe. This is the doppelgänger who is resisted and who must finally be killed off in order for the individual to survive. Of course such destruction of the self-same other is often tantamount to suicide. This is a possibility we have already encountered in Littell's *Kindly Ones* (2009). Sebald's narrator does not kill himself, although he does exhibit decidedly suicidal or self-destructive tendencies. And Austerlitz is not so much detested as adored, much like the idolized Bruno Schulz in other texts we have examined. It is the excess of emotion that the narrator feels in relation to Austerlitz that links his adoration of his double to the self-destructive aspects of rejection that typically characterize the relationship to the doppelgänger.

Whether we take Austerlitz as the narrator's projection and invention or as an actual character within the world of the text, it is clear that Austerlitz's survivor story, as told by the narrator, is a story of traumatization. For the child survivor the world is a constant reflection of loss and absence, grief and despondency, to which the narrative gives full voice:

I now think, said Austerlitz, that time will not pass away, has not passed away, that I can turn back and go behind it, and there I shall find everything as it once was, or more precisely I shall find that all moments of time have co-existed simultaneously, in which case none of that history would be true, past events have not yet occurred but are waiting to do so at the moment when we think of them, although that, of course, opens up the bleak prospect of ever-lasting misery and never ending anguish. (Sebald 2001, 101)

This no-time/all-time synthesis of everywhere and nowhere is a virtual descrip-tion of what in psychoanalytic terminology is called primary process. It is a por-trait of Austerlitz's being locked in a past that is as present to him as the present. Furthermore, shortly after his reunion with the narrator, he observes that "it has been clear to me of late why an agency greater than or superior to my own capac-ity for thought, which circumspectly directs operations somewhere in my brain, has always preserved me from my own secret" (44). Or as he puts it with even greater psychoanalytic clarity later on, as if the description has no less than been lifted from a textbook analysis of inadequate repression:

I had constantly been preoccupied by that accumulation of knowledge which I had pursued for decades, and which served as a substitute or compensatory memory. . . . Yet this self-censorship of my mind, the constant suppression of the memories surfacing in me . . . demanded ever greater efforts and finally, and unavoidably, led to the almost total paralysis of my linguistic faculties, the destruction of all my notes and sketches, my endless nocturnal peregrinations through London, and the hallucinations which plagued me with increasing frequency up to the point of my nervous breakdown in the summer of 1992. (140)

Hence Austerlitz expresses his need of a "listener" such as the narrator (41). With-out telling his story to someone, he cannot get out from behind the curtain his trauma has cast between him and the world, which has become the only optic through which he can see that world. The external world of nature and of man-made artifacts (in particular, buildings), we might say, has till now doubly con-tained his consciousness: it has become the repository of his grief, and for a long time it prevented that grief from totally overwhelming and destroying him. But it did so at an increasingly steep psychological cost, which Austerlitz himself has come to recognize and which he now needs to address.

By the end of Austerlitz's story, as the narrator records it, Austerlitz has ex-perienced a psychological recovery of sorts. He is last seen searching for more information about his father's fate. More important perhaps, he is in pursuit of the woman Marie who had once loved him but whom his personal demons had kept him from being able to love in return. By contrast, the narrator of the novel does not arrive at any such good place, not even vicariously through Austerlitz, which is to say through the story he tells of Austerlitz, for it is the narrator in this novel, I suggest, whose consciousness or mood is the subject of the novel, not Austerlitz's. In the narrator's telling of it, it may be Austerlitz who needs a "listener" in order to work through his resistances to hearing his own story, but this is only a psychological reversal on the narrator's part. It is in fact the narrator who needs Austerlitz in order to come to terms with his own internal landscape, which he projects onto the literal landscape of England and Europe and onto the survivor's view of it. In "Sebald's Uncanny Travels," John Zilcosky argues that whereas in most journey novels a character gets lost and must find his way home again, for Sebald's protagonist getting lost is virtually impossible: "no matter how far he journeys, he can never leave his home" (2004, 102–103). This, I suggest, is the symptom to which the narrator must come to pay attention. It is also a symptom of the text itself to which Sebald either does or does not attend, depending on how we put together the evidence of the text.

To stay within the world of the text for a moment, for the narrator Austerlitz's experience is that "substitute or compensatory" narrative that requires more and more energy on the narrator's part to contain. Through Austerlitz the narrator constructs the story not of his literal life, which is very different from Austerlitz's in almost all its particulars, but of his imaginative perception of the post-Holocaust (which is also the postcolonial) world into which "through no fault of his own" (to quote a phrase from the opening of the book) he has been born. Thus, to return to the opening of the novel, as the train (that most infamous vehicle of Jewish deportation) rolls into the station, the narrator, who cannot clarify the reasons for his travels to Belgium, very quickly begins "to feel unwell." It is this "sense of indisposition" that prompts him, with what he refers to as uncertain footsteps, to walk around the inner city, beginning with (of all streets) the "Jeruzalemstraat" and winding up at the recently opened "Nocturama." When he later comes to record his impressions of the Nocturama, the only animal he remembers is a raccoon "washing the same piece of apple over and over again as if it hoped that all this washing . . . would help it to escape the unreal world in which it had arrived, so to speak, through no fault of its own." The raccoon's obsessive-compulsive washing of the dirty fruit (an apple, no less) and its wish to escape—an image that contains both the German's sense of guilt and his equally powerful wish to flee an unreal world that has been created through no fault of his own—carries the narrator back to the Centraal Station, which then takes on the aspect of the Nocturama: the "railway passengers" come to seem to the narrator "somehow miniaturized," as if "they were the last members of a diminutive race, which had perished or had been expelled from its homeland. One of the people waiting in the *Salle des pas perdus* was Austerlitz" (Sebald 2001, 3–7). Thus Austerlitz suddenly materializes in the midst of the narrator's internal ruminations on a race of humans who had perished or been expelled from its homeland, the culmination of the set of Holocaust-inflected images that have externalized the narrator's Holocaust-driven inner consciousness from the opening sentence of the novel.

From the beginning, then, with his arrival in Antwerp and his walk along the Jeruzalemstraat, the narrator is obsessed with things Jewish. When early on in their relationship Austerlitz refers to his "obsession with railway stations, speaking not so much to me as to himself," we are meant to hear the narrator's own obsession (34). This "obsession with railway stations," the narrator goes on to tell us, which seamlessly blends together Austerlitz and himself, "was the only hint of his personal life he allowed himself to give me before I returned to Germany at the end of 1975, intending to settle permanently in my native land" (34). It is after he leaves his native land for a second time that he once again runs into Austerlitz, almost twenty years after they first met. In repetition of the very beginning of the book, he is feeling "slightly unwell" (38). Indeed, the proximate cause of the narrator's running into Austerlitz again is a problem with his eyesight, which is quickly revealed to be a problem as well with the narrator's will to live: he no longer can see clearly, and he is not sure he wishes to regain clarity of vision. On the one hand, the narrator experiences "anxiety." He is "considerably alarmed" and "filled with concern" when he realizes that his vision is fading (34–35). "At the same time," however, he tells us that he perceives his failing eyesight as "a vision of release into which I saw myself free of the constant compulsion to read and write" (35–36). Since he is writing this book, his wish to be free of the compulsion to write means he would prefer not to be writing this book.

The scene of Austerlitz and the narrator's reunion in London clearly is made to recall the opening of the book, accompanied as it is by the narrator's feeling unwell and by those "reasons which were never entirely clear to me" that deliver the narrator to Antwerp and produce his focus on the compulsive behavior of the raccoon in the Nocturama. The "nervous breakdown" subsequently attributed to Austerlitz, with its "endless nocturnal peregrinations through London" and "hallucinations" (140), thus belongs at least as much to the narrator as to Austerlitz. Austerlitz, we begin to sense, is only the narrator's externalization of the wandering Jew within himself. The narrator is suspended between the homing instincts of those pigeons tended to by Austerlitz's friend Gerald and the moths, who are paralyzed and stuck in position till they die, which are a part of Gerald's uncle's entomological collection. As Eric Santner notes, the name Austerlitz recalls Ahasverus, who is the prototype of the wandering Jew within Christian literature (2006, 121, 123). We've met Ahasverus already in relation to Grossman's *See Under: Love*. Not only do Austerlitz and the narrator wander endlessly throughout Europe, but images of nomadism (many of them in relation to biblical scenes) punctuate the text.

Lest we miss the doppelgänger relationship between the narrator and Austerlitz, with its various troubling implications, the narrative provides Austerlitz with a mother who sang the role of Olimpia in the Jacques Offenbach opera based on the story "The Sandman," by E. T. A. Hoffman (Sebald 2001, 161). Indeed, as his former babysitter, Vera, tells Austerlitz, his mother was so "inspired by the works of Jacques Offenbach" that she named her son (Jacques) for him (154). So, I suggest, did the narrator, not to mention Sebald. Hoffman is the writer cited by Sebald in an interview in which he describes the refusal of German culture to acknowledge its Nazi past. "There was evidence of what had occurred," Sebald explains, "evidence in no uncertain terms. And yet at the time you were sitting in your seminars at university, you know, reading a piece of romantic fiction, E. T. A. Hoffman or something, and never referring in any of those cases to the real historical background, to the social conditions, to the psychological complications caused by social conditions and so on" (Sebald 2011, 47). Those psychological complications are what are being put center stage in Sebald's novel.

They also remind us that the Hoffman tale on which Offenbach based his opera was an important work in Freud's definition of "The Uncanny" (1973c; first published 1919), to which the doppelgänger is closely related. Several important features of Freud's essay inform Sebald's novel. First, as noted, there is the phenomenon of the doppelgänger itself, which is a register of the uncanny or, in German, *unheimlich*. Insofar as the term "unheimlich" is etymologically linked to "unhomely," as Freud insists more than once in his essay (220–26), it suggests precisely the problem of the homeless German ex-patriot discovering his uncanny double in the Jewish survivor. More than the uncertainty posed by inanimate objects as to whether or not they are alive (also a feature of Sebald's text in terms of the fascination with architecture, along with photographs, which, in Sebald's words in an interview recorded in *Emergence of Memory*, "are emanations of the dead" [2011, 39; Zilcosky 2004]), the uncanny in Sebald's novel has to do with the Jewish other. It hints at the way Jews and Germans were so like each other even before the war as to have provoked the Germans' radical wish to exterminate the uncanny Jewish double. In Littell's *The Kindly Ones*, if Aue is not actually a Jew, he certainly sees the Jew as a part of himself that he wishes to destroy. Aue and the narrator in *Austerlitz* both see and do not see this. They both wish to see and not to see it. For this reason, the emphasis in Freud's essay on the "motif of the 'Sand-Man,' who tears out children's eyes" ("Uncanny" 1973c, 227) becomes a major feature in Sebald's novel as well. Freud links the "fear of damaging or losing one's eyes," the "fear of going blind," with the "dread of being castrated," and the fear of castration, of course, with the "wish" to kill the father (231). The relationship to the father has everything to do with the narrator and his father and almost nothing to do with Austerlitz and his. One of the major fears ascribed in the novel, not to Austerlitz but to the narrator, who has left behind his fatherland along with his literal father, is the "progressive decline in [his] eyesight" (Sebald 2001, 35). The novel intensifies this reference to the Hoffman story, Freud's reading of it, and the Offenbach opera when the narrator immediately recalls, as eyedrops are being put into his eyes, that "a few drops of liquid . . . used to be applied to the pupils of operatic divas before they went on stage" (35). These drops, the narrator recalls, were also applied to "young women about to be introduced to a suitor" (35), which associates Hoffman and Offenbach with the narrator's almost romantic attachment to Austerlitz. Indeed, immediately following the visit to his eye doctor the narrator once again runs into Austerlitz, after a gap of twenty years. It is at this point that the narrator becomes the confidant of Austerlitz's story. He becomes Austerlitz's "listener." The narrator listens but does not see, in more ways than one.

Since the narrator is deliberately constructed by Sebald in ways that recall Sebald himself, we are being invited by the author to see the narrator as a thinly veiled version of himself. Sebald is also a German born after the war, living primarily in England. Furthermore, his family background is hardly untroubled, both personally and politically. This closeness of the text's narrator to the author himself cannot but direct our questions about the projection of the German onto the Jew in the direction of the literal author, even if in the end we might discover ways not to implicate Sebald in the narrator's psychological problems, at least not to the same extent. To further intensify the problem of where Sebald stands in relation to his narrator and to his narrator's projections onto Austerlitz is the intentional doubling of the author and Austerlitz. Of course, in a very literal (if also literary) way, Austerlitz is Sebald's invention, not the narrator's. But the doubling goes further than this. Therefore, at one key moment in the novel, a photograph ostensibly taken by Austerlitz of himself and given to the narrator shows someone looking a lot like Sebald reflected in the shop window in Theresienstadt that the photograph records. Indeed, when the book has Austerlitz explain how he first became aware of his origins, the story he tells is virtually the same story that Sebald tells of his own first introduction to the Kindertransport. This is from the novel:

> I was listening to two women talking to each other about the summer of 1939, when they were children and had been sent to England on a special transport. They mentioned a number of cities . . . but only when one of the couple said that her own transport, after two days traveling through the German Reich and the Netherlands . . . had finally left the Hook of Holland on the ferry *Prague* to cross the North Sea to Harwich, only then did I know beyond any doubt that these fragments of memory were part of my own life as well. (2001, 141; italics in original)

This is Sebald speaking autobiographically:

> There was this story of a woman who together with her twin sister had also come to Britain on one of those *Kindertransporte,* as they were called, trains with very young children leaving Germany or Czechoslovakia or Austria just before the outbreak of war. And those two girls were, I think, two-and-a-half to three years old. They came out of a Jewish Munich orphanage and they

were fostered by a Welsh fundamentalist childless couple who then went on to erase their identity. And both foster parents ended tragically, as one might say, the father in a lunatic asylum, the mother through an early death. And so the children never really knew who they were. (2011, 110–11; italics in original).

Sebald was actually sued for plagiarism by the woman whose story he adapted.

Susi Bechhofer's book titled *Rosa's Child: The True Story of One Woman's Quest for a Lost Mother and a Vanished Past* (1999) does indeed contain details that inform Sebald's narrative, as Sebald himself suggests. Yet what Sebald most notably seems to take from the autobiography (which focuses on the sexual abuse Bechhofer suffered at the hands of her foster father and the psychological consequences of that abuse) is the idea of the twins, which emerges in his text as the twinning of both the conscious and unconscious self (in and through Austerlitz and the narrator/Sebald), and also, through this device, of the German and the Jew. "I never shook off the feeling," Austerlitz reports early in the book, "that something very obvious, very manifest in itself, was hidden from me. Sometimes it was as if I were in a dream and trying to perceive reality; then again I felt as if an invisible twin brother were walking beside me, the reverse of a shadow, so to speak" (Sebald 2001, 54–55). As I have been suggesting, that twin is the narrator, who is attributing that thought to *his* twin, Austerlitz, as perhaps Sebald is to his twins, the narrator and Austerlitz, the German and the Jew: "Jew and *goy* in magnetic gravitation," as Styron puts it in *Sophie's Choice* (1979, 170).

Of course no character or narrative voice in any book ever originates anywhere but from within the consciousness of the author. Therefore, all aspects of a literary text necessarily express something of the writer's consciousness. Yet in *Austerlitz* this aspect of literary production becomes particularly marked, enough so as to constitute a subject in its own right: the subject of subject position itself, of how we project onto others and their history our own selves and stories. Sebald does not hide behind his narrator. He insists that we see him inhabit the narrator. The interpretive question for readers is, Why?

Insofar as the narrator is searching at every turn for evidences of the Holocaust, so is Sebald. Breendonk is one more example of this. But Breendonk is also an occasion for us to reflect on another aspect of the narrator's/author's cast of mind. While looking at Breendonk for a second time, and from a distance, the narrator takes up a book first given to him by Austerlitz himself, a book by Dan Jacobson. In this book, titled *Heshel's Kingdom* (1999), Jacobson (a writer of repute and represented as Austerlitz's colleague; perhaps he was Sebald's) records his search in Lithuania for "traces of his forebears." What he finds instead are "only signs everywhere of the annihilation from which . . . his immediate family" had been preserved by his grandfather's early demise and the family's subsequent emigration to South Africa (quoted in Sebald 2001, 297). Indeed, in Jacobson Sebald's narrator finds confirmation of his sense that the landscape itself is polluted and degraded: "I have never seen more deceitfully innocent-looking landscapes than those of Lithuania," writes Jacobson (1999, 168).

The references to Jacobson seem to serve as a kind of seal of authenticity to the narrator's narrative, an authentication of what occurred in this place and its devastation of the landscape, which now tells the story in its grotesque, albeit eloquent, muteness. Like Austerlitz, Jacobson is a Jew. His is a Jewish text, recording Jewish history from inside that history. Yet for this very reason Sebald's use of Jacobson's text is problematic. It is as if Sebald would give his text a Jewish seal of approval, much like the female protagonist of Schlink's *The Reader* would do by leaving her scanty inheritance to the one survivor of her crimes against the Jews. But does Jacobson's text, any more than Sebald's, read history from within the perspective of the victim or survivor of the Holocaust? Does its claim that the European landscape is a repository of devastation necessarily express a Jewish position? In his book Jacobson writes about several Nazi photographs taken of camp victims that he comes to view in a museum in Lithuania:

> The assembling of images of war and natural calamity for display on television and in the press is always a morally ambiguous business . . . ; so is our participation as viewers and readers in the results. But this—! Sadistic prurience was not a "temptation" or a "danger" for the photographers of the scenes on show here: it was precisely what had animated them. (1999, 131)

Jacobson dramatizes the complexity of the photographic record through the story of another visitor to the museum who decides to photograph the photograph. This woman, who is one of a group of South African Jews (almost clichéd in their lack of proper reverence for the site and what it displays), points to a picture of a ghetto scene and in a Litvak Yiddish accent explains: "That's just what it was. You see it? I was here in the war. I was in the Kovno Ghetto. Afterwards they sent me to Auschwitz." And the text continues: "Then she did a strange thing. It would have seemed strange to me anyway, even if I had not been . . . thinking as I had about the origin of many of the pictures on the walls. She reached into her handbag and took out a small camera." When the camera fails to operate properly, she asks what seems to be the proper philosophical and ethical question (the question that Sebald will pose over and over again in his photographic display in the novel): "What is the good of that?" only to follow this question with evidence of the fact that she hasn't a clue as to the problem that her failed attempt at second-hand witnessing discloses: "'Why doesn't the flash flash?'" she asks "with genuine distress" (131–32).

In relation to a novel like *Austerlitz*, in which photographs are such a dominant feature that they have solicited the lion's share of scholarly commentary and critique, the scene of the photography exhibit in Jacobson's novel assumes special significance. Photographs in Sebald's text would seem to be, at least on first glance, a gesture toward claiming the historical truthfulness and accuracy of his narrative. In point of fact, however, the photographs themselves are fictive representations of often unidentified people, places, and things. The photographs confirm absolutely nothing at all except their own existence as photographs. To adapt the words of the tourist in Jacobson's book, they do no "good." As another critic has put it, the photography in Sebald's novel is not intended to be a "transparent device of historical testimony"; rather, it is "a locus of trauma" (Pane 2005, 37). These are the lines of argument followed by other critics as well (Taberner 2004; Osborne 2007). As Caroline Duttlinger (2004) suggests, the photographs picture the failure of memory to hold on to and reconstruct the past, even with the assistance of such technological aids as photographs. Sebald's highly sophisticated rendering of how historical truths and realities can never be proven beyond a shadow of a doubt by any single artifact, detail, word, or image is a stroke of genius that merits the high praise the novel has received. The point in Jacobson's book seems similarly to be that external, archival evidence cannot "prove" anything. Nor can it do our remembering for us. It cannot authenticate the past or our claims for it. Yet what is Sebald's use of Jacobson's novel in his own work of fiction but an attempt at external documentation and validation?

One needs to note in this regard that Jacobson's is not even a survivor account. Albeit Jewish, like Austerlitz, and not German, like the narrator and Sebald, Jacobson is nonetheless of the narrator's and Sebald's generation. As is the case with Sebald's novel, the pall that hangs over the European landscape in Jacobson's novel is one that Jacobson brings with him. It does not emerge from an earlier childhood memory of the place, which it now acts to replace or revive. Instead, it is the only image of the place he has ever had, and it is a product purely of his imagination, since his mother and grandmother have told him precious little about the place. Before he even arrives in Lithuania, in other words, Jacobson is disposed to see it a certain way, both because of what he already knows about the Holocaust and because of how he is psychologically constituted, which is also (as it is for writers like Spiegelman and Stollman) a consequence, albeit indirect, of the events that transpired in Europe.

The second problem with the narrator's citation of Jacobson's book is that Jacobson's family did not just migrate anywhere from Lithuania; they settled in South Africa, which is, from the beginning of *Austerlitz,* one more astounding example of European inhumanity. Colonialism is as much a subject of Sebald's text as the Holocaust (as is the case with Chabon's *Final Solution* [2004], in Stef Crap and Gert Buelen's [2011] reading of it). Indeed, one more of those unclear reasons that the narrator's journey to Austerlitz and through Austerlitz to the story of the Holocaust begins in Belgium is because of Belgium's preeminence as a colonial power. In this subjugation of blacks by whites, Jewish émigrés like the Jacobsons were hardly innocent, even if some of them (like Jacobson himself) eventually left South Africa. Indeed, in the scene of the South African tourists in the museum in Lithuania, Jacobson identifies himself as British. He knows full well what moral problems being South African raises, problems that are not so different from those of being German after the war.

What motivates Austerlitz to put Jacobson's book in the narrator's hands, which is to say since Austerlitz is a projection of the narrator, what prompts the narrator to recur to Jacobson's book at this stage in the story (or what prompts Sebald to invoke this book at this point) has everything to do with the complexity of the narrator's/Sebald's subject position.. The thinking together of the Holocaust and colonial exploitation in a book in which Jewish refugees from Europe find themselves within apartheid South Africa suggests at the very least something about the narrator's depressive, melancholic cast of mind. However, it also might suggest a certain resistance to assuming full blame for what occurred during the Holocaust. Whether the narrator is thus constructed self-consciously by Sebald, to expose the subject position of the German as not completely assuming responsibility for the Holocaust, or whether Sebald is implicated in this hedging, the reader has to decide for himself. Like Schlink's *The Reader,* Sebald's *Austerlitz* could seem more like a shame narrative than a responsible grappling with German history.

The narrator's/Sebald's portrayal of the devastated landscape of Europe following the Second World War and the murder of the Jews certainly has to be taken as a gesture on their (his) part to record and even to identify with the fate of the Jews and to acknowledge the consequences of their extermination for Europe itself. There also seems to be commonsense logic about this depiction of Europe. How else would anyone, especially a Jew, see the post-Holocaust world of Europe? we might ask. Of course the answer to this question is that anyone (Jewish or German) might see the scene quite otherwise. Impressions of the landscape, which are always projections onto it, depend on the mind of the perceiver, not the objective realities that an impersonal optic (a camera lens, for example) might see, although again we need to remember that a human mind frames even the camera's otherwise impersonal view of things. Cameras, especially as they feature in works like Sebald's, are always vehicles of subjectivity. As Simon Ward puts the case in "Ruins and Poetics in the Works of W. G. Sebald," quoting architect Robert Harbison: "The spectator's perspective is always constitutive of the meaning of the ruin" (2004, 58; Bond 2004 makes a similar point). Insofar as "Jerusalem is the archetype of the ruined city," in Sebald's work, the ruin, like the landscape, has a Jewish cast to it (Ward 2004, 59).

Therefore, the example of landscape descriptions in the writings of a Jewish survivor like Aharon Appelfeld can shed significant light on the processes of projection that are being exhibited in Sebald's text, if only to make the simple, straightforward point that the landscapes of Europe might be experienced differently from the way Sebald portrays them, even by actual survivors of the Holocaust. Throughout both his fiction and his autobiographical texts, Appelfeld recurs again and again to the sheer physical beauty of the lost homeland of the Jewish survivor, despite everything that transpired there. Appelfeld is a child survivor who is not so unlike Austerlitz: both of them are abandoned children, bereft of their beloved mothers, which means also of a mother tongue and a motherland as well, and both are left to survive largely through their own devices, whether in the confines of a loveless Welsh home, which is Austerlitz's fate and that of the woman survivor whose story is behind his, or in the forests of Romania, where the young Appelfeld survives. Yet in his memoir *The Story of a Life* (1999) and in the movie he made at about the same time he was writing the book, *All That Remains* (1999), Appelfeld portrays the landscape as anything but the repository of absence and loss that it is for Sebald's narrator and major protagonist. Quite to the contrary, for Appelfeld the landscapes of Romania are places of sacred childhood memories, which he refuses to let be expunged from his consciousness, however much others might want or expect this of him.

Appelfeld's landscape is what I would call a homescape. It is the place where the child's fondest memories of his family reside. This is true despite the fact that the adult writer Appelfeld is quite conscious of and intent upon representing the absence of Jews from contemporary Europe and the horrific circumstances that produced that absence. *All That Remains,* for example, dwells Claude Lanzmann-like on the fact that the contemporary villagers of the small town where Appelfeld lived barely remember the Jews and are painfully vague when it comes to what transpired there just several decades earlier. Yet throughout the film the camera dwells lovingly on the overwhelmingly, breathtakingly beautiful natural landscape that surrounds the now *Judenfrei* village. This beauty is not to be seen as purely ironic, although it is that, too, of course. In one extremely powerful clip, which appears in the film twice, we see several young girls (too young to have any memory of the events that transpired in their village) holding hands and simply being young and innocent and beautiful, standing in a field of wheat and flowers. We will discover momentarily, with a shock, in the second clip, that this beautiful spot may well mark the mass gravesite where Appelfeld's mother is buried. Finding this gravesite has been one of Appelfeld's chief motivations in returning to his native land. Yet even in the second clip, where this information is finally introduced, the image of the young girls is presented in straightforward simplicity. Their youth and innocence exist side by side with what once occurred there, emblematic of the way the landscape continues to serve for Appelfeld as a beloved scene of childhood, of the home he shared with his parents—in particular, his beloved, murdered mother. Indeed, it is his mother whom the young girls seem lovingly, longingly to recall as they also recall the young child Appelfeld, who was even younger than these girls when he was forced to flee.

To be sure, Appelfeld's land/homescapes are doing psychological work for him. Throughout his fiction Appelfeld is both in dialogue with his mother and also, through his reimagining of the world she loved and lost, attempting to restore her to that world, where the mother and the son might be reunited, in imagination at least. This is why the landscape is for him a homescape. He views it with the fondness and nostalgia of the child he once was. What I claim here in relation to Sebald's *Austerlitz* is that the narrator's text is similarly doing psychological work for the narrator, as is Sebald's narrative for Sebald.

In a review of Sebald's posthumously published *On the Natural History of Destruction* (2003), Daphne Merkin criticizes the book in terms that are reminiscent of the critique of Schlink's novel. She reads it as a "complex apologia . . . that attempts to absolve a son of the sins of the father by establishing a larger and more generic ground for incrimination." And she goes on: "In a sleight of hand so deft that it is easy to miss its implications, Sebald repositions the Germans as unmourned victims of 'defenseless cities' rather than as culpable victimizers of a defenseless people. . . . In the world according to Sebald . . . we are all more or less Jews bound for the slaughter" (2003, 13). I disagree with Merkin's critique. Quite the opposite, *On the Natural History of Destruction* is a not an ethically problematic text, because, like Schlink's *The Reader*, it is a text written by a German, addressed to other Germans, expressing heartfelt German grief concerning the devastation of both the physical country and of German culture. Its argument has virtually nothing to do with Jews and everything to do with the failure of German society to have properly mourned its losses, including its murdered Jews. The text does not play the game of speaking in the voice of or through the perspective of the Jewish victim as does a text like *Sophie's Choice* or *Austerlitz*.

Whatever else can be said concerning Sebald's *Austerlitz*, it is (again like Styron's *Sophie's Choice*) a highly melancholic novel. That is, it is not only that the novel concerns one melancholic character narrated by another, but, rather, that the consciousness of the text itself is deeply melancholic. This melancholic mood might therefore be understood to extend beyond the narrator to the author as well. Such melancholy might be defended. In *The Language of Silence*, Ernestine Schlant (1999) says of Sebald's *The Emigrants* (1996), that "when Sebald makes melancholy the underlying and all-pervasive mood of the four narratives, he does not follow Freud's distinction between mourning and melancholy. . . . Sebald defines melancholy . . . as a form of the labor of mourning." Yet Schlant immediately contradicts her definition of melancholy as doing the work of mourning when she goes on to argue that "the promise of renewed life and of renewed interest in life contained in Freud's hypothesis that the labor of mourning can be completed is absent in Sebald" (217–18; Taberner 2004 and Restuccia 2005 make similar points).

Endless mourning is not an expression of mourning, but, as we have seen, of its opposite. In *Inability to Mourn: Principles of Collective Behavior*, Alexander and Margarete Mitscherlich (1975), defining the postwar German position somewhat differently, come to this same conclusion. Because the postwar German population was in fact incapable of mourning the death of its beloved and idealized führer, they succumbed not to melancholy, but to an affective break with its relationship to the past. The consequences in the Mitscherliches' interpretation are problematic from the psychological and ethical points of view. The second generation, in Eric Santner's words, "inherited not guilt so much as the denial of guilt, not losses so much as lost opportunities to mourn losses. . . . The second generation inherited not only the unmourned traumas of the parents but also the psychic structures that impeded mourning in the older generation in the first place" (1990, 34, 37).

Might not all of those photographs in *Austerlitz* be evidences of a fetishistic quality of mind like that often associated with melancholy and incomplete mourning, as in Rosa's attachment to the shawl in Ozick's novella, or Vladek's to his photographs in *Maus,* or Berenice's to hers in *The Far Euphrates*? Certainly the investment in those photos—first on Austerlitz's part, and then on the narrator's, and finally for Sebald himself—makes one want to think about fetishism and incomplete mourning as features of Sebald's novel. Sebald is absolutely on target when he argues in *On the Natural History of Destruction* that the German nation has not properly mourned the destruction of their country in the Second World War. Such mourning for German losses (material and cultural) may be an essential part of the healing process that would mediate against further psychotic breaks with civilized behavior in the future. It might also produce an ethical relation to the German present and future that was lacking in the past.

Taking this observation as a point of departure, one can argue that it is the lack of an ability to mourn that compromises the text in *Austerlitz* and that Sebald corrects this in *On the Natural History of Destruction*. Yet I must claim more for *Austerlitz,* which is an extraordinary work of fiction. Trust the teller not the tale, D. H. Lawrence cautions us, and he is quite right. Self-critique of the German nation, with its call to mourn, is visible in *Austerlitz* as well, especially if we read it from a German perspective as opposed to a Jewish one. Is it possible for a Jewish reader like myself to do that?

Although I demur somewhat from Eric Santner's beautiful and affecting defense of both *Austerlitz* and *On the Natural History of Destruction* in his 2006 book, *On Creaturely Life,* I begin there in order to suggest what *Austerlitz* might require of us as readers and how this makes Sebald's novel more extraordinary, not less. Building on ideas he first expressed in *On the Psychotheology of Everyday Life* (2001), Santner argues, "In Sebald's universe one's subjective involvement with another human being is not simply a function of some sort of spiritual affinity; it depends, rather, on the degree to which one participates, at first often unknowingly, in . . . their 'spirit world.' We are, as it were, in proximity to the 'neighbor' when we have entered the enigmatic space of his or her hauntedness" (2006, 58). "Hauntedness" here refers to what Santner defines as "creaturely life."

This is the way all humans function through unconscious processes such that the relationship to the other requires acknowledging about others what we need to acknowledge about ourselves. This is our strangeness to ourselves, which is produced by the fact that we possess a dynamic unconscious. "The other," writes Santner, is "strange not only to me but also to him- or herself" (xiii). Sebald's "literary writings," Santner argues, are "singularly obsessed with developing the means to engage with the 'neighbor' in his or her creaturely expressivity, [such] that his entire oeuvre could be seen as the construction of *an archive of creaturely life*" (xiii, italics in original). In arguing for something called creaturely life, Santner is generating an alternative to the opposition between mourning and melancholy. Santner summarizes the melancholy-versus-mourning debate thus: against the argument that "melancholy is really a mode of defense . . . [which] comes very close to the modality of perversion that Freud call fetishism" and which thereby forfeits the "possibility of a radically ethical act," is

> the claim made by the partisans of the "ethical turn" in deconstruction that melancholy is the only affective posture that can maintain fidelity to those losses that the reigning ideological formation would like to disavow. Whereas mourning, which culminates in a reattachment of libido to new objects of desire (or idealization), proves to be an ultimately adaptive strategy to the governing reality principle . . . melancholy retards adaption, attaches itself *to* loss . . . and thereby—so it is claimed—holds open the possibility of alternative frameworks of what counts as reality. (89, italics in original)

Santner's idea of creaturely life forms a "third alternative." Creaturely life links "melancholic immersion in creaturely life *and* ethicopolitical intervention into that very dimension; the saturnine gaze *and* the awakening to the answerability to the neighbor, to acts of neighbor-love" (91; italics in original). In Santner's view, mourning must "'learn' from melancholy how to home in on the agitations of creaturely life that materialize the persistence of deep structural stresses in the social body" (91).

Santner's is a powerful philosophical position, and it opens up an essential element of Sebald's work. And yet there is still a problem in Sebald's producing this ethical vision through the Jewish character. This has less to do with the melancholy-versus-mourning debate than with how using the Jew as a trope replicates an old cultural position. In attaching (or reattaching) melancholy (even the more mournful melancholy that Santner describes) to the figure of the Jew, Sebald and his narrator provoke the question raised by both Dominick LaCapra (1994) and Elizabeth Bellamy (1997) in relation to those "partisans" of deconstruction, as Santner refers to them. This is the question of whether the discussion of the Jew and Jewish history in contemporary culture marks a transformation in relation to anti-Semitism or is instead an antifascist philo-Semitism that ironically replicates an important structural feature of traditional anti-Semitism: the use of the Jew as a figure for other concerns rather than as a historical subject in his own right. If the condemnation of anti-Semitism and the Nazi genocide continues to serve as a vehicle for other matters within Western culture (problems of nationalism, for example), then the structure of thinking about the Jew, which culminated in the Holocaust, cannot be said to have been transcended. For LaCapra and Bellamy this postmodern position is intimately related to the idea of melancholy, especially in relation to its significance within Freudian theory.

Thus, LaCapra argues that "the Holocaust has often tended to be repressed or encrypted as a specific series of events and to be displaced onto such general questions as language, nomadism, unrepresentability, silence, and so forth." There is, he continues, a "tendency to trope away from specificity and to reproduce problems in terms of reading technologies that function as discursive 'cuisanarts.' Such reactions inhibit processes of working-through and learning from the past" (1994, 209–10). Or as Bellamy puts it in relation to French intellectuals:

> From Sarte to Jabès to Finkielkraut, the ongoing process of "imagining the Jew" in postwar France is a paradoxical process of not just rejecting but also *intro*jecting the anti-Semitic trope of the Jew as the strange and uncanny "other." Consequently, the postwar Jewish imaginary in France has been an extended meditation of the themes of *l'altérité, déracinement, l'étrangeté*—stereotypes left over from an earlier, modernist anti-Semitism, but which experienced complex metamorphoses in the post-Holocaust. . . . Real Jews have tended to be transformed into tropes or signifiers for the decentered, destabilized postmodern subject in a theoretical system that persists in defining (or "fetishizing") them from without. (1997, 17–18, 31; italics in original)

The "much-debated 'slash' between modernism and postmodernism," Bellamy writes,

> demarcates, among other things, an obscure psychic threshold of repression, disavowal, denegation, or foreclosure of an unresolved modernism—all the psychic defenses against the violence of the divide between modernism and postmodernism, for which a melancholic strain within postmodernism has become the most observable aftereffect. . . . This unacknowledged melancholia in turns serves as the ironic backdrop for postmodernism's often contradictory engagement with psychoanalysis as a modernist 'grand narrative' that it seeks both to appropriate and to reject. . . . After all, postmodernism can be summarized as, among other things, a kind of melancholic reaction to the loss of modernity's narratives of coherence. (1–2)

LaCapra and Bellamy both proceed psychoanalytically by placing mourning—in particular, mourning the loss of narrative coherence—at the center of postmodernist consciousness. They then place at the center of that loss the Holocaust, which according to both Bellamy and LaCapra can be understood as an acting-out on the part of German and, perhaps, also French and European culture, of unacknowledged psychic impulses concerning the Jew. Since psychoanalysis can itself be understood as encrypting within itself the Jew, both in the figure of Freud and in the general association of psychoanalysis with Jews, thinking psychoanalytically (i.e., psychoanalyzing European culture) is already to be thinking about the Jew and also repressing that fact. Thus Bellamy and LaCapra produce a picture of the postmodernist unconscious in which the Jew is as much its repressed trauma as it was Germany's before the war.

The postmodernist response to "after Auschwitz," in their view, becomes its own form of acting-out rather than working-through. One lesson of Freud's "Mourning and Melancholia," Bellamy reminds us, "is that melancholia is a kind of perversion or distortion of a memory—a refusal of a salutary remembrance of loss, a refusal to mourn, that condemns the subject to a futile 'acting out'" (2–3). This accounts for the dominant note of melancholia that informs contemporary culture, in Germany as well—as expressed by the Mitscherliches (1975) and by Santner in his earlier book *Stranded Objects* (1–30).

I believe that if one puts aside, even if only momentarily, a certain subject position in relation to the Holocaust (a Jewish or philo-Jewish subject position), it has to be admitted that *On the Natural History of Destruction* is one of the most powerful and affecting laments ever written for the devastation suffered by a nation during wartime. That Sebald's topic is the Allied bombing of German cities at the end of a war perpetrated and horribly executed by the German nation itself does not change the horror and devastation of these events and their traumatizing consequences on a civilian population, into subsequent generations. However retaliatory (which might or might not be reason to excuse them), the bombings of Dresden and other German cities were also intended to be humiliating. They certainly produced as abundant and severe consequences in their wake as the bombing of Hiroshima, which was at least preemptive. However we wish to judge these events morally, both of them were as profoundly traumatic to Germans and Japanese as the Holocaust was to Jews.

This is not *to level the moral field in any manner whatsoever.* Not all military actions are equal, and the Holocaust, the bombing of German cities, and the dropping of the atomic bomb on Japan cannot be fit into the same moral paradigm. Genocide such as the Nazis perpetrated against the Jews is *not* the same as military actions taken against Germany and Japan—even if we might want to object to some of those military actions. We need to examine and understand each and every one of these events in order to render moral judgment. But the consequences of all these actions may be equally painful and equally traumatic for their individual survivors. And this means that our compassion needs to be extended to them all. This is precisely the point of Jonathan Safran Foer's novel

Extremely Loud and Incredibly Close (2005), which deals with the terrorist attack on the Twin Towers in New York City. Since Foer is a Jewish author, whose first major book, *Everything Is Illuminated* (2002), is about the Holocaust, we might hear in his later book an echo of the Holocaust experience as we do in Spiegelman's graphic novel on the same subject, *In the Shadow of No Towers* (2004), where he actually does invoke the Holocaust. The "incredibly close" in Foer's title might just signal such a link, especially since in *Everything Is Illuminated* the author extends his sympathies to the victimizers and not only the victims. In *Extremely Loud and Incredibly Close* this sympathy for the victimizers (in this case Germans and not Ukrainians) is expanded: Foer's protagonists are German refugees who, in the grandparent generation, suffered the trauma of the bombing of Dresden and who, now, in the present moment of the text, suffer the trauma of the Twin Towers. *Extremely Loud and Incredibly Close* does nothing so crude as to force an equivalency among catastrophes. Rather, it opens up the possibility that on the personal level trauma is trauma, whatever its causes and whatever the place of those events in some larger moral landscape.

Foer's *Extremely Loud and Incredibly Close* takes us back to *Austerlitz*. Can I, as a Jewish reader, not lend my sympathies (as Foer does his) to the German victim? Can I read not as a Jew, but as a German? If the Holocaust brings into view how the Nazis failed to recognize the Jews as other human beings, is it not my moral responsibility, insofar as I oppose Nazism and mourn its victims, to recognize Germans, Poles, and others as humans, who also suffer and did indeed suffer the traumas of the war? There is absolutely no reason for stories of German suffering not to be told. In constructing the narrative in *Austerlitz* the way he does, and by telling the Holocaust narrative through the consciousness of a non-Jewish non-survivor, Sebald—whether intentionally or not—poses a challenge, especially to Jewish readers. He frames the issue of subject position in such a way as to complicate the Jewish perspective, even if he in no way requires our relinquishing our moral condemnation of the German nation. In this he stands solidly beside Schlink. It may well be that *Austerlitz* is a snapshot of Sebald's own depressive tendencies of mind, his tendency to see suffering and devastation where even a Jewish survivor like Appelfeld might see beauty and rejuvenation. The book, then, might evidence the tendencies toward projection that make of the Holocaust a stage onto which individuals cast their fantasies and fears. Or the novel might be an exposé of just those distortions of subject position and projection. Perhaps, like many great works of art, *Austerlitz* exceeds its author's knowledge and intention.

Whatever the case, we must be grateful for *Austerlitz*. It is a great work of fiction. It is also the most important kind of fiction. It extends its critique out of the world of the text and into the world of the reader. It is very difficult for readers, especially of fictions that deal with horrific events like the Holocaust, to tolerate ambivalences, ambiguities, even (or especially) self-conscious self-concern. And yet how else does a literary text become fully literary (as opposed to historical or journalistic or political) except by projecting events through the distorting lens of the subjective "I." What is possibly the most difficult aspect of *Austerlitz* for the non-impartial reader of the text (like myself) is that it may finally be impossible to decide whether the text is complicit in the distortions of its narrator or is self-consciously framing them. What if we as readers cannot make this judgment call, in the same way that we cannot quite decide if Ozick's Rosa is delusional during and not just after the war? Is the text then greater or more suspect for the impossibility it presents of teasing out guilt from condemnation, identification from distancing, and subject position from epistemological objectivity and "truth"? In this the text is fully, mimetically, a picture of our psychological lives in this world of neighbors, as Santner (2006) puts it, some of whom are enemies, some of whom are friends, and all of whom suffer as we do from the unconscious life we share.

Epilogue: Holocaust, Apartheid, and the Slaughter of Animals

J. M. Coetzee's Elizabeth Costello *and Cora Diamond's "Difficulty of Reality"*

THE QUESTION OF subject position, both in relation to who writes about an event like the Holocaust and how they approach it, as well as how readers respond to these texts, seems to necessarily accompany anything we understand the literary ethics of writing and reading to be. I conclude this study of the subject of Holocaust fiction with one last text, also written by a non-Jewish author, that stages precisely the kind of application to the Holocaust that will strike some people as abusive, even reprobate, others as inspired. I am referring to J. M. Coetzee's *Elizabeth Costello* (2003b), two chapters of which were originally delivered by Coetzee as a set of lectures at Princeton University and published along with several critical essays as *The Lives of Animals* (2003a). Both the novel and the lectures revolve around a famous, aging novelist who is giving talks in the United States, not on her area of expertise, which is literature, but on animal rights. She is also visiting her son and his family. Since the two Coetzee lectures include lectures by his protagonist Elizabeth Costello, who is herself a writer of fiction (albeit female rather than male, Australian rather than South African), Coetzee's text creates a striking parallel between him and his character, which he clearly intends for us to see. In this way *Elizabeth Costello/The Lives of Animals* bears a structural similarity to Sebald's *Austerlitz*. The parallel between author and character will become pertinent in thinking about Coetzee's, or his character's, displacement of the subject of animal rights onto the Holocaust, since Coetzee, who is far better known as a writer about apartheid and postapartheid South Africa than about animal rights, may be involved in a displacement in this novel, whether in relation to Elizabeth Costello or her topic. Insofar as Costello discourses on the issue of animal rights, Coetzee does so as well, even if his lectures contextualize his character's lectures, describing her severely pained relationship with the members of her family. Along with her lectures he includes further responses that she gives to questions raised by her audience about her defense of animal rights, as well as another lecture she gives on poetry. This framing of Costello is further developed in the novel-length version of the text (*Elizabeth Costello*), which reprints the *Lives of Animals* lectures as two of the novel's "lessons" (the book's term for chapters). Of course, as in any work of fiction, the distance between the author of the novel and his protagonist is all to the point of our reading of the book. We might find the author as guilty as his character of an illegitimate use of the Holocaust in his text as, for example, we might find Philip Roth guilty when Nathan Zuckerman fantasizes that Amy Bellette is Anne Frank. Or we might defend Coetzee's and Roth's strategies. We might also defend Elizabeth Costello's allusion to the Holocaust, as several critics of the novel have indeed done. Some of these defenses are printed along with the two lectures; some appear in a subsequent volume titled *Philosophy and Animal Life* (Cavell 2008). Where the reader stands in relation to what becomes a multifaceted, multivocal conversation among writers, philosophers, literary critics, and animal rights activists is where I have chosen to deliver this final foray into the subject of the Holocaust. I utilize Cora Diamond's terminology in her essay on Coetzee's lectures to call this problem of Holocaust response: "The Difficulty of Reality" (in Cavell 2008).

The Trope of the Holocaust, the Figure of the Jew

Following is the scene that gets Elizabeth Costello into trouble with a Jewish member of her audience, who, like Costello, is a writer, although her antagonist Stern is a poet, not a novelist. Also unlike Costello (and unlike Coetzee), he is a Jew: "I have no reason to believe," Costello addresses her audience during her formal lecture, "that you have at the forefront of your minds what is being done to animals at this moment in production facilities." And after having dealt with the subject of the Holocaust at some considerable length, albeit in no more detail than her description of the slaughter of animals (Coetzee and Costello are not sensationalists), she concludes: "Let me say it openly: we are surrounded by an enterprise of degradation, cruelty, and killing which rivals anything that the Third Reich was capable of, indeed dwarfs it, in that ours is an enterprise without end" (Coetzee 2003a, 62, 65). The poet Stern, who subsequently refuses to attend the dinner in her honor, accuses Costello of "blasphemy" and excuses himself thus: "At the kernel of your lecture, it seems to me, was the question of breaking bread. If we refuse to break bread with the executioners of Auschwitz, can we continue to break bread with the slaughterers of animals?" (94). Therefore, we understand, he refuses to break bread with her.

According to Stanley Cavell, in "Companionable Thinking," his essay-length response to Cora Diamond's own essay-length response to Coetzee's novel (Diamond's essay being itself a response to other essays of Cavell), the problem with both Costello's and Stern's positions is the problem of "inordinate knowledge, knowledge whose importunateness can seem excessive in its expression" (Cavell 2008, 95). In other words, both Costello and Stern seem to Cavell to be making claims to their audiences that what they believe represents a moral and philosophical truth that others simply do not see or understand. Costello explicitly says to her audience that they are likely unaware of what she is about to tell them. Stern, in refusing to break bread with Costello, puts her on a level with the slaughterers of the Jews, which, whether or not we disapprove of Costello's analogy, is surely to overstate the case against her. In other words, where both Costello and Stern err in equal measure is that each imagines they see or know something the other does not: in one case the likeness between the slaughter of animals and the slaughter of the Jews, in the other case the utter dissimilarity between them and the "blasphemy" involved in the "comparison" (94). Each, therefore, places himself or herself above and beyond reproach, squarely leveling reproach at the other.

In his response to Diamond, Cavell's own position on the issue of animal rights and human rights (including the subject of the Holocaust), is utterly different. "What is a proper response to learning, and maintaining the knowledge, of the existence of [evil and suffering such as] concentration camps, or of mass starvation, or of the hydrogen bomb?" Cavell asks in "Companionable Thinking." And he continues, marking his departure from Diamond's text:

> I do not propose a competition between our degree of compromise with the subjection of animals to human demand and that of our compromise with the degree of injustice in our society. . . . [Yet] I confess my persistent feeling that a sense of shame at being human (at being stigmatized for having a human body) is more maddeningly directed to the human treatment of human animals than to its treatment of its non-human neighbors. I think I do not overlook the point that in relation to non-humans we can take meaningful personal measures whereas in the human case, if we are conscious of it, we readily sense helplessness. What then? Shall we unblushingly publish our guilt in remaining sane in a mad world? (2008, 121–24)

"I can never say in my defense," Cavell writes, that "'I am above reproach'" or "'I am *not* above reproach'" (122), for "I remain too impressed with Freud's vision of the human animal's compromise with existence—the defense or the deflection of our ego in our knowledge of ourselves from what there is to know about ourselves—to suppose that a human life can get itself without residue into the clear" (121).

There are many reasons to side with Stern against Costello, especially if one happens to be, like Stern, a Jew (as I am; although I admit I read *Elizabeth Costello* because of my interest in animal rights, not for its use of the Holocaust image). Do I reverse Costello's insensitivity, if that's what it is, by using her argument concerning animal rights to say something about the misuse of the Holocaust in moral discourse? Be that as it may, "Jews are not metaphors—not for poets, not for novelists, not for theologians, not for murderers, and never for antisemites," as Cynthia Ozick once put it (quoted by Young 1988, 84). To complicate matters even more, Ozick's position on Jews is strikingly similar to Costello's own stated position on animals. For Costello animals are not metaphors for something else. She makes clear, especially in her class on poetry, that they are subjects, conscious beings, unto themselves. This, she argues, is what a poet like Ted Hughes understands, and she brings in evidence of her argument Hughes's poem "The Jaguar." Yet Costello herself applies a way of looking at nonhuman animals that she adamantly rejects to looking at human animals, like her audience and like Stern. This involves her in a serious internal contradiction when she invokes the Holocaust in her lecture.

As James Young points out, figurative language (such as Costello or Coetzee employ) will inevitably create representational problems. The question is whether in a particular instance the benefits of such language may outweigh the deficits: "In the case of Holocaust metaphors, we find that figurative language is never entirely innocent and is almost always complicit in the actions we take in our world." And he continues: "Like other elements of narrative, the figures and archetypes used by writers to represent the Holocaust . . . screen as much of the realities as they illuminate" (1988, 84). Nonetheless, he suggests, although "we may not like the ways that Jews have been figured traditionally, or the ways Jews are now used to figure other peoples . . . in fact, Jewish memory and tradition depend explicitly on the capacity of figurative language to remember the past" (84). Additionally, as Michael Rothberg has eloquently argued in *Multidirectional Memory* (2009), moral discourses often bear significant similarities to each other, not because one alludes to the other, but because they are developing contemporaneously with and in relation to each other. The affinities between them are historical. Responses to slavery, the Holocaust, colonialism, and the slaughter of animals all develop within the same moral universe of historical events and discourse. And indeed, neither Elizabeth Costello nor her author is inventing the reference to Jews in the context of animal rights. The discourse comparing the treatment of animals with the treatment of Jews, as well as blacks (and what is Coetzee's major literary subject if not apartheid?), already exists within the animal rights movement. Of course, some might argue that in the animal rights movement this is already a poorly chosen comparison at best. At worst it might be downright absurd and offensive. Analogies are probably always a bad idea, because they bypass the requirements of complex analytic thinking. In relation to Coetzee's novel it has to be added that although blacks and Jews do share a species category such that comparing slavery and the Holocaust makes some sense, nonhuman animals are not humans. Thus it can be argued that it is not obvious, especially given the history of human development (hunting and farming), why the slaughter of animals is wrong or whether it is wrong in the same way that enslavement and murder of humans is wrong. Whether or not we want to protect nonhuman others against abuse and slaughter, nonhuman others are *not* the same as human others, for the simple reason that they do not share the same species category. Blacks and Jews do, and it can be argued that slave owners have always known that their slaves were humans like themselves. This is not so for animals.

So there is much to object to in Costello's, perhaps Coetzee's, analogy, although clearly there is much to defend it, since many critics have come to her defense, or at least Coetzee's. I will put the defense off for a moment in order to add one more plank in the argument against the Holocaust analogizing, this time in relation to Coetzee, not his character. In Coetzee's text Elizabeth Costello wins the day over her Jewish interlocutor. Elizabeth Costello does *not* refuse to break bread with the slaughterers of animals, even though she objects to them. She refuses to eat those slaughtered animals at dinner with animal eaters. Nor is she unwilling to have dinner with her grandchildren, even though they are eating chicken. It is her daughter-in-law who puts the children at a different table. From the perspective of Coetzee's novel, Costello occupies the higher moral ground in the exchange with Stern not because she is a vegetarian, but because she continues to break bread with those who are not. By her own admission, she is also not above reproach. "I'm wearing leather shoes," she explains to one of the members of her audience who praises her. "I'm carrying a leather purse. I wouldn't have overmuch respect if I were you." And to the objection that surely there is a difference between eating animals and wearing leather, she replies, simply, "Degrees of obscenity" (2003a, 89). She wears leather shoes and carries a leather purse in self-acknowledged contradiction of her moral principles.

Therefore, in setting out his argument, whatever Elizabeth Costello's announced position, Coetzee's text recycles an old archetype of the Jew, which may simply point to the ways that in ducking one moral problem we inadvertently, perhaps inevitably, construct another. In any event, Stern emerges in the text as the stereotype of the Jew who because of his refusal of the new law of Christian forgiveness refuses to break bread with others not of his faith. Costello's daughter-in-law makes of Costello such a Jew when she says, "The ban on meat that you get in vegetarianism is only an extreme form of dietary ban . . . and a dietary ban is a quick, simple way for the elite group to define itself. Other people's table habits are unclean, and we cannot eat or drink with them" (87). The daughter-in-law's problematic status in the text and Costello's behavior undercut her daughter-in-law's accusations against her. Unfortunately, this only enhances the text's objections to Stern, who is and acts like a Jew in every possible way.

Given Jewish history, which is at least as troubled as the history of either black Africans or nonhuman others, religiously observant Jews like myself might be troubled by the use of the Jewish example, as they might be by Costello's rather promiscuous Holocaust analogizing, although the text leads me to question the grounds on which I oppose the analogy and even the implications of the Jewish dietary laws. In other words, not only do I find myself interrogating my defense of the Holocaust as not susceptible to the kind of analogizing to which Costello subjects it, but I must also interrogate what the Jewish dietary laws are about and how they may indeed function in the service of segregating Jews from others. (Most observant Jews, I suspect, would not deny this.) Of course, I also experience delight at thinking Costello might be perceived as something of a Jew, following dietary laws and obsessed with the Holocaust. Indeed, in the final of the book's lessons, titled "At the Gate," in which Costello is cast in the role of K (i.e., Kafka, the Jew), the Costello-as-Jew note is played once again—this time, however, in a much more positive key.

However, the allusion to Costello as Kafka's K (Coetzee's C[ostello]?) at the end of the book returns me to the problem of Costello's problematic status as a "Jew" in this text, an identification that she herself establishes in the opening remarks of her first lecture, although this imagery belongs as much to Coetzee's text as to the character the text creates. This is how Costello begins her lecture:

> It is two years since I last spoke in the United States. In the lecture I then gave, I had reason to refer to the great fabulist Franz Kafka, and in particular to his story "Report to an Academy," about an educated ape, Red Peter, who stands before the members of a learned society telling the story of his life—of his ascent from beast to something approaching man. On that occasion I felt a little like Red Peter myself and said so. Today that feeling is even stronger, for reasons that I hope will become clearer to you.
> . . . The comparison I have just drawn between myself and Kafka's ape might be taken as . . . a light-hearted remark, meant to set you at ease. . . . Even those among you who read Kafka's story of the ape who performs before human beings as an allegory of Kafka the Jew performing for Gentiles may nevertheless—in view of the fact that I am not a Jew—have done me the kindness of taking the comparison at face value, that is to say, ironically.
> I want to say at the outset that that was not how my remark . . . was intended. I did not intend it ironically. It means what it says. I say what I mean. (2003a, 62)

In other words, Costello means she speaks not as a Jew, which she isn't, but as an ape, which of course she isn't as well. By the same logic, she also speaks as a Jew.

Presumably, given her emphasis on taking her statement at face value, Costello objects to interpreting Kafka's story as an allegory about the Jew performing before gentiles. Costello wants Kafka's story to attend to the ape-ness of the ape, with which Costello identifies. Therefore, she herself is an ape, not a Jew. And yet the subject she immediately launches into is the Holocaust—not the subject of apes or of other animals, but of Jews. At this moment we feel she is articulating not the position of Red Peter the ape, but Red Peter the stand-in for Kafka—that is, the Jew (Costello being Coetzee's C, as I have already suggested). In speaking about the rights of animals, in other words, Costello experiences herself as an animal and as a Jew, the outsider, the one with dietary laws who is perceived by others (her daughter-in-law, for example) as putting herself outside the human community. Insofar as her author, Coetzee, ends with a Kafkaesque allegory, Costello's position and Coetzee's have to be taken as very closely related to each other.

There is a structural similarity here to David Lurie's metamorphosis in another Coetzee novel, *Disgrace* (1999), from an ordinary white South African, perhaps like his author (which is not to implicate Coetzee in David Lurie's disgraceful behavior toward women and animals), to the Jewish victim, who becomes the defender of both women and animals. *Disgrace* has nothing whatsoever to do with Jewish history. It is about postapartheid South Africa and the traumas attendant upon the redistribution of power from whites to blacks. In the novel the epitome of such traumatization is the rape of Lucy, David's daughter, by blacks. Nonetheless, the name David Lurie has suggested to critics that the character might be taken as Jewish: Lurie is a typically Jewish name, which, in its proximity to his student turned sexual partner Melanie's last name, Isaacs, constructs an oblique reference to the name Isaac Luria, the famous rabbi and mystic. But it is really only after he has disgraced himself and been disgraced by others that David Lurie truly becomes the Jew—the Jew both as victim and as social outcast. There is his "skull cap" of a bandage, which he wears following the attack on him (it is referred to several times in the text). He insists on "justice" rather than repentance or mercy or grace in relation to both his crime against Melanie and the rape of his daughter, Lucy (119). Similarly, when he discovers his daughter's pregnancy he muses that he will become a "Joseph" in relation to his descendants (217), thus suggesting exile and the Israeli diaspora. This comment looks backward to another hint of his Jewish affiliations in the same mode: his reference to the Exodus from Egyptian slavery and the mezuzah that symbolizes that for Jews, when he says to his daughter: "do you think if you come through, you get . . . safe conduct into the future, or a sign to paint on the door-lintel that will make the plague pass you by"? (1999, 112). Jews, by Christian definition, stand in dis-relation to grace. So do Africans, unless they convert, an option that is also open to and sometimes forced upon Jews. What blacks and Jews have in common, then, is that within the white Christian world they exist in a condition of "dis-grace," which is not disgrace in the sense of something shameful, but simply being outside the law of grace in the same way that beasts and angels in the discourse of ethics exist outside the moral law (I take it that this is the point of Coetzee's introduction of Lucifer into the text, Lucy and Lucifer to some degree reflecting and illuminating each other). From the perspective of Coetzee's book, to be in dis-grace is not necessarily a bad thing at all. David Lurie can be read as the Jew as Christ figure in the new law of natural relations across species boundaries, in which human beings are every bit constrained by the moral law (to which animals are not) and not the law of grace, which pertains to neither species.

In making the figural "Jew" the repository of moral conscience in these two texts, Coetzee himself is implicated (whether for better or for worse), even if his character Elizabeth Costello is the one who is made to establish the analogy for herself within the text. In the case of David Lurie, the character either is or is not Jewish, but this is entirely Coetzee's choice, not Lurie's. As with the analogy to the Holocaust in relation to animal slaughter, whether this is Elizabeth Costello's analogy or Coetzee's, we might believe the author of the analogy (like Sebald in *Austerlitz* or Styron in *Sophie's Choice*) is taking on the burden of history. Or, given the prevalence of the image of the Jew that circulates in postmodernist discourse (or the abundance of Holocaust allusions that also abound in contemporary culture), we might believe there is a presumption and a lack of respect for the Jew as subject in this circulation of the Jew as a cultural trope. Both Dominick LaCapra (1994) and Elizabeth Bellamy (1997) have astutely pointed this out, as we have seen. The Jew as a figure of ethics and the Holocaust as paradigm of victimhood are certainly images that bespeak resistance to fascism and anti-Semitism. Nonetheless, it is still a question of whether such analogizing does not sacrifice the Jew to a new politics, unquestionably better than Nazism, but a non-Jewish politics nonetheless, in which the Jew as subject dissolves into a larger ethical undertaking.

Coetzee is a great novelist, and his fiction is not to be reduced to simple moral formulae. Far more important than whether Costello and Lurie are cast as "Jews" or "animals" is that they represent what Cora Diamond and Stanley Cavell (2008) identify in relation to Costello: the human being as wounded animal. Both Costello and Lurie, not to mention Lucy, his daughter, also speak the pain of another wounded animal in these texts: the author Coetzee, whose text forces the reader to read through her own wounded condition.

"The Difficulty of Reality," the "Wounded Animal," and the Reader

I suggested earlier that for reasons of history and religious affiliation I share a stronger subject position with Stern than with Costello in terms of the Holocaust. Nonetheless, as I have also noted, I first read *Elizabeth Costello* and *Disgrace* because of my interest in animal rights. For many years, whenever I taught courses on racism, sexism, anti-Semitism, the extermination of Native Americans, and so on, I would caution my students to look inward before directing their wrath outward to those who horribly violated the rights of others. I would suggest to my students that decades hence other people might look back on us and find certain of our customs and behaviors primitive and immoral. We cannot know now what aspects of our lives will be condemned, because from our contemporary perspectives there is nothing offensive or unethical in what we are doing. The example I consistently used was our eating animals and using them as part of our everyday economy in a variety of ways. Eventually I had to ask myself why I kept using this example, until it became clear to me that I was saying something to myself in addition to what I was saying to my students. Then I read Jonathan Safran Foer's book *Eating Animals* (2010), and I put away my *fleisich* (meat) dishes.

In both Cora Diamond's and Stanley Cavell's (2008) view of her, Elizabeth Costello is not so much a philosopher or an animal rights activist as she is a wounded animal, who puts on full display all of those wishes, desires, fears, guilt, and anguish that inhere in being a bodily constituted entity. This explains her identification with animals and their suffering and with the poems of Ted Hughes, which figure forth the animal itself and not its likeness to or dissimilarity from the human. It also explains her identification with the Jewish victim. David Lurie in *Disgrace* is similarly wounded, as is his daughter, Lucy. Indeed, both are literally wounded. David is set on fire by the same men who rape Lucy. Lurie, like Costello, embodies the all-too-human pain of living the moral compromises of a human life, which is destined to arrive where all lives (human and nonhuman) arrive: at what the novel tellingly calls the "disgrace of dying." This is the ultimate disgrace in this book of other sorts of disgraces: the failure of the body (and the mind) in death. The disgraces that are human experiences are produced by the disgrace we all share, with the animals as well: the disgrace of our mortality. In what sense can death be a disgrace?

At the risk of hopelessly simplifying Stanley Cavell's rich and nuanced philosophy, but in order to bring this study to a close, I propose that in the views of both Cavell and Coetzee, it is the limits of and the limitations placed on the human body—namely, our inevitable mortality in the future and, throughout our lived lives, our inability as humans to ever verify beyond the shadow of a doubt our knowledge of others—that produces in humans both their vulnerability and their compulsions, including a desire to possess or otherwise control other human beings. We would secure for ourselves what can never be ours: deep, internal knowledge of what others think and feel. We would also, perhaps, by killing off others live the fantasy of our own potency and even immortality. The Nazis' medical experiments and savagery toward the Jews might be an excellent example of such perversion; they would dissect, mutilate, and humiliate human beings to prove that they were not human beings so that they might with good conscience exterminate them. In the process they produced a nonhuman thing—a body. But in so doing they also proved the opposite: that the Jews were as human as other human beings. At the very least Coetzee's novels of the wounded human being and the disgrace of being thus bodily constituted contribute a powerful insight into what produces racism, anti-Semitism, and other forms of human discrimination (against nonhuman beings as well). At best they illustrate how all human beings—imagined humans like Costello and Lurie, authors like Coetzee, readers like myself—struggle with the limitations imposed by being a human being. That struggle may be what ultimately defines us as humans, as subjects in our own right, who must thus extend subject-hood and its rights (and responsibilities) to others.

I add the term "responsibilities" because I think Lucy's rapists are not to be forgiven. Nazi criminality is not to be condoned on a plea of human frailty. We might come to understand why humans behave as they do and how their behavior expresses their humanness, but immoral actions are to be condemned and punished accordingly. If that is the Jewish law of retribution and justice rather than the Christian law of forgiveness, so be it. I am, after all (like the survivor in Schlink's *The Reader,* who will not permit atonement), a Jew.

As subjects, however, we need to constantly interrogate our subjectivity and that of others through which we all perceive a world of other similarly subjective beings and through which we determine both our actions and our responses to others. The Holocaust was a failure of self-scrutiny on the parts of both national leaders and a population that followed those leaders, sometimes blindly, sometimes helplessly. It was a failure to recognize the subject-hood and subjectivity of the self and others. For us to read Holocaust texts with anything less than our own self-scrutiny and acknowledgment would be to fall into the same failure. For the writers I have discussed—from Ozick, Spiegelman, and Stollman through such Jewish writers as Roth, Grossman, Appelfeld, Krauss, Foer, Chabon, and Horn and such non-Jewish authors as Styron, Schlink, Sebald, and Coetzee—the examination of our own subject position is what gives us access not only to the depths of other people's suffering and pain but also to what is often our complicity (even if unwitting) in that suffering and pain. I recall here Eric Santner's (2006) idea that what we can recognize in others is an unconscious that is in conversation with our own unconscious. That recognition of the unconscious conversations of which we are apart, or what Stanley Cavell would call acknowledgment (rather than knowledge) of the world and of others in it, is what permits us to interact humanly and humanely with other humans and perhaps with non-human others as well. As Cavell has put it in a statement I have already quoted in the introduction to this book: "fantasy shadows anything we can understand reality to be" (1996, 97). Therefore, to see our fantasies and the fantasies of others is to see no more than our humanness and theirs. That we may fail to fully understand ourselves and others as we probe such fantasies is a risk we run. And it is a risk run by the novels themselves. But in the final analysis the willingness to acknowledge and accept the frailty and even lack of self-knowledge displayed by other people's stories (whether those of fictional or real persons or of authors) may be the ultimate instrument for recognizing those same failings in ourselves. Then we might be able to exceed simplistic moral judgments and enter into the process of ethical thinking, which alone enables us to accept other people's humanity and our own.

Bibliography

Abraham, Nicholas, and Maria Torok. 1994. *The Shell and the Kernel.* Edited by Nicholas R. Rand. Chicago: University of Chicago Press.

Alkana, Joseph. 1997. "'Do We Not know the Meaning of Aesthetic Gratification?': Cynthia Ozick's *The Shawl,* the Akeda, and the Ethics of Holocaust Literary Aesthetics." *Modern Fiction Studies* 43: 963–90.

Appelfeld, Aharon. 1981. *Age of Wonders.* Translated by Dalya Bilu. Boston: David R. Godine. Originally published in 1978 in Hebrew.

———. 1994. *Beyond Despair: Three Lectures and a Conversation with Philip Roth.* Translated by Jeffrey Green. New York: Fromm International.

———. 1998. *Iron Tracks.* Translated by Jeffrey Green. New York: Schocken.

———. 1999a. *All That Remains* [film]. Directed by Zoltan Terner. Israel.

———. 1999b. *The Story of a Life* [Hebrew]. Jerusalem: Keter.

Auslander, Shalom. 2012. *Hope: A Tragedy.* New York: Riverhead.

Auster, Paul. 1994. *New York Trilogy.* New York: Penguin.

———. 2006. *The New York Trilogy.* With a new introduction by Luc Sante and illustrations by Art Spiegelman. Penguin Classics Deluxe Edition. New York: Penguin.

———. 2004. *City of Glass: The Graphic Novel (New York Trilogy).* Adapted by David Mazzuccelli. New York: Picador.

Beatty, Jack. 1979. "Review of *The Ghost Writer,* by Philip Roth." *New Republic* 6 (October): 36–40.

Bechhofer, Susi, and Jeremy Josephs. 1999. *Rosa's Child: The True Story of One Woman's Quest for a Lost Mother and a Vanished Past.* London: I. B. Taurus.

Bellamy, Elizabeth. 1997. *Affective Genealogies: Psychoanalysis, Postmodernism, and the "Jewish Question" after Auschwitz.* Lincoln: University of Nebraska Press.

Bellow, Saul. 1970. *Mr. Sammler's Planet.* New York: Viking Press.

Benn Michaels, Walter. 1996. "'You who never was there': Slavery and the New Historicism, Deconstruction and the Holocaust." *Narrative* 4, no. 1: 1–16.

Berberich, Christine. 2006. "The Continued Presence of the Past: New Directions in Holocaust Writing." *MODERNISM, modernity* 13, no. 3: 567–75.

Berger, Alan. 1997. *Children of Job: American Second-Generation Witnesses to the Holocaust.* Albany: State University of New York Press.

Bernstein, Susan David. 2003. "Promiscuous Reading: The Problem of Identification and Anne Frank's Diary." In *Witnessing the Disaster: Essays on Representation and the Holocaust,* edited by Michael Bernard-Donals and Richard Glejzer, 141–61. Madison: University of Wisconsin Press.

Bohm-Duchen, Monica. 2003. "The Uses and Abuses in Photography in Holocaust-Related Art." In *Image and Remembrance,* edited by Shelley Hornstein and Florence Jacobowitz, 220–34. Bloomington: Indiana University Press.

Bond, Greg. 2004. "On the Misery of Nature and the Nature of Misery: W. G. Sebald's Landscapes." In *W. G. Sebald: A Critical Companion*, edited by J. J. Long and Anne Whitehead, 31–44. Edinburgh: Edinburgh University Press.

Borowski, Tadeusz. 1976. *This Way for the Gas, Ladies and Gentlemen*. Translated by Barbara Vedder. New York: Penguin.

Bosmajian, Hamida. 1998. "The Orphaned Voice in Art Spiegelman's *Maus I and II*." *Literature and Psychology* 44, no. 1/2: 1–22.

Brooks, Peter. 1994. *Psychoanalysis and Storytelling*. Oxford: Blackwell.

Budick, Emily Miller. 1989. *Fiction and Historical Consciousness: The American Romance Tradition*. New Haven, CT: Yale University Press.

———. 1994. *Engendering Romance: Women Writers and the Hawthorne Tradition, 1850–1990*. New Haven, CT: Yale University Press.

———. 1996. "The Haunted House of Fiction: Ghostwriting the Holocaust." *Common Knowledge* 5: 120–35.

———. 1998. *Blacks and Jews in Literary Conversation*. New York: Cambridge University Press.

———. 2003. "Psychoanalysis, Epistemology, and Holocaust Fiction: The Case of Cynthia Ozick's *The Shawl*." In *The Representation of the Holocaust in Literature and Film*, edited by Marc Lee Raphael, 1: 1–28. Williamsburg, VA: College of William and Mary.

———. 2004. *Aharon Appelfeld's Fiction: Acknowledging the Holocaust*. Bloomington: Indiana University Press.

———. 2007. "The Holocaust, Trauma, and the Jewish Fiction of *Tzimtzum*: Aryeh Lev Stollman's *Far Euphrates*." In *The Representation of the Holocaust in Literature and Film*, edited by Marc Lee Raphael, 2: 24–39. Williamsburg, VA: College of William and Mary.

Budick, Emily Miller, and Rami Aronzon. 2008. *Psychotherapy and the Everyday Life*. London: Karnac.

Cavell, Stanley. 1976. "Knowing and Acknowledging." In *Must We Mean What We Say? A Book of Essays*, 238–66. Cambridge: Cambridge University Press.

———. 1987. *Disowning Knowledge in Six Plays of Shakespeare*. Cambridge: Cambridge University Press.

———. 1996. *Contesting Tears: The Hollywood Melodrama of the Unknown Woman*. Chicago: University of Chicago Press.

———. 1999. *The Claim of Reason: Wittgenstein, Skepticism, Morality, and Tragedy*. New York: Oxford.

———. 2008. *Philosophy and Animal Life*. Coauthored by Cora Diamond, John McDowell, Ian Hacking, and Cary Wolfe. New York: Columbia University Press.

———. 2010. *Little Did I Know: Excerpts from Memory*. Stanford, CA: Stanford University Press.

Chabon, Michael. 2000. *The Amazing Adventures of Kavalier and Clay*. New York: Random House.

———. 2004. *The Final Solution: A Story of Detection*. New York: HarperCollins.

Clarke, Jon Henrik, ed. 1968. *William Styron's Nat Turner: Ten Black Writers Respond*. Boston: Beacon Press.

Coetzee, J. M. 1999. *Disgrace*. New York: Viking.

———. 2003a. *The Lives of Animals*. New York: Penguin.

———. 2003b. *Elizabeth Costello.* New York: Viking.

Crap, Stef, and Gert Buelens. 2011. "Traumatic Mirrorings: Holocaust and Colonial Trauma in Michael Chabon's *The Final Solution.*" *Criticism* 53, no. 4: 569–86.

Devereau, Mary. 2004. "Moral Judgments and Works of Art: The Case of Narrative Literature." *Journal of Aesthetics and Art Criticism* 62, no. 1: 3–11.

Donahue, William Collins. 2011. *Holocaust as Fiction: Bernhard Schlink's "Nazi" Novels and Their Films.* New York: Palgrave Macmillan.

Duttlinger, Caroline. 2004. "Traumatic Photographs: Remembrance and the Technical Media in W. G. Sebald's *Austerlitz.*" In *W. G. Sebald,* edited by J. J. Long and Anne Whitehead, 155–71. Seattle: University of Washington Press.

Englander, Nathan. 1999. *For Relief of Unbearable Urges.* New York: Alfred A. Knopf.

———. 2012. *What We Talk About When We Talk About Anne Frank: Stories.* New York: Weidenfeld and Nicholson.

Estrin, Elana. 2011. "Q & A: Author Nicole Krauss." *Cultural Compass.* https://blog.hrc .utexas.edu/2011/09/19/qa-author-nicole-krauss.

Ezrahi, Sidra. 1980. *By Words Alone: The Holocaust in Literature.* Chicago: University of Chicago Press.

Felderer, Ditlieb. 1979. *Anne Frank's Diary: A HOAX.* Torrance, CA: Institute for Historical Review.

Frank, Anne. 1989 [1929–1945]. *The Diary of Anne Frank: The Critical Edition.* Translated by Arnold J. Pomerans and B. M. Mooyaart-Doubleday. New York: Viking.

———. 2003. *The Diary of Anne Frank: Revised Critical Edition.* New York: Doubleday.

Feldman, Shoshana, and Dori Laub. 1992. *Testimony: Crises of Witnessing in Literature, Psychoanalysis, and History.* New York: Routledge.

Foer, Jonathan Safran. 2002. *Everything Is Illuminated.* New York: Houghton Mifflin.

———. 2006. *Extremely Loud and Incredibly Close.* New York: Penguin.

———. 2010a. *Eating Animals.* New York: Penguin.

———. 2010b. *Tree of Codes.* London: Visual Editions.

Freud, Sigmund. 1973a."Creative Writers and Day-Dreaming." *The Standard Edition of the Complete Psychological Works of Sigmund Freud.* Translated by James Strachey. London: Hogarth Press. Vol. 9: 141–53.

———. 1973b. "Mourning and Melancholia."*The Standard Edition of the Complete Psychological Works of Sigmund Freud.* Translated by James Strachey. London: Hogarth Press. Vol. 14: 243–58.

———. 1973c. "The Uncanny." *The Standard Edition of the Complete Psychological Works of Sigmund Freud.* Translated by James Strachey. London: Hogarth Press. Vol. 17: 217–56.

———. 1973d. "Beyond the Pleasure Principle." *The Standard Edition of the Complete Psychological Works of Sigmund Freud.* Translated by James Strachey. London: Hogarth Press. Vol. 18: 7–64.

Fridman, Lea Wernick. 2000. *Words and Witness: A Narrative and Aesthetic Strategies in the Representation of the Holocaust.* Albany: State University of New York Press.

Goldenberg, Myrna. 1998. "Memoirs of Auschwitz Survivors: The Burden of Gender." In *Women in the Holocaust,* edited by Dalia Ofer and Lenore J. Wietzman, 327–39. New Haven, CT: Yale University Press.

Goldfarb, David. 2011. "Appropriations of Bruno Schulz." *Jewish Quarterly.* June 14. http://jewishquarterly.org/appropriations-of-bruno-schulz.

Gopnick, Adam. 1987. "Comics and Catastrophe: Art Spiegelman's *Maus* and the History of the Cartoon." *New Republic* 196, no. 25: 29–34.

Gordon, Andrew. 1994. "Cynthia Ozick's "The Shawl" and the Transitional Object." *Literature and Psychology* 40: 1–9.

Greenberg, Moshe, ed. and trans. 1983. *Ezekiel 1–20. A New Translation with Introduction and Commentary.* New York: Anchor Bible Doubleday.

Grossman, David. 1989. *See Under: Love.* Translated by Betsy Rosenberg. New York: Washington Square Press.

Harrison, Bernard. 2006. "Aharon Appelfeld and the Problem of Holocaust Fiction." *Partial Answers* 4, no. 1: 80–105.

Hartman, Geoffrey. 1996. *The Longest Shadow: In the Aftermath of the Holocaust.* Bloomington: Indiana University Press.

Hemon, Aleksandar. 2001. *The Question of Bruno.* New York: Vintage.

Hirsch, Marianne. 1997. *Family Frames: Photography, Narrative, and Postmemory.* Cambridge, MA: Harvard University Press.

Horn, Dara. 2006. *The World to Come.* New York: W. W. Norton.

Horowitz, Sara. 1997. *Voicing the Void: Muteness and Memory in Holocaust Fiction.* Albany: State University of New York Press.

Jacobson, Dan. 1999. *Heshel's Kingdom.* New York: Penguin.

Kahlendorf, Ursula R. 2003. "Trauma Narrated, Read, and (Mis)Understood: Bernhard Schlink's *The Reader.*" *Monatsheft* 93, no. 3: 468–81.

Karay, Felicja. 1998. "Women in the Forced-Labor Camps." In *Women in the Holocaust,* edited by Dalia Ofer and Lenore J. Wietzman, 285–309. New Haven, CT: Yale University Press.

Kertész, Imre. 1992. *Fatelessness.* Translated by Christopher C. Wilson and Katharina M. Wilson. Evanston, IL: Northwestern University Press.

———. 1997. *Kaddish for a Child Not Born.* Translated by Christopher C. Wilson and Katharina M. Wilson. Evanston, IL: Northwestern University Press.

Kiš, Danilo. 1992. *The Hourglass.* Translated by Ralph Mannheim. London: Farber and Farber.

Krauss, Nicole. 2006. *History of Love.* London: Penguin.

———. 2010. *Great House.* New York: W. W. Norton.

Kremer, S. Lillian. 1989. *Witness through the Imagination: Jewish American Holocaust Literature.* Detroit: Wayne State University Press.

LaCapra, Dominick. 1994. *Representing the Holocaust: History, Theory, Trauma.* Ithaca, NY: Cornell University Press.

———. 1998. *History and Memory after Auschwitz.* Ithaca, NY: Cornell University Press.

Langer, Lawrence. 1975. *The Holocaust and the Literary Imagination.* New Haven, CT: Yale University Press.

———. 2000. *Preempting the Holocaust.* New Haven, CT: Yale University Press.

———. 2006. *Using and Abusing the Holocaust.* Bloomington: Indiana University Press.

Leys, Ruth. 2000. *Trauma: A Genealogy.* Chicago: University of Chicago.

———. 2009. *From Guilt to Shame: Auschwitz and After.* Princeton, NJ: Princeton University Press.

Littell, Jonathan. 2009. *The Kindly Ones.* Translated by Charlotte Mandell. New York: Harper.

MacKinnon, John E. 2003. "Crime, Compassion, and *The Reader.*" *Philosophy and Literature* 27, no. 1: 1–20.

———. 2004. "Law and Tenderness in Bernhard Schlink's *The Reader.*" *Law and Literature* 16, no. 2: 179–201.

Merkin, Daphne. 2003. "Review of *On the Natural History of Destruction.*" *New York Times Book Review* 4, no. 6.

Meyer, Nicholas. (1974) 1993. *The Seven-Per-Cent Solution.* New York: Dutton. Reprint, New York: W. W. Norton. Citations refer to the Norton edition.

Michaels, Anne. 1998. *Fugitive Pieces.* New York: Random House.

Mikics, David. 2003. "Underground Comics and Survival Tales: *Maus* in Context." In *Considering Maus: Approaches to Art Spiegelman's "Survivor's Tale" of the Holocaust,* edited by Deborah R. Geis, 15–25. Tuscaloosa: University of Alabama Press.

Mintz, Alan. 1984. *Hurban: Responses to Catastrophe in Hebrew Literature.* New York: Columbia University Press.

Mitscherlich, Alexander, and Margarete Mitscherlich. 1975. *The Inability to Mourn: Principles of Collective Behavior.* Translated by Beverly R. Placzek. New York: Grove Press.

Newman, Lesléa. 1988. *A Letter to Harvey Milk: Short Stories.* Ann Arbor, MI: Firebrand.

Niven, Bill. 2003. "Bernard Schlink's *Der Vorleser* and the Problem of Shame." *Modern Language Review* 98, no. 2: 381–96.

Osborne, Dora. 2007. "Blind Spots: Viewing Trauma in W. G. Sebald's *Austerlitz,*" *seminar* 43: 517–33.

Ozick, Cynthia. 1971. "Envy; or, Yiddish in America." *Pagan Rabbi and Other Stories.* New York: E. P. Dutton.

———. 1976. "Usurpation; or, Other People's Stories." *Bloodshed and Three Novellas.* New York: Alfred A. Knopf.

———. 1983a. "I. B. Singer's *Book of Creation.*" *Art and Ardor: Essays,* 217–23. New York: Alfred A. Knopf.

———. 1983b. "Literature as Idol: Harold Bloom." *Art and Ardor: Essays,* 178–99. New York: Alfred A. Knopf.

———. 1983c. "The Phantasmagoria of Bruno Schulz." *Art and Ardor: Essays,* 224–28. New York: Alfred A. Knopf.

———. 1983d. "Toward a New Yiddish." *Art and Ardor: Essays,* 151–77. New York: Alfred A. Knopf.

———. 1987. *The Messiah of Stockholm.* New York: Random House.

———. 1989. *Memory and Metaphor: Essays.* New York: Alfred A. Knopf.

———. 1990. *The Shawl.* New York: Random House.

———. 1997a. *The Puttermesser Papers.* New York: Alfred A. Knopf.

———. 1997b. "Who Owns Anne Frank?" *New Yorker* (October): 76–87.

———. 1999. "The Rights of History and the Rights of Imagination." *Commentary* 107, no. 3: 22–27.

Pane, Samuel. 2005. "Trauma Obscura: Photographic Media in W. G. Sebald's *Austerlitz.*" *Mosaic* 38, no. 1: 37–54.

Patterson, David. 1992. *The Shriek of Silence: A Phenomenology of the Holocaust Novel.* Lexington: University Press of Kentucky.

Phillips, Adam. 2002. *Promises, Promises: Essays on Psychoanalysis and Literature.* New York: Basic Books.

Q & A. "20 under 40." *New Yorker,* June 14, 2010. "Conversation with Nicole Krauss," https://www.randomhouse.com/boldtype/0502/krauss/interview.html.

Raphael, Lev. 1990. *Dancing on Tisha B'Av.* New York: St. Martin's.

Reik, Theodor. 1949. *Listening with a Third Ear.* New York: Farrar, Straus, and Co.

Restuccia, Frances L. 2005. "Sebald's Punctum: Awakening to Holocaust Trauma in *Austerlitz.*" *European Journal of English Studies* 9, no. 3: 301–22.

Ringelheim, Joan. 1985. "Women and the Holocaust: A Reconsideration of Research." *Signs* 10: 741–61.

———. 1998. "The Split between Gender and the Holocaust." In *Women in the Holocaust,* edited by Dalia Ofer and Lenore J. Wietzman, 340–50. New Haven, CT: Yale University Press.

Rosen, Norma. 1989. *Touching Evil.* Detroit: Wayne State University Press.

Rosenbaum, Thane. 2000. *Second Hand Smoke: A Novel.* New York: St. Martin's/Griffin.

———. 2003. *The Golems of Gotham: A Novel.* New York: Harper Perennial.

Rosenfeld, Alvin. 1979. "The Holocaust According to William Styron." *Midstream* 25, no. 10: 43–49.

———. 1980. *A Double Dying: Reflections on Holocaust Literature.* Bloomington: Indiana University Press.

———. 1991. "Popularization and Memory: The Case of Anne Frank." In *Lessons and Legacies: The Meaning of the Holocaust in a Changing World,* edited by Peter Hayes, 243–78. Chicago: Northwestern University.

———. 2011. *The End of the Holocaust.* Bloomington: Indiana University Press.

Roskies, David. 1999. *Against the Apocalypse: Responses to Catastrophe in Modern Jewish Culture.* Syracuse, NY: Syracuse University Press.

Roth, Philip. 1975. "'I Always Wanted You to Admire My Fasting'; or, Looking at Kafka." In *Reading Myself and Others,* 247–70. New York: Farrar, Straus, Giroux.

———. 1985. *Zuckerman Bound: A Trilogy and an Epilogue.* New York: Farrar, Straus, Giroux.

———. 1987. *The Counterlife.* New York: Farrar, Straus, Giroux.

———. 1993. *Operation Shylock.* New York: Simon and Schuster.

———. 1995. *The Ghost Writer.* New York: Vintage. Originally published in 1979.

———. 2007. *Exit Ghost.* London: Jonathan Cape.

Rothberg, Michael. 2000. *Traumatic Realism: The Demands of Holocaust Representation.* Minneapolis: University of Minnesota Press.

———. 2009. *Multidirectional Memory: Representing the Holocaust in the Age of Decolonialization.* Stanford, CA: Stanford University Press.

Rubin-Dorsky, Jeffrey. 1989. "Philip Roth's *The Ghost Writer:* Literary Heritage and Jewish Irreverence." *Studies in American Jewish Literature* 8: 68–85.

Santner, Eric L. 1990. *Stranded Objects: Mourning, Memory, and Film in Postwar Germany.* Ithaca, NY: Cornell University Press.

———. 2001. *On the Psychotheology of Everyday Life: Reflections on Freud and Rosenzweig.* Chicago: Chicago University Press.

———. 2006. *On Creaturely Life: Rilke/Benjamin/Sebald.* Chicago: University of Chicago Press.

Saposnik, Irving S. 1982. "Bellow, Malamud, Roth . . . and Styron? or, One Jewish Writer's Response." *Judaism* 31: 322–32.

Schlant, Ernestine. 1999. *The Language of Silence: West German Literature and the Holocaust.* New York: Routledge.

Schlink, Bernhard. 2008. *The Reader.* New York: Knopf/Doubleday.

———. 2010. *Guilt about the Past.* Berkeley, CA: House of Anansi Press.

Scholem, Gershom. 1971. *Messianic Idea in Judaism and Other Essays of Jewish Spirituality*. London: Allen and Unwin.

Schulz, Bruno. 1978. *Sanatorium under the Sign of the Hourglass*. Translated by Celina Wieniewska. New York: Penguin. Originally published in 1937.

———. 1992. *The Street of Crocodiles*. Translated by Celina Wieniewska. New York: Penguin. Originally published in Polish in 1934 and first translated into English in 1963.

Sebald, W. G. 2001. *Austerlitz*. Translated by Anthea Bell. New York: Random House.

———. 2003. *On the Natural History of Destruction*. Translated by Anthea Bell. New York: Random House.

———. 2011. *The Emergence of Memory: Conversations with W. B. Sebald*. Edited by Lynne Sharon Schwartz. New York: Seven Stories Press [Kindle edition].

Singer, Isaac Bashevis. 2011. *Collected Stories of Isaac Bashevis Singer*. London: Penguin Modern Classics.

Sokoloff, Naomi. 1988. "Reinventing Bruno Schulz: Cynthia Ozick's *The Messiah of Stockholm* and David Grossman's *See Under: Love*." *AJS Review* 13: 171–99.

Spargo, R. Clifton. 2001. "To Invent as Presumptuously as Real Life: Parody and the Cultural Memory of Anne Frank in Roth's *The Ghost Writer*." *Representations* 76, no. 1: 88–119.

Spiegelman, Art. 1998. *Comix, Essays, Graphics, and Scraps; from* Maus *to* Now *to* Maus *to* Now. Osnabrück: Kulturgeschichliches Museum.

———. 2004. *In the Shadow of No Towers*. New York: Pantheon.

———. 2011a. *The Complete Maus: A Survivor's Tale/My Father Bleeds History* and *Here My Troubles Began*. New York: Pantheon.

———. 2011b. *MetaMaus: A Look Inside a Modern Classic, Maus*. With CD-ROM. New York: Pantheon.

Stollman, Aryeh Lev. 1997. *The Far Euphrates*. New York: Riverhead.

Styron, William. 1966. *The Confessions of Nat Turner*. London: Cape.

———. 1979. *Sophie's Choice*. New York: Random House.

———. 1992. *Darkness Visible: A Memoir of Madness*. New York: Vintage.

Suleiman, Susan. 2009. "When the Perpetrator Becomes a Reliable Witness of the Holocaust: On Jonathan Littell's *Les Bienveillantes*." *New German Critique* 106, vol. 36, no. 1: 1–19.

Sundquist, Eric. 2007. "Witness without End." *American Literary History* 19, no. 1: 65–85.

Swales, Martin. 2003. "Sex, Shame, and Guilt: Reflections on Bernhard Schlink's *Der Vorleser (The Reader)* and J. M. Coetzee's *Disgrace*." *Journal of European Studies* 33, no. 7: 7–22.

Tabensky, Pedro Alexis. 2004. "Judging and Understanding." *Law and Literature* 16, no. 1: 207–28.

Taberner, Stuart. 2004. "German Nostalgia? Remembering German-Jewish Life in W. G. Sebald's *die Ausgewanderten* and *Austerlitz*." *German Review* 79, no.3: 181–202.

Translation of the Treatise Chagigah from the Babylonian Talmud. 1891. Introduction by A. W. Streane. Cambridge: Cambridge University Press.

Tye, Larry. 2013. *Superman: The High-Flying History of America's Most Enduring Hero*. New York: Random House.

Volkan, Vamik D. 1981. *Linking Objects and Linking Phenomena: A Study of the Forms, Symptoms, Metapsychology, and Therapy of Complicated Mourning*. New York: International University Press.

Ward, Simon. 2004. "Ruins and Poetics in the Works of W. G. Sebald." In *W. G. Sebald: A Critical Companion,* edited by J. J. Long and Anne Whitehead, 58–71. Seattle: University of Washington Press.

Weissman, Gary. 2004. *Fantasies of Witnessing: Postwar Efforts to Experience the Holocaust.* Ithaca, NY: Cornell University Press.

Winnicott, D. W. 1971. *Playing and Reality.* New York: Basic Books.

———. 1987. *Holding and Interpretation: Fragment of an Analysis.* New York: Grove Press.

Wisse, Ruth. 2000. *The Modern Jewish Canon.* New York: Free Press.

Young, James E. 1988. *Writing and Rewriting the Holocaust: Narrative and the Consequences of Interpretation.* Bloomington: Indiana University Press.

———. 1998. "The Holocaust as Vicarious Past: Art Spiegelman's Maus and the Afterimages of History." *Critical Inquiry* 24 (Spring): 666–99.

———. 2000a. "Against Redemption: The Arts of Counter-Memory." *Humanity at the Limit: The Impact of the Holocaust Experience on Jews and Christians.* Edited by Michael A. Signer. Bloomington: Indiana University Press.

———. 2000b. *At Memory's Edge: After-Images of the Holocaust in Contemporary Art and Architecture.* New Haven, CT: Yale University Press.

Zemel, Carol. 2003. "Emblems of Atrocity." In *Image and Remembrance,* edited by Shelley Hornstein and Florence Jacobowitz, 201–19. Bloomington: Indiana University Press.

Zilcosky, John. 2004. "Sebald's Uncanny Travels." In *W. G. Sebald: A Critical Companion,* edited by J. J. Long and Anne Whitehead, 102–20. Seattle: University of Washington Press.

Žižek, Slovoj. 1991. "The Truth Arises from Misrecognition." In *Lacan and the Subject of Language,* edited by Ellie Ragland-Sullivan and Mark Bracher, 188–212. New York: Routledge.

Index

Abraham, Nicholas, 75–76, 109–10
Alkana, Joseph, 63–64
Appelfeld, Aharon, 52, 155, 163, 237; *The Age of Wonders*, 5, 16, 35, 127, 130–31, 132, 150, 151, 153, 163, 164–66, 169, 170, 171, 202, 205; *All that Remains*, 219–21; *Beyond Despair*, 5; *Iron Tracks*, 171–72, 174; *The Story of a Life*, 53, 220
Arendt, Hannah, 6
Aronzon, Rami, ix, 13, 38–39
Auslander, Shalom: *Hope: A Tragedy*, 15, 26–28
Auster, Paul: *New York Trilogy*, 155–56, 158, 168

Babel, Isaac, 135, 146
Barthes, Roland, 111
Bechhofer, Susi, 216
Beckett, Samuel, 93
Bellamy, Elizabeth, 10, 223–25, 235
Bellow, Saul: *Mr. Sammler's Planet*, 5, 35, 52
Benigni, Roberto, 54
Benjamin, Walter, 61
Ben-Zakkahi, Yochanan, 131, 133
Berberich, Christine, 16
Berger, Alan, 8, 154
Bernstein, Susan, 19
Bloom, Harold, 205
Bohm-Duchen, Monica, 109
Bond, Greg, 219
Borowski Tadeusz, 128
Bosmajian, Hamida, 96
Brooks, Peter, 13, 60, 61
Budick, Emily, 5, 9, 13, 21, 22, 23–24, 35, 38–39, 186; reading Anne Frank, 15–16
Buelens, Gert, 156, 218

Cavell, Stanley, 6, 7, 9–10, 14, 199–200, 229–30, 235–36, 237
Chabon, Michael, 155, 163, 237; *Amazing Adventures of Kavalier and Clay*, 16, 127, 130, 133, 135, 136, 137, 138–40, 141, 143, 144, 145, 156, 167–69, 172, 178, 182, 205; *The Final Solution*, 16, 127, 129–30, 132, 145, 155–60, 163, 167, 168, 208, 218
Chagigah, 65

Coetzee, J. M.: *Disgrace*, 234–35; *Elizabeth Costello*, 17, 228–37; *Lives of Animals*, 17, 228–37
Crap, Stef, 156, 218

Dante, 192
Der Nister, 161–62
Devereau, Mary, 195
Diamond, Cora, 229–30, 235–36
Donahue, William, 195
Doppelgänger (double), 33, 157–59, 209–10, 213–14
Duttlinger, Caroline, 218

Eliot, T. S., 2
Englander, Nathan: "The 27th Man," 149; "What do we talk about when we talk about Anne Frank?" 15, 28
Ezekiel, Book of, 65
Ezrahi, Sidra, 2, 4–5

Feldman, Shoshana, 38, 94
Felderer, Ditlieb, 24–25
Fetish, 44, 45, 66, 68, 92, 111, 112, 122–23, 125, 131, 134, 136, 139, 145, 173–74, 222–24
Feuermann, Emanuel, 135
Fink, Ida, 50
Foer, Jonathan Safran, 134, 155, 237; *Code of Trees*, 16, 127, 132–33, 134, 143, 147, 152, 153–54, 156, 157, 176; *Eating Animals*, 236; *Everything is Illuminated*, 132; *Extremely Loud and Incredibly Close*, 225–26
Frank, Anne, 137; author's relationship to, 20–21, 228–30, 33, 125; controversy over *Diary*, 15, 19–20, 69, 125, 135, 146; Roth's use of *Diary*, 20–21
Frank, Margot, 29
Frank, Otto, 23–25
Freud, Sigmund, ix, 12–13, 44, 59, 95, 137, 156, 157, 175, 179, 223–25, 230; "Beyond the Pleasure Principle," 108, 113; "Creative Writers and Day-dreamers," 44–45, 60, 123; "Mourning and Melancholia," 122, 136–37, 221, 224, 225; "The Uncanny," 214

Fridman, Lea, 8
Friedländer, Saul, 66, 71

Gilbert, Sandra, 27
Goldenberg, Myrna, 50
Goldfarb, David, 127
Gopnik, Adam, 144
Gordon, Andrew, 44
Greenberg, Moshe, 65
Grossman, David, 155, 166, 237; See Under:
   Love, 16, 83, 95, 127, 129, 130, 132, 135, 142, 143,
   145, 146–47, 150–53, 154, 155, 157, 159–160, 162,
   164, 167, 168, 175, 180, 202, 213
Gubar, Susan, 27
Guilt, 14, 16, 40, 52, 56–58, 63, 71, 79–80, 91–93,
   95, 147, 148, 150, 159, 164, 165, 167–68, 184,
   187–88, 190, 196–202, 204, 206, 212, 222,
   227, 230

Harrison, Bernard, 3–4, 61–62
Hartman, Geoffrey, 2, 10, 116
Hawthorne, Nathaniel: The House of the Seven
   Gables, 189; "Wakefield," 168
Hemona, Aleksander, 127–28
Hirsch, Marianne, 2, 109, 111
Historical Fiction, 9–10
Hoffman, E. T. A., 214; "The Sandman," 213–15
Holmes, Sherlock, 155, 157–60
Horn, Dana, 163, 237; The World to Come, 16,
   128, 131, 134, 135, 136, 142, 148, 149, 160–62,
   169, 170, 182
Horowitz, Sara, 7–8, 159

Jacobson, Dan: Heshel's Kingdom, 216–19
James, Henry, 146, 147
Judgement in Nuremberg (film), 27

Kafka, Franz, 128–29, 131, 143, 152, 164–65,
   233–34
Kahlandorf, Ursula, 195
Karay, Felicja, 50
Kertesz, Imre: Fatelessness, 98–99; Kaddish for
   a Child Unborn, 5, 170
Kiš, Danilo, 127–28
Kosinski, Jerzi: The Painted Bird, 34
Krauss, Nicole, 134, 155, 163, 237; Great House,
   16, 128, 131, 132, 133, 141, 154, 171–78, 182; His-
   tory of Love, 16, 127, 132, 133–34, 135, 136–37,
   139, 140, 141, 142, 143–44, 151, 162, 163–64, 168,
   172, 175, 178–82, 205
Kremer, S. Lillian, 8

Lacan, Jacques, 123
LaCapra, Dominick, 10, 12, 75, 76, 110, 116, 201,
   223–25, 235
Lang, Berel, 3–4, 61–62
Langer, Lawrence, 2, 5, 8–9, 19, 20
Lanzmann, Claude, 27
Laub, Dori, 38, 94
Lear, Jonathan, 16
Levi, Primo, 10, 27, 34, 72–73; Survival at Aus-
   chwitz, 192
Levin, Meyer, 23–25
Lewis, C. S., 64
Leyb, Mani, 161
Leys, Ruth, 52, 196
Littell, Jonathan: The Kindly Ones, 15, 30–34,
   184, 208, 210, 214

MacKinnon, John, 199
Malamud, Bernard, 135, 146; "The Mourners,"
   179; The Tenants, 191
Manger, Itsik, 161
Merkin, Daphne, 221
Meyers, Nicholas: The Seven-Percent-Solution,
   158–60
Michaels, Anne, 16, 95, 128, 131–32, 139, 151, 154,
   155, 169–71, 173
Michaels, Walter Benn, 9
Mikics, David, 89
Mintz, Alan, 8
Mitscherlich, Alexander, 221–22, 225
Mitscherlich, Margarete, 221–22, 225
Morrison, Toni, 186
Mourning, 44–45, 55, 58, 61, 80, 82, 111, 121–25,
   127–34, 136–42, 163–71, 180, 181, 192–93, 201,
   222–25
Munch, Edvard, 153, 167

Nabokov, Vladimir, 156
Nachman of Bratslav, 161
Nadir, Moyshe, 161
Niven, Bill, 196, 205
Newman, Leslea, 118
Nietzsche, Frederich, 37
Nussbaum, Martha, 199

Osborne, Dora, 218
Offenbach, Jacques, 213–15
Ozick, Cynthia, 101, 144, 145, 155, 161, 163, 231,
   237; "Envy; or, Yiddish in America," 129,
   154; "I. B. Singer's Book of Creation," 154; The
   Messiah of Stockholm, 16, 26, 127, 128, 129, 137,
   141–43, 144–45, 146, 147, 148, 149, 150, 152, 154,

160, 161, 162, 163, 164, 167, 171, 173, 178, 180; "The Pagan Rabbi," 64; "Phantasmagoria of Bruno Schulz," 141; "Primo Levi's Suicide Note," 185, 188; *The Puttermesser Papers*, 143, 144, 145; "The Rights of History" and the Redemptive history, 60–62, 66; "Rights of Imagination," 195; *The Shawl*, 5, 14, 15, 16, 38, 41–69, 70–71, 72, 80–81, 82, 83, 100, 102, 106, 119, 121, 122, 124, 134, 136, 163, 170, 171, 207, 227; "Toward a New Yiddish," 147, 161; "Usurpation; or, Other People's Stories," 129; "Who Owns Anne Frank?," 19

Pane, Samuel, 218
Patterson, David, 8
Peretz, I. L., 161
Phillips, Adam, 61
Poe, Edgar Allan: Doppelgänger, 210; Dupin, 33, 155–59; "The Purloined Letter," 159; tales of conscience and revenge, 32–33
Prager, Emily: *Eve's Tattoo*, 9
Psychoanalytic theory, 11–16, 37–39, 43–45, 68, 75, 90–95, 123, 157–58, 211, 224–25

Rabbi Hanina, 169
Rabbi Yehuda Low ben Bezalel, 169
Rand, Nicholas, 109–10
Raphael, Lev: *Dancing on Tisha B'Av*, 118
Redemptive History, 61–62, 78
Regan, Ronald, 20
Reik, Theodor, 37, 39, 60
Restuccia, Frances, 221
Ringelblum, Emanuel, 135
Ringelheim, Joan, 50
Rosen, Emily: *Touching Evil*, 9, 26
Rosenbaum, Thane: *Golems of Gotham*, 144; *Second Hand Smoke*, 154
Rosenfeld, Alvin, 2, 4, 9, 19, 20, 183, 185, 188
Roskies, David, 8
Roth, Philip, 155, 161, 163, 237; *Anatomy Lesson*, 26; "Conversion of the Jews," 144; *The Counterlife*, 21, 148, 150; "Defender of the Faith," 23; *The Ghost Writer*, 13, 15, 19–28, 30, 33, 130, 133, 134–35, 137, 146, 150, 152, 185–86, 187–88, 191, 229; *Goodbye, Columbus*, 191; "I Always Wanted You to Admire My Fasting; or, Looking at Kafka," 128, 133, 149–50; *Operation Shylock*, 26; Other Europe project, 128, 148; "The Prague Orgy," 16, 22, 28, 127, 128, 130, 131, 132, 133, 134, 143, 146–50, 157, 163, 164, 165, 167; *Zuckerman Bound*, 127

Rothberg, Michael, 2, 7, 9, 10, 51, 116, 231
Rubin-Dorsky, Jeffrey, 21

Santner, Eric, 16, 213, 222–23, 227, 237
Schlant, Ernestine, 221
Schlink, Bernhard, 158; *Guilt About the Past*, 184, 190, 200; *The Reader*, 7, 16, 25–26, 33, 183–84, 195–208, 219, 220, 237
Schnitzler, Arthur, 151, 164
Scholem, Gershon, 137
Schulz, Bruno, 16, 127–82, 210; *The Messiah*, 129, 144, 145, 152, 173; *Sanatorium under the Sign of the Hourglass*, 128; *The Street of Crocodiles*, 128, 131, 132, 133, 136, 143, 145, 152
Sebald, G. W.: *Austerlitz*, 16, 183–84, 209–27, 228, 235; *Emergence of Memory*, 214; *The Emigrants*, 221; *Natural History of Destruction*, 221–22, 225
Shame, 6, 37, 43, 46–50, 52, 58, 63, 71, 102, 165, 166, 196–207, 219, 230, 234
Sholem Aleichem, 161
Singer, Isaac Bashevis, 135, 146, 154; "The Manuscript," 129, 135
Sokoloff, Naomi, 127
Spargo, R. Clifton, 21
Spiegelman, Art, 101, 156, 237; *Comix, Essays, Graphics*, 73, 74; *Complete Maus*, 5, 10, 14, 15, 38, 42, 51, 52, 53, 71–99, 100, 103, 105, 106, 109, 112, 113, 115, 121, 122–23, 124, 129, 132, 136, 143–44, 145, 153, 154, 168; *MetaMaus*, 72, 82, 86, 88, 97
Stollman, Aryeh Lev, 237; *The Far Euphrates*, 13, 14, 15, 16, 42, 100–19, 121, 124, 130, 133, 140, 170, 176, 185
Styron, William, 210; *The Confessions of Nat Turner*, 187–89, 195; *Darkness Visible*, 192–93; *Sophie's Choice*, 16, 183–95, 216, 220, 221, 235
Subject Position (subjectivity), 1–4, 7–8, 10, 12–13, 15–17, 19, 21, 30, 34, 37, 61, 69, 91–92, 119, 121, 183, 191, 200, 202, 206–207, 216, 219, 224–25, 227, 237
Suleiman, Susan Rubin, 30–31
Sundquist, Eric, 9
Swales, Martin, 196

Tabensky, Pedro, 199
Taberner, Stuart, 218, 221
Teleology, 64, 194
Trauma, 27, 29, 43–45, 52, 75–76, 81–82, 94–95, 101, 105, 108–10, 112–13, 118, 154, 171, 174, 201, 210–11, 218, 222, 225–26, 234

Torok, Maria, 75–76, 109–10

Tye, Larry, 138

Uris, Leon, 34

Volkan, Vamik D., 44, 55

Walker, Alice: *Meridian,* 186

Ward, Simon, 219

Wassermann, Jakob, 151, 166

Weissman, Gary, 14

Wiesel, Elie, 4, 10, 27, 34

Winnicott, D. W., 61, 67, 68

Wisse, Ruth, 127, 153–54

Wouk, Herman, 34

Yad Veshem, 107

Young, James, 2, 10, 12, 29, 51, 66, 71, 75, 231

Zemel, Carol, 109

Zilcosky, John, 212, 214

Žižek, Slavoj, 16, 123

Zweig, Stephan, 131, 164

EMILY MILLER BUDICK holds the Ann and Joseph Edelman
Chair in American Studies at the Hebrew University of Jerusalem,
where she is also chair of the Department of English and director of
the Center for Literary Studies. She has published essays and books in
the fields of American literature, Jewish and Hebrew literature, and
Holocaust literature. Her major publications include *Fiction and Historical
Consciousness* (1989), *Engendering Romance* (1994), *Blacks and Jews in
Literary Conversation* (1998), and *Aharon Appelfeld's Fiction* (IUP, 2004).

Lightning Source UK Ltd.
Milton Keynes UK
UKOW02f1223160415

249755UK00003B/43/P